ALFREDO JAAR

ALFREDO JAAR

DECOLONIAL TIME AND THE AESTHETICS OF THE UNFINISHED

FLORENCIA SAN MARTÍN

WITH A FOREWORD BY WOLFGANG KALECK

Duke University Press
Durham and London 2026

Printed in the United States of America on acid-free paper ∞
Project Editor: Lisa Lawley
Designed by Dave Rainey
Typeset in Arno Pro by Westchester Publishing Services

Library of Congress Cataloging-in-Publication Data
Names: San Martín, Florencia author | Kaleck, Wolfgang writer of foreword
Title: Alfredo Jaar : decolonial time and the aesthetics of the unfinished / Florencia San Martín ; with a foreword by Wolfgang Kaleck.
Other titles: Decolonial time and the aesthetics of the unfinished
Description: Durham : Duke University Press, 2026. | Includes bibliographical references and index.
Identifiers: LCCN 2025049998 (print)
LCCN 2025049999 (ebook)
ISBN 9781478038788 paperback
ISBN 9781478033905 hardcover
ISBN 9781478062417 ebook
Subjects: LCSH: Jaar, Alfredo | Jaar, Alfredo—Criticism and interpretation | Decolonization in art | Political art—Chile | Art—Political aspects—Chile | Art—Political aspects—Latin America | Neoliberalism—Latin America | Art, Chilean—20th century | Art, Chilean—21st century
Classification: LCC N6669.J33 S26 2026 (print) | LCC N6669.J33 (ebook) | DDC 709.2—dc23/eng/20260305
LC record available at https://lccn.loc.gov/2025049998
LC ebook record available at https://lccn.loc.gov/2025049999

Cover art: Alfredo Jaar, *The Garden of Good and Evil*, 2019. Ten stainless steel cells, each 1 sq. m. Courtesy of the artist.

Publication of this book has been aided by a grant from the Millard Meiss Publication Fund of CAA.

Advancing
Art&Design

MM

To my parents, Eduardo and Verónica

CONTENTS

ILLUSTRATIONS

PLATES

FIGURES

FOREWORD

Vivimos adentro, pero en contra

Wolfgang Kaleck

A life without art would be unlivable. Art is life.
—Alfredo Jaar

In her inspiring new monograph, art historian Florencia San Martín addresses two of the most critical topics in Jaar's work: his decolonial spirit and his aesthetics of resistance, which, as she argues, will always remain an aesthetics of the unfinished and of failure. Failure, alongside mourning and the fight for accountability, shapes the three chapters in this book.

Since the beginning of President Donald Trump's second term in office, there has been considerable discussion that his measures and announcements would mean the downfall of the Western liberal, rules-based order. What an unbelievable ignorance of history! Alfredo Jaar's work exemplifies the contrary, as San Martín's book shows, recalling the history of the post–World War II record of US foreign policy, with the September 11, 1973, US-backed military coup led by General Augusto Pinochet in Chile as the point of departure. Jaar presents in his typical manner—subtle and persistent at the same time—the content of a conversation between then President Richard Nixon and Henry Kissinger that goes far beyond Trump's current boastful announcements about the takeover of Greenland and the Panama Canal:

> P: Hi, Henry.
>
> K: Mr. President.
>
> P: Where are you. In New York?
>
> K: No. I am in Washington. I am working. I may go to a football game this afternoon if I get through.
>
> P: Good. Good. Well it is the opener. It is better than television. Nothing new of any importance . . . ?
>
> K: Nothing of very great consequence. The Chilean thing is getting consolidated and of course the newspapers are bleeding because a pro-Communist government has been overthrown.

P: Isn't that something. Isn't that something.

K: I mean instead of celebrating—in the Eisenhower period we would be heros [*sic*].[1]

All three politicians are united by their cynicism and their complete lack of human empathy—except that Nixon and Kissinger, beyond a mere declaration of intent, went into action and supported the military coup of September 11, 1973, which cost the lives of multiple leftist oppositionists. Thousands were tortured, disappeared, and driven into exile. To acknowledge the ongoing struggles of victims of human rights violations in Chile and beyond is San Martín's primary purpose in chapter 1, "Mourning." And, as she offers in the next chapter, "Accountability," for the global left, Kissinger and the 1973 putsch in Chile marked a historical turning point: Even when a democratic socialist like Salvador Allende, the overthrown Chilean president, came to power by election, Kissinger reiterates, "I don't see why we need to stand by and watch a country go communist due to the irresponsibility of its own people."

Kissinger's contribution to this and other crimes against humanity was never prosecuted, as San Martín further elaborates in chapter 2. Instead, the politician was honored all over the world until his last days; he died on November 20, 2023, and to this day, his conception and practice of Realpolitik are considered exemplary. Alfredo Jaar, on the other hand, works against this lack of historical memory and the ongoing impunity. It becomes his obsession, as Florencia San Martín meticulously elaborates. In multiple museums around the world, Jaar has borne witness to the monstrosity of the crimes of the military dictatorship and their impunity and mourns the victims of society. San Martín's monograph is about such mourning and unfinished actions for justice, which, as Jaar's art proposes, can take place in cultural and public spaces.

One of his many stops took Jaar to Berlin, where, in 2012, together with the author of this foreword, he placed advertisements in Berlin's daily newspapers calling for Kissinger's arrest in the various languages of the countries in which he had wreaked havoc: "Arrest Kissinger" was the message. It was meant as a wakeup call for the German leftist, social democratic, and liberal majority to apply the same standards of international criminal law to a powerful actor like the former US foreign secretary as to the war criminals of Serbia and Rwanda who were prosecuted at the time in UN tribunals in The Hague but also in German, French, and Spanish courts. This cooperation between an artist and a human rights lawyer in a common artistic and legal intervention presented an opportunity to think and practice justice as a shared goal and a common task, together with lawyers, but not only within and directed to the legal community, in transdisciplinary efforts to overcome legal and political boundaries. The idea of concrete utopian interventions, which this book applies from a transdisciplinary approach to art history, connects to existing legal frameworks and possibilities but at the same time provides an overarching vision of absolute justice as a destination that will never be achieved. And that, too, is part of the story: this demand was favorably received in museums by a culturally minded, progressive public who, after visiting the exhibition, returned to everyday life, whatever that meant.

The legal regulations for an investigation into Kissinger's war crimes of the 1960s and 1970s and his prosecution were not yet in place. After all, today's legal norms allow for the prosecution of powerful violators of the law, but there is still a long way to go from the norm to its application to the crimes of former President George Bush and others in establishing a system of extraterritorial prisons and systematic torture in the aftermath of September 11, 2001, for example. To think ahead along this path, to undertake artistic and legal interventions in this direction, connects the author with the artist. And failure also connects the two—the mentality to deal with and overcome failures as part of our lives and our political and professional engagement is somehow lacking in these dystopian times. Weren't the times dark in other decades as well? Probably not for most US citizens and Western Europeans. But for many people, the world has been in disorder for most of the past decades, and this disorder was called "order" by the profiteers of the unjust world order.

Florencia San Martín's assessment of Alfredo's artistic work as decolonial, and more specifically as a transdisciplinary project that exposes together the tropes of mourning, accountability, and failure, is needed and urgent in any case. Even more than that, it's the seemingly minor details that Alfredo points out.

Putting the huge country called Chile, which extends over several different vegetation zones, on the map, Alfredo Jaar, in his 1982 installation, *Stars*, says: "Well, I know it looks like the flag of Texas, but it is not. It is the flag of Chile. Yes, Chile, in South South America."[2] The blatant expropriation of the emblematic date of September 11, 1973, for all eternity and globally, 9/11 means, even for the progressive left and liberals in the Global North, September 11, 2001. There is no consciousness of what the date means for South America. And, of course, as San Martín demonstrates in chapter 3, "Failure," this shows us a progressive US American who says "America" and actually means the entire Americas, not just the United States.

Alfredo Jaar's art denounces blatant and subtle violence all over the world. Mourning, accountability, and failure are relevant in too many places of the world, as San Martín's monograph shows. Jaar works on famine in Sudan, the genocide in Rwanda, violence against migrants and refugees, and right extremist violence in Germany. *Aesthetics of Resistance*—the magnum opus of the German writer Peter Weiss—presents a political, historical, and art-historical view of struggles on the side of the world's marginalized. Alfredo Jaar, as San Martín elaborates in the conclusion, thinks and creates within this tradition. As such, for his public intervention in 2012, he chose one of the novel's settings, the Pergamon Museum in Berlin. Inside the museum, the Pergamonfries can be seen, and Weiss interprets them in his own way as a human uprising against the oppression of the gods. In Alfredo Jaar's work, several panels are displayed on the steps of the museum, with neon signs showing the right-wing extremist bombings and murders in the old and new Federal Republic of Germany. Consistently taking a stance and engaging with the context of his surroundings, Jaar explores both historical and contemporary events across his work; these are public artistic interventions in the best sense of the word, not merely in name. Through Jaar's unwavering intention to expose systems of oppression, they reveal the underlying structures of oppression and actively confront them. In his own words: "I select wrongs within the very system and create works departing from those wrongs."[3]

But will it change anything? We don't know. As San Martín's book offers, Alfredo is aware of the failure and incompleteness of his and our work. But not a little despondent, he sets to work. Doubting, yes, but doubting in the sense of rational thinking and philosophizing. Jaar leaves no doubt about his own intentions: knowing that we often fail but that we have no other option but to fight against it, in the spirit of Antonio Gramsci, an intellectual pessimist and an optimist of the will. As one of his works spells out, using Samuel Beckett's words—and which San Martín signals repeatedly in this monograph—"I can't go on. I'll go on." Or, as San Martín also quotes Aníbal Quijano throughout this book, "Vivimos adentro, pero en contra."

In *Alfredo Jaar: Decolonial Time and the Aesthetics of the Unfinished*, Florencia San Martín reconstructs all of this through a wealth of stories, shaped by many conversations. With a firework of references to history, philosophy, decolonial thinking, art history, and activism, she explores the intellectual depth of Alfredo Jaar's work, further offering a transdisciplinary paradigm for thinking about art and justice from the perspective of decolonial time and the aesthetics of the unfinished. She hereby demonstrates that the impact of Alfredo Jaar's work is not restricted to the places and museums where the work is presented—in fact, mourning and accountability are collective actions of societies, and justice can only be achieved by broader transdisciplinary alliances. The work of artists and legal experts can spark ideas, trigger dynamics, and contribute to justice, but to communicate, they would need readers and interpreters like art historian Florencia San Martín, who translates and communicates and hereby democratizes their specific knowledge. And her book also means an important milestone in building historical memory, which, as both the artist and his interpreter show, shall not freeze the past but help tackle the challenges of today's injustices in so many places in the world. It seems that historical progress came to a halt; it seems that we cannot go on, but the message of Jaar and San Martín is that we should go on.

INTRODUCTION

Decolonial Time and the Aesthetics of the Unfinished

Linear time is a Western invention; time is not linear, it is a marvellous entanglement.
—Lina Bo Bardi

October 12, 1992, New York City. The sky is hazy; the streets are crowded. A parade moves uptown from Forty-Second Street and Fifth Avenue to Eighty-Sixth Street and Third Avenue. Two beauty queens in sparkling blue and pink dresses greet the masses from a sixteenth-century carriage replica, Christopher Columbus between them. A re-creation of the three sailing ships that brought Columbus and the Spanish *conquistadores* to the other side of the Atlantic joins the spectacle. So does Uncle Sam, the US Army's orchestra, and a pop-like hackney carriage drawn by eight horses promoting the US American pale lager Budweiser.[1] Providing information about that day, the *New York Times* states that federal offices and schools will be closed, while financial markets will remain open. No, the market never closes. In our colonial capitalist system instituted five hundred years ago, it is structurally understood that the market generates and infuses joy. As such, it must stay operational as an allegory of Columbus Day.

A few blocks south, in the Spring Street Subway Station, a public innervation turns the aboveground celebratory narrative about the quincentenary into a question about freedom, race, migration, and capitalism (plate 1). Made by Alfredo Jaar, the work is a photograph in an advertising billboard showing the barbed-wire entrance of the Whitehead refugee detention center in Hong Kong, where thousands of Vietnamese awaited the beginning of a new life.[2] Rendered in blue and earthy tones, the image is symmetrically composed. Adopting the regime of vision and representation developed during the Renaissance, a historical moment in global culture and politics that championed humanism and expansionism towards the "backward" lands of the so-called New World, the image shows two identical fences forming four diagonal lines that lead the viewer's gaze toward a vanishing point that converges on the fenced entrance in the lower quadrant. Beyond is a hilltop and in the distance, slightly covered by fog, a larger hill. At the center is a text. Printed with a thin, vintage-style font reminiscent of imperial lettering, the text, just as the title of Jaar's work, reads "1992." As Jaar affirms in his proposal for this work: "1992 will mark the 500th anniversary of the first 'encounter' in history and the beginning of a Common Market structure in a Europe without borders. [Yet] the gap continues to widen between the so-called Third World and the so-called First World. . . . My proposal [is to] depict that reality."[3]

Three main aspects of Jaar's art and thinking are revealed in this statement: First, the recognition of the origins of capitalism with the conquest in 1492 and the global expansion five hundred years later of its current phase—neoliberalism, a market-driven system that dismisses the welfare state through policies of deregulation, commodification, privatization, and corporate success. Second, the continuity of the colonial binary logic of life under free-market rule—conqueror and conquered, civilized and barbaric, savior settler and backward ignorant, developed and underdeveloped, nationalist and terrorist, citizen and refugee, human and alien, and so on. And third, the fact that Jaar's main aim as an artist is to make visible the catastrophic consequences of colonialism not only in the Americas but also in the world, as we deduct in *1992* through the representation of a date celebrating the conquest and a photograph showing the refugee crisis five hundred years later in East and Southeast Asia. There was no encounter in 1492, as Jaar ironically notes by using quotation marks to denounce the infamous way in which Spain and advocates of the "discovery" were celebrating the quincentenary as the "Encuentro de Dos Mundos" (Encounter of Two Worlds).[4] And there is still no encounter today. In the post–Iron Curtain era, the global economy had not opened borders and provided more opportunities for all; in other words, the free economy is not as free as its name implies. Yet there is critical hope, that is, ways of inhabiting, knowing, and creating that imagine and work toward more just and reciprocal worlds. Therein lie the presence, insistence, and urgency of the arts and critical discourse. As Jaar once said: "A life without art would be unlivable. Art is life."[5]

Born in Santiago, Chile, in 1956, Alfredo Jaar created his early works in the 1970s, joining a generation of Latin American artists working under right-wing regimes in the Cold War context. In 1982, he moved to New York City and further developed a multimedia project by means of public space interventions, memorial monuments, performances, drawings, films, and large-scale installations composed of photography, text, mirrors, light, and press archives. Today, having moved to Lisbon, Portugal, in late 2025 in response to the political climate imposed by the Trump regime, Jaar is one of the most celebrated artists working in the global context—his work has been exhibited at multiple art biennials, museums, and galleries; numerous art institutions collect it; and it has been the subject of more than eighty monographs and thousands of interviews and reviews. As the object of multiple awards, including a MacArthur Fellowship in 2000, a Hiroshima Art Prize in 2018, a Hasselblad Award in 2020, and a MacDowell Medal and a Prix Pictet in 2025,—Jaar's art certainly has not been ignored. What has been ignored is the decolonial time that drives his art and thinking.

This book offers a new understanding of Jaar's art by arguing that the decolonial in general, and decolonial time specifically, has been centrally informing Jaar's art from the very outset of his career in the early 1970s, propelling him to create an aesthetic project that refuses to give up, to stop the fight, to erase, to forget. Elaborating on what I call here the aesthetics of the unfinished through the concepts of mourning, accountability, and failure, this book examines how Jaar has been identifying and critiquing coloniality in the global neoliberal present, inviting us to think that things could be otherwise, although they are not yet. As such, this study reads Jaar's oeuvre as fundamentally incomplete, just as the decolonial itself. More specifically, it maintains that Jaar's art has been informed by two interconnected historical events: the 1973 US-backed military coup that initiated the Chilean dictatorship and its corollary neoliberal economic system, adopted in Chile for the first time in the world. It further contends that this twofold experience has been central in Jaar's art and thinking ever since—from works related to Chile and Chile-US relations to projects that expose the devastating humanitarian consequences of neoliberalism throughout the world, as he does in *1992*.

Based on ten years of archival research, interviews with the artist and his contemporaries, and the analysis of iconic, lesser-known, and totally unknown works, this book further reframes the discussion around the photographic and the ethics of representation in Jaar's art through the perspective of decolonial time, revealing the crucial role of critical journalism and radical poetry in Jaar's art and thinking. "I am a kind of frustrated journalist [who] want[s] to bring the news to the world . . . with poetry," Jaar once said.[6] Across an introduction, a conclusion, and three chapters—"Mourning,"

"Accountability," and "Failure"—*Alfredo Jaar: Decolonial Time and the Aesthetics of the Unfinished* ultimately proposes decolonial time as a critical analytic that reimagines memory studies and art history together, proposing an understanding of Jaar's and other contemporary art by relating them first to the legacies of colonialism globally from the perspective of the Americas.

REPRESENTING DECOLONIAL TIME

Modernity is a cultural construction that began to develop in the sixteenth century with the conquest and the simultaneous establishment of mercantile capitalism and the production of the idea of "race." Coloniality, on the other hand, is the conceptual continuity of traditional colonialism in current social orders and forms of knowledges.[7] Modernity and coloniality are constitutive of one another; they are "two sides of the same coin."[8] Specifically regarding the question of time, at the outset of modernity, the colonial tropes of newness, innovation, and progress came to justify Europe's expansionism toward the "New World" as well as the development of new methods of labor control that were possible only through Indigenous denigration and slave trafficking from the Western part of the African continent. Enacted as if the past had never existed, a destruction of all human and nonhuman life in the "remote" and "backward" lands of Abya Yala (the Americas) had to occur to build every institution in society "virtually ex nihilo," as sociologists Aníbal Quijano and Immanuel Wallerstein have argued.[9] In this sense, the Americas were "not incorporated into an already existing capitalist world economy"; their very "discovery" propelled such order.[10] This is why, as Quijano and Wallerstein further maintain, "we can speak about Americanity as a concept."[11] A central heuristic in this book, Americanity means that since the nineteenth century, with the different paths taken between the United States and Latin America, with the former embracing global power and the latter hemispheric subordination, coloniality has operated at both the hemispheric and the global levels.[12] Standing against modernity's progressive time and its machine of denigration and oblivion, Quijano explains, "Vivimos adentro, pero en contra" (We live inside it, but against it).[13] Jaar's art represents that living inside and against from the perspective of decolonial time, critiquing what Quijano calls "coloniality of power" or the world as it is.[14] "I select wrongs within the very system and create works departing from those wrongs," Jaar said.[15]

Such is the case of Jaar's 2016 *I Can't Go On, I'll Go On* (figure I.1). Created in response to Donald Trump's election as the forty-fifth president of the

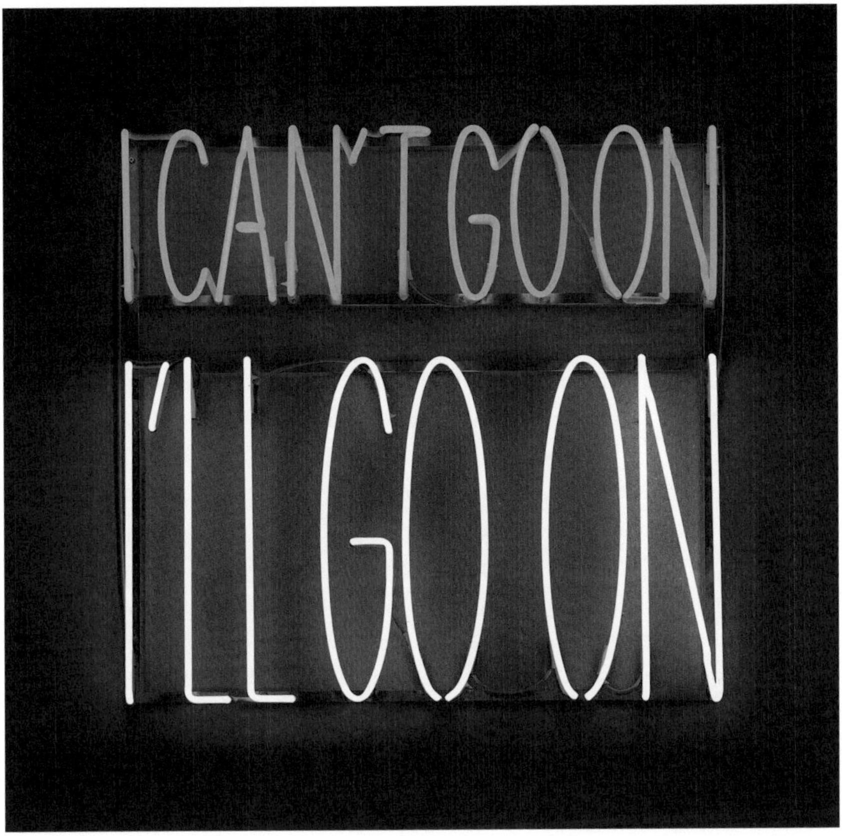

I.1 Alfredo Jaar, *I Can't Go On, I'll Go On*, 2016. Courtesy of Alfredo Jaar.

United States and installed since in different cities worldwide, this work uses neon to write the famous statement from Irish playwright Samuel Beckett's 1953 novel, *The Unnamable,* which Jaar divides into two rows.[16] The fragment on the top is rendered with red neon and reads, all in capitals: "I Can't Go On." The phrase at the bottom is rendered with white neon light and reads, also in capitals: "I'll Go On." As Jaar often explains in his public lectures, Beckett's phrase was inspired by Italian Marxist philosopher Antonio Gramsci, who, while witnessing the rise of Italian dictator Benito Mussolini's Fascism in interwar Europe, defined himself as intellectually pessimistic and optimistic in will.[17] A fervent reader of Gramsci, Jaar identifies with this mode of lamenting and creating, revealing that while coloniality punishes social change, it cannot paralyze the struggles for liberation. It cannot paralyze hope.

Importantly, this form of identification is not binominal, as it is not aimed at replacing power positions within structural coloniality. As I show throughout this book, Jaar's art is not about providing solutions but about exposing the problem, propelling critical aesthetic modes of representing and enacting reparation, reciprocity, and certainly decolonial time. It is about recognizing that *vivimos adentro, pero en contra,* disobeying pessimism while knowing that we will fail.[18] In Jaar's words, "It's about our incapacity to change this reality; even though I keep going, I keep trying."[19] And while it is true that Jaar emphasizes his position of radical hope by enlarging the scale of the words "I'll Go On" in his installation, that does not mean that coloniality has withdrawn. After all, "I can't go on" is still there, rendered in red and at the top of the sentence, showing Jaar's acknowledgment of coloniality's continuum.

"What can we do when apparently nothing can be done, and doing nothing is not an option?" asks Diana Taylor in her 2020 book, *¡Presente!* Advocating for being there, next to migrants on the US-Mexico border and to those seeking legal options once in the United States, Taylor argues that the action of *acuerpamiento* (to embody) may advance in the process of going through a togetherness that resists oppression from intellectual inequity and performance as activism.[20] While for Taylor the response is being present, for Jaar, it is representation of decolonial time. "I don't know what art can do in the face of war and global warming of our planet," Jaar said in 2022.[21] "I don't know what to do so I offer a space of uncertainty," he continued, with those spaces embodying relational aesthetic forms that expose no solutions but spaces nonetheless that still exist in the realm of representation as a means to convey hope.[22]

In Jaar's art, these narratives have also involved the body, a political act of *acuerpamiento* as a sense of solidarity and togetherness. In 2019, for instance, when he installed *I Can't Go On, I'll Go On* at the Bridge of Sighs in Edinburgh, Jaar, alongside a group of collaborators—most of them local art students—walked together under the bridge and through streets of the Scottish capital wearing sandwich boards as minimalist design covering their torsos (plate 2). This wearable design contained text on both sides. The text on the front, rendered with white lettering over a black background, reads, "I Can't Go On." The text on the back, rendered with black lettering over a white background, reads, "I'll Go On." This dialectic of positive and negative shows again the fission and coexistence of pessimism and optimism in the thought of Gramsci, Beckett, and many others, reminding us about the complex and never-fixed identity of the photographic, a central empiric in

Jaar's art and thinking. "The fact that a photograph is often split between negative and positive manifestations means that its identity is always simultaneously divided and multiplied," writes photography theorist Geoffrey Batchen.[23] Photography from this perspective offers a metaphor—whether formal, processual, technical, and/or narrative—of the unfinished essence of the decolonial, propelling aesthetic modes to exist that contest modernity's binary logic. In the words of Afro-Indigenous artist and poet Alan Pelaez Lopez, whose work is a call for justice for undocumented migrants on the US-Mexico border, "I would like to live in a world where my work was not necessary."[24]

From the perspective of the Americas, Jaar's art exposes that in the time of coloniality, the oppressed are deprived of their memory and their culture, simultaneously signaling the potential of art to resist and therefore exist in relational pasts, presents, and futures.[25] In reading Jaar's art through the concept of the "aesthetics of the unfinished," this study joins what philosopher and decolonial theorist Nelson Maldonado-Torres has defined as "an increasingly self-conscious and coalitional effort to understanding decolonization, and not simply modernity, as an unfinished project."[26] Importantly, as modernity only acknowledges "human cultural activity [through] finished products . . . expressed in an habitual past tense," these efforts have faced multiple obstacles.[27] Contesting such a mode of understanding humans and society, the art of Jaar, Pelaez Lopez, and many others in cultures of resistance proposes unfinished inquiries that imagine a world that is yet to come through the relational times that modernity denies.

Embracing this idea of the unfinished from critical science fiction literature, that is, from decolonial time, in his 1920 short story "The Comet," Pan-Africanist writer and sociologist W. E. B. Du Bois tells the story of a comet that suddenly hits New York, unleashing toxic and fatal gas that kills everyone in the city but Jim Davis, a Black man.[28] As Du Bois narrates, in the aftermath of the catastrophe, Jim wanders around the rubble of a city in ruins; he wanders around the wreckage of modernity. Suddenly, Jim enters a restaurant on Fifth Avenue, where he previously would not have been allowed because of the color of his skin, and then he finds a car and drives uptown. Upon arriving near Seventy-Second Street, he hears a woman's cry from a window. Jim has found another survivor: a young, wealthy, and white woman called Julia. Together, Jim and Julia walk toward a future beyond and away from coloniality's obstructions, which seem to have been transformed into a concluded inequitable past. There was hope, or at least that was what Jim believed at the time. However, that future is not yet there, as Jim soon realizes that only New York was affected by this cosmic disaster and that the world continues as it is. And in the world as it is, the oppressed—in this case Jim—although trying while wandering in the search for hope, fails at overcoming the racial capitalism that defines modernity.

As in "The Comet," Jaar's art is about critiquing hegemonic time as a fascist totality that "rejects the past [and] praises the present as the site of the real and the future as the horizon of expectation and the ultimate source of meaning," as philosopher Rolando Vázquez maintains.[29] With the time of modernity systematically devaluating the narratives of the oppressed and the traumas of past violence, the emancipatory hopes for otherwise futures as those imagined by Du Bois are eradicated or ignored by the colonizing culture. Still, as Vázquez continues, "we live in a time of open wounds," with such openness propelling the in-process cultural analysis created by visual, textual, sonic, or bodily forms and a collective practice of humility aimed toward radical hope.[30]

Art and art history from this angle, and for that matter aesthetics, are contingent, humble, and committed to reparation struggles that question the universalization of an art history understood from a linear approach.[31] Standing against Immanuel Kant's theory on judgment, where aesthetics regards a formal process that aims at universal and transcendental beauty, art from this perspective affirms neither progressive time nor art history as we know it, in which events are set to advance and thus erase. It rather acknowledges that art history and its public face, the museum, are colonial institutions that arose at the height of imperialism in the late eighteenth and early nineteenth centuries and have since designated what art is and is not and thus what value is placed on it, with that value following a temporal linearity though a victorious locus of enunciation.[32] Advocating for an unfinished, relational art history that does not aim for modernity's success, Māori art historian Ngarino Ellis writes: "As they say, history is typically written by the victors."[33] Or, as Beckett wrote in *Worstward Ho* (1983): "Ever tried. Ever failed. No matter. Try again. Fail again. Fail better."[34]

In 1958, the Mexican historian Edmundo O'Gorman brought a pivotal argument to the decolonial debate: that America was not "discovered" but "invented."[35] Representing not two different interpretations but two different paradigms, "discovery" embraces the European imperialist, victorious perspective of the world's linear history, and "invention" the perspective of those who have been left aside and who are expected to continue the steps of progress within a history in which they do not perceive themselves to belong.[36]

Thinking from the paradigm of the "invention" therefore means thinking from the decolonial. Within this paradigm, also in the mid-twentieth century, intellectuals from the Caribbean started challenging the global legacies of the conquest from their Afro-descendant experiences, adding to the decolonial its understanding as an incomplete project, as described by Maldonado-Torres. "To see clearly, to think clearly—that is, dangerously—and to answer clearly the innocent first question: what, fundamentally, is colonization?" wrote the Martinican poet and politician Aimé Césaire.[37] Urging the reader to observe modernity's sweeping away of all it "encounters," from modes of knowing, learning, and relating to forms of living in the incompleteness of decolonial time, Césaire uses the term *danger* as a call for epistemic, *ongoing* revolution.[38] It is nothing short of a call for the unfinished nature of the decolonial.

Half a century later in New York City, Jaar responded to such a call, countering the colonial rhetoric of the encounter with works such as *1992*. A few years earlier, in the years leading up to the quincentenary, he did the same with his little-known installation *Motherland, Motherland. What Mother, What Land?* (1984) (plate 3). Shown one time only in a group exhibition at the Fisher Gallery at the University of Southern California in Los Angeles, the work includes mounds of earth on the floor, neon tubes, and four images mounted to the wall.[39] The image on the far left is taken by Jaar from a drawing in the Boturini Codex or "Tira de la Peregrinación" (The Pilgrimage Strip), one of the earliest documents of migration in the Americas.[40] Showing the migration of the Chichimeca and the Mexica from Aztlán to Tenochtitlán in the Valley of Mexico, the image is organized in a geometrical composition. Turning singularity and collectivity, and figuration and abstraction, into relational modes rather than hierarchical oppositions within a fixed colonial cartography, the image "does not show the contours of the geographical territory but rather the events, motion, and internal relations between and among beings: divine, natural, human, animal."[41] Quite different than in Jaar's *1992*, migration here is depicted through an aesthetics of relational hope, with the act of walking, in Taylor's words, conveying a "way of becoming in motion [that is] never a simple practice, never one foot in front of the other."[42] In this sense, the line—that is, that horizontal continuity that forms at the center through the footprints of the Mexica—represents *not* modernity's time as "the single-track logic of . . . analytical thought."[43] Indeed, this logic is what Jaar shows and critiques by placing next to "Tira de la Peregrinación" a reproduction of a 1594 copper plate engraving from the series of volumes *America*, by Flemish engraver Theodor de Bry.

Representing the foundational moment in which time became linear, de Bry's plate manifests the European rhetoric of salvation through oppositional binaries—conqueror and conquered, dressed and naked, leaning forward and leaning back, foreground and background. Depicting assimilation by means of oppression, it further reproduces a one-sided location of meaning based on the event/paradigm of the discovery, which de Bry had learned about from testimonies of superiority narrated by conquerors back in Europe.[44] As an image of testimony and as a site of "encounter," it shows the backward Other offering their "gifts," seen by the receiver as profit, to the *conquistadores,* who have saved them from their less-than-human experience. After all, the debate in sixteenth-century Spain between Bartolomé de Las Casas and Juan Ginés de Sepúlveda was whether the Indigenous had souls and therefore were human at all, a condition they could obtain only if educated properly by submissively immersing themselves in the path of Christianity.[45] In this context, considered essential in providing unpaid labor for imperial capitalist expansion, Indigenous populations who resisted what Amílcar Cabral calls "cultural alienation" were targeted as "uncivilized" and "temporally remote," risking their life and therefore the erasure of their memory.[46] They were "given a residual status that . . . converts them into minorities [and] savages."[47] As such—that is, as people from the past—Indigenous peoples have been "turned into multicultural adornment for neoliberalism," as Bolivian theorist Silvia Rivera Cusicanqui maintains.[48] Justifying a culture of land appropriation and exploitation of labor, this distinction between the time of humans ensures the presence and dominium of cultural capitalism. "The fundamental characteristic of culture is its intimate interaction with the economic and social realities of the environment, and with the level of the forces of production and the means of production of the society which created it," writes Cabral.[49]

In 2011, Jaar created an installation criticizing such a characteristic by inscribing the linguistic equation "Culture = Capital," which is also the title of the work (figure I.2). Using neon lights to show formally and allegorically what coloniality hides under the global promise of "technological advances," Jaar's equation displays, *clearly* and *dangerously,* that in our neoliberal world, culture sells. And, because it sells, colonial silence and strategies of invisibility regarding the violence that produces that culture *as* capitalism *must* continue. There is no wonder why de Bry's engravings have become so famous and why decolonial readings of them, as in Jaar's *Motherland,* are so urgent. "There is an important reason to engage in a decolonial reading of De Bry," writes decolonial theorist Walter D. Mignolo. "Not only De Bry silences the Indians (as objects rather than persons), but scholarship on De Bry has tended to maintain that silence."[50]

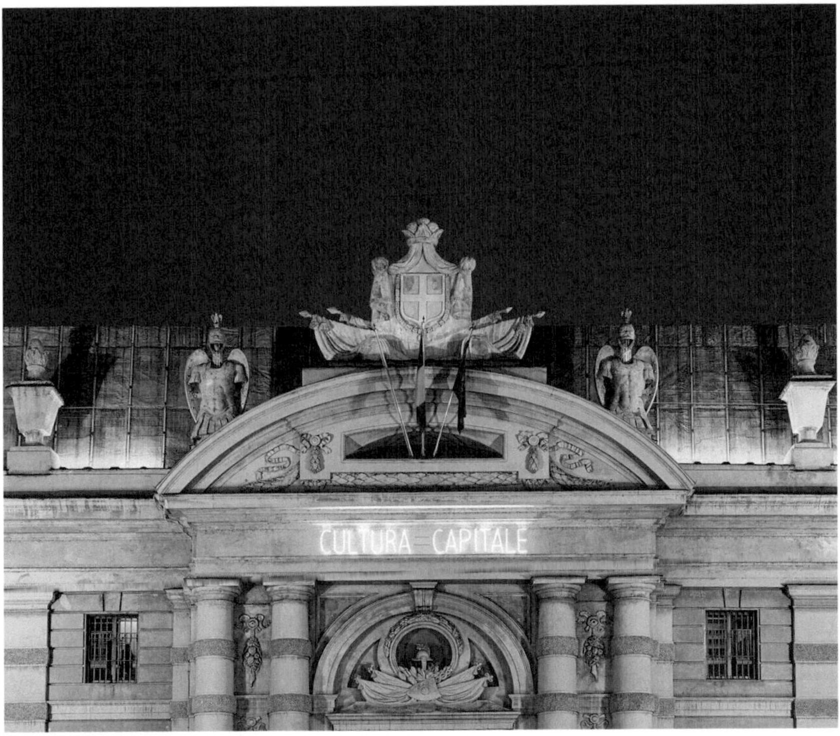

I.2 Alfredo Jaar, *Culture = Capital*, 2011. Courtesy of Alfredo Jaar.

In *Motherland*, Jaar further exposes that silence by reading de Bry's engraving together with that of "Tira de la Peregrinación," highlighting their formal differences as an extension of their approaches to the discovery. For the Indigenous people in Tawantinsuyu, for instance, the "encounter" depicted by de Bry was seen as *Pachakuti*, with the word *Pacha* meaning "mother," "world," "life," "space," and "time," and *kuti* meaning "drastic shift."[51] As a "violent invasion, merciless destruction, disdain for existing life forms in the continent, and convulsion at all levels of existence," *Pachakuti* means the origins of Americanity.[52] In Jaar's *Motherland*, it means that the earth, in the shape of four conical piles, may represent the Andes Mountain range in South America as a symbol of ecological resistance, and the neon tubes, with their arrow-like shape, may symbolize the outset of the colonial wound. Relating meaning to form and metaphor rather than to monolinguistic materiality, in Jaar's iconography, neon also means the merging of aesthetics and politics and the understanding of culture through what anthropologist Johannes Fabian calls "temporal coevalness," where the Other is not placed outside the flow of time.[53] It further means that culture can, and should, fight capitalism, even, or perhaps precisely, because of coloniality's aims at ignoring that fight.

Two more images are reproduced in Jaar's *Motherland*. The third one from the left shows a 1983 photograph of US troops moving ashore in a mock landing as part of the Pig Pine II exercises, a US Army operation that trained Honduras counterforces against Nicaragua's Sandinista government. The fourth and final one, a close-up photograph of the Chilean military during the dictatorship, lacks any specific markers of time and site, thereby representing fascist values of uniformity and restraint. This image thus could have been taken any time between 1973, when the dictatorship started, and 1984, when Jaar did the work. It could also have been captured *before* the third one, made in 1983 Nicaragua, showing that, in Jaar's narrative, history's progressive temporality, which goes from past to present and left to right, is confronted and criticized. Indeed, we may go even further and say that, allegorically, this photograph could have been taken *after* 1984, as photography in Jaar's art, as I will elaborate later, is not only about what happened in the past but also about what *should not* happen again in the future. Yet, in life under modernity, the future is the inevitable reproduction of the past. In the case of Chile, the country this image represents, neoliberalism reproduces the logic of capitalism, just as does the military coup with the paradigm of discovery. This is why Jaar places the image of the Chilean military at the "end" of his narrative, exposing the temporal circles within coloniality. In so doing, he shows one of the main arguments in this book: that his oeuvre is centrally informed by a twofold historical paradigm—the Chilean dictatorship and the neoliberal system it inaugurated—and that said paradigm, in which human repression is needed for profit, dominates in the global order today, in the ongoing neoliberal present.

THE ONGOING NEOLIBERAL PRESENT

On the morning of September 11, 1973, a US-backed military coup led by General Augusto Pinochet overthrew the democratically elected socialist government of Salvador Allende in Chile. Injecting a machine of terror that tortured, assassinated, and disappeared thousands, the coup's main aim—and that of the dictatorship that followed—was the implementation for the first time in the world of an advanced form of capitalism: neoliberalism. A cultural model that celebrates market-oriented life through harsh forms of austerity and individualism, neoliberalism reduces the influence of the communal and thus of reciprocal forms of inhibiting and relating among human and nonhuman beings. It also limits rights for nonhegemonic subjects and political subjectivities through relations of submission and domination. In this context, that is, under free-market rule, if justice is "the ethical norm that should govern the whole, [justice] could also be the mask of terror, an absolute principle of sovereign demand that attempts to leave no residue, an ideality that justifies cruel dehumanization," as literary scholar Fernando J. Rosenberg maintains.[54] In the "laboratory" of Chile, the implementation of this model of cruelty was so successful that its conceptual designer, the US economist and winner of the 1976 Nobel Prize in Economic Sciences, Milton Friedman, called it a "miracle."[55] "Chile is an economic miracle," he wrote for *Newsweek* on January 25, 1982, proudly assessing the effects of his economic policies, applied in Chile by the Chicago Boys, a group of young Chilean economists who studied under him at the University of Chicago. "Chile is an even more amazing *political* miracle," he continued, praising the politically severe military scenario in which such a miracle is possible.[56] And thus the dictatorship developed, benefiting the elite and multinational market-oriented life while displacing and humiliating the Othered majority. Meanwhile, Friedman's best student, a disciplined Augusto Pinochet, "was torturing people so prices could be free," as Uruguayan writer Eduardo Galeano so pointedly said.[57]

This is what Friedman meant in a letter he sent to Pinochet after their April 1975 meeting in Santiago. "The only way to fix the 'coercion' in Chile [resulting from] collectivism . . . and welfare state [is by a] severe, drastic, and shock treatment," he wrote. "With the many measures you have already taken [you have offered] more room for individual initiative and for a private sphere of life [and thus a] chance of a return to a democratic society."[58] Recalling the drastic shock imposed by Europe with the conquest, the Chilean dictatorship was nothing but a *refoundational* project of colonialism, that is, an "epochal transition that closes the cycle of the modern liberal and populist states in the region and ushers in the third, telematics and planetary phase of capital," as cultural theorist Idelber Avelar has maintained.[59] With the term *epoch* meaning a period of time characterized by a distinctive series of memorable events, the Chilean regime was an indelible moment in history, yes, but one operating *within* modernity's colonial foundations designed in 1492.

In the neoliberal phase of modernity, multiple linguistic terms have been used to transform traumatic events into incidents and measures of salvation, such as the word *encounter* or slogans such as "Encuentro de Dos Mundos." The same can be said about the term *freedom*. Adopting the latter, in 1976, Richard Nixon's US Secretary of the Treasury, William Simon, "congratulated Pinochet for bringing 'economic freedom' to the Chilean people."[60] And the general, of course, was quite gratified with such a compliment. He may have thought: a shock policy has worked, Chileans are now "free," and the United States is giving Chile the highest grade in the course on Americanity. As Pinochet told Henry Kissinger, Nixon's secretary of state and the main intellectual architect of the Chilean regime: "We are behind you. You are the leader."[61]

And thus the 1970s passed by, and Pinochet, the economic elite, and the military class consolidated their power through a constitution that meant, in short, the textbook of neoliberal authority. A task started by the conservative Jaime Guzmán as early as two days after the coup, in the next decade, Chile's 1980 constitution eradicated political dissent through severe measures that interpellated the subject as consumer, securing a culture of individualism, racism, sexism, and extractivism.[62] And, since fascism is always contested by revolution, whether this latter fails, the 1980s also saw the rise of popular discontent and increased pressure from the international community, revitalizing the hopes of liberation of a mourning society in collective pain.[63]

Writing from my own positionality as an art historian born and raised in the 1980s in Santiago, I recall overhearing with my sister from our bedroom in our family home the passionate conversations about politics that my parents had with their colleagues and friends until late at night. I knew that my father, an architect, had served as mayor of Santiago's commune of La Reina from 1972 until September 11, 1973, the date of the coup. I also knew he was held for three days in the detention camp of Tres Alamos in Santiago and that his architecture office's partner, Allende's nephew, was exiled to Mexico and later to Cuba. Like many kids my age, I also recall the chants and songs of the "No," a campaign created by the opposition to propel Chileans to cast their votes against the continuity of Pinochet in the 1988 National Referendum. I remember those hymns and songs, streamed from television in the weeks before the elections, being intonated everywhere, from the streets and organized public events to my friends' homes and recess at school. The "No" won, surprising the economic and military class and their supporters. On March 11, 1990, the transition period began, and a day later, on March 12, my younger sister was born. "She was born in democracy," my mother often said. A climate of hope was felt in Chile. Or, at least, that is how I recall it at the time.

Yet the end of the dictatorship was hardly as it sounds. Pinochet, right after leaving office, appointed himself senator for life, becoming commander in chief of the military and thus remaining *inside* the country's leadership. Furthermore, the neoliberal constitution injected during his regime stayed intact, securing amnesty for the perpetrators and maintaining the harsh economic differences and cultural policies of heteronormativity and extractivism in "democratic" Chile. With the dictatorship's neoliberal ghost defining all modes of life in the early 1990s, "Chilean political democracy was a fragile enterprise."[64] A series of Center and Center-Left administrations followed until 2010, when the late right-wing billionaire Sebastián Piñera, who had made his fortune in Chile's neoliberal heaven, won the presidential election. Piñera succeeded the socialist government of Michelle Bachelet, herself a victim of Pinochet's regime. In 2014 Bachelet was reelected, and four years later Piñera won the presidency again, denoting a highly polarized society living under harsh neoliberalism in the late 2010s.[65]

In 2018, the same year he returned to office, Piñera traveled to Washington, DC, to meet with Donald Trump, then serving his first term as president of the United States. Replicating the pitiful assumption of obedience from the part of the assimilated Other regarding the empire that Pinochet had so proudly voiced to Kissinger in 1976, Piñera, after telling Trump at the Oval Office that Chile shared with the United States its values of democracy, human rights, and freedom, offered his US counterpart a gift: a print of a small Chilean flag delineated in the middle of a large US flag (figure I.3).[66] Using the white and red stripes and the last star at the bottom right from an altered version of the US emblem, the Chilean flag was simply denoted by a "witty" Piñera through a white rectangular contour. There is no need to create another flag, stripe, or star, Piñera seems to tell us with his "conceptual" print, in which a unified entity is built through an overlapped two-nation flag. As he proudly told Trump and the dozens of journalists with a big smile: "Chile is in the heart of the US."[67]

Piñera's gesture rapidly became viral and mocked through thousands of memes in social media. In decolonial terminology, this irony means that the Chilean president, in reducing a nation to a fragment of another, showed no heart or collaborative friendship. Instead, it demonstrates the continued presence of imperialism in the age of global neoliberalism and the support of this presence by the elite Piñera so well represented. Maybe that is why Trump, witnessing Piñera's flag, laughed and pleasantly agreed. A behavioral pattern of modernity, Piñera's flag, just as Pinochet's response to Kissinger, represents nothing but "the sad dreams of Latin American elites of becoming

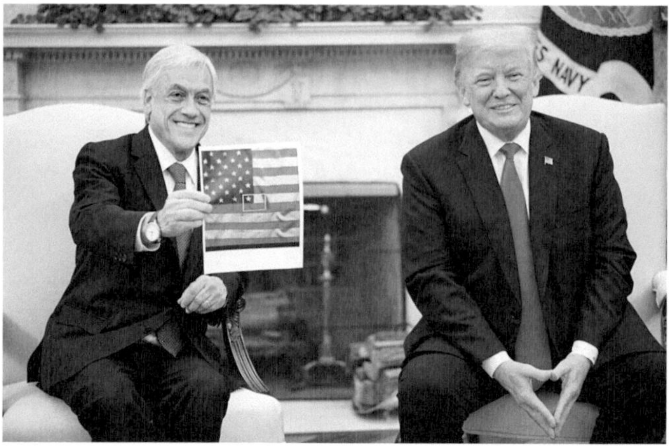

I.3 President Donald Trump meets with Chilean President Sebastián Piñera at the White House, September 28, 2018.

modern while diving deeper and deeper into the logic of coloniality," as Mignolo so pointedly states.[68] After all, since the nineteenth century, a key historical moment in Americanity, imperialism has equated the prevalence of Manifest Destiny in successive and successful hemispheric programs of imperial US strategies. And in this context, so the story goes, Latin America has been "naturally" and derogatorily understood as "America's backyard."

"For over a century—beginning with the Monroe doctrine—Latin Americans resisted, often violently, both the United States' self-assigned mission to reform humanity . . . and the militarism that such mission inevitably generated," writes historian Greg Grandin.[69] In so doing, Latin Americans, as Grandin continues, "forced the United States, often against the worst impulses of its leaders, to develop more pragmatic and flexible imperial strategies, strategies that proved indispensable in its postwar rise to global superpower."[70] This means that, regardless of collective and organized resistance, liberatory projects against imperialism have failed, allowing Americanity to continue ruling culture and society through neoliberal tactics of interventionism. In recent years, such "pragmatic and flexible imperial strategies" have been replaced by blatant derogatory and dehumanizing language. In 2018, for instance, just days before Trump's meeting with Piñera at the Oval Office, Secretary of State Rex Tillerson, in acknowledging the threat of China's growing relations in Latin America, said: "Latin America does not need new imperial powers."[71] And on September 3, 2025, when the United States

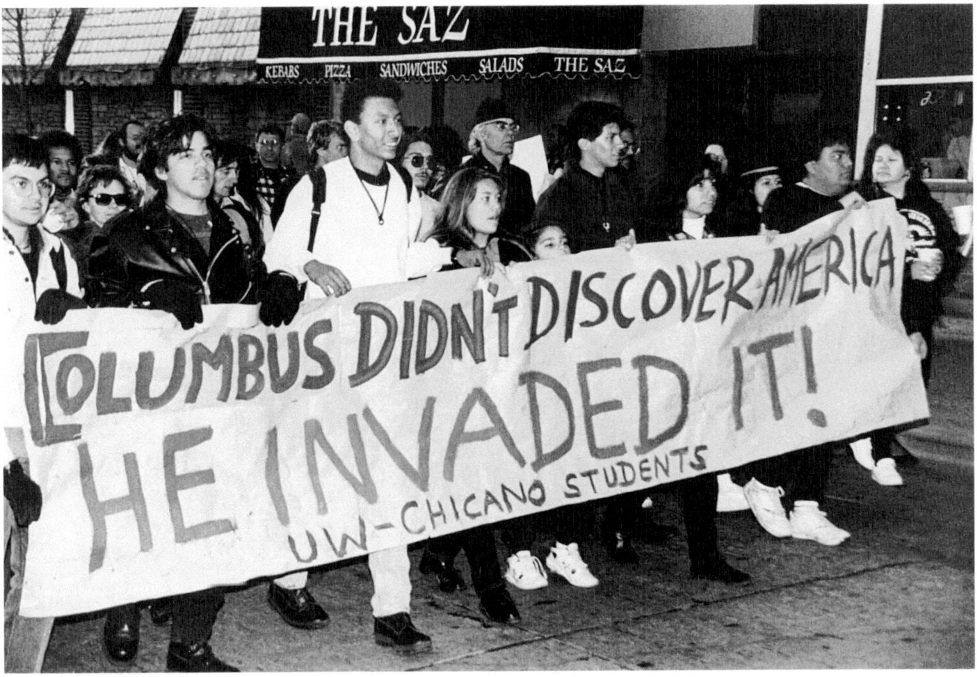

I.4 Chicano students from the University of Wisconsin–Madison protesting on Columbus Day, October 12, 1992.

blew up a vessel that the Trump administration accused of smuggling drugs out of Venezuela, Secretary of State Marco Rubio, sidestepping Latin American nations' sovereignty and the legality of such actions, said, "[They will only stop] when you blow them up, when you get rid of them. [Otherwise, this will] happen again."[72] And so it has been, with more vessels being blown up in the Caribbean waters through operations managed by the defense department recently renamed, plainly and shamelessly, the U.S. Department of War.

Jaar's art on decolonial time critiques coloniality's more and less flexible imperial strategies, showing and honoring in turn different waves of revolutions in diverse periods and sites. One of these revolutions occurred during the quincentenary, when Jaar created *1992* and millions took to the streets across the hemisphere and beyond to say no: "Columbus didn't discover America; he invaded it," as reads, for instance, a sign carried by a group of Chicano students at the University of Wisconsin–Madison in a protest of Columbus Day (figure I.4). Another recent revolution was Chile's *estallido social,* the largest civil unrest in Chile since the end of the dictatorship.

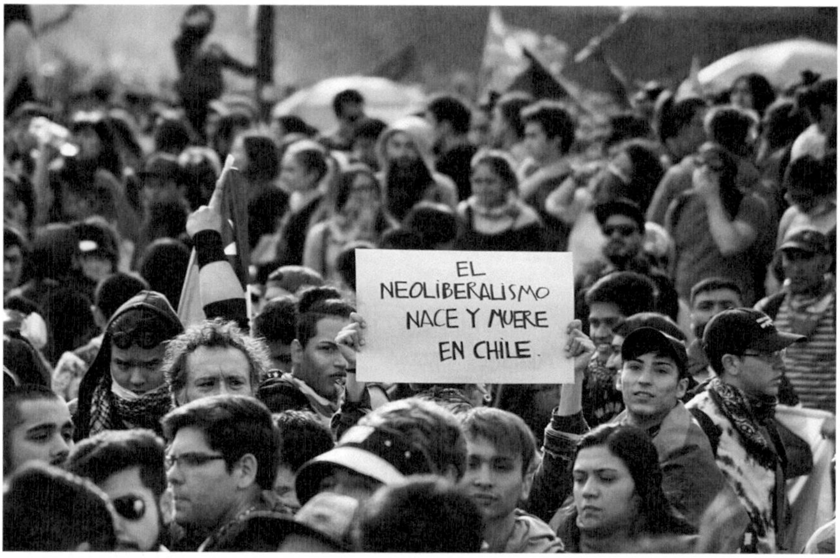

I.5 Protest in Santiago, Chile, October 2019.

Commenced on October 18, 2019, when hundreds of high school students took to the streets in Santiago responding to a subway fare hike imposed by the Piñera administration, the *estallido* was soon joined by millions across generations and social, ethnic, and racial backgrounds, all while solidarity chapters were being formed in cities like Barcelona, Beirut, Berlin, Istanbul, London, Lima, Mexico City, New York, Tokyo, and more.[73] Demanding the end of the dictatorship's neoliberal legacies and centuries of colonial rule, one of the revolt's main mottos reads: "Neoliberalism was born and will die in Chile" (figure I.5).

Witnessing the spread and scope of the revolt, Piñera, who two weeks before the protests' outset had described Chile as Latin America's "oasis," for which he meant neoliberal heaven, announced on public television: "We are at war."[74] He called the military to the streets and ordered a state of siege. Thousands were arrested, dozens were killed, and hundreds suffered ocular injuries through pellets fired by state security agents directly into their eyes. Observing the events from the United States, the Trump administration said: "The United States stands with Chile, an important ally, as it works to peacefully restore national order."[75] Discipline, punishment, and the restoration of neoliberal order were central, just as shown in Piñera's gift to Trump in the form of an obedient and assimilated flag.

Pressure from international human rights organizations, however, left no option to the Piñera administration but to agree to a referendum to resolve two questions: first, if citizens wanted a new constitution; and second, if this should be written by elected members of the Parliament or by a Constitutional Convention formed by elected civilians. On election day, in October 2020, almost 80 percent of the population voted yes to both questions. A renewed sense of hope was felt in and beyond Chile. In Jaar's words: "Have we finally reached the end of the dictatorship? I hope so, and this would be the achievement of the street."[76] In May 2021, Chileans returned to the polls to elect the members for a gender parity Convention with Elisa Loncón, a Mapuche linguist, academic, and Indigenous rights activist, serving as its first president. Later that year, left-wing former student leader Gabriel Boric won the presidency, while the constitution's draft became available for citizens to review and vote on. This time, however, the opposition lost, and quite overwhelmingly. This means that while in 2020 the large majority voted yes to replace Pinochet's constitution, two years later, the majority voted no to the same ontological question. "How could this be explained?" we all wondered. The answer is, again, Americanity. For the traditional political spectrum, neoliberalism was *not* related to decolonial demands. Put differently, capitalism was detached from issues of race, gender, reparation, and environmental justice. And so, under Americanity's rule, it should come as no surprise that, in 2025 Chile, Pinochet's fervent admirer, far-right conservative José Antonio Kast, won the presidential election with an overwhelming 58 percent of the vote, reflecting the current far-right turn in Latin America.

In this context, Taylor's question "What can we do when apparently nothing can be done, and doing nothing is not an option?" emerges as ever so urgent, just as Jaar's aesthetics of the unfinished becomes ever so contingent. As Jaar said when asked about what motivated him to exhibit *I Can't Go On, I'll Go On* in Edinburgh: "We have seen winds of fascism emerge all around Europe, the United States, Asia, and Latin America. I went through . . . Pinochet's regime in Chile [and] when I read this statement by Beckett, I was fascinated; I felt it reflected my mood, a mood of impotence, a feeling that I cannot go on, I do not understand, I am lost."[77] Revealing an ongoing state of mourning that began in his native Chile, Jaar's words expose that the ruins of the dictatorship are relational, exceeding the nation-state. They also reveal that language is not separated from coloniality and that words, such as the terms *encounter* and *freedom*, are perpetuated in those ruins.

The chapters in this book are about those ruins; they are about how Jaar has been denouncing linguistic formulas of inclusion within a "free world without borders" by insisting on the fact that America was not invented twice but once, as O'Gorman would say. This means that, regardless of Columbus's name being removed from the holiday, known in New York since 2022 as "Italian American Heritage Day and Peoples' Day," and of the many monuments of the conquest being destroyed in recent years in the wake of Black Lives Matter protests, Columbus's legacies still define life under modernity. Indeed, considering that the federal holiday was never eliminated and that the history of victors is not burned in the debris of the past, Trump's 2025 announcement at the outset of his second term in office of "reinstating Columbus Day" by bringing the explorer "back from the ashes" is nothing but a linguistic tactic to keep modernity as is.[78] It is nothing but a blatant imperial statement of Americanity. As Māori scholar Linda Tuhiwai Smith writes from Aotearoa (New Zealand): "There is one particular figure whose name looms large . . . : Christopher Columbus. [He] sets its modern time frame (500 years) and defines the outer limits of that legacy, that is, total destruction."[79]

Responding and reacting to such destruction, Jaar's art exposes forms, methods, and experiences that refuse to forget, to lose hope. As linguist and activist Noam Chomsky said when asked about the colonial pressure to forget *Nakba* in 1948: "To forget about the past means forgetting about the future because the past involves aspirations, hopes."[80] And because forgetting informs the textbook of the world, or *el mundo, le monde,* and so forth, as a masculine and singular noun that obstructs emancipatory temporalities in the sequential progression of modernity, "those who cannot remember the past are condemned to repeat it."[81] Forgetting thus means the semantic tactic of repeating cruelty, genocide, and the justification of war. And art, as art historian Boreth Ly maintains, "cannot solve this moral and ethical conflict or provide complete healing for the wound."[82] Still, as she continues, it can "help to engage us in this difficult dialogue and serve as catharsis."[83] Acknowledging the never-completed task of creating, relating, and remembering and the role of art in the interpellation of modernity in both communal (dialogical) and personal (catharsis) realms, Jaar maintains: "Art is our attempt to change the order of reality. How do we accomplish such an impossible task? I don't know. That is why I am an artist. During decades, I have searched for an answer to this question."[84]

HEMISPHERIC AND GLOBAL ENTANGLEMENTS

Jaar's critique of neoliberal coloniality is not detached from his own experiences in different periods, sites, and diasporic memory accounts. Jaar was born in 1956 in Chile during the second presidency of former dictator Carlos

Ibáñez del Campo. When the artist was five and right-wing president Jorge Alessandri's policies of austerity and freezing of public sector pay unleashed widespread industrial and social unrest, his father decided to move the family from Chile. They moved to Martinique, coinciding with the moment when Caribbean intellectuals such as Césaire were starting to think about decolonization as an unfinished project.[85] Once on the island, Jaar attended the Lycée Schœlcher in Fort-de-France, the same place where Césaire, his wife Suzanne (a surrealist poet and feminist activist), and the decolonial novelist Joseph Zobel had been teachers. Jaar's schooling was thus informed not only by Western "classics" but also by the legacies of educators and alumni such as Frantz Fanon and Édouard Glissant, both students of Césaire. Named after Victor Schœlcher, the nineteenth-century abolitionist and writer who played a leading role in the emancipation of enslaved people in France and its colonies during the Second Republic, the school building was later designated by Césaire, who served as Fort-de-France's mayor and was a deputy in France's National Assembly from 1945 to 2001, as a national monument.[86] Further embracing this understanding of monuments, where what's honored is not modernity's narrative of independence but a hemispheric and global poetics and politics of a decolonial project in becoming, Jaar was recently invited to propose a monument to Césaire. "This is a tremendous honor for me," he said.[87]

In retrospect, it was during his middle and high school years in Martinique that Jaar started to absorb critical histories of racial justice, emancipation, and liberation, a rare learning experience within a world whose restricted pedagogy "limit[ed] the imaginative capacity of youth and non-youth alike." Indeed, one can further say that Jaar's experience was based on an abolitionist teaching, where "the radical imagination of collective memories of resistance, trauma, survival, love, joy, and cultural modes of expression and practices . . . push and expand the fundamental ideas of democracy."[88] Art from this perspective, as education scholar Bettina L. Love argues, "is freedom dreams turned into action because 'politics is not separate from lived experience.'"[89] With the noun *freedom* here meaning not the countless offerings of the globalized market but the communal and shared actions of movements of liberation, Love's statement recalls the title of Angela Y. Davis's 2016 book *Freedom Is a Constant Struggle*, a collection of interviews, presentations, and essays on global justice and transnational solidarities in the aftermath of the Ferguson unrest and the question of Palestine. Importantly, since these actions are global, it should come as no surprise that in 1971, when Davis was arrested as one of the FBI's Ten Most Wanted Fugitives, students in Santiago from the Universidad de Chile organized a week of solidarity that included street rallies, graphics, and petitions demanding her liberty.[90] It should come as no surprise either that a year later, when Davis was released from prison, she visited Chile at the height of Allende's government and that a day after the coup, on September 12, 1973, she organized a rally in New York protesting the role of the Nixon administration in Allende's overthrow.[91] Meanwhile, solidarity committees were being formed all over the world. From France, Italy, Sweden, the United States, and the German Democratic Republic (GDR) to Algeria, Japan, and Palestine, the transnational solidarity movement with the victims of the Chilean dictatorship was of significant proportions. "Every day, an act of solidarity was created in some locality in the closest or most remote corners of the planet," said architect, dictatorship survivor, and 2019 National Architecture Award winner Miguel Lawner.[92] And while it is true that this movement reached a global scope during the coup, it started before, when hundreds of people from all over the world traveled to Chile to experience firsthand Salvador Allende's socialist revolution.

Alfredo Jaar was one of them. In 1972, a year before the coup, the then fifteen-year-old returned to Chile from Martinique. His father, a fervent reader with a great passion for critical information and social justice, wanted his family to directly live the social reforms of Allende, who had been democratically elected president of Chile in 1970.[93] He wanted his children to experience such hope. In March 1973, with Allende still in office, Jaar, after performing well in the national college entrance exam, was accepted into the Universidad de Chile's Facultad de Arquitectura y Urbanismo (FAU, Faculty of Architecture and Urbanism), where he enrolled in three "continuous" studios that were part of the "creative" curricula.[94] In these studios, conducted by architects Hernán Montecinos, Pedro Murtinho, and Ramón Méndez, assignments were divided into phases and students were encouraged "to find the political, cultural, and sociological skin of space by analyzing space and light," as Jaar's classmate, Jorge Dalmazzo, recalls.[95] Another classmate, Isabel Devés, remembers: "We were prompted to go out to the street and observe to find the context's essence and then translate those findings through different modes of representation, which were not necessarily architectural plans."[96] "We were encouraged to think about the city as an open book," said another classmate, Bernardo Urquieta.[97] And in this "book," as Montecinos's teaching assistant Jorge Iglesis recalls, "instead of following conventional formulas, as was the case in other workshops from the 'non-creative' curriculum, students came with their own conclusions and observations, and then exchanged them with their classmates and teachers, leaving the studio with even more questions."[98]

As a mode of searching, embracing observation, experiential learning, and collective analysis, this methodology in which architecture is an ongoing process has been applied by Jaar throughout his more than five-decade career. "As a trained architect my art responds to context," he often says, with *context* meaning what he does and does not see from the media, the streets, and the city's urban planning; and what he does and does not hear from political addresses, the masses, and the public space. After identifying context through extensive research, which includes archival gatherings of media clips and other forms of visual, textual, and sonic documentation, Jaar signals said presences or absences regarding the orchestration of the real, that is, regarding the manipulation of truth by modernity's power channels: "I edit, edit, and edit, in order to arrive at the essence of what I want to say."[99]

With its heart in the public space and in how the political, cultural, and social develop within that space, Jaar's method of art as a response to context recalls art historian Eddie Chambers's take on art history and by extension art itself: "In writing art history and/or art criticism, context is everything. Without the art we study and teach being considered from the perspectives of multiple contexts—including social, racial, historical—it is unlikely to be sufficiently or properly understood," he argues. "Except for those invested in social history, mainstream art historians frequently disregard context as a significant area of inquiry."[100] Likewise, Jaar's education at FAU embraced neither universal narratives and rules nor predetermined formal, theoretical, and experiential sources, methods, and temporalities. It acknowledged that "to think of history as one is to posit the equivalence between three ideas: one time, one humanity, and one history," as Paul Ricoeur has said.[101] In this sense, Jaar's thinking about time allies with architect Lina Bo Bardi, who explains that "linear time is a Western invention; time is not linear, it is a marvellous entanglement."[102] And in that entanglement, the path for becoming creates relational traces with no beginning or end, nor one way or another, or civilized or barbaric, modern or postmodern, colonial or postcolonial, or any other binarism from what the Venezuelan anthropologist Fernando Coronil coined as a modality of Occidentalism, in which "the question [is] presented as a problem *for* the Self, not *of* the Self or *for* the Other."[103] Art from this perspective, and education about culture for that matter, embraces a sense of mobility, ongoing observation, an unfinished search for hope, and a collective building of projects that are essentially *in* progress.

In Jaar's art, that sense of decolonial motion is oftentimes formulated by overlapping images and text and the building of complex spatial forms that portray light and lighting as aids for remembrance. As such, light and lighting are never just that: a radiation that makes visible the appearance of things or a symbolic source of knowledge beyond and away from representation. They are rather ongoing grooves that acknowledge the multiple pasts and thus times that modernity buries in the remote sites of non-history. Such was the case of Allende's Chile, whose peoples, murals, songs, and hopes were all aimed to be destroyed with the coup. So was the university and thus Allende's dream of transforming Chile "into one big school."[104] Indeed, beginning with the coup, public universities became controlled by different military divisions, extending the brutality of the regime into the realm of education. With its "creative" line, however, FAU managed to continue its studio offerings. After all, the military did not see "creativity" as disobedient or revolutionary. It was not part of Occidentalism's "rational" mental binarism; thus, it was not considered a threat.

Nor was the idea of happiness, whose meaning in dictatorial Chile propelled Jaar to develop one of his most famous projects, *Studies on Happiness*. In this series, created between 1979 and 1981, Jaar asked the inhabitants of Santiago if they were happy by different means, including interviews in the public space and images of eight advertising billboards with the question "¿Es usted feliz?" (Are you happy?) (figure I.6).[105] Rendered in stark black text on white backgrounds, Jaar's question invited people to think critically about the nation's freedom regime, that is, the machine of censorship, torture, and repression led by the US-backed Dirección de Inteligencia Nacional (DINA, National Intelligence Directorate)—renamed in 1977 as the Central Nacional de Informaciones (CNI, National Information Center.) Saying no in this sense means a critique of the public secret that propelled the coup in the first place and that was starting to materialize with the 1978 plebiscite and its resulting neoliberal constitution of 1980. It means no to a free-market culture that was soon to be injected all over the world. It means no, in feminist scholar and activist Lynne Segal's words, to "the contemporary [capitalist idea of] happiness agenda [that] may be better described as its opposite: a misery agenda."[106] As Jaar said in 2017 when asked about what motivated him to create this project: "A neoliberal model was strongly being established. I wanted to question [that model, so] I asked: Do we want this? Are we happy with this?" The journalist then asked: "What are you looking for with this question today?" Jaar responded: "The same as before. To question the existent model."[107]

Through a conceptual strategy depicting the ostensibly innocent question about happiness, Jaar circumvented censorship, subverting the one-sidedness of the emitter in the speech under dictatorship while signaling the

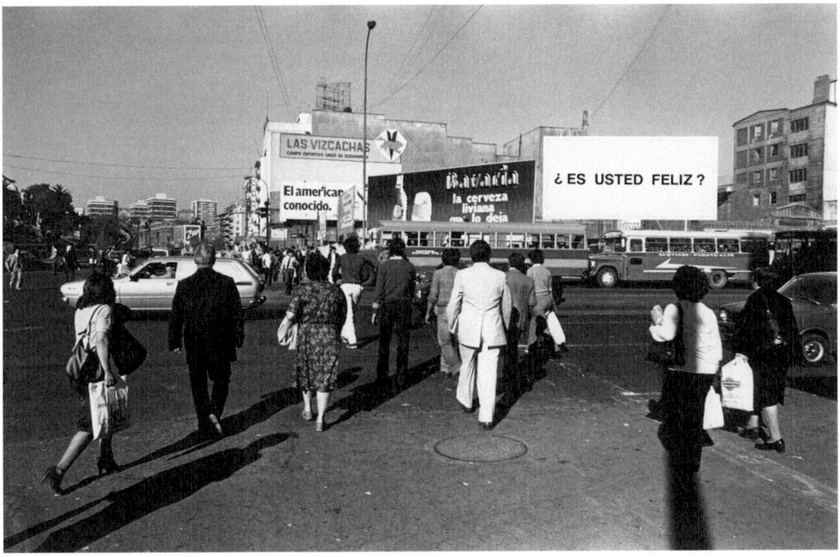

I.6 Alfredo Jaar, *Public Interventions*, 1981, from the series *Studies on Happiness* (1979–81). Courtesy of Alfredo Jaar.

humanitarian and ecological constraints that the new model of neoliberal freedom was starting to inject into society. And, as neoliberalism has become a global phenomenon, Jaar has been reenacting the question in multiple cities worldwide, from the port city of Valparaiso in Chile to Monterrey in Mexico, Austin in Texas, and more (figure I.7).[108] Rendered in stark white text on black backgrounds, the work disrupts the partiality of those who speak in the free market's planetary regime, highlighting the question's reproducibility by turning negative into positive and vice versa through graphic design. And just as the negative-positive identity of the photographic can reproduce the image—or the referent—into endlessness, so does Jaar through language and the inquiry of happiness. As novelist Clarice Lispector writes in *The Hour of the Star*, "[As] long as I have questions to which there are no answers, I shall go on writing."[109] In Jaar's art, the inquiry about happiness is what keeps him going, *writing* an artistic project that remains urgent, open. "In a way, throughout the years, I have been repeating the same question about happiness again and again in different projects and geopolitical contexts," Jaar once said.[110] Recalling Césaire's *Discourse on Colonialism*, which, paraphrasing English scholar Bret Benjamin, is first and foremost a denouncement of the role of capitalism in humans' happiness, Jaar's project says no, the question of capitalism and

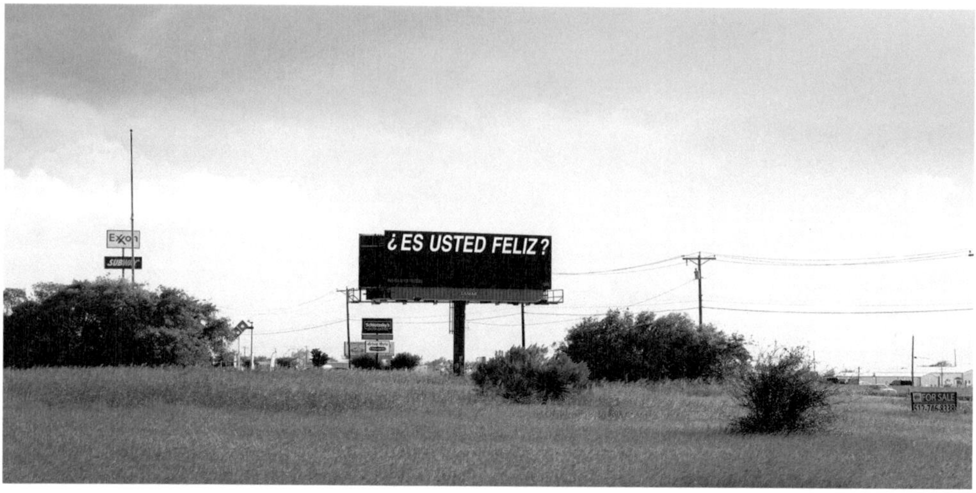

I.7 Alfredo Jaar, *For Freedoms*, 1981/2018, from the series *Studies on Happiness* (1979–81), Austin, Texas. Courtesy of Alfredo Jaar.

coloniality is not detached from the question of happiness.[111] Furthermore, this happiness, which is thought from the decolonial, is not detached from the incomplete struggle for a world yet to come.

As a mode of being and becoming, happiness from this perspective was central in anti-imperialist experiences and discourses in dictatorship Chile. Understood not as the result of the struggle but as the struggle itself, happiness regards the hopes in the present for an imminent decolonial future. Miguel Enríquez, for instance, one of the founders of the Movimiento de Izquierda Revolucionaria (MIR, Movement of the Revolutionary Left), wrote: "My happiness is my fight."[112] Evoking Karl Marx's 1865 "Confessions," for Enríquez (who in 1974 was assassinated by DINA while living clandestinely), happiness occurs "when people can surrender completely to the moment they are living; when being and becoming are the same."[113] In this scenario, the answer no in Jaar's work means to give up, to assimilate with the regime, to break oneself and betray to survive death while simultaneously falling into the obscenity of torture.[114] The answer yes, on the other hand, means the persistence of the fight, even, or perhaps precisely, in life under dictatorship. Jaar's work from this perspective offers the possibility of embracing such a fight while also preventing risking one's life, challenging the assumption that words are transparent and that the relation between signifier and signified is always fixed, universal. Through a multilayered question that exposes the complex decolonial meaning of happiness and freedom together, Jaar's work "conceive[s] affect, happiness or otherwise, as an entry into political subjectivity and the legitimate ground for political act," as scholar of contemporary art and literature Esther Gabara maintains.[115] And in that space, the answers yes and no mean not simply the rejection or affirmation of fascism and imperialism by adopting and adhering to a two-party system. They also mean a negation of binarism as the single source of subjectivity. In this sense, Jaar's series "create[s] another form of (realist) fiction [that] need not be the opposite of avant-garde critique, and it should not be collapsed with ideology."[116] And this is why, as Gabara continues, in the epigraph of Jaar's book *Studies on Happiness* the artist paraphrases a famous line by Nigerian novelist, poet, and critic Chinua Achebe about the capacity of art to create otherwise realities.[117] The epigraph reads: "Art is our constant effort to create for ourselves a different order of reality from that which is given to us."[118] Such understanding of *aesthetics* as an *unfinished* effort impulses Jaar to continue posing the same question—he knows that while neither yes nor no can do much to change the course of modernity and dismantle its linear time, their relational inquiries can still imagine otherwise realities. In so doing, the graphic content in Jaar's work, that is, the seemingly binominal poll about happiness, raises the following questions: How has happiness as a form of decolonial fight existed within neoliberalism? What forms has it taken and how have these forms addressed the restrictions of the free market? The answer proposed by Jaar is art: art as a mode of insisting over and over from different conceptual forms on the question of liberation—art as a form of radical hope.

In 1982, finding himself "completely suffocated by the political situation," Jaar decided to leave Chile.[119] He moved to New York, where the Chilean economic "miracle" and its semantics of freedom were rapidly being injected by the Ronald Reagan–Margaret Thatcher axis, causing even more harm to humans and the planet.[120] Importantly, as Reagan's New Right relied on modernity's rhetoric of "democracy," speaking against it, that is, saying no openly and loudly, was *not as dangerous* as in a formal fascist autocracy, as in Chile. "[Fascism] sees its salvation in granting expression to the masses—but on no account granting them rights," writes Walter Benjamin.[121] And the people know. From the realm of the decolonial, they know that the liberation project is ongoing as revolution is likely to fail in the world as it is. They know, in other words, that modernity continues denigrating peoples, cultures, and subjectivities that embrace and expand the narratives on nonlinear times and that that is precisely why they won't stop the fight. "The more conservative things became under Reagan, the more space I found for my work. [In this] environment, an opposition developed, and there was a space for the kind of things I was doing," Jaar recalls.[122]

This is why, in 1985, Jaar appropriated the June 7, 1985, cover of *The Economist*, which featured the following headline: "What will they leave behind?" (figure I.8). Here, the artist simply reproduces the cover and shows it as such, with the image of Reagan and former UK Prime Minister Margaret Thatcher walking away, their backs to the camera, while readers, or the world, see them bailing out as a symbol of impunity in the global justice system. Responding to the rhetorical question of *The Economist* of "What will they leave behind?" Jaar proposes the following answer: the linear past. What Reagan and Thatcher turn their backs on, Jaar seems to tell us, is the time of crime they helped develop and then escaped from. It is the time of victors' history that regards progress but also walking away from coloniality, death, oblivion, and certainly accountability. In representing the cover twice, that is, as cover and as art, Jaar invites us to think about another time, the time of behind, where dynamic and active memories indeed exist, even if only in images.

In the next decade, when Jaar made *1992*, neoliberalism, in the words of anthropologist Anna Lowenhaupt Tsing, was "whiz[zing] around the globe."[123] In this context, Jaar developed his most famous series, *The Rwanda Project* (1994–2000), where he addresses the indifference of the Western mainstream media regarding the 1994 genocide in Rwanda. In the project's 1994 installation, *Untitled* (*Newsweek*) (plate 4), Jaar appropriates the covers of the US weekly magazine *Newsweek* published from April 11 to August 1, 1994. Beneath each cover, he adds text describing events in Rwanda taking place at that same moment. Aiming to provide strategies to protect individuals' stock shares while ignoring massacres across the hemisphere and overseas, *Newsweek*'s headline on the first cover reads: "Focus. On Your Money: How to Survive in a Scary Market." The headline on the last cover, on the other hand, reads: "Hell on Earth: Racing Against Death in Rwanda," to which Jaar adds: "August 1, 1994: Newsweek magazine dedicates its first cover to Rwanda" (figure I.9). Alongside the text is a photograph showing people lying dead in the dry dirt in Rwanda, while others stand up in the rubble of the past *as* a representation of the present. A young child in the foreground witnesses the ruins, their expression simultaneously of pain, consciousness, and commotion. The child's expression is the testimony of modernity's denial of happiness.

"The conviction that another acknowledged crime against humanity was perpetrated against the Africans by slavery and its catastrophic and far-reaching, later colonial, effects, is the central problematic of Alfredo Jaar,"

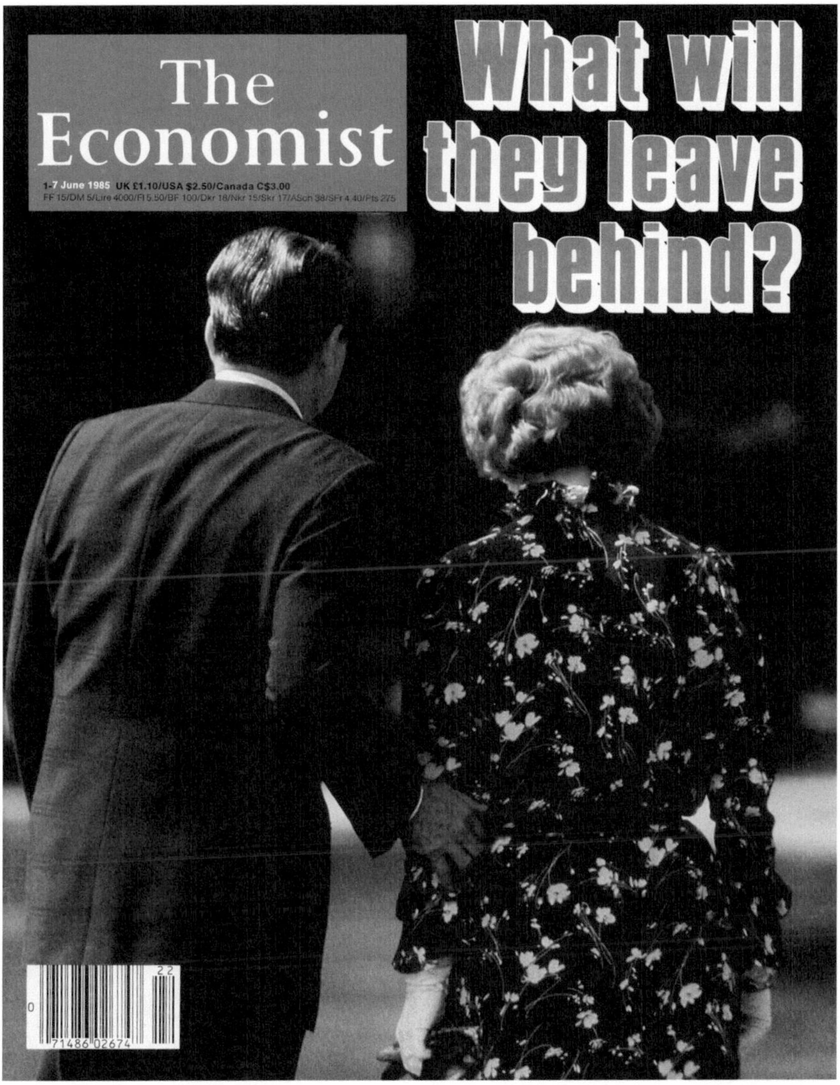

I.8 Alfredo Jaar, *What Will They Leave Behind?*, 1985. Courtesy of Alfredo Jaar.

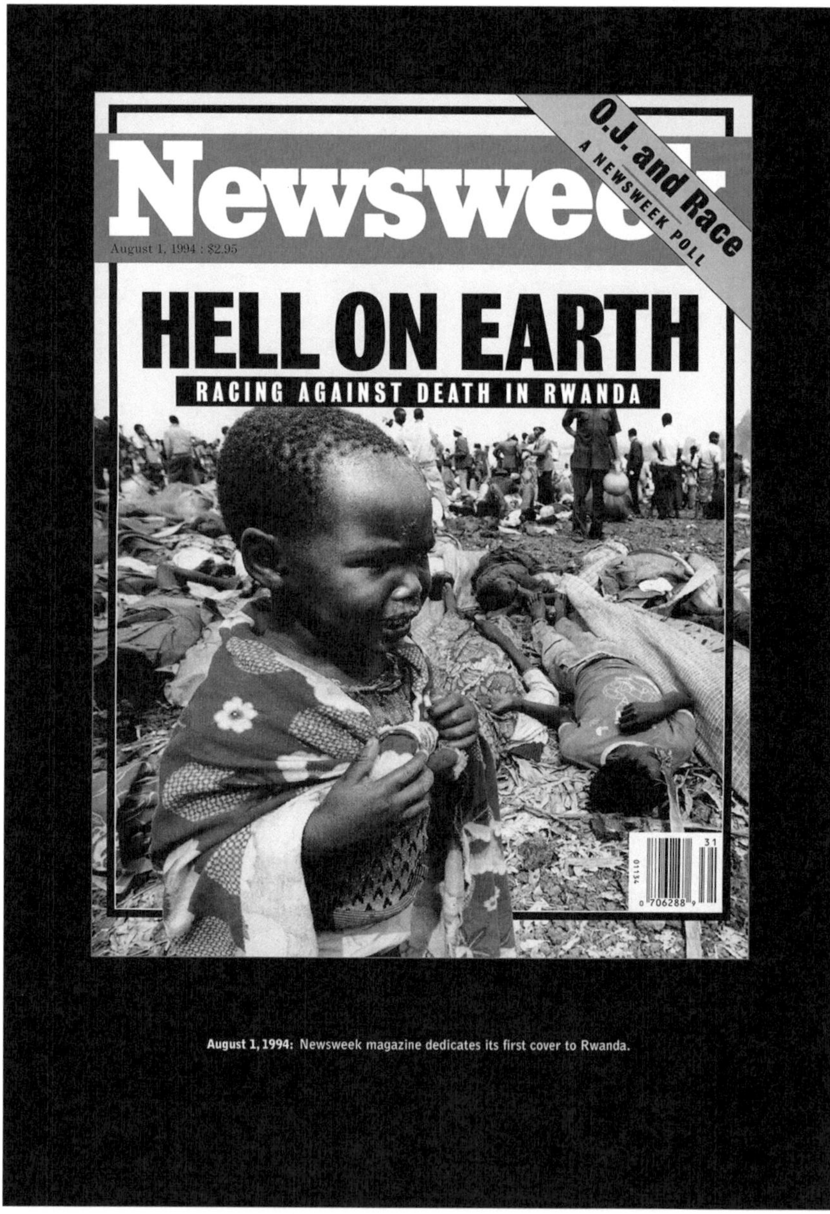

I.9 Alfredo Jaar, *Untitled (Newsweek)* (detail), 1994, from the series *The Rwanda Project* (1994–2000). Courtesy of Alfredo Jaar.

writes art historian Griselda Pollock. "Jaar feels called upon, by his refusal to look away from what is happening in the world to and around Africa, to examine . . . what our current regimes of representation do in this double bind of representation."[124] In Jaar's critique of the media and the regimes of representation it imposes, however, it is key to note that the artist's own experience growing up in Martinique has informed his interest in Africa and the African diaspora. "I lived for ten years [in] Martinique, which was the birth country of Aimé Césaire, one of the founders of Négritude. I had these very strong links with Africa through Martinique, and I immediately realized the wrongful, racist portrayal of Africa in the media. To focus on these issues became quite natural," he said.[125] In turn, in Jaar's understanding of "history," there is no "later colonial" but coloniality of power, that is, an ongoing system begun in the sixteenth century alongside the invention of the Americas. In Jaar's words: "This idea of 'postcolonial' is as illusory as 'postwar.' Unfortunately, the 'colonies' are pretty much alive [as they] are extremely dependent on the former colonizers. And conflicts exist now because these former colonies that are still colonies are trying to distance themselves from that system of oppression."[126]

Jaar's art is about connecting the conceptual locus of the conquest with neoliberalism's capitalist violence in the global context, questioning the idea of happiness in free-market narratives embracing liberty, access, and success. It is about exposing the colonial dangers of modernity and the complicity of the media and intellectual discourse in such dangers, signaling that words such as *openness, cooperation, freedom, democracy*, and so on have indeed multiple and, most of the time, opposing meanings. From the perspective of capitalism, these words are well established in linear time. As Princeton University professor of political science John Ikenberry proudly reported in 2018: "The liberal international characteristics of order—openness, rules, multilateral cooperation—are deeply rooted and likely to persist."[127] Jaar's art, in all, is about showing the world *just* as it is, one in which the life of the majority has a lesser value than that of those replicating and benefiting from economic freedom. And in this binominal equation, millions are censored, tortured, and sometimes—many times—killed or made to disappear. Many others are criminalized, incarcerated, deported, and dehumanized, as shown in Jaar's *1992*.

This is what Jaar meant in his proposal for this work. He offered: "One of the most tragic consequences of this situation is the movement of peoples searching for a better life. My [work] depicts the 'reception' being given to Vietnamese refugees arriving in Hong Kong Whitehead Detention Center, where more than 25,000 people wait for a screening procedure to define their status."[128] By "this situation," Jaar refers to the legacies of the conquest in the neoliberal present, where "reception" means no encounter but imprisonment, erasure, and denial of mourning. If Jaar's work, installed in SoHo, the heart of New York's art world at the time, and displayed underground beneath the Columbus Day parade, addressed the "social, political, [and] economic . . . shifts affecting us all at the close of the 20th century," as prompted by the Public Art Fund (the art organization that, alongside the Whitney Museum of American Art and the American Center in Paris, had invited Jaar to create *1992*), it was precisely to state that in 1992, the foundations of capitalism as established five hundred years ago have not only remained but expanded further. And today, in our digital, globalized world built on smart technologies, frenetic consumerism, and social media spectacle as forms of reality, there are more prisons, despair, genocide, and deaths; more freedom, connectivity, progress, and linear success.

As I write in 2025, the global migration crisis represented in Jaar's *1992* has exacerbated even further. In the United States, for instance, the Trump administration has adopted the infamous Alien Enemies Act of 1798 to deport immigrants to inhuman detention centers abroad regardless of evidence of criminal records, all while creating fear in society through political and media spectacle. In this context, humans considered "aliens," a disparaging term used since 1798 to describe lawful permanent residents in the United States, are seen by the administration literally as "enemy."[129] The same is the case with the university. Enacting to the letter Vice President JD Vance's statement from 2021—"universities are the enemy"—federal funding has now been removed or threatened to be removed if requests for epistemological and cultural exceptionalism are not met.[130] Demanding higher education to obey Americanity in their curriculum, research, and reparation programs, the Trump administration, in Jaar's words, is "forcing people to remain silent. It's Pinochet, again."[131] And here we are, with the war against the university recalling the Chilean dictatorship, where cultural institutions were taken over and freedom of speech was reproved. In this context, Jaar's question about happiness is today, just as ever, immanently urgent.

So is the question about Palestine. As a fourth-generation Palestinian whose paternal family migrated to Chile from Bethlehem during the Ottoman Empire in the last quarter of the nineteenth century, Jaar, since an early age, has not been estranged from this question. He recalls: "I grew up witnessing my father's suffering upon the issue of Palestine, and in a way that pain was transferred to me."[132] Within the decolonial framework of this book, such pain—which Jaar absorbed through oral tradition from his father's diasporic grief vis-à-vis other experiences he has lived firsthand, such as the coup—has materialized in his art throughout a refusal to forget the global catastrophe of progressive time. This is what the artist meant when referring to Palestine and the mainstream media. He said: "The Western media conveniently starts the narrative from October 7th, ignoring the historical context. Consequently, the aggressor is portrayed as the good guy while the victim becomes the villain."[133] In this context, as Jaar explains elsewhere, "when students in the U.S. started protesting and asking for a cease fire, for the end of the genocide, the Biden-Harris administration sent the police." And today, Jaar continues, "this is going even further."[134] Yet, as the artist further denotes, referring to the 2024 student solidarity encampments with Palestine across university campuses in the United States from the lens of decolonial time and radical hope, "the younger generation is the consciousness of the world."[135] Referring to this all in his acceptance speech at the MacDowell Medal ceremony in Peterborough, New Hampshire, on June 29, 2025, Jaar said, "As an architect making art, I respond to context. And what is the context today? Censorship is emerging everywhere. . . . We are sponsoring a genocide and supporting an apartheid system. Students have faced threats of imprisonment, yet they continue to speak out. . . . Their courage in the face of adversity is a beacon of hope.[136]

In 1985, Jaar had his first solo exhibition in the United States at New York University's Grey Art Gallery (now the Grey Art Museum). In *Installation Projects*, with the selection of the word *projects* for the title, Jaar was introducing himself to Manhattan's downtown art world as an artist whose aesthetic was essentially unfinished. However, said aesthetics went unnoticed at the time. As one critic wrote in relationship to *Motherland*, which Jaar displayed as a sketch on a sheet of paper: "By placing neon in conjunction with natural materials such as earth, [Jaar] draws attention to the gap between technology and nature, between developed and underdeveloped countries, evok[ing] the magic realism associated with South American liter[ature]."[137] Equating earth with nature and neon with civilization, that is, progressive time, this critic's comparison of a work by a Latin American artist with the genre of magical realism in Latin American literature is not surprising. After all, in the words of literary scholar Matthew Bush, magical realism "provided global audiences with an exotic look of Latin Americanness that has proven hard to shake."[138]

In the 1980s, with the emergence of a Latin American art market, US art institutions created reductive and homogenizing cultural stereotypes, linking the arts of the time with the literature boom of the 1960s and 1970s.[139] Solidarizing with the boom as an axis from which to think about Latin American art's new global identity, art curators and scholars celebrated the boom's most famous writer, Colombian Nobel Prize in Literature winner Gabriel García

Márquez, whose best-known novel, *Cien años de soledad* (*One Hundred Years of Solitude*, 1967), creates a cultural project inseparable from what García Márquez called Latin America's "monstrous reality."[140] "Our aim, perhaps ambitious, has been to take up this challenge in relation to the visual arts: we would argue that the way to understand contemporary Latin American art must be to see it in the context or reality, the 'monstrous reality' of world politics," note Latin American art scholars Oriana Baddeley and Valerie Fraser in their landmark 1989 volume of Latin American art.[141] Yet, to paraphrase literary critic Jean Franco, the myth of Macondo—the fictional city in *Cien años de soledad*—not only contrasts with the reality of Latin American cities, then in the process of disintegration through a series of military dictatorships, but also represents a virgin state disconnected from US oppression and dominion.[142] In turn, as Cuban novelist and thinker Arturo Benítez Rojo states, the book further shows a recurrent theme in the Caribbean novel in which at stake is the search "toward a Utopian territory" or "a hypothetical center of origins," recalling the search for El Dorado and the strong presence of Western enunciation in the representation of culture and thus time.[143] By adopting, expanding, and marketizing cultural subordination through the circular novel in the search of roots, a critical take on Americanity is exactly what García Márquez's novel lacked.

Also in 1985, the same year as his exhibition at NYU's Grey Art Gallery, Alfredo Jaar made *Cien años de soledad [no realmente]* (plate 5). Using neon to politicize the material in its temporal dimension, Jaar writes the title of García Márquez's novel in cursive script with white neon lettering. Below it, written with red neon and all in capitals, he adds: "No realmente" (Not really). "As you know, García Márquez's novel gives a completely wrong idea of Latin America," Jaar said.[144] Showing that aesthetics and politics, or art and life, are not *always* mirrored, García Márquez's most famous novel not only reproduced but also marketized—and quite successfully—the colonial time of modernity. Seeking to substitute the region's "backwardness" by repudiating any link to tradition and advocating for "newness," writers of the boom insisted "in the foundational role of their generation in erasing the past to 'catch up' with history's present," as Avelar has argued.[145] In his *Cien años de soledad* specifically, Avelar continues, García Márquez presents "allegories of an 'author' doubled in the foundational character, who appears without predecessors and often operates outside the system of change, hierarchy, and power that has condemned Latin American countries to anachronism and dependency."[146] This means that, by removing the self from the past, García Márquez and his most famous novel advocate for literature's autonomy, secularity, and globality. They advocate for sales, aligning with "the Chicago-school modernization theories" and exposing "the need for reconciliation between fables of identity and teleologies of modernization, [that is, between] the circular time of myth versus the linear, onward-flowing time of secular history."[147]

No wonder why Jaar appropriates this title and novel and shows it just like that: an allegory of the refoundational project of neoliberalism in life under modernity. Contrasting the temporality of *Cien años de soledad,* the phrase "Not really" in Jaar's installation means "No, this is not Latin America." Turned into a decolonial negation, this conceptual gesture further underscores the historical conditions that propelled Jaar to create this work and thus a second negation: "No, Latin America is not alone." As Reagan had just publicly revealed his support to the Contras in Nicaragua, the negation of the word *solitude* thus means intervention, memory annihilation, ruins.[148] It means Americanity. After all, as Quijano and Wallerstein remind us, "independence did not undo coloniality; it merely transforms its outer form."[149]

Informed by different hemispheric and global entanglements, Jaar's art on decolonial time shows the ongoing state of mourning by those in cultures of resistance as well as the centrality of culture in indicting perpetrators in society and the fact that the struggles for reparation and justice have so far failed and thus decolonial efforts must continue. Jaar's art, in total, is about mourning, accountability, and failure, a threefold decolonial paradigm that he enacts through what I call in this book his exercises of memory.

EXERCISES OF MEMORY

In 1993, thirty-two-year-old South African photojournalist Kevin Carter traveled from his hometown in Johannesburg to Sudan, where he photographed the famine crises during the Second Civil War. In one of these photographs, a starving child is being observed by a vulture. Positioned in the foreground, in the lower right quadrant of the frame, the child hides, laying the elbows in the dirt. The vulture, on the other hand, depicted a few feet behind at the center right, stands defiant and sees, as if witnessing Carter's presence, his lens, while waiting for its prey. Appearing first in the *New York Times* and then circulated worldwide, in 1994, this photograph earned Carter a Pulitzer Prize. It also prompted him to commit suicide three months later in response to the media scandal around the image, which accused Carter of his "vulture-like ethics."[150] As one critic wrote: "The man adjusting his lens to take just the right frame of [the child's] suffering might just as well be a predator, another vulture on the scene."[151]

This and other commentaries published by the media were appropriated by Jaar in his 2006 installation *The Sound of Silence*, in which he contextualizes Carter's photograph by creating a theater-like space with an eight-minute video loop inside it (figure I.10). In the video, using white lowercase lettering over a black background, Jaar narrates Carter's story, from his birth during apartheid and his trip to Sudan to his suicide and the image's afterlife. Midway through his account, Jaar details the moment Carter captures the photograph of the vulture and the child, which, in turn, appears suddenly and shortly while a single flash discharges. Interrupting the viewer's vision and modernity's linear time, Jaar repeats Carter's name over and over. "kevin, kevin, kevin carter," he writes at the beginning; "kevin, kevin, kevin carter," he repeats by the end. Through a linguistic operation that insists on a word—a proper name—Jaar pays homage not only to Carter but also to the capacity of photojournalism to shape people's consciousnesses, creating a linguistic, photographic, and architectural memorial that honors the photojournalist's ethical sense of responsibility regarding the suffering of humans caused by modernity and its homologue of war. "Such images cannot be more than an invitation to pay attention, to reflect, to learn, to examine the rationalizations for mass suffering offered by established powers," writes Susan Sontag.[152] Equating imperial power with humanitarian catastrophe, Sontag asks: "Who caused what the picture shows? Who is responsible? Is it excusable? Was it inevitable?"[153] Jaar's response is the vulture as both presence and allegory—as a figure provoking starvation, sorrow, and death, the vulture in Jaar's work is neither the photographer nor the bird but the capitalist society in the context of modernity that creates these conditions in the first place.

Eight years later, in 2014, Jaar created another theater-like installation to contextualize a second image: Dutch photojournalist Koen Wessing's *Estelí, Nicaragua, September 1978* (figure I.11). Taken in 1978 during the Nicaraguan Revolution, this photograph shows two young female peasants crying in desperation upon learning about the assassination of their farmer father by the US-sponsored National Guard. Titled *Shadows*, the installation begins with a dark and narrow hallway, with a series of light boxes displaying contact prints from the same 35 mm film used by Wessing for his *Estelí* in the walls. At the end of the corridor, in an isolated dark room, *Estelí* appears to the viewer's eye through a projection that gradually illuminates the image, as the women become glowing silhouettes (figure I.12). In becoming silhouettes, they become anonymous bodies, representing society under modernity's state of terror, or society in collective pain.

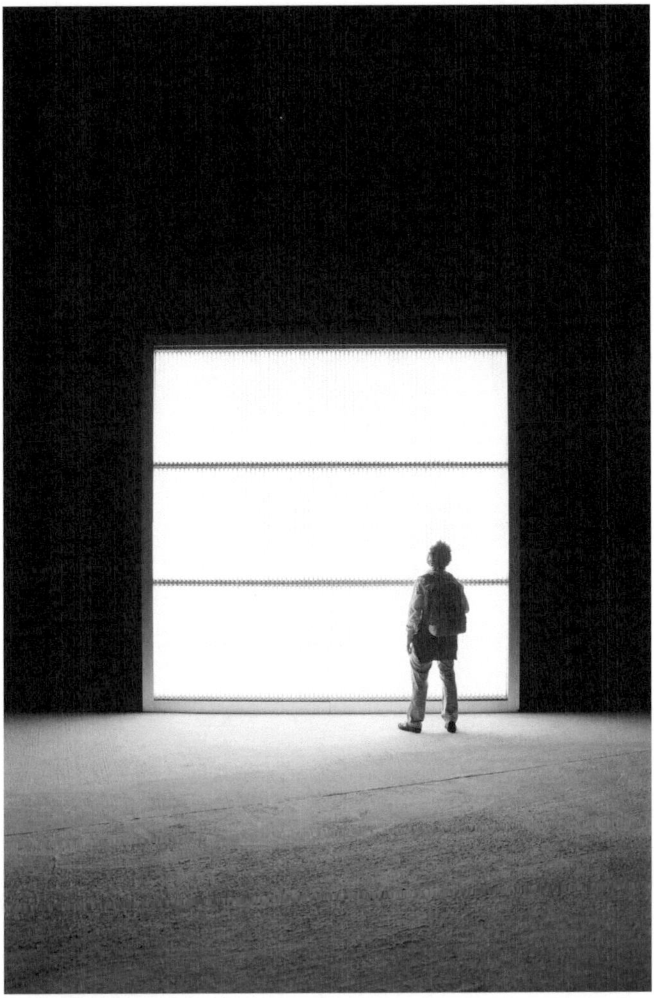

I.10 Alfredo Jaar, *The Sound of Silence*, 2006. Courtesy of Alfredo Jaar.

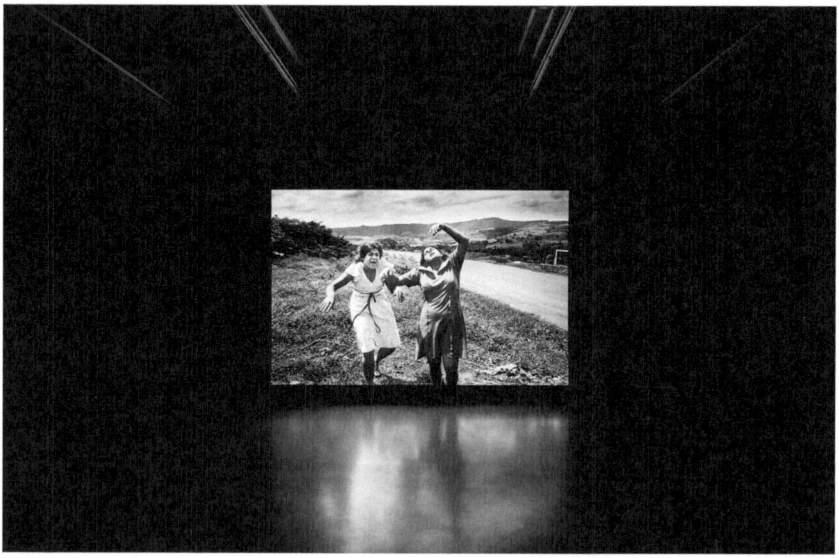

I.11 Alfredo Jaar, *Shadows*, 2014. Courtesy of Alfredo Jaar.

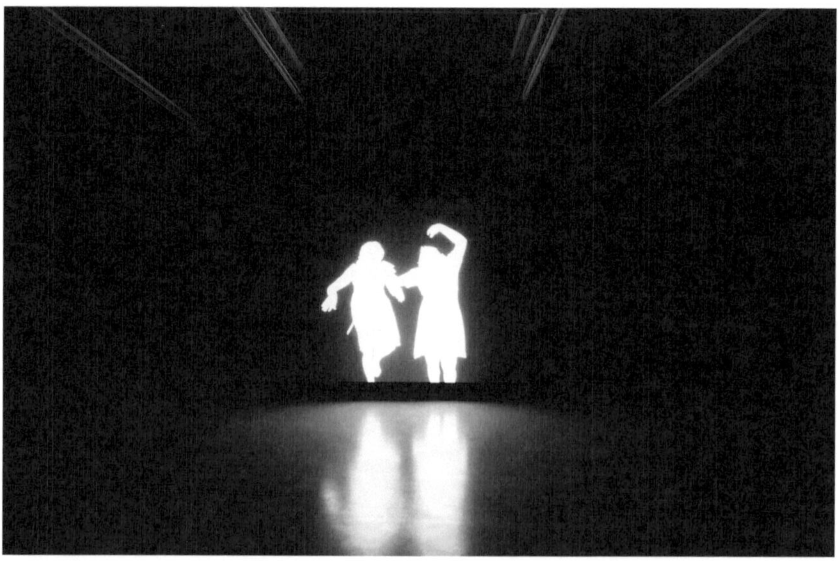

I.12 Alfredo Jaar, *Shadows*, 2014. Courtesy of Alfredo Jaar.

Turning a local story into the story of many, *Shadows* also includes a testimony by Wessing in the form of a video in which the photographer narrates the moment before the shooting: "We were in Managua in the north of Nicaragua, and suddenly we saw a man lying on the road. . . . He had a big hole, like this, in his head. They shot him five kilometers from his house. His colleagues arrived and they put his body in a van and took him home."[154] Wessing's words provide information that every family of victims of atrocities deserves to know: a testimony of how their loved ones were killed so that justice may eventually be achieved. In incorporating this testimony, Jaar honors those fallen under modernity and those who mourn, including photojournalists such as Wessing and their fight for representing the existence and thus the past of the oppressed. In this sense, the glowing silhouettes, just as the flash discharged in *The Sound of Silence*, are allegories of photojournalism's capacity to interface in our forms of seeing and judging within the art gallery, the museum, the media, the world.

Important to the discussion in this book about global coloniality, in *Shadows* Jaar displays, next to Wessing's testimony, a photo book made by the Dutch photojournalist immediately after the Chilean coup (figure I.13). Indeed, shortly after the military took over, thirty-one-year-old Wessing flew to Santiago to document the brutal images of the repression so that the world could "see," creating the photo book *Chili September 1973*. Published in Amsterdam in 1973, both the book and its images were censored in Chile, just as with any image documenting the brutality of the dictatorship. This is why Jaar, only upon his arrival in New York in the early 1980s, was finally able to *see* thousands of photographs made by socially committed photojournalists such as Wessing; thousands of images showing people behind bars, crying, hidden, searching, and mourning; images of the military burning everything, from revolutionary literature to bodies and people, even when alive.[155] To modernize the nation, so the narrative of coloniality says, the past must be forgotten in the invisible debris of history. And today in "democratic" Chile, when many of these images have entered the country's imaginary, millions remain to be seen. Connecting shared histories of repression under the rule of Americanity, *The Sound of Silence*, *Shadows*, and Jaar's entire body of work are conceptually elaborated *with* the victims instead of *for* them, in an aesthetic project embracing collective reciprocity and hope. The line is fine, but it is also quite marked.

Jaar's art on photojournalist images of human suffering has propelled some art critics to accuse him of "aestheticizing horror," "exploit[ing the] subject," and "manipulat[ing] the viewer."[156] Reviewing *The Sound of Silence* for the *New York Times*, art critic Roberta Smith, for instance, states that the story

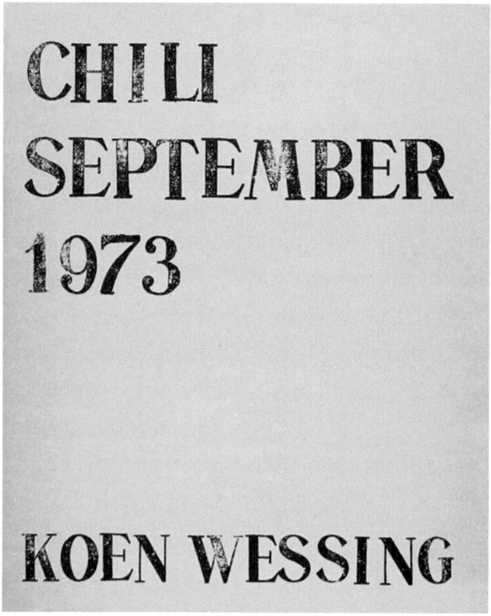

I.13 Koen Wessing, *Chili September 1973*, 1973.

"is trivialized and exploited by the art . . . , leav[ing] you moved yet irked, feeling raw yet manipulated. You may wonder whether Mr. Jaar is an artist or just some finely tuned hybrid of set designer, art director, editorial writer and graphic designer."[157] Smith's critique, however, not only presupposes a finalized and polished result by overlooking Jaar's relational temporality. It also situates the artist in the position of a Western savior, while simultaneously nullifying the presence and agency of the photographed and by extension the more complex temporal and spatial dimension within the photographic. Yet, as philosopher Jacques Rancière writes by denoting the differences between pity (or Occidentalism) and compassion (of nonhegemonic reciprocity): "Humanism or compassion are words people like to use with regard of Alfredo Jaar. . . . But compassion is not pity for the unfortunate, it is the capacity to feel with them, which equally entails the capacity to make them feel with us."[158] In turn, as media scholar Ariella Azoulay has argued, the space between the photographer, the photographed, and the viewer "is a political space where human beings look at one another, speak and act in a manner that is not solely subordinate to disciplinary constraints, not to ones of governance."[159] This means that judgments formulated from the lens of "universal" aesthetics, as those appropriated by Jaar in *The Sound of Silence*, where the photographer—or Carter—is called "a predator, another vulture," invalidate "the presence of the persons photographed and the relations of reciprocity that exist between them and the photographer."[160] What is negated is the very reciprocity that documentary images can indeed offer, challenging the idea that photographs of violence exploit their subjects to provide sensational material and thus feed voyeuristic tendencies. Quite differently, Jaar's art on photojournalism embodies reciprocity through a process of learning that is ethically and politically necessary, one that, in line with social and cultural theorist Susie Linfield's take on photography, may connect us to our history of violence and human cruelty.[161] It further represents the extended political spaces between lens, subject, and unfinished instances of reception, offering aesthetic modes of speaking (or making), existing (or performing), and listening (or critically understanding) through compassion, reciprocity, and humility together. Viewed from this perspective, critical photojournalism has the potential to advance toward decolonial approaches to human rights and photography as an ethical means to respond to our ever-increasing arrogant and nihilistic modernity. This is why photography, as used by Jaar, reminds us that photographs of atrocity show not only what *has been* but also that *things like this* should not happen again.[162] It reminds us of the motto "Nunca más" (Never again), used by families of victims in Latin America and beyond, recalling a collective performativity that relies on photographs of the deceased to prevent the reproduction of their death in other bodies, epochs, genocides, and wars. In this sense, Jaar's art turns the *index* of the past, in singular, into a dynamic and activist sign of decolonial pasts, presents, and futures, in plural, reframing photography's ontology as a sign not only and essentially related to its reference or to what the lens has touched through the action of light. Photography is also what *could* be touched, that is, what *could* be witnessed or lived in within a world of radical hope that is yet to come.

As Jaar's art refuses to leave the struggles and memories of the past in oblivion, below the ashes of sequential time, he has called his works on Chile "exercises of memory." As this book considers the global impact of the Chilean coup and its neoliberal implementation as a laboratory of the world, I will refer from now on to Jaar's entire oeuvre as such, that is, as exercises of memory elaborated through and within an unfinished aesthetics, one where national, regional, and global decolonial debates all intersect. Viewed as representational practices that interrupt the frozen past of Western art, art history, and intellectual discourse, Jaar's art represents the "ongoing reactivation of what every image related to the disappeared purports to achieve: that they appear, alive; and that those responsible are brought to trial and punished for their crimes."[163] As such, it develops, expands, complicates, and rethinks the ongoing present *as* presence, challenging, in Avelar's argument, the “evolutionary narrative where the present emerges as the inevitable overcoming of a failed past.”[164] Jaar’s exercises of memory therefore aim at mobilizing historical and political consciousness so that crimes like those that happened in the past in Chile, the Americas, and the world “won’t happen again.” They thus remind us of Walter Benjamin’s always urgent statement about modernity, suffering, and ruins. Writing about the philosophy of history, Benjamin states: “There is no document of civilization which is not at the same time a document of barbarism.”[165] Insisting on a colonial temporality that repeats the horrors of the world by reproducing the archive of justifiable war, Benjamin continues: “And just as such a document is not free of barbarism, barbarism taints also the manner in which it was transmitted from one owner to another.”[166] Thinking of himself as a pessimist in thought and optimist in will, Jaar knows that by appropriating and intervening in documents of the world as it is, he is portraying exactly that: that being modernity’s world and its corollary barbarism, oppression, criminalization, genocide, and war. Yet at the same time, Jaar refuses to give up, to give away his radical hope, creating an unfinished aesthetic project in which photography is central.

So is the case with poetry, which in Jaar’s art is formulated from a temporal dimension that rebuffs the erasure of sites of knowledges built upon decolonial chaos and ruptures. Like photography, poetry in Jaar’s art has taken multiple forms, from installations and images including verses and stanzas honoring anti-imperialist writers, to bibliography and archival resources informing his project on decolonial time. He has also invited poets to write about his works, intersecting and expanding his aesthetics of the unfinished in collaborative and relational ways. Importantly, considering the role of Caribbean intellectuals in decolonial thought in general and Jaar’s art in particular, one of these poets is Glissant, whom Jaar met in 2010 at a conference on the Caribbean at the National Arts Gallery in Nassau in the Bahamas. “After listening to Glissant, I was marveled,” he recalls.[167] What marveled Jaar was what Glissant called poetics of relation, where language and thought are “forever conjectural . . . latent, open, multilingual in intention [and] directly in contact with everything possible.”[168] And since relation “interweaves” instead of “projects” in “a line of energy curved back onto itself,” Glissant’s poetics interpellates modernity’s desire for ultimate achievements in the temporal continuity of the universal.[169] Glissant’s poetics, in this sense, as his English translator Betsy Wing tellingly describes it, is “based more on associative principles than on any steady progress toward irrefutable proof.”[170]

This is why Jaar, after meeting Glissant in the Bahamas, invited him to write about a portfolio of fifteen photographs he took in Robben Island,

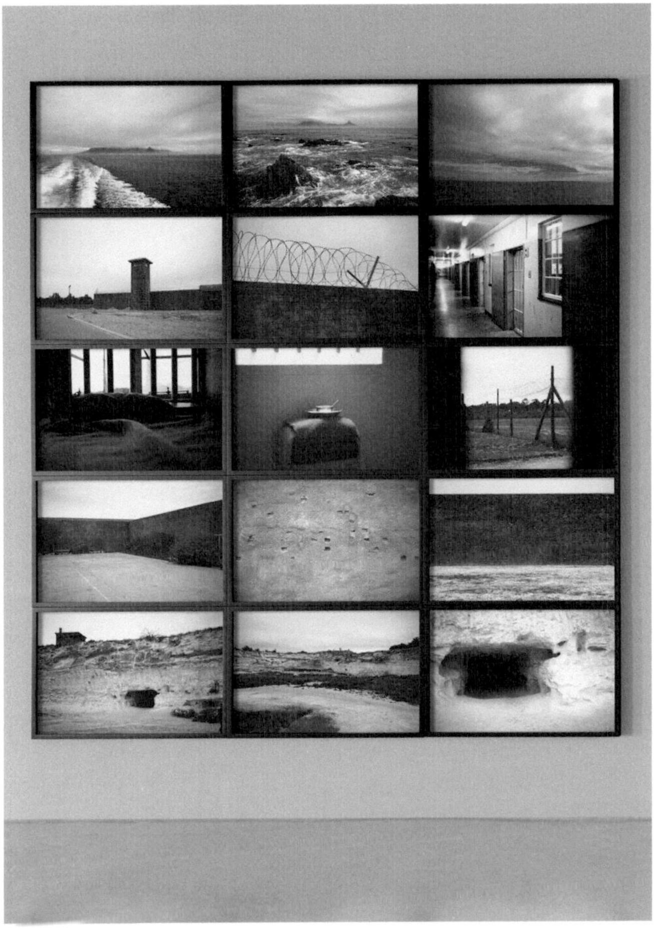

I.14 Alfredo Jaar, *The Sound of Silence*, 2006. Courtesy of Alfredo Jaar.

the prison off the coast of Cape Town where Nelson Mandela was incarcerated during apartheid (figure I.14). The coloniality of time is not detached from the coloniality of the cell, Jaar may have thought. Recalling his *1992* (plate 1), in which he denounces our binominal order by confronting freedom and confinement, here Jaar critiques modernity's Cartesian logic by showing together ocean waves and barbed wires, the horizon and the prison's walls, and the clouds merging into the sea next to a solitary hallway in cold green tones. Titled just as his 2006 installation, *The Sound of Silence*, the work honors Mandela's tireless fight for liberation and that of all those imprisoned in modernity's oppression, mingling modes to remember and mourn as open forms *in* relation. And thus Glissant wrote: "[we] hear out the world with equipoise and with fairness . . . where one minute is no less than a century . . . learning that the infinite grows in the green death of a hallway, and that the seas rush to places on earth."[171] Thinking from the fluid dimension of the Caribbean archipelago as a site from where to imagine a non-totalitarian world or the *tout-monde,* in this stanza, sound emerges from that world in becoming, resonating in a minute that is never just that but the ongoing time of the decolonial, and inhabiting the endless process of mourning as hope in the interweaving of seas, earth, sounds, and the ongoing search for reciprocity.[172]

There are circles within circles. Neoliberalism, as I have argued in this introduction, is the current phase *within* capitalism, just as globalization is the current phase *within* modernity. Exposing this coexistence by responding to different historical contexts at the national, regional, and global levels, in 1992, for instance, observing the expansion of the Chilean free market's "miracle" into the world, Jaar made his little-known and yet critically important *1992* (plate 1). Indeed, *1992*—as artwork and epoch—represents the moment in which Jaar started incorporating into his exercises of memory interconnected situations of coloniality within a global context. In doing so, the work shows that "cultures of the world have always maintained relations among themselves," as Glissant wrote, and that by the early 1990s, when Glissant published *Poetics of Relation,* "the right conditions came together to speed up the nature of these connections," as Jaar said.[173] In this sense, *1992* shows that Jaar's focus on "global" issues does not simply follow "trends" in the art world or the art market as an extension of the world, that is, our capitalist-oriented system. Rather, Jaar's art is about critiquing these trends by showing them twice, appropriating a word, an image, a cover, a stanza, or a verse, and representing them through conceptual strategies engaging with decolonial time.

The chapters that follow address such aesthetics of the unfinished by reading Jaar's art in relation to critical discourses around the photographic, journalism, poetry, transnational solidarity, human rights jurisdiction, and hope, offering a new paradigm from where to think about global contemporary art from the concepts of mourning, accountability, and failure. Chapter 1, "Mourning," offers a comparative analysis of Jaar's art regarding victims of the Chilean dictatorship and of other regimes globally through the analytic of mourning, a concept that challenges a culture of oblivion by means of emancipatory temporalities. Chapter 2, "Accountability," focuses on victimizers during and after the Cold War from the starting point of Jaar's project on Henry Kissinger, the conceptual architect of the Chilean dictatorship and of other genocides worldwide, further maintaining that since accountability exceeds a person's physical life as it perpetuates in modernity's institutional systems, demands for justice *must* continue.[174] Chapter 3, "Failure," centers on the idea of "America" in Jaar's oeuvre to discuss its colonial and anti-colonial meanings, recalling that since practices of liberation, including those regarding language, have so far failed, art as symbolic means toward reparation has not given up. Finally, the conclusion, "The End of the World," provides some closing remarks on how Jaar's lesser-known works addressing our planetary crisis in the age of digital totalization expose and expand on the three main concepts in this book, positing a narrative of hope where, perhaps, in Césaire's words, "the only thing in the world worth beginning [is] The End of the world."[175]

As a book on mourning, accountability, and failure, this book is also about protest, archives, and language, and about death, justice, and active listening. As such, art as aesthetics is understood through contingent relationalities that are always in process and thus rendered linguistically in the present tense. Joining an ever-expanding scholarship that "refuses to be written about in the past tense without the unpredictable—and persistent—intervention of the present tense," as Boreth Ly has argued, this book shows that "memories of traumatic events . . . always continue to hunt us," as Ly further maintains by quoting Raymond Williams.[176] It also reminds us what the Chilean biologist Humberto Maturana called *lenguajear* or languaging, where a noun-turned-verb allows us to use and interpret language and thus culture not as a finished product but as a continuous activity.[177] This is why, in all, this book's temporal flows, entanglements, conjectures, and transdisciplinary are rendered through a languaging that inhabits the present both formally and metaphorically, challenging the completed outcome of cultural analysis and aiming to be continued in future forms, epochs, sites, and art history writings.

1

MOURNING

Power cultivates forgetfulness. But under the country's layer of amnesia, memories emerge. They resonate under the skin.
—Patricio Guzmán, *Allende*

In 1974, Alfredo Jaar created his earliest series of drawings, commencing his project on decolonial time. In one of these drawings, *September 11 (White)*, Jaar repeatedly writes the number 11 on a sheet of paper previously extracted from a sketchbook and arranged vertically (figure 1.1). The reiteration of the number 11 framed by the sheet's edges offers an allegory of a time that is stopped, abruptly interrupted by the social and cultural shock of the military coup in Chile on September 11, 1973. Yet, despite the coup's dreadful effect on people's minds and hearts, the artist continues writing and repeating the same number, slightly altering its shape as a mirror of the exhausted body, as seen in the 11 at the lower right corner. The hand never stops; representation never ceases. No, it cannot stop because the pulse continues and days continue, even in a time of war that is progressive and amnesiac. Simultaneously, that same linear time drives Jaar to repeat the same date forever, revealing a time when grief cannot be denied, much less made to disappear. What Jaar represents in this early work is the presence and urgency of decolonial time in representational practices showing mourning, and he does so by filling the page with repetition. He fills the sheet with the same number to reveal the continuity of the coup in the temporal subjectivity of the collective body that lives, and because it lives, it writes in mourning. "The date of September 11, 1973, . . . was the determining factor in our lives. . . . The first thing that came to mind [when I made these drawings] was that fatal date," Jaar said.[1]

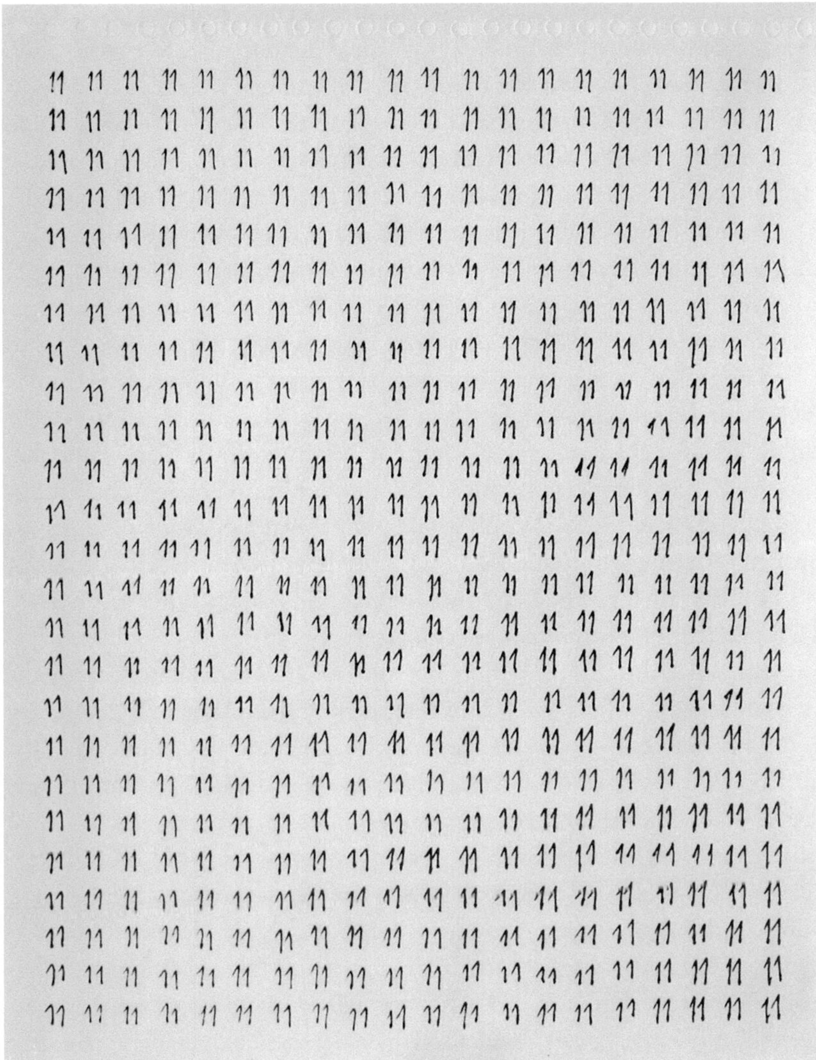

1.1 Alfredo Jaar, *September 11 (White)*, 1974. Courtesy of Alfredo Jaar.

On that date, a civic-military coup drastically changed all forms of life in Chile, inaugurating a dictatorship that would last for seventeen years. The Presidential Palace in downtown Santiago was bombed by earth and sky, and the democratically elected socialist president, Salvador Allende, died inside La Moneda in flames. Supporters of Allende's left-wing coalition, Unidad Popular (Popular Unity), were systematically persecuted, detained, tortured, or forced into exile. Many others were killed, and the bodies of thousands are still disappeared.[2] Suddenly, the newly imposed regime and its technology of violence emptied the streets of Chile, denying free speech while creating a massive architecture of repression whose legacies are still felt today.

From the perspective of the decolonial, the visual paradigm of the coup is not only the image of the military bombarding La Moneda or La Moneda in flames.[3] It is also the unforgettable ruins of the entire Chilean landscape that witnessed its drastic transformation, with those ruins, as literary scholars Michael J. Lazzara and Vicky Unruh would put it, meaning "dynamic sites shot through with competing cultural narratives, palimpsests on which memories and histories are fashioned and refashioned."[4] In his *September 11 (White)*, Jaar represents those ruins by repeating a number that metaphorically overflows the paper, the city, the nation. Repetition in this sense is not copy, lethargy, or abstraction. It is the acknowledgment of a drastic shift in life under modernity that continues to resonate vividly and loudly in Chile's social fabric, propelling the creation of acts and forms of resistance. From truth committees and human rights organizations to public-space protests and critical cultural practices, such as Jaar's, these acts and forms show that mourning is still happening, as people refuse to forget. They show that to remember is to mourn and that to mourn is to remember not only the deceased but also their own memories *as* existence. In the process of this ongoing mourning, the past and the present are revised through emancipatory temporalities, creating, as literary scholar Saidiya Hartman argues, "an opening for counter history, a story written against the narrative of progress.[5]

This is how Jaar's art relates to the coup, the dictatorship that followed, and its neoliberal continuity in Chile's amnesic present, honoring the existence and resistance of victims before and after their physical death. This is also how Jaar's art relates to the transnational conditions that enabled the dictatorship and to a genealogy of hemispheric solidarities opposing this massacre from the realm of culture. This chapter examines these mourning relationalities and the central role of poetry, journalism, and photojournalism in shaping them. Further arguing that global resistance against neoliberalism preceded the coup in linear time, this chapter ultimately offers an understanding of the coup not only as a national event but also as a global one. As such, it provides a comparative analysis of the intrinsically transnational dimension of memory, examining works by Jaar related to the victims of the Chilean dictatorship as well as other humanitarian massacres globally.

STANZAS OF REMEMBRANCE

In 1972, during Allende's second year in office, Chilean society was highly polarized. Inflation, fiscal deficit, and foreign public debt reached their highest levels in the country's history. Strikes from both the right and the center were part of daily life. Union organizations paralyzed transportation and production, and people had to wait in long lines to buy basic groceries, such as bread and milk. Protesting food shortages, bourgeois women mobilized the domestic opposition by banging on pots and pans in public-space protests known as El Cacerolazo.[6] Meanwhile, the right-wing conservative newspaper *El Mercurio* published daily headlines such as "There Is No Milk," "There Is No Bread," and "This Is the Truth."[7] As economist Paul Rosenstein-Rodan wrote in the *New York Times* a year after the coup and thus of Allende's death, Allende's main slogan, "Children are born to be happy: milk for all," was only a metaphor of his own "incompetence," leading the Chilean "people [to] almost wish for a military coup."[8] In justifying the coup through Allende's supposedly disastrous political and economic agenda, the idea of an "incompetent" president has remained in market-oriented discourses. In 2013, the then-president of Chile, the late right-wing billionaire Sebastián Piñera, maintained that Allende "didn't have any respect for the law," propelling the coup.[9] Combining ineptitude and authoritarianism, in 2023 José Antonio Kast—Pinochet's impassioned far-right defender and, since March 2026, Chile's president—went even further and said that Allende's government was, literally, "a dictatorship."[10]

Declassified documents tell quite a different story. In 1972, a year before the coup, the release of the secret documents of International Telephone and Telegraph (ITT)—a US company that owned 70 percent of the Chile Telephone Company (Chitelco) and financed *El Mercurio*—made public a main secret of coloniality: the inextricable relationship between capitalism and humanitarian devastation. Writing for the *Washington Post*, the US investigative reporter who uncovered the ITT documents, Jack Anderson, stated: "[ITT and the CIA] were plotting together to create economic chaos in Chile, hoping this would cause the Chilean army to pull a coup that would block Allende from coming to power."[11] Revealing that while US efforts to prevent

Allende from becoming president failed (Allende assumed the presidency on November 3, 1970), Anderson's findings also exposed that the plan to destabilize the Chilean economy should continue when Allende assumed office. As ITT's vice president told Henry Kissinger, Richard Nixon's national security advisor at the time: "There should be no hesitance on the part of the United States to confront the new President."[12] Fearing Allende's agenda to nationalize natural and consumer goods, the United States developed a second interventionist plan. Known as Track II, it consisted of undermining Allende's economy by denying international credit and banning imports of copper and other products and vital exports, such as, once again, bread and milk. In this way, declassified documents tell us, an "economic chaos" would develop, and the Chilean armed forces would have to "step in and restore order."[13]

A few days after he published his article in the *Washington Post*, Anderson appeared during prime time on the Chilean public service broadcaster Televisión Nacional de Chile (TVN), providing even more information. He said: "ITT [approached] other companies—Ford, General Motors . . . , oil companies [and other] businesses such as Pepsi Cola regarding its campaign to ruin Chile's economy, goad the military to act and to establish a dictatorship. . . . So there you have it: ITT, that gigantic company [would] go so far as to work jointly with our government—under the utmost secrecy—and . . . our CIA in a plot to save its investments in Chile."[14] Considering the severity of said disclosure for Chilean democracy, in April 1972, the Popular Unity's publishing house, Quimantú, meaning "sun of knowledge" in Mapudungun, the language spoken by the Mapuche, published a 170-page book with photocopies of the ITT memos. Including Spanish translations next to the originals in English, the publication, which circulated widely among Chileans, opened with the following introduction: "These documents . . . are a testimony of the economic and political penetration in dependent countries of large imperial companies and the governments linked to them. [It is our] duty to inform . . . all the Chilean citizens about . . . their extraordinary gravity."[15]

And citizens responded. Chilean poet Pablo Neruda, the Nobel Laureate in Literature who, as cultural theorist Mary Louise Pratt argues, belonged to a generation for whom "literature and revolution were joined at the hip," published his last collection of poems informed by the ITT release.[16] Titled *Incitación al nixonicidio y alabanza de la revolución chilena* (*A Call for the Destruction of Nixon and Praise for the Chilean Revolution*) and written from his coastal home in Isla Negra, the book includes forty-four poems and was published in February 1973, also by Quimantú. In one of the most revealing stanzas included in the poem "Victory," Neruda wrote, "[Nixon] decided to close us with wire: / They would no longer trade with us / so that Chile would die of hunger."[17] He was right. The plan was to destroy everything: that is, to "make the economy scream" and thus to "save Chile!" as Nixon told the CIA director on September 15, 1970, a few days after Allende was elected president.[18] Allende, on the other hand, also informed by the ITT declassification, pronounced his emblematic speech of December 4, 1972, at the United Nations in New York. Standing before a packed Assembly, Allende said,

> We are faced by a direct confrontation between the large transnational corporations and the states. The corporations are interfering in the fundamental political, economic and military decisions of the states. The corporations are global organizations that do not depend on any state and whose activities are not controlled by, nor are they accountable to any parliament or any other institution representative of the collective interest. In short, the entire world's political structure is being undermined.[19]

Alerting about the danger of a new economic phase that was starting to conceptualize in Chile as a "laboratory" of the world, Allende, as historian Greg Grandin notes, "offered a pretty good definition of neoliberalism."[20] Indeed, we can further say that this is why, at the end of his speech, in a widely watched televised episode of transnational solidarity against imperialism, the Assembly stood up and enthusiastically applauded, loudly, chanting for minutes: "Viva Allende!"[21]

Allende's speech was largely covered by the US media. The *New York Times*, for instance, included responses to Allende's accusations from US corporations, with an ITT spokesman countering that the company "never intervened or interfered in the internal affairs of Chile in any way."[22] Less ambiguous about what had already proven true was the coverage by the Puerto Rico–based English-language daily *San Juan Star*, broadly read among the Puerto Rican community in New York's El Barrio. As shown in a photograph by Nuyorican photographer and Taller Boricua member Máximo Rafael Colón, Latino activist Humberto Cintrón presents the *San Juan Star* to Colón's camera, emblazoned with a headline reading: "ITT Foments Civil War in Chile, Allende Says" (figure 1.2).[23] In further evidence of a common fight against the neoliberal threat, Cintrón organized an interview with Allende's wife, Hortensia Bussi, while Allende was in New York for his speech at the UN. The interview was broadcast on *Realidades*, the first national Latino show, launched in 1972 and hosted by Cintrón at Channel THIRTEEN, an educational public television station in New York.[24] As Colón recalls, "When Allende and the Chilean Ambassador to the United States,

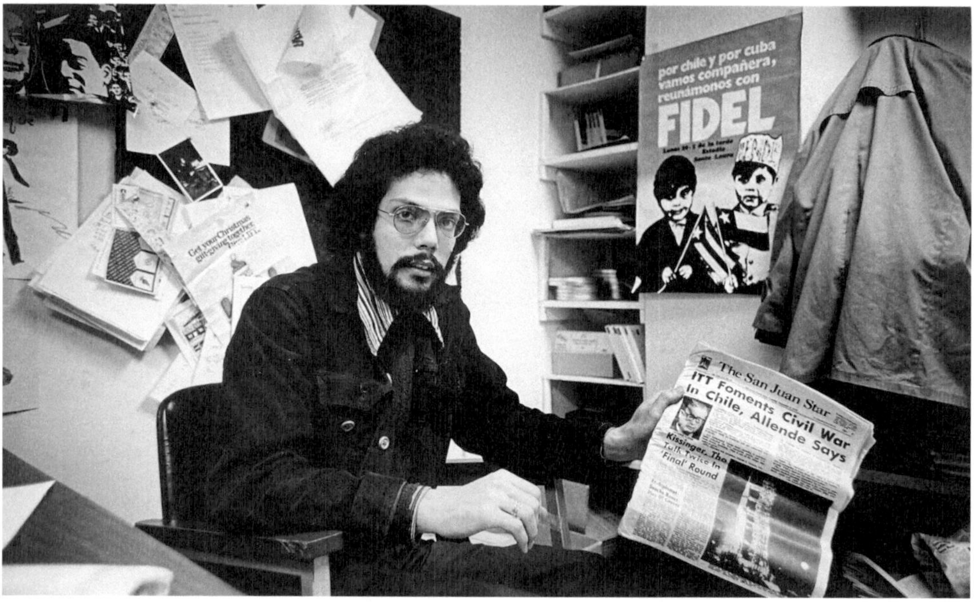

1.2 Máximo Rafael Colón, Humberto Cintrón holding a copy of the *San Juan Star*, 1972. Courtesy of Máximo Rafael Colón.

Orlando Letelier, arrived at the interview's site, Hortensia Bussi told them: 'These comrades support the struggle of Chile.' Then, they all shook hands."[25]

Also in 1972, art critic Dore Ashton was likewise shaking hands with Letelier—in her case, on a weekly basis. That year, Ashton was working as the US representative of the soon-to-be inaugurated Museo de la Solidaridad (Museum of Solidarity), a Chilean museum whose collection was assembled through donations in solidarity with the decolonial praxis of liberation. Well-known artists, including Pablo Picasso, Victor Vasarely, Lygia Clark, and the Chilean Roberto Matta, among many others, donated works.[26] Allende himself was involved in the development of the project, which was led by Brazilian art critic Mario Pedrosa, then exiled in Chile from the US-backed military dictatorship in Brazil (1964–85). In the museum's inaugural speech, Allende said: "On behalf of the people and the Government of Chile, I wish to express my profound gratitude to the artists who have donated their work to constitute the basis for the Museum . . . inaugurating an unprecedented kind of relationship between the artists and the people."[27]

In the United States, as Ashton recalled, Letelier was one of the project's "most enthusiastic" participants. "[He] would call me every Monday morning . . . to say, 'Have we got some new things?'"[28] As Ashton later explained, "It was his voice that kept [me] attentive to the cause."[29] And thus, in her call for participation to US artists, Ashton wrote: "An 'International Committee of Artistic Solidarity with Chile' has been formed for the purpose of supporting the ideals represented by the first elected socialist government in our hemisphere. . . . It is my hope . . . that American artists will be well represented [by] donat[ing] an important work."[30] Artists responded, among them, Alexander Calder, Philip Guston, Sol Lewitt, and Robert Motherwell. And Letelier, "on behalf of the Chilean government," wrote them back expressing Chile's "deepest appreciation for [their] generous contribution[s]."[31]

These histories reveal a complex aesthetic program that went far beyond traditional donations, public protests, and beneficiary exhibitions, as in the case of the solidarity movement with Vietnam in the previous decade.[32] In the case of Chile, there was a sense, or at least a call for a sense, of geopolitical belonging, as is revealed in Ashton's identification of Allende's revolution as collective and hemispheric.[33] Furthermore, unlike the case with Vietnam, many art workers, journalists, activists, and intellectuals actually traveled to Chile to learn firsthand from the Popular Unity's revolution. In the words of investigative journalist John Dinges, "For me and for many, 1972 was the year to live the revolution. . . . Thousands of academics, veterans of the U.S. antiwar movement [went to] Chile, where a socialist had become president in impeccably democratic elections."[34] Indeed, what Dinges describes from the United States was a global phenomenon, as thousands of activists from around the world travelled to Chile to live the experience of the Popular Unity. Among those was Alfredo Jaar, who, after living for ten years with his family in Martinique, returned to Chile. "My father wanted us to live Allende's revolution, so we returned."[35]

Jaar's experience in revolutionary Chile was short-lived, however, as the coup followed shortly thereafter, establishing a fascist junta presided by General Augusto Pinochet. In his earliest works addressing the date of the coup, Jaar created a series of calendars interrupting progressive time. In his *September 11, 1973 (Drawing)* from 1974 (figure 1.3), on a sheet of paper previously placed vertically, Jaar draws two calendars with black ink, one on top of the other. The calendar at the top shows the month of September 1973 with the number *11* replacing the days after the coup. Under this monthly calendar Jaar writes: "solo once después del once" (only eleven after eleven), enclosing the word *once* in a circle as a graphic pattern of continuity. The drawing at the bottom shows the yearly calendar of 1973, under which the artist adds: "un

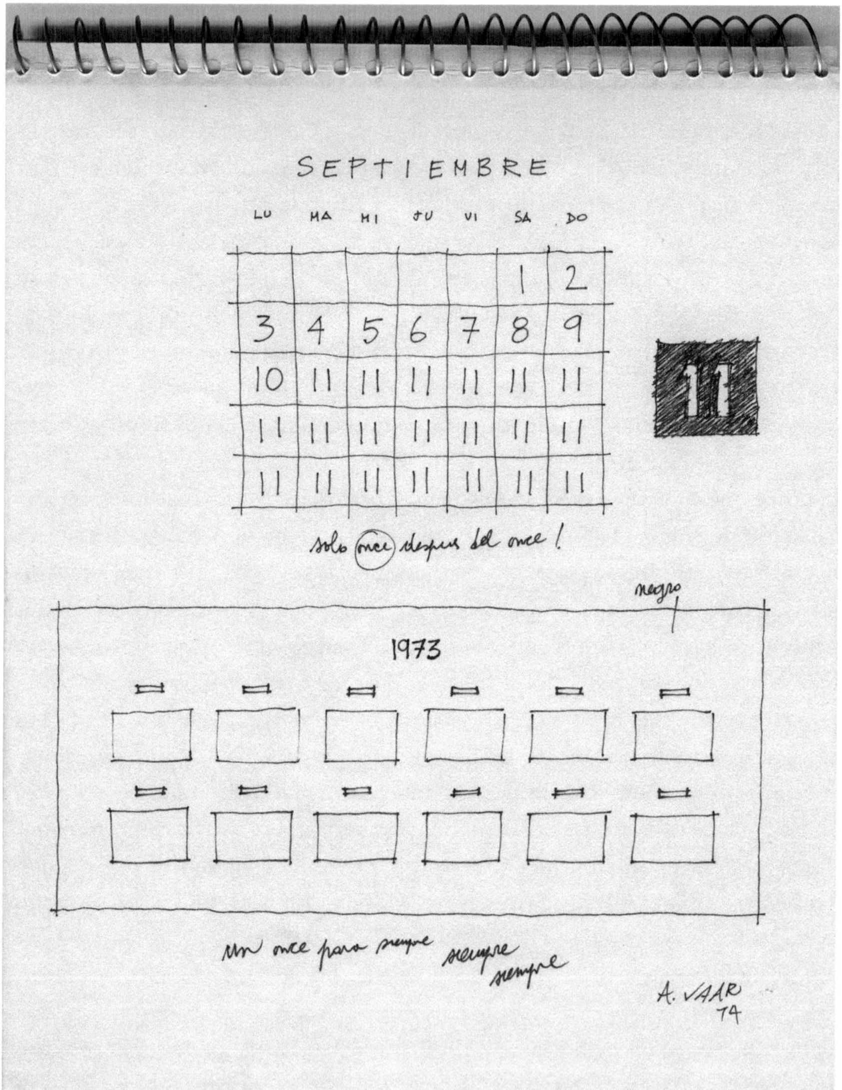

1.3 Alfredo Jaar, *September 11, 1973 (Drawing)*, 1974. Courtesy of Alfredo Jaar.

once para siempre, siempre, siempre" (an eleven forever, always, always), deliberately excluding the final period as a prolongation of mourning. Jaar goes even further and calls the entire experience of drawing the number *11*, as we observe in a third diagram to the right of the monthly calendar, which is rendered through a negative space as a means of reproduction. Through a conceptual strategy that intersects images and text, Jaar invites us to consider how mourning cannot disappear twice, in the time of modernity and the arts.

By creating this work a year *after* the coup, Jaar portrays a time that is repeated in the everyday experience of dictatorship. In this experience, which he calls "11," the junta converted the Popular Unity's architecture of hope into one of uniformity and repression, prohibiting and punishing all political activities and left-wing movements while simultaneously persecuting, torturing, killing, and disappearing thousands. The building in downtown Santiago that housed the Museum of Solidarity was turned into the junta's very headquarters, and Letelier, having returned to Chile to serve as Allende's minister of defense, was arrested, tortured, and exiled. Public-space murals with social and political content made by different left-wing muralist brigades were covered under many layers of paint, and books that did not represent the junta's values of patriotism, severe Catholicism, and privatization were systematically burned. Recalling the massive destruction of codices that followed the conquest in the sixteenth century, this burning ranged from publications on general sociology to declassified documents and poems, such as Quimantú's ITT memos and Neruda's *Nixonicidio*.[36] No wonder that Neruda, then a sixty-nine-year-old supporter of Allende fighting fascism and cancer, died in a hospital in Santiago two weeks after the coup. He was poisoned, as the most recent forensic report suggests, which dismantles the official narrative that he died from a heart attack and cancer complications.[37] And yet, in September 2023, in the context of the fiftieth anniversary of the coup, the Court of Appeals, following the linear time of modernity's history, closed the Neruda investigation.[38] Still, in the ongoing, *unclosed* case of decolonial time, justice for the victims has not yet come, and for this reason, the search for justice must continue.

In another drawing from his earliest series, Jaar traces a grid and uses Letraset, a tool commonly used by architectural students at the time to label plans. He also writes four times with black ink the Spanish name "Pablo" in capital letters (figure 1.4). Creating a vertical column at the center of the sheet, three of the four "Pablos" in the drawing represent various Pablos who died from different circumstances in 1973. One is Neruda, one is Picasso, and one is the Catalan cellist Pablo Casals. The identity and the date of death of these Pablos are handwritten by Jaar at the bottom of the drawing, so that

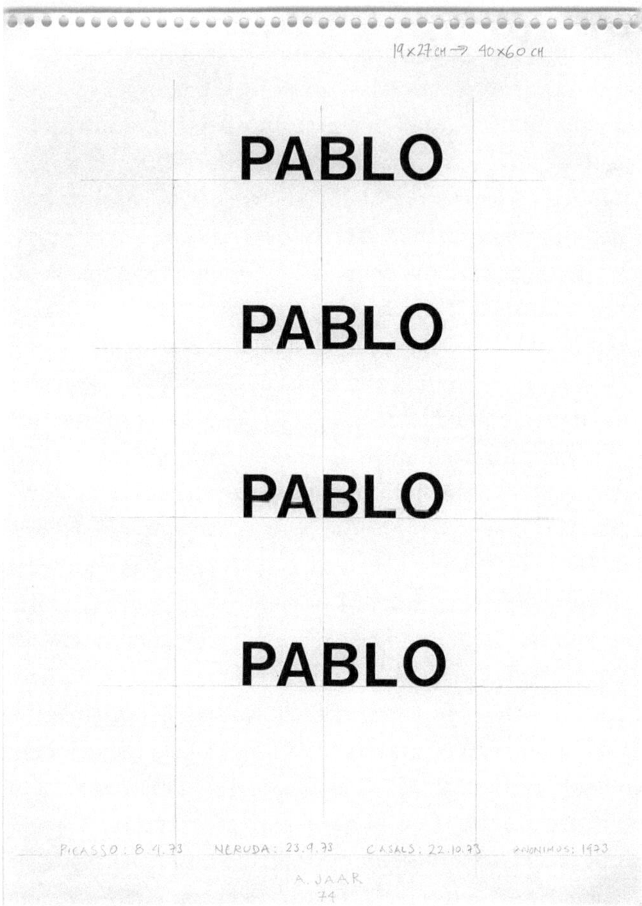

1.4 Alfredo Jaar, *Pablo, Pablo, Pablo, Pablo (dibujo)*, 1974. Courtesy of Alfredo Jaar.

we read: "Picasso: 8.4.73"; "Neruda: 23.9.73"; "Casals: 22.10.27." Though I will address the identity of the fourth Pablo below, for now, it is important to note that these three Pablos were "deeply admired [by Jaar] for their understanding of art as politics and vice versa."[39] Casals and Picasso were fervent critics of Francisco Franco's military dictatorship in Spain. So was Neruda, who, as consul in Paris during the left-wing administration of Pedro Aguirre Cerda, helped more than two thousand Spaniards flee Franco's regime, arriving in the city port of Valparaíso in 1939. Welcomed by thousands, including a thirty-one-year-old Allende, who at the time was minister of health, among the refugees was Catalan painter José Balmes. And, as the story goes, three decades later, in 1972, in an act of transnational solidarity that comprised policies of insertion in the country of exile, Allende, then president of Chile, appointed Balmes, then dean of fine arts at the Universidad de Chile, to work with Pedrosa in the creation of the Museum of Solidarity. As a practice of anti-imperialist liberation, solidarity from this perspective is a relational mode of caring, resisting, and belonging that is essentially transnational, and, as such, it operates beyond the nation's borders through shared histories and projects of decolonial liberation.

This transnational dimension of solidarity, which is also aware of its danger under modernity or within our world as war, is also denoted by Neruda in the prologue of *Nixonicidio*: "This may be an ephemeral operation. But I will carry it out. And I have recourse to the oldest arms of poetry, the song and the pamphlet used by classicists and romantics alike, and destined to destroy the enemy. Steady now, I'm going to fire."[40] Calling poets and activists with shared histories of imperialism to act in the spirit of transnational solidarity, in the first poem of *Nixonicidio*, titled, "I Begin by Invoking Walt Whitman," Neruda writes, "I claim you, essential brother / old Walt Whitman with your gray hands /so that, with your special help / line by line, we will tear out by the roots / and destroy this bloodthirsty President Nixon."[41] The statement is clear: The essence of poetry is to resist hemispheric coloniality by denouncing the relation between human rights violations and multinational profit that was already taking place in Chile. Yes, death by means of the neoliberal threat was already happening before the coup.

The first victim of this pattern within the neoliberal phase of modernity was René Schneider. Commander in chief of the army under Allende, Schneider opposed the US plan to prevent Allende's election, resulting in his assassination on October 25, 1970, right after Nixon ordered the Chilean "economy to scream."[42] He was kidnapped by CIA operatives and murdered by Chilean forces, to which Neruda in his *Nixonicidio* responded, "Like a diamond your memory will live on / in the highest peak of the cordillera. / The country will go with you always / on the road to spring."[43] A document of decolonial time, stanzas like this show that memory practices in Chile were already underway *before* the coup. In fact, Jaar's reference to Neruda's death and by extension to *Nixonicidio* and the ITT release locates the artist's temporal understanding of the dictatorship's catastrophe before, during, and after the coup. Put differently, Jaar's earliest series of work places the coup not at the outset of the regime in clock time but at the historical moment when the tyranny became massive and totalitarian, inaugurating a new epoch in linear time.

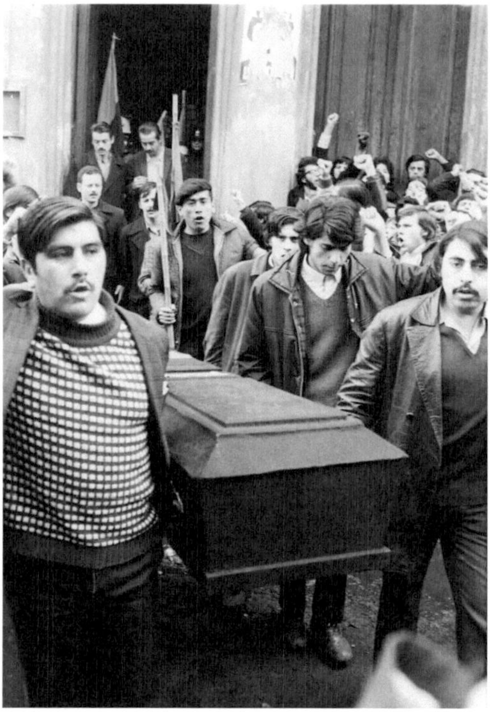

1.5 Armindo Cardoso, *Funeral de Nilton Da Silva*, 1973. Cardoso Archive, Biblioteca Nacional de Chile.

Before the coup, other deaths followed Schneider's assassination. In July 1973, for instance, a twenty-two-year-old poet and student of literature at the University of Chile, Nilton Da Silva, was murdered by the extreme right in downtown Santiago. The funeral of Da Silva, a militant of the Movimiento de Izquierda Revolucionaria (MIR) who was living in Santiago as a political refugee from the US-backed Brazilian dictatorship, was the first massive protest *anticipating* the coup. The event was documented by photojournalist Armindo Cardoso, who in 1969 arrived in Chile as a political refugee from António de Oliveira Salazar's dictatorship in Portugal (figure 1.5). In the image, a group of young men carry Da Silva's coffin. Dozens march behind the scene, their fists and left-wing flags raised. Miguel Enríquez, one of MIR's founders, is depicted in a medium-full shot at the bottom left of the frame. Enríquez has the iconic mustache of the revolutionary youth, his hair is parted on the side, and his gaze is directed forward. He chants, holding the coffin with his left hand, and lifts his right arm, which is cut off by the frame. In the background, to Enríquez's left, is another founder of MIR, Bautista van Schouwen, his left arm pressed to his thigh. As we looked together at this photograph at the National Center of Contemporary Art in Chile in 2023, filmmaker Carmen Castillo, a dictatorship survivor and Enríquez's domestic partner at the time, told me: "We knew what was coming."[44] What she meant was that the coup was already sounding, anticipating the massacre, all while the crowds were already taking to the streets to protest in the present the inevitable dictatorial future within modernity's linear time.

Writing about Da Silva's funeral, art historian Amy Conger, a leading scholar of photographer Edward Weston—who at the time was living in Santiago while teaching art history at the Universidad de Chile—contended: "It was the largest procession I saw in Chile."[45] And in 1974, a year after Da Silva's assassination and a year into the dictatorship, Conger herself was detained by DINA, the regime's intelligence agency. Fed bread and water only, she was interrogated for hours, kept handcuffed, and threatened to be raped, all while witnessing the horrors of torture and the cry of other prisoners.[46] She was released thirteen days later after signing a false confession under orders, and upon her return to the United States, she started working with Amnesty International in solidarity with victims of the Chilean and other regimes around the world until she died in 2023 at her home in Riverside, California.

In a book like this one, in which the coup, diverse forms of solidarities, and memory practices are understood through transnational dimensions, it is key to note that although Conger and Cardoso did not suffer the same fate as Da Silva, Conger was still imprisoned and Cardoso was forced into exile, again. This means that just as the coup did not start overnight, it affected more than the nation-state of Chile and Chileans within that nation. In France, for instance, where Carmen Castillo was exiled, "the coup and the dictatorship were treated as a state issue," as she recalls.[47] And in the Americas, in the words of Dore Ashton, Allende's political project was regarded as "our hemisphere." Furthermore, chapters of cultural solidarity developed not only in Europe and the Americas but also in places such as Algiers, China, Palestine, the former Soviet Union, and more, clearly indicating the global impact of the coup before and after clock time.[48] And, as transnational memory acts, these practices also developed *within* Chile, as shown during the Popular Unity period in the committed photojournalism of Cardoso, a Portuguese exile, and in the activism and radical poetry of Da Silva, a Brazilian exile. Chileans' comrades, on the other hand, acknowledged and honored those practices. As the poet Jorge Etcheverry wrote in stanzas: "Nilton da Silva / We will see your face again / In the first concentration we do in the center."[49] "We will see your face again," Etcheverry writes, with the collective *we* and the adverb *again* reminding us that representational acts, such as poetry *as* protest, keep the memory of the victims alive. "We" and "again" thus remind us of the decolonial practice of mourning that is essentially unending and collective; they mean, in the words of performance studies theorist Sandra Ruiz, that "if we must perpetually mourn, let's not do it alone."[50]

Such is the case of dozens of women who go every day to the Atacama Desert in northern Chile and search; they search for their loved ones who were disappeared by the dictatorship in a collective and endless practice of mourning. They know that the vastness and dryness of the desert, where the world's largest radio telescope is located and where the military buried thousands of bodies in secret graves, will not stop their practice of searching, even if in calendar time the atrocities of the regime happened twenty, thirty, forty, fifty years ago or more. "I wish the telescopes didn't just look into the sky but could also see through the earth so that we could find them," says the mother of a disappeared in *Nostalgia for the Light*, a 2013 documentary film by the Chilean filmmaker Patricio Guzmán.[51] "I wish . . . we could find them," she remarks, revealing that her search is not an individual act but a collective one—her search, just as Jaar's works on mourning, is shared by a society that lives as it duels. "This . . . is the story of many, . . . a plural story," says a victim and mourner in *Chile, Obstinate Memory*, another documentary by Guzmán.[52] And *plural*, as Chilean cultural critic Nelly Richard has noted, pertains to a nation "coming to terms with" the legacy of the dictatorship in the present, connecting to the famous motto *¿Dónde están?* (Where are they?) used in street protests since the very beginning of the dictatorship by the families of the disappeared and to the testimonies of victims.[53] In a present that refuses to forget, the mothers, grandmothers, and all who stand in solidarity with the victims go and search in and beyond the desert in the hopes of finding the disappeared. If remains are found, they hope that forensic scientists might determine the date of their deaths to commemorate their loved ones properly, with a funeral, an obituary, and a grave.[54] In this manner, the continuity of the dictatorship through its neoliberal policy of oblivion is challenged and interrupted. It is confronted through a collective effort that, regardless of failing, still endures and persists in the public court of social justice. Philosopher and art historian Georges Didi-Huberman puts it this way: "Victims of oppression are mourned by survivors [and] in these tears, in these gestures of lament [is] a call for justice."[55] Enacting an aesthetic praxis of collective mourning *as* hope for a world that has the potential to be otherwise, the decolonial mind and heart know that justice has not yet come, and thus it keeps going, keeps searching. "And we go on and on," writes the Chilean poet and winner of the Nobel Prize in Literature Gabriela

Mistral in *Lagar*, recalling Samuel Beckett's words from 1953, also echoed by Jaar in his 2016 *I Can't Go On, I'll Go On* (figure I.1). "And we go on and on" says Mistral, because, as she continues, "we are still time."[56]

All this considered, we can now better understand the identity of the fourth Pablo in Jaar's 1974 drawing (figure 1.4). As mentioned previously, the identity and the date of death of each of the Pablos are handwritten by Jaar at the bottom of the drawing. In the case of the fourth Pablo, however, Jaar's handwriting is almost invisible, inviting us, as active viewers, to try looking harder. He invites us to see and think about these images as translations of historical accounts embracing a politics of visuality that acknowledges the victim's existence through acts of remembering and thus through *active* mourning. In this way, we see and read the small letters at the bottom right of the drawing: "Anonymous: 1973." The fourth Pablo, in Jaar's words, "symbolizes all the Pablos who disappeared in 1973 after the coup."[57]

Turning a word, a proper name, into a concept that embraces anonymity, disappearance, and collective mourning and searching in dictatorship and postdictatorship life, Jaar titled the work *Pablo, Pablo, Pablo, Pablo (dibujo* [drawing]*)*. It is neither one nor two but many, and those many are framed not only in the strict period of the dictatorship but also within its neoliberal injection and aftermath, that is, within its neoliberal continuity. A memory politics in which an ongoing search for the disappeared in poems, critical journalism, and declassified archives is central. It is thus not surprising that Jaar has described this work as his "first memorial."[58] In this sense, Jaar's *Pablo, Pablo, Pablo, Pablo* is both a memorial and a work on memory as well as a recognition of the role of poetry in mobilizing historical and political discourses aiming to reframe not only the present and the future but also the past.

As poet Gonzalo Millán wrote in *La Ciudad*, a collection of poems published in 1979 while in exile in Quebec, Canada, "The river reverses its flows. / Waterfall rise. / People begin to recede. // Those who were being tortured stop shaking. / Those who were being tortured close their mouths. / The concentration camps are emptied. / Those who were missing appear."[59] Altering the flow of progressive time to dismantle the teleology of capital that seems infinitely reproducible, the poem, in line with Quijano's statement about living inside but against, invites us to imagine a space outside modernity in which the past can be something other than the strict historical past. As Millán continues: "September 11. / Planes full of refugees return. / Chile is a democratic country. / The Armed Forces respect the Constitution. / The soldiers return to their barracks. / Neruda is reborn."[60]

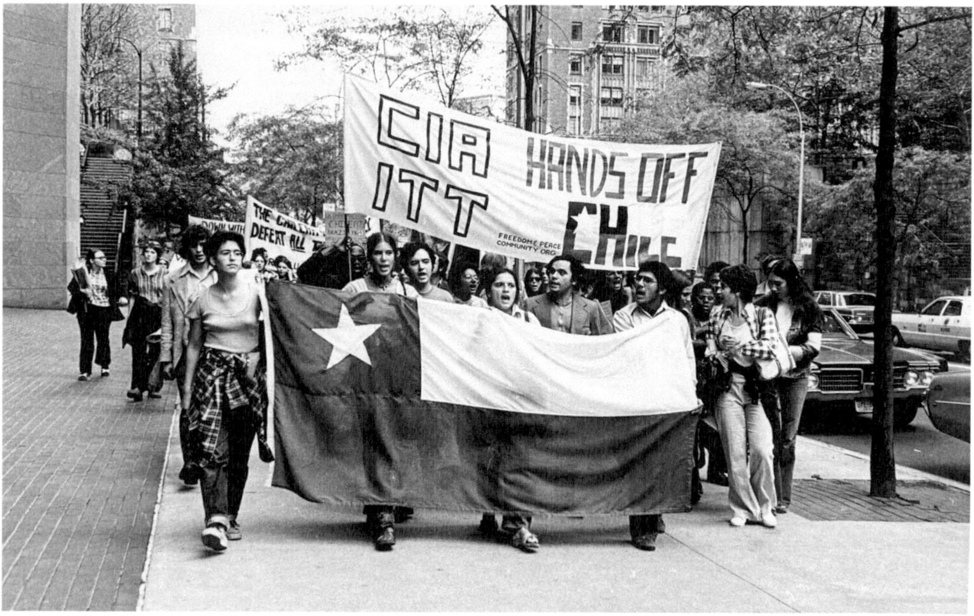

1.6 Máximo Rafael Colón, *Progressive Forces in New York Demonstrate Against Imperialism*, 1972. Courtesy of Máximo Rafael Colón.

URGENT SOLIDARITIES

In New York, where Jaar would self-exile in the early 1980s, anti-imperialist artists, activists, and intellectuals took to the streets right after the coup. Organized by the US Committee for Justice to Latin American Political Prisoners (USLA), which evolved in the late 1960s from the North American Congress on Latin America (NACLA), these early rallies brought out large conglomerations of people, such as a demonstration at Columbia University with more than 1,200 participants.[61] Other public demonstrations were smaller in size but no less significant. Such was the case of a march in which activists walked from the ITT headquarters at 437 Madison Avenue and Fiftieth Street toward the United Nations Headquarters, where Allende had delivered his emblematic speech on the global danger of neoliberalism in December 1972.[62] As recorded in another photograph by Máximo Colón, protesters from different racial and ethnic backgrounds walk together holding the Chilean flag and a sign reading "CIA, ITT, HANDS OFF CHILE" (figure 1.6). Enacting solidarity as a collective fight against multinational totalitarianism that is transnational in scope, protestors also marched with signs demanding the autonomy of Indochina, Chile, and Puerto Rico together in the context of the Cold War.

As evident in these events, cultures of resistance knew that human rights violations in Chile were intrinsically linked to the role of multinationals in the design of Pinochet's Chile. As was published in the November 1973 newsletter of USLA: "The U.S. government, one of the first to extend recognition to the military junta, is preparing huge loans to shore up the military government and help carry out its work. A major portion of blame for this destruction to democratic rights in Chile must be assigned to the U.S. government and corporations which, as revealed by the publication of secret ITT memos, were involved in covert sabotage of Allende's regime from the time of its election."[63] No wonder why a month later, USLA's offices on New York's Fifth Avenue were bombed.[64] Nonetheless, USLA continued fighting from many fronts—one being the arts, which members understood as a tool of political resistance and aesthetic solidarity. Not coincidentally, Dore Ashton, who learned about the Chilean news mostly through clandestine sources, was one of USLA's founders. "I am surprised you know about this," she told an interviewer in 2012 at the age of eighty-four, implying that this history had not yet been revealed.[65]

Examples of collaboration between USLA and art workers in New York seeking to activate memory through collective solidarity acts abound.[66] On November 5, 1973, for instance, Ashton and US artists Leon Golub and Rudolph Baranick organized a workshop at Golub's studio in SoHo. Inviting "artists and writers" to "an evening of solidarity with the victims of repression in Chile," organizers aimed to help those persecuted by the military in Chile through fundraising.[67] Another example is the *Chile Emergency Exhibition*, which opened on March 2, 1974, at Ivan Karp's Gallery, also in SoHo.[68] Organized by art critic Lucy Lippard and artists who had previously participated in the solidarity movement with Vietnam, including Irving Petlin and Chilean Enrique Castro Cid, among others, the exhibition featured roughly two hundred artists who donated their works in solidarity with the movement for freedom in Chile.[69] The exhibition poster shows a small bird-like figure with a red dot at its center atop a black background, representing repression but also hope for freedom (figure 1.7).[70] Following that hope, organizers aimed to aid victims with concrete actions, which they did: they raised $33,000 from sales (about $210,000 today), and more than two hundred victims were helped in various ways, from plane tickets to health supplies.[71] As a survivor wrote to the exhibition's organizers: "It would have been impossible for us to leave Chile without [your help.]"[72]

Other modes for merging art, politics, and solidarity included arranging faculty positions for detainee or exiled artists in academic institutions

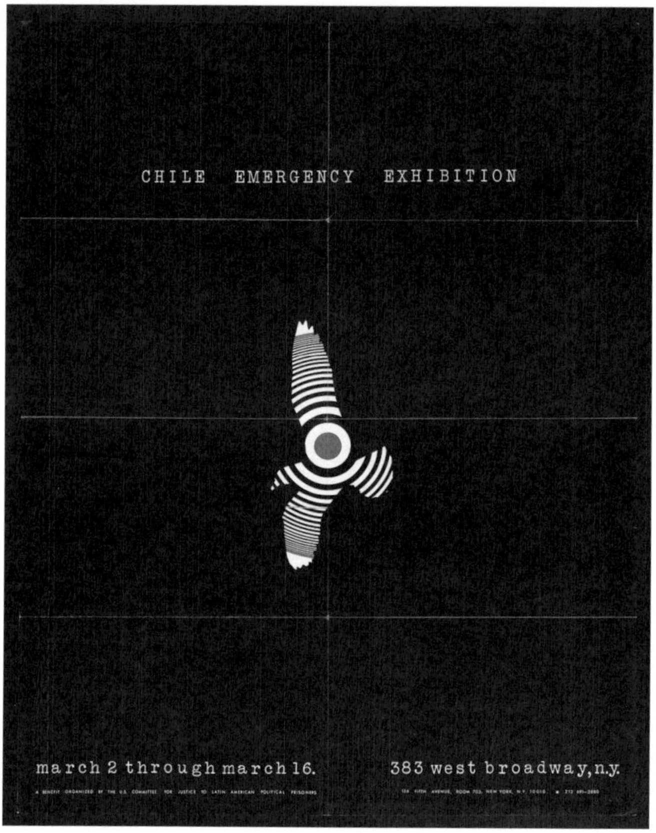

1.7 Poster for *Chile Emergency Exhibition,* 1974.

across the United States.[73] As head of the Art Division of USLA, Ashton played a pivotal role in these actions. Artist René Castro Ruiz, for instance, while detained in a concentration camp in northern Chile, was hired by the Center for Advanced Visual Studies at the Massachusetts Institute of Technology (MIT). Only then was he able to leave Chile.[74] Rumors about these events started to circulate among Chilean artists and intellectuals in detention centers and among those living in exile. Such was the case of art teacher Ximena Rojas, who, exiled in Quito, Ecuador, wrote to Ashton addressing her as a "dear friend of the Chilean people."[75] And Ashton indeed was so, before and after Pinochet's dictatorship. As Lippard made clear in her notes on the solidarity movement with Chile: "The Museum of Solidarity [which Ashton significantly helped shape] is the precedent for this sense of artistic solidarity."[76] Lippard's words prove that in New York, where Jaar would move in 1982, these practices were understood as collective gestures of solidarity with the Chilean victims offered by those with shared histories of oppression in life under modernity. They were made not through pity but through an aesthetic of belonging that encompassed urgency, contingency, and commonality.

Referring to this solidarity paradigm, Orlando Letelier, then the leader of the opposition in the United States, said in his September 10, 1976, speech at the Felt Forum in New York: "We have representatives of the United Auto Workers, and several other labor unions; many community leaders, particularly of the black, Puerto Rican and Chicano people; and representatives of Amnesty International, that have played such an important role in obtaining the freedom of hundreds of Chilean political prisoners."[77] And as the story goes, Letelier, who two weeks before had published his famous article in *The Nation* criticizing the coexistence of repression and economic freedom in Chile, to which I will refer more extensively in the next chapter, was, just as Allende and Neruda, assassinated shortly thereafter.[78]

A memorial exhibition for Letelier took place the following year at Cayman Gallery, a nonprofit art space dedicated to promoting Latin American and Latinx artists on West Broadway.[79] The event was organized by Ashton and Mario Toral, a Chilean exile in New York, among others, and funding from the show went to help sustain refugees in need, defray legal expenses, and "maintain the promise of the first Popular Unity government in Chile."[80] Many well-known artists living in New York donated works, from abstract expressionists such as Lee Krasner and Willem de Kooning and conceptual artists such as Walter de Maria and Rafael Ferrer to feminist artists such as Nancy Spero and May Stevens. The list is long, further revealing a sense of collective urgency that responded in concrete ways to the call for participation, which described the exhibition as "an act of memory and as a symbol of our outrage in solidarity with artists all over the world engaged in protesting repression in Chile."[81] The event also included a brochure, which reproduced on the cover the signature black-and-white portrait of Letelier by Chilean photojournalist Marcelo Montecino and included a poem for Letelier by English art critic and poet John Berger. Highlighting the global impact of the coup and the agency of poetry within transnational anti-imperialism, a stanza in the poem reads: "he lived in many places / and he died everywhere."[82] Empowering the role of memory and thus decolonial time in the ongoing struggle against neoliberal coloniality, Berger adds, "he will be here too / in the spring / every spring."[83]

"[Allende] was a remarkable man, and when they assassinated him, I was very distraught," says Ashton in a short film interview from 2015. She continues: "Then we had a committee that was going to try to get even with those sons of [——] but it never worked, unfortunately. . . . Allende was very impressive, as you know, I guess you know" (plate 6).[84] Revealing a memory aesthetic that refuses to give up while acknowledging that the anti-imperialist revolution has so far failed, the film was made by Alfredo Jaar, who had met Ashton in 1983, a year after he moved to New York.[85] They immediately became close friends, maintaining weekly conversations after Ashton's art history lectures at the Cooper Union. These conversations continued through the years, engaging with issues such as conceptualism, censorship, and, importantly for the discussion in this book, poetry. In 2009, for instance, in the *Brooklyn Rail*, Jaar said that in dictatorship Chile he "started to learn how to speak in between the lines, to evoke, instead of speaking directly. It was a strategy, but it was also a matter of survival. There was no other way to speak," to which Ashton responded: "They used songs a lot, or poems, to substitute what they couldn't express verbally."[86] Indeed, what Jaar's art is about is the power of words to fabricate and intervene into the political, representing in form and content his aesthetics of the unfinished.

Such is the case with his 1988 *El poder de las palabras (Para R. W.)* (*The Power of Words [For R. W.]*) (figure 1.8). A series of prints sandwiching a name and date to create a memorial, Jaar here honors writer and investigative journalist Rodolfo Walsh, who was murdered on March 25, 1977, during Argentina's Dirty War (1976–83). The day before his assassination, Walsh published his famous "Open Letter to the Military Junta," in which he denounced the constitutive relation between human rights violations and neoliberalism in Argentina. Acknowledging that this twofold model was first implemented in Chile by means of US multinational interests, Walsh wrote: "By privatizing banks, you are placing the savings and credit of the country in the hands of foreign banks; by indemnifying ITT and Siemens, you are rewarding companies that have swindled the State. . . . Faced with all these facts, we are left to wonder: Who are the mercenaries working at the service of foreign interests? Which is the ideology that is threatening the nation?"[87] Jaar's work comprises a triptych of three panels of white text over a black background. The panel at the left reads, "24 Mar. 1977," the date Walsh wrote the letter.[88] The panel at the right reads, "25 Mar. 1977," when Walsh was killed. Between these two dates—one representing resistance and life and the other punishment and death—Jaar reproduces a phrase in which Walsh anticipates his fate and proclaims a larger commitment to speak out, to exist, to live: "These are the thoughts I wanted to pass on to the members of this Junta on the

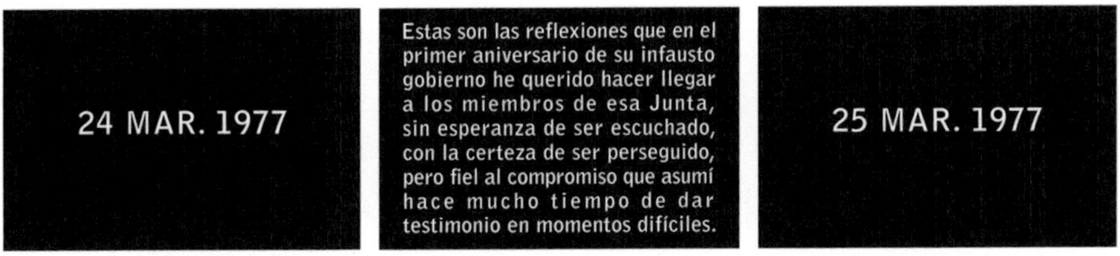

1.8 Alfredo Jaar, *El poder de las palabras (Para R. W.)*, 1988. Courtesy of Alfredo Jaar.

first anniversary of their ill-fated government, with no hope of being heard and with the certainty of being persecuted, but faithful to the commitment I made a long time ago to bear witness during difficult times."[89] Challenging modernity's temporal logic of a beginning and an end through the power of words, Jaar's memorial honors the life and journalism of Walsh as well as the lives and struggles of modernity's victims, even after their deaths. In doing so, it demonstrates that images *and* or *as* words have the potential to advance the fight for representation, visibility, and existence, reclaiming a memory politics built through decolonial time.

IMAGES OF EXISTENCE

> When I arrived in New York in 1982, I began a series of works on memory because, during the dictatorship's first week, images on that week were not allowed to be seen. There was censorship, and I wanted to see what had happened in that fatal week of September 11. . . . I bought old newspapers and magazines, and I made a series of works titled *Faces*, where I simply cut the photograph of a scene and made a blow-up of a face. No words. I thought that I didn't need to say anything, that these faces, in that moment, said it all. This man, for example, is photographed at the National Stadium. He knew he was going to die, and his face communicates it.[90]

This is how Alfredo Jaar, in a 2015 public lecture, explained his series *Faces* (figure 1.9).[91] Blowing up a "face that is lost" in a photojournalistic record, Jaar aimed to search for facial expressions that he thought contained "everything you need to know about the [Chilean] dictatorship."[92] Placing the fragment alongside the photograph from which it had been extracted, the image of the man described

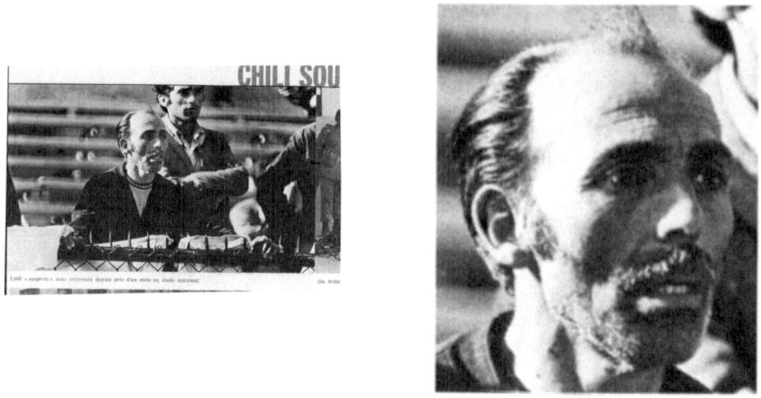

1.9 Alfredo Jaar, *Faces* (diptych, detail), 1982. Courtesy of Alfredo Jaar.

here, for instance, shows that same man alongside others standing behind a security fence at the National Stadium's stands, which had become the largest detention, torture, and kidnapping center immediately following the coup.

Providing more information about that moment of atrocity, including the country's new policy of censorship, is the image's original caption. Because it was written in French, we deduce that this image had an international rather than domestic circulation. The image on the right, however, which is cropped and printed significantly larger by Jaar, directs the viewer's attention to a single victim of the regime, with an expression of horror and pain. The victim, that is, the persecuted, tortured, or disappeared, used as a noun instead of an adjective, is emphasized in the work by the fragment—that which is defeated, lost, and forgotten in the political and cultural discourse and law of dictatorship and postdictatorship Chile. And since they are photographs, these faces function not only as vestiges of what "has been" but also "as recognition and reconstitution of a certain degree of existence to the disappeared," remembering the appeals of "¿Dónde están?" (Where are they?) and "¡Que aparezcan vivos!" (That they appear alive) that reject progressive reconciliation policies intending to close, that is, to forget, the issue of the disappeared.[93] Past and present are thus fused together, inviting the viewer to become simultaneously involved in a politics of reparation and reconstitution.[94]

Jaar's aim in this series, just as in his exercises of memory overall, is to engage the viewer in a memory politics that "keeps the relation between the past and the present open . . . preventing history from turning itself into the aesthetic figure of a closed time."[95] *Faces*, therefore, means presence, life: It means existence. Affirming the victims' presence in history and images, Jaar challenges the neoliberal agenda embracing both destruction (killing, disappearance, torture) and erasure (censorship). This explains why *Faces* was the very first work he made in New York. Finding himself in a space with no censorship—at least not as he experienced in Chile—Jaar, in his words, "wanted to see what had happened in that fatal week of September 11."[96] As he continues: "I bought old newspapers and magazines, and I made . . . *Faces*, where I simply cut the photograph of a scene and made a blow-up of a face. No words. I thought that I didn't need to say anything, that these faces, in that moment, said it all."[97]

Jaar's series is composed of eleven diptychs. Each diptych includes a reproduction of an image he appropriated from the media and a detail of a face from that reproduction, which the artist reproduces larger in size and places next to the "original." One of the diptychs shows Neruda's internationally covered funeral on the left (figure 1.10). Since Jaar created his earliest memorial to the victims of the Chilean regime in 1974 from the starting point of Neruda's *Nixonicidio* and the poet's consequential death, it is not surprising that in 1982, this was one of the images that Jaar "wanted to see."[98] Jaar, just as in the image of the man at the National Stadium, appropriates this photograph from a French newspaper, as one can understand from reading the upper portion of the capital letters located at the bottom edge of the image that read, "*camarade*," comrade, or *camarada*. The photograph was taken with a wide-angle lens; the pueblo, the crowds, walked alongside the coffin, which is at the center and covered with a Chilean flag. On the first row surrounding the coffin, the woman on the far left cries and frowns. Behind her, a man looks at the casket as if time had stopped, while a younger man to his left looks beyond the frame. Neruda's compañera, Matilde, is at the center, her gaze directed down in silence. Next to Matilde is a man, a young woman, and another man. The two men look at the coffin, but the young woman's gaze is directed upward, lost. At the far right, a man looks slightly to his right, his face straight. For the detail component of the diptych, Jaar blows up a fragment, which he describes to the audience as follows: "This young woman, which is behind three men, at the right. We don't see her in a photo, but if we make a blow-up, then we see her in her totality. No words . . . [this] is the saddest image . . . *Faces*."[99]

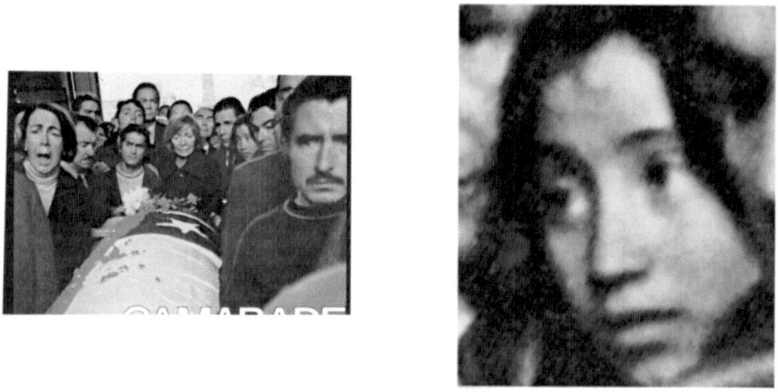

1.10 Alfredo Jaar, *Faces* (diptych, detail), 1982. Courtesy of Alfredo Jaar.

Another diptych from this series shows, on the left, a man looking intensely at the camera from behind two national police officers (*carabineros*) (figure 1.11). Here, Jaar reveals more information about the source and gives the viewer the full caption, "anchoring" the image, in Roland Barthes's terms.[100] Likewise published by the French media, the caption reads in English: "The eyes of the vanquished. Left-wing activists and above all foreign revolutionaries gathered by the government of Allende."[101] The name of the journalist is also provided: Georges Menant, a veteran of the May 1968 protests in France. In including this entire text as part of the image, Jaar exposes both the transnational dimension of the Chilean regime and the solidarities it awoke from the capacity of critical textual and visual records to create decolonial discourses on time, honoring the names and works of journalists and their politics of hope.

A few weeks after the coup, on September 22, 1973, the Chilean junta permitted the international press to tour the National Stadium. Among those photojournalists was US photographer David Burnett, who, in turn, captured the photograph used by Jaar that accompanies Menant's article. Describing

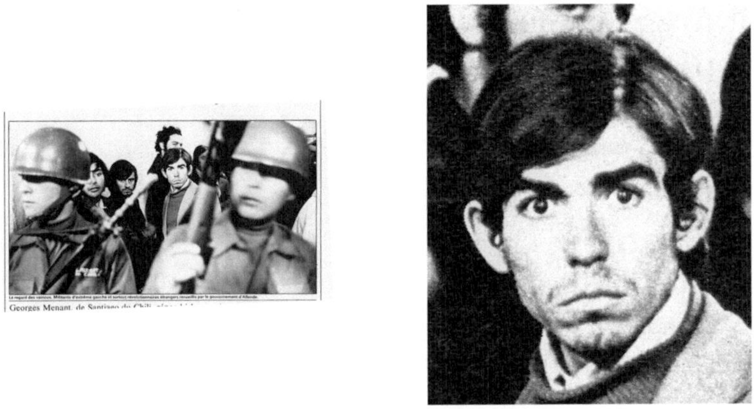

1.11 Alfredo Jaar, *Faces* (diptych, detail), 1982. Courtesy of Alfredo Jaar.

this photo, which has become so famous today, Burnett remarked, "The haunting gaze of one man in particular, whose figure was framed by two armed soldiers, caught my eye. The picture has always stayed with me."[102] As he put it elsewhere: "I wanted the rest of the world to know that in that one moment, a young man about my own age, anonymous to me as I was anonymous to him, was experiencing the kind of terror which spoke a great deal about the politics of Chile."[103] That expression, that face described and captured by Burnett, is precisely the fragment of the image that Jaar extracts. He blows up that face, reproduces it larger in size, and places it next to the "original."

In a way, this operation recalls Barthes's famous distinction between *punctum* and *studium* in *Camera Lucida*, a book that has significantly influenced Jaar's thinking on photography.[104] For Barthes, the *punctum* is that "stinging accident" that "pricks" the viewer past what can be said beyond the photographer's intention, or the *studium*, in this case a Chilean detention site.[105] In other words, the *punctum* is the "element which rises from the scene, shoots out of it like an arrow, and pierces" the viewer.[106] And yet, after trying over and over in *Camera Lucida* to find a word for the *punctum*—an arrow, a wound—Barthes, by the end of the first part of the book, states that "what I can name cannot really prick me."[107] The *punctum* is thus *ineffable.* As such, as photo historian Geoffrey Batchen reminds us, the *punctum* is found in an image that Barthes decides not to reproduce in *Camera Lucida,* insisting on the singular, irreplaceable nature of his pain.[108] As is well-known in the history of photography, this late nineteenth-century image shows Barthes's beloved mother Henriette as a child in a winter garden, and it was found by Barthes while he was mourning her death in 1977 in their apartment in Paris. The *punctum,* thus, as represented in this image, has a crucial temporal component. Paralleling that temporality in which remembrance is at stake but considering mourning as a shared experience and not from a personal and transcendental dimension, Jaar, in opposition to Barthes, reproduces those images: faces that "said it all," representing memory as both located and collective. In other words, while for Barthes the winter garden photograph found only after his mother's death and related to his process of mourning "would be nothing but an indifferent picture" for the reader-viewer of *Camera Lucida,* for Jaar, reproduction is essential for the construction of plural collective memory.[109] Past and present and the individual and the collective fuse together in ways that drive Barthes's *punctum* beyond its original set of assumptions, leading the viewer of Jaar's *Faces* to become involved with the historical events Jaar references and the politics of reconstitution.

Aligning itself with a definition of art as "more than that" and "never complete," Jaar's *Faces* also aligns with photographer and theorist Allan Sekula's critique of capitalism and the role of the arts in such critique.[110] "[Our] capitalist society [is controlled by] academic thuggeries like Dr. Milton Friedman's overtly instrumentalist 'free market,'" he wrote in 1978, three years after Friedman's meeting with Pinochet in Chile. "If we consider art as a discourse anchored in concrete social relations rather than as a mystified, vaporous, and ahistorical realm . . . meaning is contingent rather than immanent, universally given, or fixed," he remarked.[111] Art from this perspective mirrors the ongoing, always pending nature of human rights demands. Therein is the significance of artistic practices that circulate photographs of the disappeared, the tortured, and the families of the victims of Latin American state terror in different geopolitical spaces and throughout time.[112] This is what Jaar does in *Faces* and his exercises of memory overall, reframing the *punctum* as the collective body in mourning and highlighting photography's capacity to engage in different aesthetics and political projects embracing decolonial time.

The photograph of Neruda's funeral, for instance, was published for the first time in Chile in 1990, when democracy was "recovered" and the country entered into the transitional period. This means that this image was censored for seventeen years despite the military attending Neruda's funeral. After all, Neruda was the 1971 Nobel laureate, and apart from his *Nixonicidio*—which was condemned by Neruda's bourgeois admirers "for abandoning lyricism and turning to blatant polemic"—his poetry, as the military put it on the date of the funeral, was "one of the sources of pride in our national culture."[113] And thus we wonder: If, according to official records, Neruda died from cancer in Santiago on September 23, 1973, and if his poetry was a "source of pride of national culture," why did the military still ban the images of his funeral? The message was clear: Memory practices such as those that took place at Neruda's funeral—that is, a memory act that was essentially temporal, contingent, and political—were not permitted, and if performed, were punished.

Importantly, Neruda's funeral was not only *his* funeral but the first massive protest *after* the coup, succeeding in clock time the funeral procession of Nilton Da Silva, which took place *before* the dictatorship "officially" started (figure 1.5). On that day, September 25, 1973, thousands marched through Santiago alongside Neruda's coffin, pronouncing Popular Unity slogans such as "El pueblo unido, jamás será vencido!" (The people united, will never be defeated!). They also chanted: "Neruda presente," "Allende presente," and "Víctor Jara presente," relating that "presence," that "existence," to other early victims of the regime such as Allende and Víctor Jara, the latter the iconic folklore musician, teacher, and poet whose hands were smashed while being tortured so that he could not play his guitar again, only to be assassinated a few days later with forty-four bullet wounds.[114] Embodying that same sense of presence and hope, in his poem *La Ciudad*, where time is narrated backward, Gonzalo Millán writes, "Víctor Jara plays the guitar. He sings."[115] And concludes: "The workers march, singing / *Venceremos!*"[116]

In pronouncing their names at the funeral, mourners remembered and memorialized victims within an aesthetics that recovered the Popular Unity's paradigm of collectivity, solidarity, contingency, and resistance to capitalism: at least for one day. As a noun that is singular and plural at the same time, in both Spanish and English languages, "presente," as Diana Taylor argues, "conveys the ontological condition that one is/we are never fully present alone, and plurality always entails singularity."[117] Similarly, invoking this same presence, in September 1976 in Washington, DC, two thousand anti-imperialist activists gathered to protest the killing of Letelier.[118] They carried posters reproducing Letelier's portrait by Montecino and headshots of his associate at the Institute for Policy Studies, the twenty-five-year-old Ronni Moffitt, both killed in 1976 when a car bomb exploded as they drove around Sheridan Circle in Washington, DC. Accompanied by signs reading,

"Solidarity among nations," mourners walked to the Washington Cathedral of St. Matthew in Dupont Circle chanting: "Comrade Orlando: Presente, your death will be avenged" and "Comrade Ronny: Presente, your death will be avenged."[119] Thus is the role of accountability, which I examine in the following chapter, and its relation to remembering, which I discuss here, in the ongoing practice of invoking presence.

Presence, from this perspective, as shown in the image of Neruda's funeral in *Faces*, represents not the wake of a "lyric" poet nor the idea of "death" that is immanent in photographic images, as Barthes made clear in *Camera Lucida*. It represents the continuity of a past that is still unfolding. In this sense, Jaar's *Faces* is a work on memory and thus a work on mourning, a denouncement of military intervention aiming to interfere in people's consciousness, that is, in their aesthetics, affects, and modes of knowing and remembering. This is also represented in the fact that in each image, Jaar finds not one or two but many *punctums*, in plural. In the photograph of Neruda's funeral, for instance, Matilde is also blown up by Jaar in a second diptych of his series. So is the case with the young man to Matilde's right. As such, Jaar incorporates the conceptual strategy of repetition begun in his earliest exercises of memory from 1974 (figure 1.1), creating a metaphor of collective loss, grief, resistance, and ongoing existence through the representation of decolonial mourning.

In 2010, twenty years after the so-called return of democracy to Chile and twenty-eight years after Jaar made *Faces*, the socialist government of Michelle Bachelet commissioned Jaar to create a memorial for the recently inaugurated Museo de la Memoria y los Derechos Humanos (MMDH, Museum of Memory and Human Rights in Santiago). Viewers access the memorial, titled *The Geometry of Conscience* and located underground at the museum's plaza, by descending thirty-three steps (plate 7). Inside a cube-like installation, after one minute of complete darkness, hundreds of silhouettes of heads start to light up on the front wall, each created by Jaar after photographs of living and dead Chileans. Rendered in the form of a grid, the silhouettes multiply to infinity in mirrors located on contiguous walls. The process lasts for ninety seconds, projecting an increasingly intense light. Suddenly, the room plunges back into darkness, leaving a strong lingering imprint on viewers' retinas. Refusing the possibility of passive spectatorship, Jaar's memorial interrupts the frozen past of most commemorative monuments and resists a fixed temporality that remembers the past as past. Through the juxtaposition of silhouetted heads, Jaar's work embodies the idea that the regime has not yet come to an end.

In turn, as the silhouettes are multiplied to infinity, in Jaar's memorial, just as in his 1974 *Pablo, Pablo, Pablo, Pablo* (figure 1.4), portraits represent not only one or a specific, fixed number of victims but an entire society that is still affected by the dictatorship and its ghostly neoliberal continuity. Jaar's memorial thus highlights a conflict that remains unresolved. It highlights the fact that, as civil rights attorney Wolfgang Kaleck has argued, "disappearance and torture are not only individual problems; and that crimes did not just happen in the past, as they have a serious impact on the survivor, their families, the social environment, and the society overall."[120] Turning photographic images into silhouettes, Jaar invites the viewer to participate in a memory politics that produces dynamic meanings of the present and the past, engaging through the agency of active viewing in the ongoing politization of society in postdictatorship life. Denouncing the neoliberal system of reconciliation, pardon, and oblivion, Jaar's memorial shows that the ruins of the past continue to resonate in a society that hasn't given up on its demands against neoliberal totalitarianism.

GRIEF UPRISINGS

In the early 2000s, new bodies and voices started organizing in massive protests demanding the end of neoliberalism in Chile. Notably, among these is the student movement, whose first demonstrations took place in 2006 and were resumed from 2011 to 2013, and then again in 2019, coinciding with the social uprising.[121] Protesting the high cost of education and consequent indebtedness through massive marches, strikes, sit-ins, and flash mobs as well as flooding social networks with radical songs and videos, students and their families forced a debate on education and political reforms by promoting democratization through participatory social practices. In doing so, they have prompted a strong critique of the economic model established with the coup and subsequently protected with the 1980 Constitution. More specifically, they have demanded free education for all as a central right that the state should provide, recalling Allende's famous words about youth and revolution, which he proclaimed in Mexico only two days before his address about neoliberalism at the United Nations in New York. On December 2, 1972, standing before hundreds of students at the University of Guadalajara, Allende said: "To be young and not revolutionary may even be a biological contradiction."[122] Thinking about youth not only as a phase in human life but as a cultural and political construction in which the concept of the student is intrinsically linked to social and political change, for Allende, learning goes hand in hand with anti-imperialist revolution.[123] Youth in this sense is not necessarily an epoch in one's life or in the time of Chronos, the personification of time in Greek mythology that regards the calendar of the clock that advances and thus erases. It means the relentless efforts for liberation in relational pasts, presents, and futures that, more massively yet not exclusively, is embraced by youth. Significantly, in his public presentations and interviews, Jaar often quotes Allende's phrase given here. In a recent interview from March 19, 2024, for instance, Jaar was asked: "What is the message you would offer to the new generations? Is there hope?" To which he responded: "I find that the new generations are very aware of the political and social moment in which we live. And this awareness makes them see and act on contingency in a very activist and natural way, [remembering] Salvador Allende who said, 'To be young and not revolutionary may even be a biological contradiction.'"[124]

In spring 2024, students across the world organized to protest higher education's complicity with Israel's genocide in Gaza through their investments. Building encampments on university campuses, organizing peaceful protests and gatherings, and creating performances, songs, graphics, signs, and more, the students critiqued, in short, the constitutive relation between human atrocities and neoliberalism from the realm of education. In this context, students at the Rhode Island School of Design (RISD), for instance, invoked a shorter version of Allende's phrase about youth and revolution as part of their demonstrations, as shown in a banner made by Puerto Rican–born student Daniel Enrique Torres Marrero, then a senior in illustration and furniture design (plate 8).[125] Written in all capitals with white lettering atop a red fabric, the banner reads: "To be young and not a revolutionary is a contradiction." Alongside the banner, as documentation of the protest shows, is a Palestinian flag, and lying in the grass, waiting to be hung all over campus, is a pile of black-and-white posters of the genocide's victims. One of these posters, taped to a marble pillar of one of the school's signature brick buildings, shows a female Muslim journalist wearing a press vest and a hijab. She smiles, her eyes are wide open, and her gaze is directed toward the viewer. To her left is her name: Narmeen Qawwas. To her right is the date she was murdered inside her bombed home in Gaza: December 11, 2023. With her memory rendered via her distinct expression of radical hope, she is remembered and mourned by the students as a young revolutionary female who fought for liberation through her socially committed journalism. She is remembered and mourned collectively by those whom Allende once called "revolutionary youth," and in that revolution, whose time is not linear and whose space is global, she exists and resists by her politics, her body, her name. Remembering the agitated aesthetics of the US solidarity movement of the 1970s and 1980s against imperialism and genocide in Cold War Latin

America, this movement demonstrates that transnational solidarities against neoliberal oppression are always ongoing, always collective, and ever more urgent. And, as such, they mourn.

Writing about mourning, Judith Butler proposes that we "consider a dimension of political life that has to do with our exposure to violence and our complicity in it, with our vulnerability to loss and the task of mourning that follows, and with finding a basis for community in these conditions."[126] This dimension of mourning does not replace another form of grief, or what Sigmund Freud calls melancholia.[127] For Freud, melancholia develops in the unconscious when a person is unable to understand and/or identify their grief, while mourning is a conscious process that has the potential to succeed if the person forgets or exchanges for an object what they have lost.[128] For Butler, on the other hand, mourning is neither the opposition of a pathological form of depression—or melancholia—nor the path to the individual's healthy recovery through overcoming, that is, the oblivion of their loss. Involving a dynamic temporality that not only remembers the past but also informs the future, mourning, in Butler's words, means "accept[ing] that by the loss one undergoes one will be changed, possibly forever."[129] As such, mourning recalls Jaar's thinking about the coup: "On September 11, 1973, everything started. I was seventeen years old," he said.[130] And in our capitalist modernity, as Butler further contends, "certain lives [are] highly protected [and others do] not even qualify as 'grievable' [and this is why] we seldom, if ever, hear the names of the thousands of Palestinians who have died by the Israeli military with United States support."[131] By saying their names, like those of Narmeen Qawwas, Ronni Moffit, Orlando Letelier, or Victor Jara, we remember victims as humans with affects, joys, and personal histories. They are remembered in conjunction with the multiple and ongoing historical moments in which different decolonial duels have begun.

Importantly, victims of these massacres are not only those who have died but also those who live in ongoing grief, as in the women in the Atacama Desert who enact their grieving *through* searching. This is why Jaar, in one of his most well-known series, *The Rwanda Project,* which he made from 1994 to 2000 in response to the media indifference to the genocide in Rwanda, repeats over and over and by different means the same name, the same presence, the same gaze: that of Gutete Emerita. As we learn from the series, in 1994, during the Rwandan genocide, Gutete Emerita, a thirty-year-old member of the Tutsi minority, was attending Mass at the Ntamara Church in Kigali. There, right before her eyes, she witnessed her family killed by Hutu militias. They were killed with grenades, spears, machetes, and clubs, and while

Emerita was able to survive, the horror she witnessed initiated her mourning and "changed her forever," as Butler would say. Alfredo Jaar, who in 1994 traveled to Rwanda to document the genocide, photographed Emerita's eyes right after the massacre, and upon his return to New York, he reproduced this image 100,000 times and spread the slides all over a large low-light table (plate 9). He also placed magnifiers for audiences to make the image larger, isolated from the world. In the interaction process between viewers and the work, the slides are stirred and rearranged, creating impermanent, fluid organic shapes that resemble piles of earth, hills, and molds: archives of a technology *seemingly* from the past. But as the past *is* the now and death is forever mourned, Jaar's installation, in all, invites us to see, think, and feel together with Emeritas's eyes as *punctums* of the ongoing present. Yes, in Jaar's art, as mentioned earlier, the *punctum* is always collective, just as decolonial mourning is always a political agency that aims at advancing in the cultural project of reparation and justice, even if only from the realm of representation. Furthermore, in this case, the *punctum* is also the original frame, that cut that "pierced" the artist, the image, the viewer, the world. The *punctum* here, in other words, is the global shared practice of existence and mourning.

In another work from *The Rwanda Project* series, Jaar narrates Gutete Emerita's story in two light boxes with rotating images. In one of these diptychlike images, he contextualizes the scene that he sees and photographs, filling the entire light boxes with text. In another, he uses the boxes' lower halves to analyze the image of Emerita's eyes. In a third one, Jaar writes at the bottom of the left box, "I remember her eyes," and at the bottom of the right he continues: "The eyes of Gutete Emerita." And, in a fourth image, the artist reproduces the photograph by placing each eye on each of two light boxes (figure 1.12). In this memorial to a massacre survivor, mourning is enacted as a mode of collective remembering. As such, it involves victims and photojournalists, images and spectatorship, past and present, and history—or war—and decolonial solidarities.

This same sense of solidarity has been enacted by students in relation to Palestine—in saying the victims' names, they revisit their present and presence through emancipatory temporalities, as Saidiya Hartman has argued.[132] Also embracing that presence and temporality, in his 2014 installation *22 Women*, composed of twenty-two tiny photographic portraits of women activists, Jaar reproduces a photograph of Amira Hass (figure 1.13). A renowned Israeli journalist, Hass has been reporting for more than thirty years on the occupation in Gaza and the West Bank for the left-wing Israeli daily newspaper *Haaretz*. In Jaar's work, each photograph, including that of Hass, is illuminated through

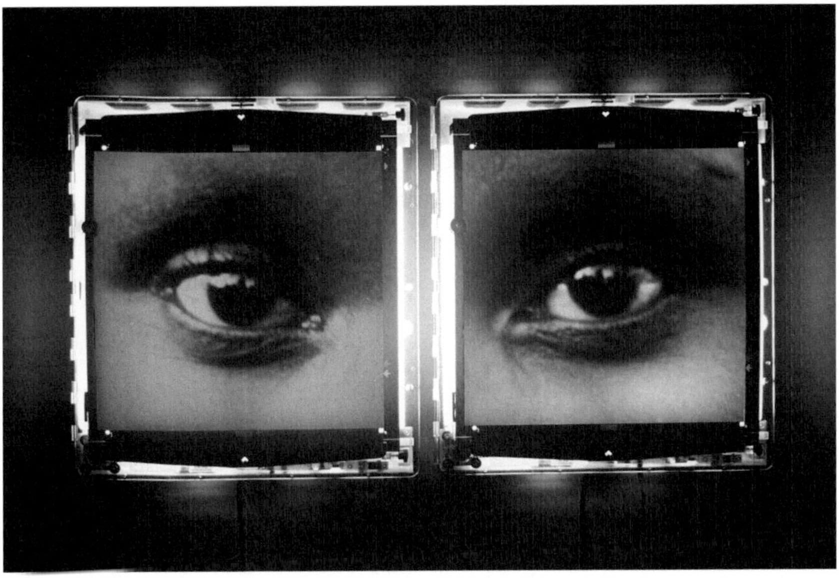

1.12 Alfredo Jaar, *The Eyes of Gutete Emerita*, 1996, from the series *The Rwanda Project* (1994–2000). Courtesy of Alfredo Jaar.

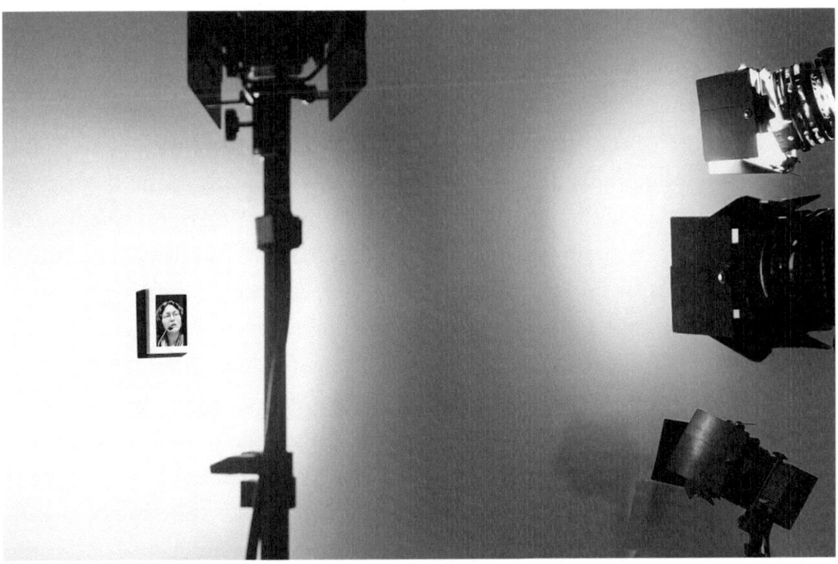

1.13 Alfredo Jaar, *22 Women*, 2014. Courtesy of Alfredo Jaar.

large paparazzi-like tripods. Scale is reduced to just that, to specific data instead of a cultural convention that relates larger size to power and smaller size to submission. Using light to illuminate these women's presence, aesthetics, and politics—both literally and symbolically—Jaar turns the paparazzi's fascination with spectacle into new directions in the public's interest, critiquing the mainstream media's indifference to emancipatory discourses on liberation such as Hass's. As Hass said on October 19, 2023, in relation to Gaza: "The majority of mainstream media don't want to deal with . . . the bureaucratic evilness [and] violence that has been accumulating for years."[133]

Embracing the same hopes of the past in the struggles of presents and futures, in October 2014, Hass joined Jaar in a conversation about genocide, journalism, and decolonial time at the Sørlandets Kunstmuseum in Kristiansand, Norway, where *22 Women* was then on view (plate 10). Despite it all, Jaar's exercises of memory tell us the present cannot kill the past. "Even if they kill them all, the trees in Gaza will continue growing, and the birds will continue singing," Mapuche descendant scholar and musician Marcelo Garzo Montalvo recently said. "This is why genocide is always incomplete."[134] Incompleteness, from this angle, regards not only the decolonial but also colonial genocide, ecocide, and epistemicide, with hope meaning a presence in and beyond the human in the fight for decolonial reciprocity.[135]

In 2010, when he created *Geometry of Conscience* at the MMDH in Santiago (plate 7), Jaar was observing the Chilean student movement's development, witnessing the ways the students were revitalizing Allende's idea of a revolutionary youth, where grieving is enacted *as* decolonial action and resistance *as* collectivity. The infinite multiplicity of heads in the mirrors in his memorial symbolizes that plurality, that ongoing action of seeking justice by those alive, those belonging to generations that did not live through the dictatorship or even the transition, yet that experience doesn't make them less witnesses, less victims of the regime's neoliberal ruins. Significantly, also informing Jaar's memorial was a new type of protest that emerged in Chile in the early 2000s. In *funas*, meaning "rotten" in Mapudungun, people demonstrate against the impunity of perpetrators of the dictatorship and the fact that said impunity has been typically backed by Chile's neoliberal justice. In so doing, protestors expose victimizers' crimes at their residences, chanting their names, personal identification numbers, and wrongdoings. Aiming at canceling their exemption in "democratic" Chile, protestors carry signs with phrases such as "En Chile se sigue torturando" (In Chile torture continues) and "Si no hay justicia, hay *funa*" (If there no justice, there is *funa*), incriminating victimizers within society.[136] *Funas* thus offer an alternative mode of inculpation, challenging the state's "limited renditions by suggesting that memory-making is complex, fluid, unending, and incomplete."[137]

In 2016, for instance, a *funa* took place at the residency of Alejandro Saez Mardones, a carabinero responsible for the 1985 kidnapping of three members of the Communist Party whose corpses were found on the outskirts of Santiago, their throats cut and bodies disfigured. In this series of murders known locally as the "Caso Degollados" (Slit-Throat Case), the victims were teacher and union leader Manuel Guerrero, graphic designer Santiago Nattino, and human rights organization Vicaría de la Solidaridad staff member José Manuel Parada.[138] More than thirty years later, in 2016, Saez Mardones was granted conditional freedom by Chile's Supreme Court, propelling the people to enact a *funa*. Standing before the victimizer's residence, protestors recalled the victims' names, lives, resistances, and fights, joining the practice of mourning that takes place from multiple realms, including the visual arts. In Jaar's *Faces*, for instance, one of these victims, Manuel Guerrero, is depicted in one of his fights: he is the man who, in the diptych depicting Neruda's funeral, is in the front right and is looking slightly toward the center (figure 1.10). He is depicted in mourning and present, rejecting the prohibition and erasure of the struggle against injustice during and after the dictatorship. In this sense, Jaar's *Faces* is a testimony of dynamic memory, where victims are not forgotten or exchanged to achieve what Freud considered successful grief but mourned collectively, in and beyond the time of their deaths.[139]

In Jaar's art on mourning, such sites as the Museum of Solidarity, poems such as the *Nixonicidio*, archives such as Ashton's notes on hemispheric belonging, and images such as those appropriated by Jaar in *Faces* have not really "disappeared," albeit Allende and Popular Unity fell *historically* within modernity's narrative of progressive time.[140] Today, when the Museum of Solidarity has been rebuilt, the *Nixonicidio* is circulating again, and many archives and images regarding the dictatorship are available, the urgency to demonstrate the ruins of the past continues to be key. In a memory politics that is essentially incomplete, there are many memory sites to be built, many poems to be written, many archives to be declassified, and, again, many images to be seen. From an aesthetics of the unfinished, these practices dwell in relational pasts, presents, and futures, resisting neoliberal efforts to erase memory and memory sites. Embracing what historian Pierre Nora calls *lieux de mémoire*, that is, sites of memory considered broadly to include not only monuments and museums but also novels, cities, personages, drawings, archives, poems, images, and more, in Jaar's *Geometry of Conscience*, the aesthetics, poetics, and politics of an expanded and ongoing memory practice are certainly not buried despite, or perhaps precisely because of, the work being located under the museum's plaza.[141] As Patricio Guzmán narrates in his 2004 documentary *Allende*: "Power cultivates forgetfulness. But under the country's layer of amnesia, memories emerge. They resonate under the skin."[142]

In her 2022 book *Planetary Longings*, Mary Louise Pratt connects Pinochet's dictatorship and its legacies in Chile with "Trump's regime" in the United States in the context of his first term as president, linking both experiences of neoliberal authoritarianism and economic and racial inequalities with massive decolonial demonstrations in recent years.[143] "Like Chileans [in the 2019 social outbreak,] in the summer of 2020, [US] Americans, too, were in the streets en masse, protesting the continuing string of police murders of Black citizens," Pratt writes. As she continues: "As in Chile, these protests faced campaigns of police brutality directed and encouraged by the president [leading] one Twitter user [to] declare: 'The Pinochetization of America cometh.'"[144] These historical connections resonate in artworks by Jaar, a self-exiled Chilean from the Pinochet regime who, in the wake of Black Lives Matter massive protests in the United States, was, in his words, "observing [how] students [in Chile] were also marching and protesting in the streets."[145]

Thinking, living, and mourning from the Americas in the wake of the massive solidarity demonstrations that followed the brutal killing of Breonna Taylor and George Floyd in March and May 2020, respectively, and of so many other women, men, and nonbinary Black people by the police's systemic racism, Jaar, in 2022, created a memorial-like installation voicing and representing support for the Black Lives Matter movement (plate 11). Shown at the 2022 edition of the Whitney Biennial in New York, the work is a multimedia installation composed of a square black-box-style gallery room, a five-minute video projected onto one of the walls, and six fans installed overhead. The film was made using three hours of found video footage Jaar gathered online from different sources documenting Black Lives Matter protests in Washington, DC, on June 1, 2020, six days after the murder of George Floyd in Minneapolis. Jaar turned all the footage to black and white and exaggerated their contrast to create a united, collective image of social uprising and revolution. The film is divided into three parts. The first shows peaceful protestors mourning the death of an innocent Black man as a symbol of modernity's racial capitalism. The second displays the moments in which mourners were shot with tear gas, stun grenades, and rubber bullets, remembering the protestors in Chile's social outbreak who lost their eyes from the same shots in the same modernity war. The final section of the film shows the National Guard helicopters bearing down on mourners, as Trump had ordered the dispersal of protesters ahead of the city's 7 p.m. curfew so that he could stage a photo op in front of St. John's Church holding up a Bible.

Leaving authoritarianism hypocrisy disguised as Christian faith and tales of salvation aside, international human rights law prohibits the militarized use of helicopters. In this case, one swooped as low as one hundred feet above the ground. Still, the traditional media barely covered this illegal measurement of rapid "cleanliness" for a quick fake or hyperreal portrait. This is why most of the footage in Jaar's video was taken from mourners reporting *while* mourning. This is also why, in the third part of the video, the six fans placed overhead start moving fast and loud, producing in the audience a sense of chaos and fear to commemorate a specific date, June 1, 2020, and time, 18:39, when the helicopters entered the scene. Hence, the title of the work: *06.01.2020 18.39*, remembering Jaar's earliest series made in 1974 to memorialize the victims of the Chilean coup (figures 1.1 and 1.3). "Coming from Chile, from Latin America, helicopters are for me a synonym for death-flights [as] hundreds of bodies were dropped from helicopters into the ocean by the military dictatorship," said Jaar to an art journalist when asked about this work. "When I saw the helicopters being used in D.C., totally illegally, to disperse the peaceful protesters, I was shocked and enraged. In that moment, I decided to do [the] piece." "How did you feel seeing these [Black Lives Matter] protests going on across the whole nation?" the journalist asked. "The civil rights movement and Martin Luther King Jr. made a big difference [but] not enough to say that there's no racism," Jaar responded, evoking his aesthetics on decolonial time and the fact that justice in the court has so far failed.

"[Not only photography] had an impact on African American social movements, by publicizing aims, mobilizing participants, and visually narrating histories," contends African American studies scholar Leigh Raiford. "African Americans' changing relationship to the photograph itself, as evidenced in the deployment of the medium in political activism, reveals that African American social movements have profoundly shaped the ways we understand the politics of photography specifically and of black visuality more broadly."[146] Understood as a significant site of anti-racist struggle, photography has been used by Jaar to commemorate such fights. In his 1995 piece *Life Magazine, April 19, 1968*, for instance, a memorial to Martin Luther King Jr., Jaar intervenes in the iconic photograph of the Baptist minister and civil rights activist's funeral procession published in *Life* magazine in an article written by African American photographer Gordon Parks (plate 12). With the title denoting the source, *Life* magazine, and the date on which this image was originally published, April 19, 1968—that is, fifteen days after King's assassination—Jaar reproduces the photograph in the left panel of a triptych. For the other two components, he turns the hues, contrast, and intensity of the image into a pale atmosphere just at the edge of invisibility. In the center panel, he uses a black marker to signal the presence of Black people in the procession. In the panel on the right, he uses a red marker to do the same in relation to white people. Highlighting the disparity between the number of Black and white attendants, mourning is here defined by race and solidarity (or its lack) with Black people. Made in 1995, almost three decades after this image was originally published, the work shows the persistence of such disparity, connecting the archive and the present. It also shows the persistence of decolonial hope, recalling King's famous words from a speech at a Chicago church in 1966, when he said: "We must accept finite disappointment, but never lose infinite hope."[147]

Similarly, in his 1989 installation *The Fire Next Time*, Jaar enlarges and reframes photojournalist records of demonstrations against racial inequality he collects from archival documents from the 1960s (figure 1.14). Titled after civil rights activist and writer James Baldwin's 1963 nonfiction testimonial-like book on racial relations in the United States, the installation prominently shows the famous image of the sanitation workers' strike in Memphis in 1968 in which Black laborers walk in a single file wearing sandwich boards covering their torso that read: "I am a Man." Demanding better working conditions and higher pay, that is, demanding the end of what would later be known as neoliberalism, the strike drew Martin Luther King Jr. to Memphis, where he would deliver his last speech on freedom before his assassination. In Jaar's installation, the chaotic stacking of lightboxes—each roughly the size of a person or coffin as a metaphor for a proper funeral that victims of modernity deserve—honors the many lives of victims taken by white supremacy, then and now. It honors and shows that photography has the power and agency to intervene in the political despite modernity's ongoing racial and capitalist constructions.

Connecting different histories of authoritarianism and grief in Chile, the Americas, and the world, Jaar's exercises of memory and the decolonial transnational solidarity context in which they inscribe offer alternative spaces from which we can think about mourning as a form of representation that seeks reparation in multiple forms. They also affirm a collectivity that informs

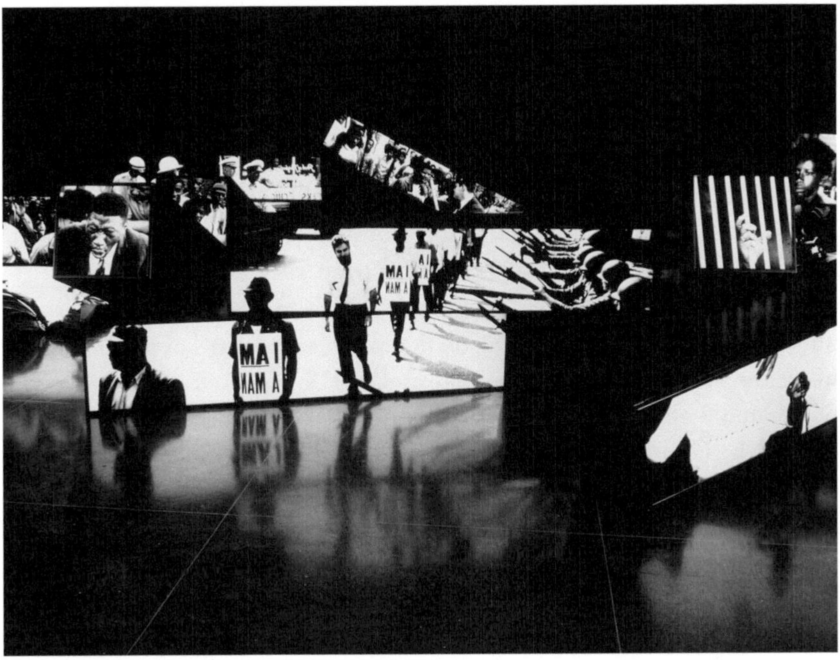

1.14 Alfredo Jaar, *The Fire Next Time*, 1989. Courtesy of Alfredo Jaar.

dissident discourses and actions, radically differing from the individuality that propels neoliberal-driven protests such as El Cacerolazo in early 1970s Chile or, let us say, Latino rallies in support of Donald Trump's 2024 presidential election.[148] "There is the unpleasant fact that [a lot of] immigrants . . . from Latin American countries . . . come to the US not to change it but to succeed in the system or, as Todd McGowan put it: 'They want to create a better life for themselves and their family, not to better their social order.'"[149] Considering that these demonstrations aim at neoliberal desires for individual prosperity and success, the relational dimension of time within collective practices of decolonial mourning enacted by Jaar is, in these cases, absent and denied.

And the people know. During a massive demonstration in solidarity with Palestine that took place in March 2024 in downtown Santiago, for instance, Chilean political commentator and renowned *pinochetista* Sergio "Checho" Hirane was asked to leave the site. "Fascist! Fascist! Go away . . . you're not from here! When we were killed [during the dictatorship], you were happily celebrating," said a protester, recalling that for those in cultures of resistance, marching for Palestine means marching for human rights, past and present and in and beyond the nation.[150] So is the case with the Jewish slogan "Never again," which, in the words of Judith Butler, "should apply to all people."[151] In cultures of resistance, this all means that not all forms of protest are conceptually the same, even if they share the same subject matter, such as Palestine. Indeed, Chile is home to the largest Palestinian diaspora outside the Middle East, including Jaar's paternal family, and while the right to return is a unifying concept, there are significant differences in the diaspora's experiences, including that of those who supported the coup, such as Hirane.[152]

Examples of protests that formally if not conceptually share the same subject matter abound. One may think, for instance, of the series of public-space demonstrations regarding the subject of free speech that emerged in the United States in the wake of right-wing activist and media personality Charles Kirk's assassination on a university campus in Utah on September 10, 2025. With the lives of some being euphorically celebrated and thus massively mourned for their fearless enactment of free speech and the lives of others who assert the same right being systematically threatened and/or silenced through modernity's machine of violence and exclusion, what differs within such protests is a different understanding of modernity, racial hierarchy, spiritual ethicality, and universality. What differs, in short, is a different understanding of the world from the perspective of decolonial time.

Jaar's works discussed in this chapter invite us to think about mourning and thus life from such a perspective, linking decolonial instances of grief and resistance with the ongoing presence of shared solidarity networks globally that operate against and beyond the strict parameters of Chronos, or clock time. They also contend that the 1973 coup in Chile, both historically and conceptually, was not a national but a regional and global event, rejecting modernity's ideals of singularity and transcendentalism within the nation-state paradigm through emancipatory practices of collective remembering. "There are many coups, and they all keep sounding loud and together, propelling us all to continue developing creative practices of resistance in the search for social justice, dignity, joy, and love," explains theater scholar and queer activist Cristian Aravena.[153] Mourning, therefore, as an action *in process* that exceeds and resists the authority of the nation-state and the narrative of progressive time opens up spaces not only for defiance but also for decolonial joy and love. Psychologist and gender studies scholar Lynne Segal puts it this way: "Love offers us the potential to think about different worlds, communities [and] spaces of hope and resistance imagined or created for promoting greater social harmony, justice, political education and enjoyment of life."[154] And these spaces, which modernity denies, are spaces for becoming *in* liberation and togetherness, spaces that, in Noam Chomsky's thinking regarding Palestine, know that the past is built upon relational hopes.[155] Jaar's art about mourning is about the possibility of such hope, which, as I show in the following chapters, he enacts simultaneously with an aesthetic fight for accountability and the acknowledgment of decolonial failure. Jaar's art knows, in other words, that while modernity continues to design life and death in the world as we know it and thus failure is likely to continue, it cannot stop the search for accountability, justice, and liberation. It cannot stop the collective practice of mourning within and toward decolonial hope.

2

ACCOUNTABILITY

What happened you know, horrible story, and definitely Kissinger is the villain . . . but people still don't say that, do they?
—Dore Ashton

In a 2015 public lecture at the Barcelona Museum of Contemporary Art, right after displaying portraits of victims of the Chilean regime, Alfredo Jaar showed a 2007 portrait of Henry Kissinger (figure 2.1). "This is another face," he said.[1] "As we know, Kissinger and Nixon financed the military coup in Chile. I got obsessed with Kissinger and made a series of works on this man."[2] Jaar's selection of this portrait is telling. In this image taken by Martin Schoeller, a German-born, New York–based photographer known for his hyperdetailed close-up portraits, Kissinger is staring straight ahead and illuminated by neon rather than flash. His pores, wrinkles, and eye bags are uncomfortably intensified through this very simple yet charged studio lighting technique, resulting in a tired and desolate expression. This appearance of sadness and defeat is quite different from the extensive photographic archive portraying Kissinger throughout his life in which his active gaze and self-confident pose convey a respected statesman, a world strategist, and a notorious authority, even when he is deplored as a villain. In contrast, in Schoeller's photograph, Kissinger's pupils—his presence—are decentered and lost, suggesting his absence within the political discourse and international leadership at the time. Himself a wise connoisseur of the power of photography to persuade meaning, Kissinger was clearly not happy with this image. This is why this face, this expression, as was captured by Schoeller, is recurrently used by Jaar to introduce his project on Henry Kissinger.

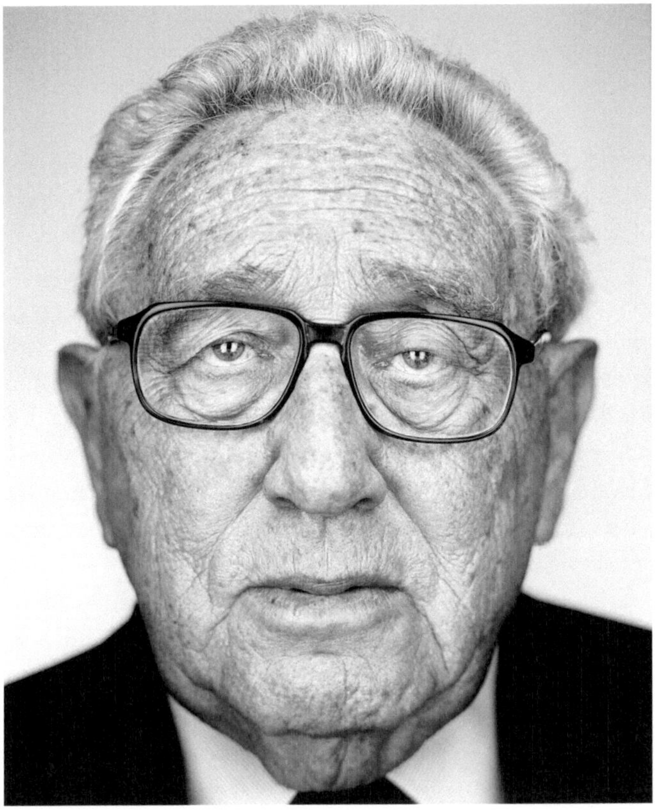

2.1 Martin Schoeller, *Henry Kissinger*, 2007.

Begun in 1983, one year after he moved from Chile to New York, Jaar's series is grouped together under the title *The Kissinger Project*. In it, Jaar appropriates and intervenes in declassified archives, print media, postcards, signed letters, autographed portraits, and pages of books, which all address Henry Kissinger's central role in plotting the overthrow of Chilean democracy, engendering the dictatorship that followed, and leading to its aftermath in the ongoing present. Comprising more than a dozen artworks, Jaar's series reveals a multifaceted, threefold phenomenon that is political, historical, and cultural: It highlights Kissinger's central role during his tenure as national security advisor and secretary of state under Richard Nixon and Gerald Ford in undermining Chilean democracy; it demonstrates that Kissinger's legacy still shapes the country's public policies; and it shows that previous condemnations of Kissinger for crimes against humanity have so far failed and thus they *must* continue, regardless of Kissinger's death in late 2023 at the age of one hundred. Jaar's project is therefore essentially unfinished, as are the ways his project underscores the fact that justice has not yet been achieved.

In the early 1980s, when Jaar commenced his series, Kissinger was not only a free man but one with significant political, economic, and even ethical influence. In the late 1990s, when the United States declassified thousands of secret documents demonstrating the degree of Kissinger's intervention in Chile—an unprecedented release that followed the dictator General Augusto Pinochet's detention in London for crimes against humanity—Kissinger went unpunished, prompting Jaar to create more works. In the early 2010s, when Jaar exhibited this project for the first time publicly, more documents were declassified and more denunciations were made. And in 2023, when Jaar opened a solo exhibition centered on this series at the National Museum of Fine Arts in Chile, Kissinger was still alive and quite active. A key strategist in international affairs, at the time, he continued to advise Republicans and Democrats alike, impacting new generations in the study of political science and international relations. "Every U.S. president since John F. Kennedy has sought Henry Kissinger's counsel, as have CEOs and political leaders worldwide," write three Harvard professors in a recent volume on Kissinger.[3] "By studying a great negotiator like Kissinger . . . we can learn to be far more effective in . . . business, legal [environments], and government," they continue, highlighting the relevance of Kissinger's "remarkable strength as a negotiator" for future generations.[4]

Publishing widely on current foreign policy, in 2022, for instance, Kissinger wrote *Leadership: Six Studies in World Strategy*, in which he examines six world leaders in the context of the Cold War to elaborate on two types of leaders: the strategist, who cautiously manipulates circumstances to their favor and works with the essence of societies until they change; and the prophet, who is prepared and even eager to break with the past at any risk. In this scholarly record describing his philosophy of power, Kissinger outspokenly rewarded both the conspirator and the genocidaire, that is, the one who designs colonial time in the favor of modernity, and the one who annihilates the memory of the multiple pasts by imposing a "progressive" and "new" beginning. To start from scratch and break with the past through a cautious strategy planned by the empire is precisely what happened in Chile on the day of the coup. Jaar's aim is to expose the consequences of Kissinger's philosophy of colonial time as well as the visual strategies used by Kissinger to promote said philosophy. In this sense, Jaar's series demonstrates the key role of images in forming and disseminating world leaders' policies and thus the never unconscious links between visual culture and politics, or between art and life. This is also revealed through Jaar's own philosophy, which advocates instead for a decolonial time through images that expose and expand on the power of representation to activate the public's consciousness for accountability. And because images—unlike humans—don't die, as Jaar seems to tell us, they will continue exposing Kissinger's crimes.

This chapter takes *The Kissinger Project* as a point of departure to examine the trope of accountability in Jaar's art, analyzing the conceptual strategies the artist employs to expose Kissinger's darker side and the dreadful and ongoing consequences of his international policies in the lives and dignity of millions. Expanding on the relationship between progressive time and neoliberalism, this chapter further elaborates on works by Jaar denouncing other perpetrators globally and the complicity of the media in their crimes. Together, works in this chapter show that while legal aims at liability have failed, the representation of wrongs has continued, even after the perpetrators' deaths. It shows, in other words, that the relationship between representation, resistance, and existence regards not only victims but also victimizers, reframing the linear time of trial and crime through nonhegemonic forms of ongoing accountability.

AN IMPERIAL HANDSHAKE

The central piece of Jaar's *The Kissinger Project* is an archival-based work for which he appropriated photographic reproductions from the first two volumes of Kissinger's memoirs, published in 1979 and 1982 (figure 2.2).[5] Titled *Searching for K* (1984), here Jaar, who at the time worked at the architectural firm SITE in New York, uses a red marker and an architectural stencil with circular apertures to trace perfect rings of differing diameters and thicknesses around Kissinger's head, repeatedly leading the viewer's gaze back to the main subject. One hundred and eight red rings interplay with the black-and-white photographs—equal to the number of times Kissinger appears photographed in the first two volumes of his memoirs—creating graphic contrasts between monochrome and color and between mechanical and manual procedure. In the photographs, Kissinger is accompanied by key political figures or "world leaders," many of whom Kissinger would later describe as "strategists" or "prophets," as well as family members and celebrities worldwide. Significantly, Jaar did not cut the photographic images out of the books but appropriated the entire pages containing them, making available the captions accompanying each reproduction, such as "Actress Jill St. John, Leonid Brezhnev, and Adrei Vavilov (interpreter) at Nixon's San Clemente reception, June 1973" and "With President Hafez al-Asad in Damascus, January 20, 1974."[6]

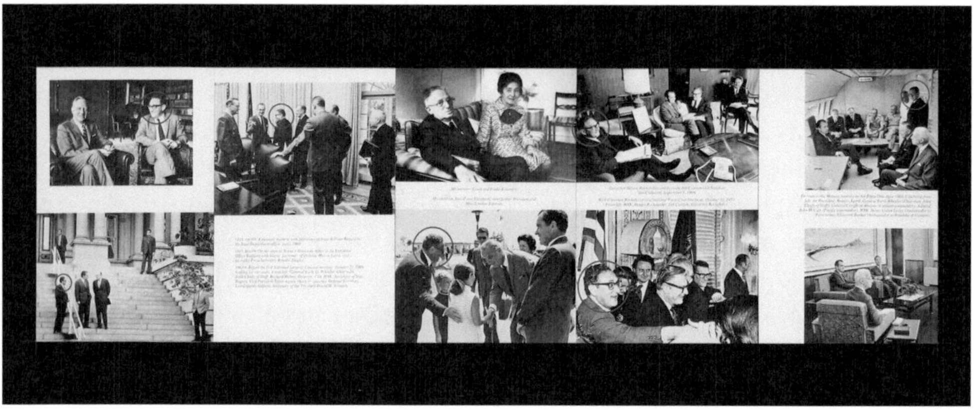

2.2 Alfredo Jaar, *Searching for K* (detail), 1984, from the series *The Kissinger Project* (ongoing from 1983). Courtesy of Alfredo Jaar.

Noticing the absence of any photograph and by extension caption related to Chile, a country that is the main topic of two lengthy chapters in Kissinger's memoirs and where Kissinger met with Pinochet in 1976, Jaar included a photograph of that meeting at the end of his visual archive (figure 2.3). Shot from below, this black-and-white photograph is set in the corner of a room and depicts Kissinger in profile shaking hands with General Augusto Pinochet. Both figures are dressed in their iconic attire: Pinochet in a military uniform and Kissinger in his signature bold black glasses and dark suit. Two guards stand in the background; one looks at Kissinger, while the other gazes at the camera. Freezing the moment in which Pinochet, displaying a slight smile, appears to be speaking to Kissinger, who in turn looks at the general and smiles back, the photograph conveys a warm exchange. The overlapping historical and symbolic consequences of this meeting in dictatorship and postdictatorship Chile are not only one of the main points in *The Kissinger Project* but also a key aspect of memory studies, anti-imperialist journalism, and human rights policies related to Chile, past and present.[7] And thus, we ask: How did that moment happen, and what are the handshake's meanings?

On June 8, 1976, at the height of the repression, when Dirección de Inteligencia Nacional (DINA) officers were committing crimes such as torture and disappearances in and beyond detention camps in Chile, the Kissinger/Pinochet meeting occurred.[8] Taking place in the presidential suite of the Diego Portales building, an office used during repairs of La Moneda Palace after being bombed during the coup by the armed forces and the national police,

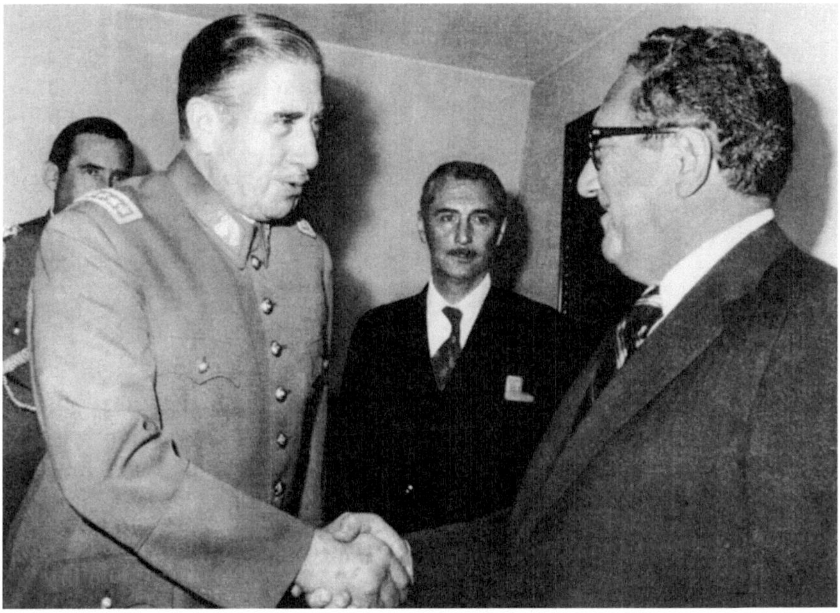

2.3 Alfredo Jaar, *Searching for K* (detail), 1984, from the series *The Kissinger Project* (ongoing from 1983). Courtesy of Alfredo Jaar.

the meeting was scheduled for the day before Kissinger's speech, ironically on human rights, at the Sixth Annual Assembly of the Organization of American States (OAS), held that year in Santiago. At the OAS assembly, in a "carefully calculated response to the main topic of the meeting, a report on the hemisphere by the Inter-American Human Rights Commission detailing allegations of violations by 16 nations," Kissinger publicly warned the Chilean junta that "the condition of human rights has impaired our relationship with Chile and will continue to do so."[9] As he continued, "Human rights are the very essence of a meaningful life, and human dignity is the ultimate purpose of government. A government that tramples on the rights of its citizens denies the purpose of its existence."[10] In contrast, and reversing his speech at the OAS, in his private meeting with Pinochet a day before, Kissinger, as shown in the Memorandum of Conversation (MEMCON) of the gathering declassified in 1999 by the National Security Archive (NSA), told the general:

> In the United States, as you know, we are sympathetic with what you are trying to do here. . . . In my statement [at the OAS] I will treat human rights in general terms, and human rights in a world context. . . . The

speech is not aimed at Chile. I wanted to tell you about this. My evaluation is that you are a victim of all left-wing groups around the world, and that your greatest sin was that you overthrew a government which was going Communist.[11]

Kissinger, clearly, was giving the green light to the regime and supporting its continuity, and his OAS speech was a rather diplomatic screen to cover the true purpose of his visit to Chile. Indeed, as a 1999 declassified document shows, it was Kissinger himself who controversially encouraged OAS representatives to choose Santiago for their annual meeting.[12] "I encouraged the OAS to have its General Assembly here. I knew it would add prestige to Chile. I came for that reason. We want to help, not undermine you," Kissinger told Pinochet, evidently considering that in a climate of a hemispheric diplomatic gathering they could *naturally* meet, preventing the US Congress's suspicion of support, as four months prior, Congress had passed the embargo of US arms to the Chilean regime as the "Kennedy Amendment."[13] Years later, when publishing a report on the meeting after Pinochet's detention in London, contradicting himself in public writing, Kissinger stated that "as *fate* would have it, the meeting was planned to be held in Santiago. . . . Neither Ford nor I considered it desirable to run from the challenge."[14]

A day after the meeting on June 9, the conservative right-wing and dictatorship-friendly press controlled by the daily *El Mercurio* and its affiliates published written and visual information on the gathering. Indeed, despite the content of the meeting being kept secret until its declassification in 1999, it was well documented in the Chilean press. Emphasizing Kissinger's "sympathy" to Pinochet, headlines of these reports read, "With Promise of Love, Kissinger Leaves Us" and contained such captions as "Augusto Pinochet and U.S. Secretary of State Henry Kissinger had a cordial meeting yesterday at the Diego Portales building."[15] The celebration of Kissinger's very persona is evident in many of those articles; he was portrayed in triumphant biographies and shown as a celebrity who, along with his wife Nancy, was welcomed by more than three thousand enthusiastic Chileans "simply to catch a glimpse of the secretary," and who, in turn, were "touched by the popular reception when [he] arrived."[16] Similar results happened with Televisión Nacional de Chile (TVN), which documented Kissinger's visit with a celebration of his "extraordinary position as chancellor of the world." "Here he is in Chilean soil, the great U.S. Secretary of State," stated a journalist reporting Kissinger's arrival at Santiago's airport. He continued, asking the attendees: "Did you imagine him like this? What did you think about his outfit?"[17] Kissinger, for Chileans supporting the regime, was "the most important celebrity to ever come to the country in years."[18] And television, which during the dictatorship not only censored information but also turned it into a spectacle, was a key axis of the regime's cultural intervention.[19]

Because TVN was controlled by the army and the media by the regime and its supporters, such as notoriously right-wing conservative tycoon and *El Mercurio* owner Agustín Edwards Eastman, these broadcasts and reports are not surprising. In turn, because the exposure of media power is so important in Jaar's art, a more detailed examination of these reports is necessary. For one, and regarding the enthusiastic tone of the press about the supposedly secret meeting, a 2014 version of a MEMCON partially released in 1999 demonstrated that Edwards's anti-communist propaganda was part of a larger imperial agenda he commenced with Kissinger in the late 1960s.[20] Fearing for the future of his Chilean assets in the wake of the socialist agenda of Popular Unity, the Kissinger/Edwards program reached its pinnacle right after Allende was democratically elected president on September 4, 1970.[21] As detailed in the report, Kissinger himself arranged a meeting on September 10, 1970, in Washington, DC, between former Central Intelligence Agency (CIA) director Richard Helms and Edwards, whose name was previously redacted from declassified documents to protect his identity as a confidential source.[22] Ignoring the recommendation made that same day by Viron Vaky, Kissinger's deputy at the National Security Council (NSC), Kissinger supported Edwards's idea of "a conspiracy for a coup d'état and how the United States could support it."[23] In other words, despite Vaky's warning that plotting a coup in Chile was "patently a violation of our own principles and policy tenets" and that "Allende's threat to the U.S. [was] hard to argue," the resulting Edwards/Helms gathering orchestrated by Kissinger was, as investigative journalist and senior adviser of the NSA Peter Kornbluh has argued, "key in the impetus that was given from that day to the destabilizing action taken by the Nixon administration against Allende."[24] Hence, it is not by chance that the next day, Nixon, in a fifteen-minute meeting with Kissinger at the Oval Office, ordered Helms to "make the [Chilean] economy scream."[25]

To "make the economy scream" resulted in a radical conspiracy to lower the value of copper, the pillar of the economy, as well as financing activities covering both media propaganda manipulation and center-right and right-wing political parties interfering in the public opinion regarding the Chilean economic crisis. Indeed, this was the main plan of CIA covert actions, whose principal aim was to prevent Allende from coming to power or, if in power, to withdraw him from the presidency. While the first attempt at a coup in

1970 failed, the second in 1973 succeeded. In both cases, however, the plan, which resulted in numerous strikes and a highly polarized country, was clear: to impose a dictatorship to maintain an order adequate for the development of a new model of capitalism, that of neoliberalism.[26] This means that the aim of the dictatorship, in the words of literary and cultural critic Idelber Avelar, was "the imbrication between the doctrine of national security and the transnational market . . . between, in a word, political authoritarianism and capitalist class interest."[27]

And the people knew it. Critical investigative journalists, politicians, poets, students, and artists in and beyond Chile were all well aware of this relation, as stated in the previous chapter. So was Alfredo Jaar, who in the 1980s commenced his project on Kissinger. In *Searching for K*, the artist exposes Kissinger's crimes and their aftermath from the perspective of the critical media. An "obsessive" press reader from an early age, as he has defined himself, Jaar, as philosopher and art historian Georges Didi-Huberman notes, makes "clear-sighted criticism of the disinformation that surrounds us."[28] In this sense, the juxtaposition of celebratory reports of Kissinger's visit to Chile and others that maintained a critical posture has been central for Jaar in the development of this project. In fact, in the same month Kissinger visited Chile, June 1976, the first opposition magazines, such as *Solidaridad* and APSI, began publication. In covering the OAS meeting, an opposition journalist wrote: "There are not harmonic relations, but rather relations of domination of the north toward the south [and] the OAS is nothing but a part of this domination apparatus."[29] Another writer from *Solidaridad* accused *El Mercurio* of abuse of pro-regime propaganda and thus censorship and human rights violations.[30] In a more direct critique of Kissinger, a third article questioned his policies in Latin America, noting his promotion of "international order directed by the great powers."[31] And while an article in the opposition magazine *Mensaje* even celebrated Kissinger's speech at the OAS, the majority of these anti-imperialist reports highly contrast with those published in *El Mercurio* and *La Tercera de la Hora* as well as with TVN broadcasts.[32]

In the context of these differing narratives, in 1984 Jaar created a diptych of two prints titled *Dear Mr. Jaar, 1976* (figure 2.4). For the first image, Jaar appropriated a signed portrait of Kissinger that he had found in a flea market in New York.[33] Wearing a gray suit, a white collared shirt, and a checkered tie, Kissinger, elegantly illuminated by a lateral soft flash, directs his gaze at the viewer, his eyes looking upward and his mouth sporting a pleasant smile. Conveying an expression of responsibility, efficiency, and morality, quite different from Martin Schoeller's 2007 portrait (figure 2.1), this autographed photograph was taken the same year as the Chilean coup, Kissinger's

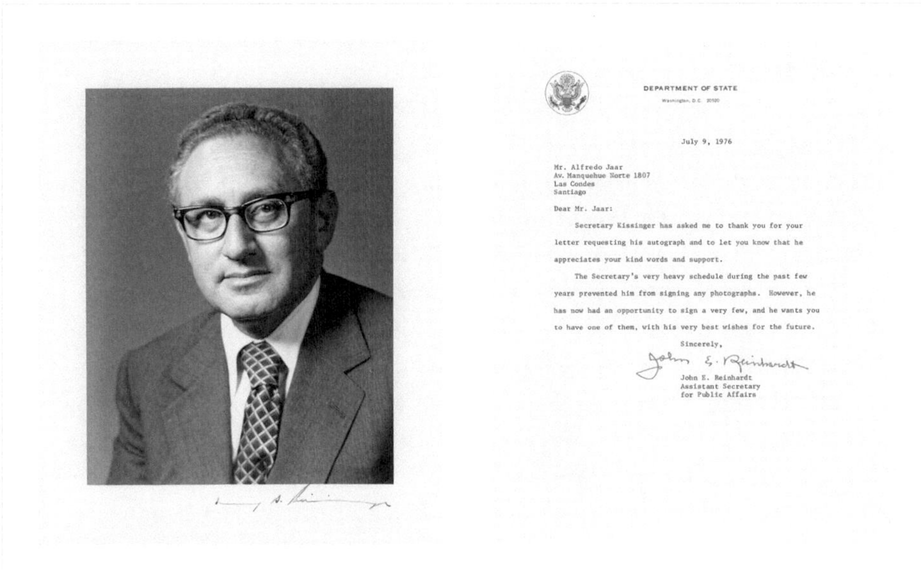

2.4 Alfredo Jaar, *Dear Mr. Jaar, 1976*, 1984, from the series *The Kissinger Project* (ongoing from 1983). Courtesy of Alfredo Jaar.

involvement in the bombing of Cambodia and Laos, and his receiving the Nobel Peace Prize for his role in the Vietnam War. Indeed, this is the image commemorating the Nobel. For the second print, on the other hand, Jaar replaced the recipient's name in a letter written by the US assistant secretary for public affairs on behalf of Henry Kissinger with his own, as if he had asked Kissinger himself for an autographed portrait.

Dated July 9, 1976, that is, only a month after Kissinger's speech at the OAS and his meeting with Pinochet, the letter reads:

> Dear Mr. Jaar,
>
> Secretary Kissinger has asked me to thank you for your letter requesting his autograph and to let you know that he appreciates your kind words and support. The Secretary's very heavy schedule during the past few years prevented him from signing any photographs. However, he has now had an opportunity to sign a very few, and he wants you to have one of them, with his very best wishes for the future.
>
> Sincerely,
> John E. Reinhart

By choosing this photograph and placing it next to a letter suggesting that Jaar asked Kissinger for an autographed portrait in 1976, the artist ironically echoes the congratulatory tone of Pinochet's regime-controlled media regarding a prized ally and celebrity. In turn, by creating this work in 1984, right after Kissinger published his second memoir, Jaar alludes to the censorship of the photograph in which Kissinger is shaking hands with Pinochet, additionally underscoring how this censored image by Kissinger conflicts radically with the media-created hero-like portrait of a Nobel Peace Prize laureate.

Three factors propelled Jaar to commence his series on Kissinger in the early 1980s in New York. During a period lacking Chilean censorship and within a massive yet still overlooked climate of US cultural solidarity toward Latin America in the context of Reagan-sponsored civil wars in Central America, the first critical account of Kissinger's memoir was published in 1983, one year after Jaar moved to New York. *The Price of Power: Kissinger in the Nixon White House* was written by Seymour Hersh, a Pulitzer Prize–winning investigative journalist described by Jaar as "the greatest U.S. American journalist alive."[34] Offering crucial revelations of Kissinger's condescending attitude toward Chile and Latin America broadly, one passage in the book discloses Kissinger's arrogance toward the Chilean foreign minister at the time, Gabriel Valdés, during a June 1969 meeting with Latin American ambassadors at the White House. After listening to Valdés's complaint about the inherently exploitative nature of US "assistance" in Latin America, Kissinger told the Chilean diplomat: "You come here speaking of Latin America, but this is not important. Nothing important can come from the South. History has never been told from the South. The axis of history starts in Moscow, goes to Bonn, crosses over to Washington, and then goes to Tokyo. What happens in the South is of no importance. You're wasting your time."[35] In 1984, a year after the publication of Hersh's book, Jaar summarized these words on a sheet of paper by using a typewriter (figure 2.5). Typing "Henry Kissinger, 1969" below the phrase, at the center Jaar included a black rectangle that is not added to the sheet but belongs to the mount. It represents censorship, lack of information, hidden operations. It represents the dictatorial state in which "Latin America," for someone like Kissinger, was not important. In this work, tellingly titled *Latin America*, Jaar exposes and resists a Latin America whose culture and identity depend on imperialist multinational interests, one whose history is dictated by the global structure of coloniality and its sad disciples: the economic class and the military. Jaar's work exposes and resists, in short, an idea of Latin America that celebrates Kissinger's persona while ignoring his colonial agenda.

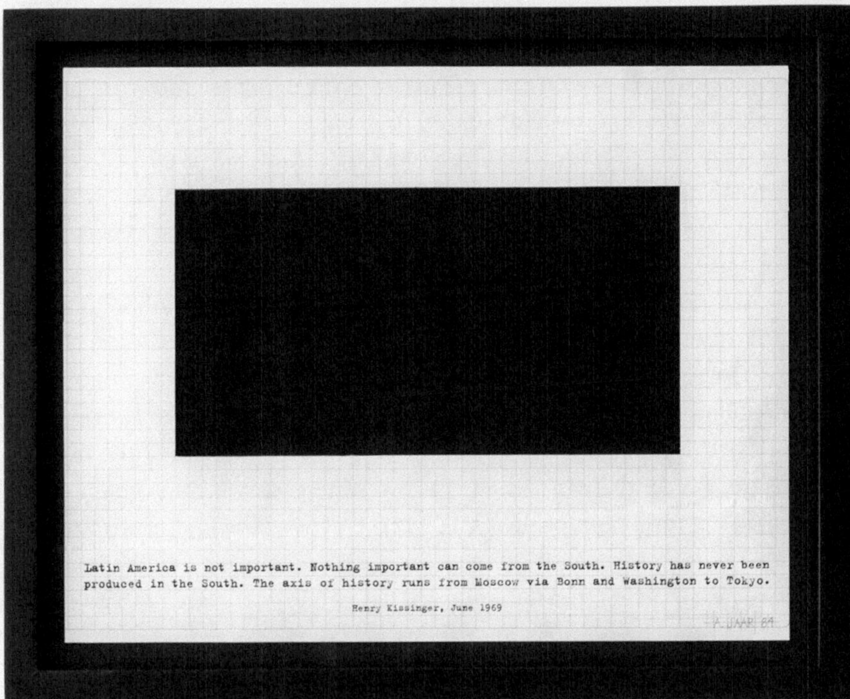

2.5 Alfredo Jaar, *Latin America*, 1984, from the series *The Kissinger Project* (ongoing from 1983). Courtesy of Alfredo Jaar.

Significantly, Jaar's project not only exposes Kissinger's dreadful intervention in Chile—a located geopolitical case—but also the paradigm from which Kissinger operates: modernity. In *Searching for K* (figure 2.2), Jaar points out this model by drawing red rings around Kissinger's head, recalling a well-known method of identification of criminals used by legal organizations. This tactic is also a metaphor for photography's essence, famously described by Roland Barthes as an index indicating that "this has been," which, in this case, works as evidence of accountability.[36] Considering that said accountability is perversely disguised by Kissinger through a cautious creation of an empathic world leader image, Jaar repeats his tactic of circling from beginning to end. In so doing, he reveals Kissinger's real intention: to persuade the reader/viewer that he (Kissinger) is the protagonist, the hero, of these moments that indeed *have been*, and photography is there to prove it. Yet, as Jaar's series shows, Kissinger carefully selected only those photographs in which he is shown in the right place, at the right time, and with the right people. It shows that Kissinger has created a linear narrative of US international affairs through the thread of his own achievements embodying modernity's progressive, universal, and heroic aesthetics and its tendency to erase the histories of traumatic forgotten pasts, in plural. Jaar's red circles thus show Kissinger's perverse idea of truth, authorship, and universality, and his vast knowledge of the capacity of documentary images to persuade actuality.[37] This is why there is always a circle when Kissinger is present, as his presence, according to himself, always means victory, development, modernity. Further, this is also why, when Kissinger is absent, as is the case in 25 photographs out of a total of 158, there is no circle to draw.

Predictably, this second type of photograph depicts defeat and shame, as in the image from August 9, 1974, showing Nixon departing the White House after resigning from the presidency over the Watergate scandal (figure 2.6).[38] In a vertical reproduction printed across a full page at the end of Kissinger's second memoir and thus at the end of Jaar's archive, Nixon, with the corners of his lips down, covers his face while waving goodbye. Nowhere to be seen, Kissinger detaches him from accountability in the realm of representation and therefore of politics and life. After all, as this image seems to tell us, Nixon resigned *alone*, and the scandal leading to his guilt and for that matter to any other form of political corruption was only *his* responsibility. By prominently including this image in his archive, Jaar highlights Kissinger's conceptual strategy to represent his "impeccable morality" by blending absence and innocence through a cunning photographic maneuver in the postproduction moment. But since representation is what matters in political persuasion, this specific shot selected and deliberately enlarged by Kissinger shows the opposite paths taken by Nixon and himself after Watergate, with one embracing dishonor, downfall, and loneliness, and the other ethics, integrity, and political power. Jaar's conceptual strategy consists simply of showing Kissinger's keen knowledge about images as forms of power. And just like modernity's progressive time, Kissinger, a master editor of images, grants himself a happy and victorious ending as the Cold War's main secretary of state.

Declassified documents and archival research, however, prove that Kissinger was the main architect of the destabilization of the Chilean economy that sought to prevent Allende from assuming the presidency. They also show that in light of Allende's ratification by the Chilean Congress in 1970, Kissinger supported the 1973 coup and the dictatorship that followed. By placing the censored photograph of Kissinger with Pinochet right after the image of a desolated, defeated

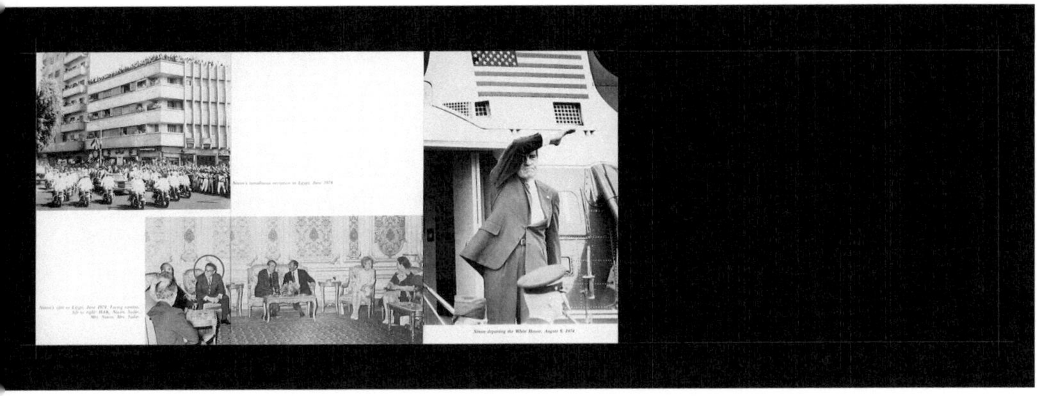

2.6 Alfredo Jaar, *Searching for K* (detail), 1984, from the series *The Kissinger Project* (ongoing from 1983). Courtesy of Alfredo Jaar.

Nixon—where Kissinger is shown in the wrong place, at the wrong time, and with the wrong person—Jaar interrupts Kissinger's triumphant ending. Mirroring Kissinger's own photographic strategies, Jaar uses the imagery to warn us about the aesthetic means used by Kissinger to persuade the public, in which at stake are tactics of revealing and censoring, of showing and hiding, and of colonial and decolonial time. Kissinger, a double-sided strategist par excellence well aware of the relation between images and massive information, predictably sought to prevent this historic and aesthetic finding. As he wrote in his chapter on Chile, included in his second memoir, published in 1982:

> It may seem strange that in a book describing my stewardship of affairs I should feel obliged to include a chapter on the downfall of Chile's President Salvador Allende. . . . Our government had nothing to do with planning his overthrow and no involvement with the plotters. . . . The Nixon Administration did not view our foreign policy interests through the prism of the financial concerns of American companies. . . . The mythology that the United States relentlessly assaulted Allende after he was installed is the opposite of the truth.[39]

Ironically, in this passage, Kissinger openly exposes his condescending take on Latin America—as Jaar demonstrates using Kissinger's own words in his 1984 artwork *Latin America*—as well as the relationship between neoliberalism and ethnic superiority, a colonial paradigm first rehearsed globally in Chile with the coup.

Importantly, neither Hersh's book nor the Chilean press, and certainly not Kissinger's memoirs, published or interpreted the photograph of Kissinger shaking hands with Pinochet. This image, so famous today and seemingly unnoticed by US public opinion at the time, first appeared in the June 21, 1976, issue of *Time* magazine accompanying an article by John Dinges, a special correspondent in Chile from 1972 to 1980 for *Time*, the *Washington Post*, and ABC Radio. The main focus of the article, accordingly titled "A Harsh Warning on Human Rights," was the most "unprecedented" cautioning about human rights that Henry Kissinger had ever made.[40] Dinges writes: "When Chile's military government asked to play host to last week's annual meeting in Santiago of the OAS, the junta hoped the occasion might be a good chance to change its widespread image as the most repressive regime on the continent. No such luck."[41] And yet, even recognizing human rights violations in Chile and the eventual consequences of such crimes in the international community, it is striking, to say the least, that a photograph connoting empathy between Kissinger and Pinochet was chosen to illustrate an article describing the opposite. Whereas through the pose the press photograph connotes and denotes support and mutual respect, the text refers to warning and distance.

Further, considering that Dinges was one of the founders of *APSI* in 1976, skepticism—and, perhaps, irony—by Dinges and his editor at *Time* are visible within this double game of image and text, which, in turn, goes a step further in Jaar's work: by unveiling through a photojournalistic record an episode censored from Kissinger's memoir, Jaar *directly* undercuts Kissinger's chameleonic personality and the brutal consequences of his international policies. Extracted from its original source and placed alongside other press records celebrating his kindness, polite behavior, and leadership, the photograph serves to both convey information and critique Kissinger's hypocrisy and opportunism. As the artist once said, "From the beginning I was interested not only in [written] information but also in visual information, in images. Later, I realized that I was interested in the 'politics of images,' although I did not have a name for it at the time."[42]

POLITICS OF IMAGES

Jaar's "politics of images" considers that photojournalist images have been typically and morally blamed by society for their complicity in the devastating events they capture and that these very accusations have prompted artists such as himself to think critically *through* these images about the political events they represent.[43] Images "not only respond to political events but also play an

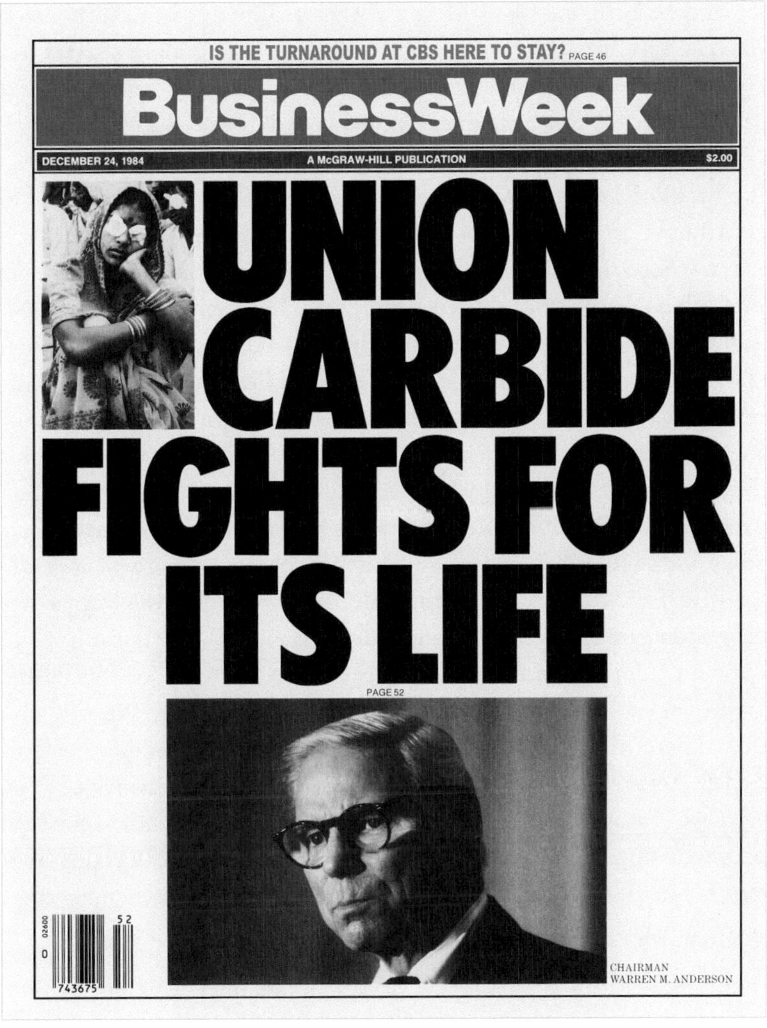

2.7 Alfredo Jaar, *BusinessWeek Magazine Cover, December 24, 1984*, 1984. Courtesy of Alfredo Jaar.

important role in shaping them," writes film scholar Nikolaj Lübecker.[44] This is what Jaar does in *BusinessWeek Magazine Cover, December 24, 1984* (figure 2.7), in which he appropriates the December 24, 1984, cover of *BusinessWeek* magazine to denounce the crime of other perpetrators benefiting from modernity's linear time—in this case a chemical company and its CEO—as well as the media's involvement in such crimes through the reframing of its victims.

The headline on the cover, written in Futura Condensed Extra Bold font, reads: "Union Carbide Fights for Its Life." It is accompanied by two photos. Following the magazine's capitalist editorial, the headline focuses on the life of the Union Carbide Corporation (UCC), a prominent US chemical company, instead of the thousands of victims of a gas tragedy provoked by the company's pesticide plant in the city of Bhopal in central India, in the largest industrial disaster in history to date. On the morning of December 3, 1984, the plant leaked roughly forty tons of methyl isocyanate gas into the air, exposing thousands of people in nearby small towns to highly toxic fumes. About 22,000 were killed, and more than 100,000 are still suffering from chronic health problems.[45] This hierarchy in the life and suffering of humans and the fight for recovery of a prominent US company is mirrored in the magazine's decisions regarding the images reproduced. Echoing the headline, the central image is placed at the bottom center of the cover and touts a horizontal portrait of Warren M. Anderson, the businessman who was chair and CEO of UCC at the time of the disaster. Wearing a black jacket and tie, a white shirt, black-framed glasses, and with his gray hair parted on the left, Anderson is theatrically illuminated, showcasing an image of power and success. A second image on the cover is positioned vertically at the top left corner, rendering visible one victim of the massacre. It features a young woman resting her face on her left palm, her eyes covered with patches, highlighting the effects of the gas on her capacity to see. Regarding this work, Jaar said:

> The week before I produced it, there was this huge accident in Bhopal in India, due to a company called Union Carbide—thousands of people died, and thousands of others were blinded. It was one of the first huge industrial accidents in the history of humankind, and it was all over the news. And that week, *BusinessWeek* comes out, headlined "Union Carbide fights for its life." They give the main photograph to the chairman of the company. That was utterly shocking for me. I couldn't believe it.[46]

Jaar's conceptual gesture consists simply of extracting the cover from the magazine, framing it, and displaying it as such, showing the complicit politics of the mainstream media in crimes against humanity and the ecosystem, together. It confirms that, paraphrasing Latin American studies theorist Mary Louise

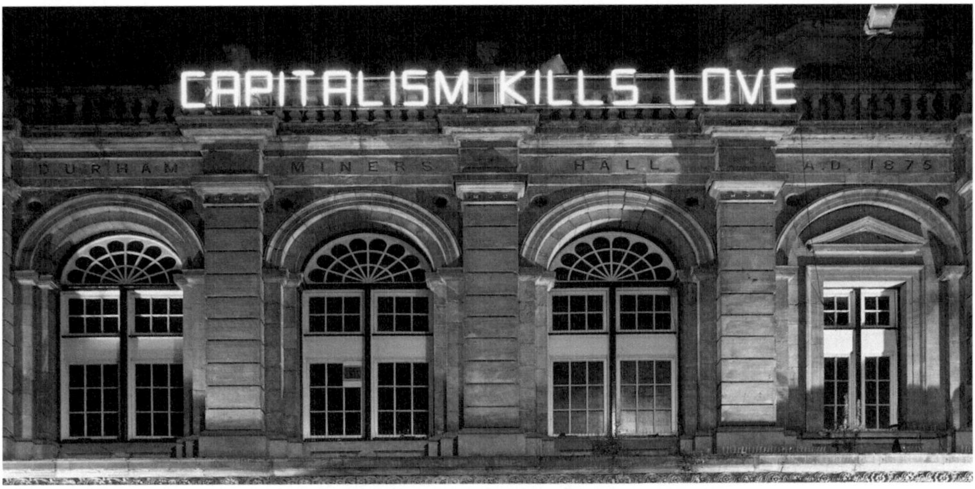

2.8 Claire Fontaine, *Capitalism Kills (Love)*, 2008. Courtesy of Studio Claire Fontaine.

Pratt, neoliberalism has transformed the planet into an ecological catastrophe.[47] It also indicates that in our brutal modernity, images of victims in the mainstream media are minimized in scale and generalized by *not* naming them as individuals and, consequently, by *not* adding a proper caption. The victimizer, on the other hand, who is represented here as a businessman embracing a politics of whiteness as a metaphor for the company he leads, is not only rendered larger in size but also turned into the victim himself. He is represented as one who suffers and thus as one whose company is now "Fight[ing] for Its Life." Exposing the power of the media in fabricating hierarchies of human suffering from the perspective of economic profit, Jaar seems to tell us, in this image, that what is absent and deprived is reciprocity. Put differently, what is lacking is decolonial love, understood, in the words of Humberto Maturana and Gerda Verden-Zöller, as "those relational behaviors through which the other arises as a legitimate other in coexistence with oneself."[48] As a 2008 neon installation by French artist Claire Fontaine reads, "Capitalism Kills Love" (figure 2.8). This is why Jaar's *BusinessWeek Magazine Cover, December 24, 1984* is as urgent today as it was in 1984, as UCC, owned since 2001 by the US multinational Dow Chemical Company, has failed to provide compensation for the victims, and more than 500,000 people continue to suffer in the sacrifice zone.[49] Since justice has not yet come and Anderson died unpunished in 2014 in his retirement in Florida at the age of ninety-two, survivors, advocacy

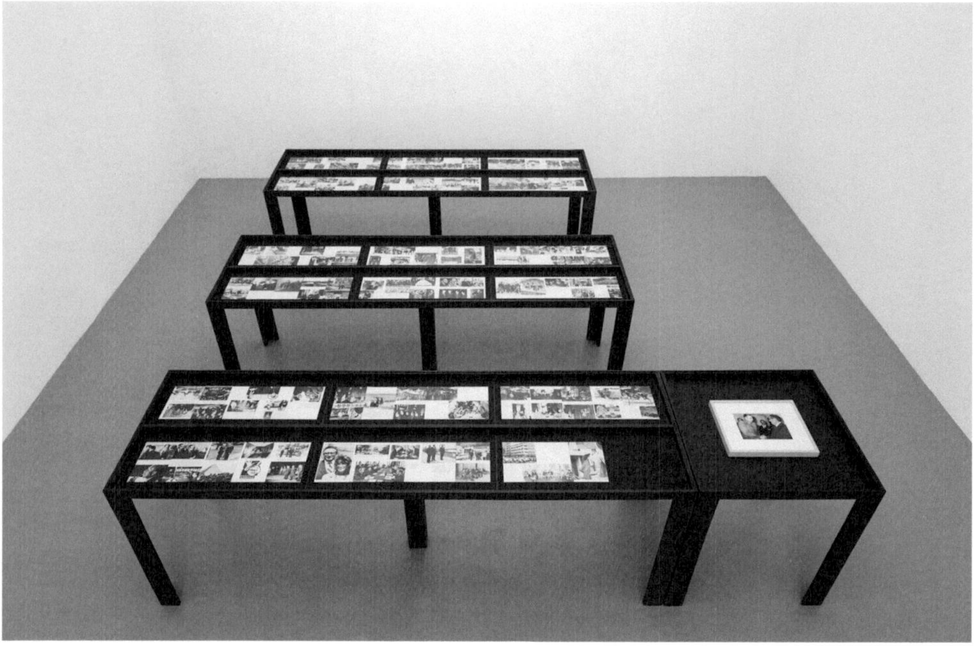

2.9 Alfredo Jaar, *Searching for K*, 1984/2012, from the series *The Kissinger Project* (ongoing from 1983). Courtesy of Alfredo Jaar.

human rights campaigners, and international solidarity organizations continue fighting for reparation on the streets of India. The natural death of perpetrators is not enough; justice is still to be made.

In Jaar's project on Kissinger, this critique of the media is also shown in a 2012 installation he designed from his 1984 *Searching for K* (figure 2.9). Here, three long black tables are isolated in perfect rows, featuring clear glass under which rest the pages extracted from Kissinger's memoirs and imprinted by Jaar with red circles around Kissinger's head. A fourth square table at the end of the third row contains the 1976 photograph of Kissinger's meeting with Pinochet. By isolating this photograph within a frame and refraining from intervening in it in any way, Jaar makes a distinction between what is in the books and what has been censored, thereby interrupting the symmetry of the rows and exceeding the space of them as a metaphor for Kissinger's distorted "truth." Jaar, as British journalist Christopher Hitchens would say, "decodes the usual relationship between fact and falsehood in Kissinger's ill-crafted memoir."[50] Since that relationship is ongoing, it is significant that the title, *Searching for K*, is in present participle, invoking in 1984, 2012, and today a project that is made through and within a time that is neither fixed nor progressive or reconciliatory but rather open and repeatedly built over upon its own ruins.

Jaar's selection of an image taken by the US embassy and published in the US media is telling.[51] Instead of choosing one of the many friendly handshakes published by the Chilean press, Jaar picks an image that highlights Kissinger's intervention in Chile from the perspective of the US media, which had closely followed Allende's fourth and finally successful presidential campaign in 1969. To keep its power in the Cold War global order, the United States' strategy was to use the media to make US Americans believe that Allende's Chile was a communist threat to the West. In effect, if there is anything that does not contradict speech and secret strategies in Kissinger's private meeting with Pinochet, it is when he tells the general: "You did a great service to the West in overthrowing Allende. Otherwise, Chile would have followed Cuba."[52] This campaign, as featured in US media, is depicted in *Untitled (Handshake)*, another work from this series created in 1985 (plate 13). Here, five covers from *Time* magazine illustrated with portraits of Kissinger and Allende are isolated in a row. By using these covers, ranging from 1969, when Allende was campaigning for the presidency, through September 1973, the date of the coup, Jaar suggests how Kissinger, and by extension Nixon, designed the conditions for political and social instability in Chile that would eventually lead to the coup by the subtle yet historically and theoretically grounded gesture of putting together these covers along with their corresponding headlines. Appropriating particular covers from a specific period, the artist crafts a narrative absent from the images themselves and consequently from their related articles.

Jaar's alternative narrative begins with the February 1969 cover illustrating Kissinger's then-recent appointment as national security adviser. The October 19, 1970, cover follows, showcasing an overlaid double portrait of Allende after winning the elections and before his inauguration on November 3. Cornered at the bottom right is a smaller image of Allende raising one arm as a sign of leadership. Yet, because of the intense overhead light that seems to prevent him from looking forward, his gesture becomes uncomfortable, as if he were covering his face from the light. It is well known in the technical aspect of photography that light, depending on its location and intensity, can easily connote the villain, the mediocre, the unpopular, just as in Kissinger's portrait by Schoeller (figure 2.1). In the background of this same image appropriated by Jaar, and using most of the space, a second portrait of Allende is rendered in red, the symbol of international communism.

Extending the signature red frame of *Time*'s covers to the face of the subject or the image's background was a tactic widely used by the magazine to identify

Cold War communist leaders and thus their policies toward the United States. Adding to this is the headline rendered within a stripe-like diagonal at the top right corner, reading: "Marxist Threat to the Americas." Although *Time*'s anti-Allende campaign was evident through a text that "anchors" the image's meaning, it is important to note that by the time this cover was published, Kissinger was well aware that, as Viron Vaky told him, "Allende's threat to the U.S. [was] hard to argue."[53] Yet that didn't stop him from convincing Nixon that Chile, a country he once disparaged as "a dagger pointed at the heart of Antarctica"—that is, dangerous to nothing—could establish a model for democratic socialist change and thus "significantly affect the world balance and our own position in it."[54] Still, as revealed in one of the most recent declassified documents, released in 2023 on the occasion of the fiftieth anniversary of the coup, Kissinger indeed feared that countries in Western Europe could follow Chile's model of democratic socialism and thus shake US power in global politics during the Cold War.[55] Kissinger, in other words, was aware of the global impact of the coup, one of the primary arguments presented in this book. Indeed, this is why it would be shortsighted to think about Jaar as a Chilean or a Latin American artist or to limit decolonial thinking as a theoretical school only centered in the Americas. From a decolonial approach, both the Chilean case and Jaar's art connect and complicate complex political and cultural exchanges across time and space, including the neoliberal linguistic trap of globalization as a time in which everyone equally belongs. In the historical context of US-Chile relations in the early 1970s, a media campaign that turned Allende's nonviolent socialist revolution into a communist menace to the hemisphere and the world was needed. Since Marxist revolutions were traumas for the Western elite because of their threat to private interest in favor of the people and the state, anti-communism, as famously noted by Noam Chomsky and Edward S. Herman, was one of the "five editorially distorting filters" embraced by the US media during the Cold War.[56]

Jaar's work exposes this political propaganda not only in the covers depicting Allende but also in those featuring Kissinger. In the first cover, from February 7, 1972, Kissinger gazes at the viewer with a relaxed pose and a small smile, echoing the tone of the article inside the magazine that narrates his "pursuit of peace and power."[57] In the third cover showing Kissinger (the fourth in Jaar's narrative), published on September 3, 1973, when he was appointed secretary of state, a self-confident and active Kissinger looks upward beyond the frame as if he were thinking deeply while speaking convincingly. Mirroring this heroic iconography, and aware of US popular culture fascination with DC and Marvel and the subsequent conversion of their characters into the hyperreal (and thus the real), the headline reads: "The Super Secretary: Ready to

Shake Up State."[58] The last image of the series shows an issue of *Time* dated September 24, 1973, that is, thirteen days after the coup. Here, a large black-and-white banner with Allende's portrait hangs from the neoclassical facade of the headquarters of the Communist Party in Santiago, the first building attacked by military troops and the national police on September 11, 1973. On the building's roof and at the center top of the image, the illustrator added the five-pointed red star of international communism with the symbol of the hammer and sickle. Allende's name is written in red bold font at the bottom of the banner, and there are red paint stains superimposed over Allende's face and name. Symbolizing blood and death and consequently the fall of Allende, the headline of the cover reads: "After the Fall."

Jaar's alternative narrative in *Untitled (Handshake)* goes further, as below the covers he adds the same photograph he used in *Searching for K* and originally extracted from Dinges's 1976 article. With the word *Handshake* in the title interrupting the linear display of color images by the addition below of the black-and-white photograph of Kissinger's friendly encounter with Pinochet, Jaar's work shows that Kissinger's interventions in Chile not only *preceded* the coup but also *continued during* the dictatorship, underscoring Kissinger's anti-Allende campaign *before* and *after* his death and the date of the coup. This same understanding of decolonial time shows that Jaar's series is as important today as it was in November 2023 when Kissinger was still alive, as Kissinger's legacy still defines imperialist policies toward the world and the US role in that world, as I will explain next. Yet, as I argue in the previous chapter, just as the memory of the disappeared can be restored through their representation, that is, through the ongoing protests of their families who carry photographic portraits of their loved ones while claiming justice, the memory of Henry Kissinger can also be defined in terms of his crimes. Further, while it is true that neither Kissinger nor Pinochet were prosecuted and punished in life, the work of artists, writers, filmmakers, journalists, and archivists can do much for collective healing and war prevention through a memory politics that exists far beyond physical life and death.

The task at hand is challenging, to say the least. Take, for instance, historian Jeremi Suri's 2007 book, *Henry Kissinger and the American Century*, in which the infamous photograph of Kissinger shaking hands with Pinochet is reproduced with the following caption: "Fearful of Cuban and Soviet influence in Chile, Kissinger provided support for coup plotters who brought Augusto Pinochet to power in September 1973."[59] While this caption conflicts drastically with information provided in declassified documents, what matters is not so much the "truth" of a certain text but how that "truth" relates to a certain image. Indeed, as explained previously, it is not at all rare to see photojournalist records shaping political events. Such is the case of the cover of Suri's book, which shows *Time*'s cover of the heroic statesman Henry Kissinger alongside the text "The Super Secretary."[60] From a decolonial approach, however, it is important to recognize the epistemology of knowledge from where those "events" are shaped, visually and textually. In the case of Suri, echoing the temporal coloniality in Kissinger's memoir, he provides a progressive history of Kissinger's feats, leading him to even include the photograph with Pinochet censored by Kissinger. Describing his idea of the Cold War, Kissinger, and the United States, Suri writes:

> The Cold War was very good for the United States. . . . American society quickly amassed more wealth and power than any peer in recent memory. Ordinary citizens consumed more cars, clothes, movies, and especially food than anyone could have imagined just a few years earlier. . . . Wealth and power were not shared equally in the United States, but even those groups subject to discrimination lived better than they had before. The United States became—as Henry Luce, the founder of *Time* magazine predicted—"the dynamic center of ever widening spheres of enterprise" . . . the self-proclaimed "Global Samaritan." This was the "American Century." This was also Henry Kissinger's century.[61]

Responding to this publication, Greg Grandin ironically commented that Suri's Kissinger as Global Samaritan is a "man of passion who sought to do good in the world by making tough choices [and in so doing he] entered [into] politics for moral reasons."[62] Historian Niall Ferguson, on the other hand, a fellow at Stanford's conservative Hoover Institution think tank, praised Suri's book as "surely the best book yet published about Henry Kissinger."[63] More than a decade later, in a 2019 presentation of his own celebratory biography on Kissinger at Harvard Kennedy School's Institute of Politics, Ferguson remarked: "[For Kissinger] the Cold War [was] about ideals, not about rival economic systems."[64] Suri's and Ferguson's publications on Kissinger, and Kissinger's own 2022 monograph on world leadership, speak of the continuous effect of his "Global Samaritan ideals" in the current generation of history and public policy students as well as young policymakers and international affairs strategists. At stake is the question of the temporal effect of the "power of Kissinger's ideas, or how those ideas tapped into deeper intellectual currents within American history and influenced later generations," as Grandin wrote in a 2015 article in *The Nation* suggestively titled "The Kissinger Effect."[65]

Today, with Kissinger's memory literally "resting in power" and his world philosophy applied to the letter—as seen in the multiple US-sponsored wars globally—Grandin, and for that matter Jaar, knows that Kissinger's temporal effect is quite profound, just as neoliberalism is "deeply rooted and likely to persist."[66] In the United States today, as I complete this book in fall 2025, this means, in the words of Australian scholar Adriano Tedde, that the current administration is keeping "decades of unipolarity and neoliberal[ism], a political doctrine dictated primarily by economic goals and an ideology steeped in the firm conviction that every action is a transaction and that every organisation is a 'business.'"[67] In this context, as Tedde further contends, the "true innovation [is] the blunt language [of] 'America First' priorities, while [the] country's goals of world supremacy remain the same."[68]

In Jaar's *The Kissinger Project*, he appropriates the 1976 photograph of Kissinger's meeting with Pinochet to show not only its calamitous results and that of neoliberalism in the life of humans both locally and globally but also its shattering of time and call for oblivion. Jaar's project portrays Kissinger *as* the institution of modernity along with its linearity of time and the complicity of the media within such time. In critiquing media temporal progression, Jaar also proposes an otherwise form of journalist narrative that challenges a definitive end, in which a binominal result is provided with a victor and a defeated. This is seen in the last *Time* cover in Jaar's *Untitled (Handshake)*, where the "Super Secretary" fights against and wins over the Latin American red villain of Allende, whose portrait overlaps with red stains symbolizing the blood of both his and socialism's fall.

In 1983, two years before creating *Untitled (Handshake)*, Jaar addressed the US "anti-Allende" campaign by appropriating postcards of influential districts and buildings in New York City and imposing on their front sides the Spanish text *Buscando a Kissinger* (Searching for Kissinger), which is also the title of the work (plate 14). In this case, he relates anti-communist propaganda with capitalist interest, showing that, as the leader of the international resistance, Orlando Letelier, wrote in August 1976 in *The Nation*, "repression for the majorities and 'economic freedom' for small privileged groups are two sides of the same coin."[69] Exposing the role of Milton Friedman and the Chicago Boys in the implementation of a complete neoliberal turn in Chile, which encompassed the privatization of services such as education and health, the encouragement of foreign investment, and the role of the market in politics and culture, this transformation was only possible through the "brutal violation of human rights" and "drastic control of any form of dissent," as Letelier writes.[70] And, indeed, this was no secret.

In the United States, as shown in the previous chapter, various forms of denunciation of Nixon's economic agenda in relation to the Chilean dictatorship were prevalent, even before the coup. Circulating more often in independent media outlets and political and public space platforms, this is shown, for instance, on the cover of the September–October 1974 issue of the Chile Solidarity Committee bulletin (figure 2.10). Here, positioned at the right edge, as if he were secretly sneaking into the site, is Kissinger, who passes a US bill with multiple zeros to Pinochet. Wearing his iconic eyeglasses and a suit, Kissinger smiles, while Pinochet, wearing his military uniform and dark shades, holds a rifle, his facial expression one of rage. With Kissinger representing the intellectual statesman from the North, and Pinochet the material author of modernity's international crimes from the South, this type of political satire, just as Letelier's article in *The Nation*, was visible for anyone who wanted to see. And, indeed, activists, artists, poets, and politicians not only saw but also responded. In the words of journalist Naomi Klein, Letelier's article in the United States "rocked the political establishment."[71]

In Chile, however, censorship rendered Letelier's activism, publishing, and support by many US outlets and people invisible, and if his article circulated at all, it was only through dangerous clandestine circles. And yet it still propelled Pinochet to issue a decree depriving Letelier of his Chilean citizenship. Signed by eighteen top military officials and government ministers, among them Pinochet and the ministers of economy and treasury, both former students of Friedman at the University of Chicago, the decree stated that Letelier was "carrying out an international advertising campaign aimed to achieve Chile's economic and cultural isolation."[72] On September 10, 1976, in his public speech at the Felt Forum at Madison Square Garden in New York, Letelier responded to this decree. Preceding a benefit concert for "The Restoration of Human Rights in Chile" featuring US folk singers and activists Joan Baez and Pete Seeger and Aparcoa, a band of the Chilean New Song genre, Letelier, standing before a packed stadium, said: "I was born a Chilean, I am a Chilean, and I will die a Chilean. They were born traitors, live as traitors, and they will be remembered forever as Fascist traitors."[73]

Two weeks later, Letelier was killed by a car bomb in Washington, DC, through Operation Condor, a CIA-backed campaign of state terror conducted in the 1970s and 1980s by civic and military fascism in the Southern Cone.[74] The material authors of the crime were the US expatriate and DINA agent Michael Townley and the former Chilean army officer Armando Fernández Larios. The mastermind, on the other hand, was the former head of DINA, Manuel Contreras, and, as later revealed, Pinochet himself. In 2010,

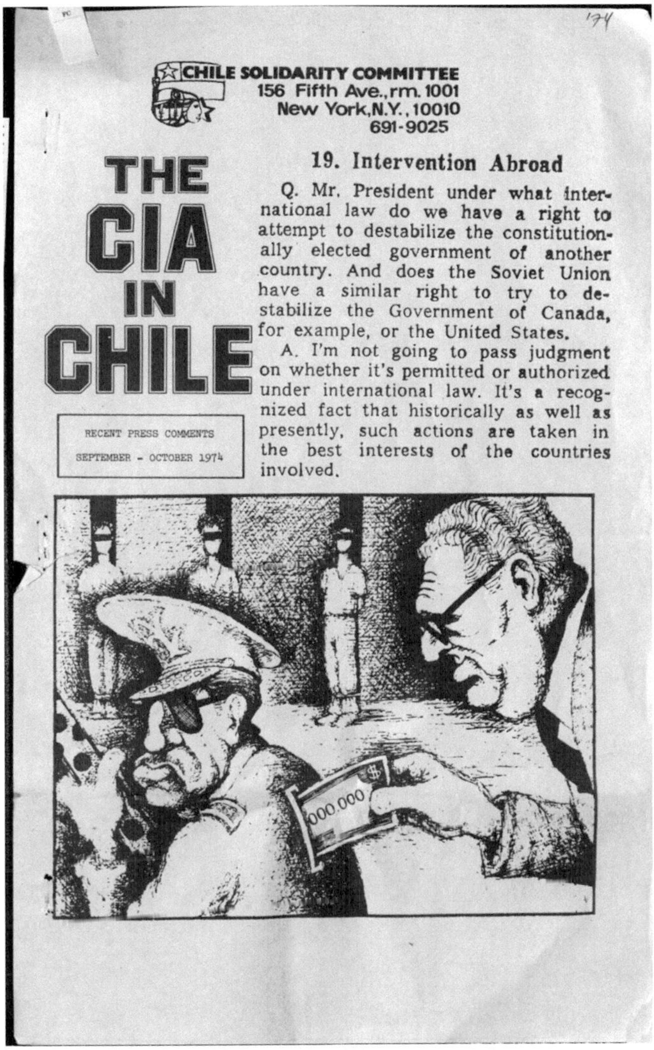

CHILE SOLIDARITY COMMITTEE
156 Fifth Ave., rm. 1001
New York, N.Y., 10010
691-9025

THE CIA IN CHILE

RECENT PRESS COMMENTS

SEPTEMBER – OCTOBER 1974

19. Intervention Abroad

Q. Mr. President under what international law do we have a right to attempt to destabilize the constitutionally elected government of another country. And does the Soviet Union have a similar right to try to destabilize the Government of Canada, for example, or the United States.

A. I'm not going to pass judgment on whether it's permitted or authorized under international law. It's a recognized fact that historically as well as presently, such actions are taken in the best interests of the countries involved.

2.10 Chile Solidarity Committee bulletin, September–October 1974.

declassified documents about Letelier's murder, widely regarded as the biggest international crime on US soil before 9/11, revealed not only that the US State Department was aware of Operation Condor, particularly of its plan to assassinate Letelier. These documents also showed that Henry Kissinger himself blocked the warnings about Letelier's murder.[75] We may thus wonder if Letelier's assassination at the nation's capital was indeed an international crime and if covering Kissinger's accountability at home was yet another strategy of modernity to maintain his image as the Cold War's Global Samaritan.

In *Buscando a Kissinger*, Jaar exposes Letelier's denouncement of capitalism and human atrocities by showing politically charged souvenirs associating Kissinger's international policies with the very symbols of world banking and investment (plate 14). One of these postcards features the Rockefeller building, pointing directly to US economic interests in Chile and their relation to the dictatorship: The Rockefeller family owned Anaconda, a mining company that alongside Kennecott Copper controlled the copper industry in Chile, and that cooperated with and benefited from Kissinger's and the CIA's plan to overthrow Chilean democracy.[76] A second disclosure in Hersh's *The Price of Power* influenced the subject matter of this work. Hersh's 1983 book includes testimony from the former US ambassador to Chile, Edward Korry, admitting that the Rockefellers' interest in Chile was what motivated him to support the US anti-Allende campaign and thus the neoliberal project it entailed in the first place.[77] In effect, as journalist David Stout stated in Korry's 2003 obituary in the *New York Times*, coming from a "fervent anti-Communist" US diplomat as Korry and "not from the left-leaning media or the opposition, this was a key demonstration of truth and liability."[78]

Korry's testimony more specifically confirms that Allende's plan to nationalize large-scale industries such as copper as well as the health and educational systems and media networks, and to redistribute land to farmers and the working class, was a serious preoccupation to US CEOs, who warned Kissinger and Nixon of their concerns over their investment and potential lost profits. It is no coincidence that in their 1976 meeting, Pinochet expressed to Kissinger his deep concern about Letelier, who had strong ties to influential politicians in the United States, notably Senator Ted Kennedy of Massachusetts, and who, according to Pinochet, was "giving false information [to U.S. Congress]."[79] Not only was there nothing false in Letelier's accusation about multinational aims at profiting and death; it was truth itself as denoted in his piece in *The Nation*, which led to his assassination by direct orders from Pinochet and a green light from Kissinger. As modernity's history goes, it is important to repeat that Pinochet, just as Kissinger, Milton Friedman, Margaret Thatcher, Warren M.

Anderson, Agustín Edwards, and a long list of others, all died unpunished and even with honors. Meanwhile, perpetrators of crimes against humanity and the planet who are alive and belong to the economic elite are not only promoted by the media but also well protected by modernity's judicial system of truth and progressive time. As denoted at "the end" of the 2019 legal thriller film *Dark Waters*, Mark Ruffalo, in the role of Robert Bilott, the lawyer who sued the chemical manufacturing corporation DuPont for contaminating the water and land of Parkersburg in West Virginia and causing thousands of deaths of humans and animals, says: "The system is rigged. We protect us, we do. Nobody else. Not the companies, not the scientists, not the government. Us."[80] This reflection and statement resonate quite mimetically with Jaar's criticism of capitalism and media complicity on the one hand, and in the acknowledgment of people's awareness of coloniality evilness on the other. As shown in his 1984 piece *You and Us*, Jaar reverses a message of a CBS advertisement that rolled out on New York City subways in the mid-1980s, altering the original announcement, "If it concerns you, it concerns us," by swapping the words *you* and *us* (figure 2.11). Denouncing the original message as fallacy, Jaar further commented that "in this instance, a TV channel owned by the General Electric Company that manufactures refrigerators but also bombs [was] setting the media agenda."[81]

But as resistance continues, art continues. As Jaar writes in 2019 in *And Yet* (plate 15), a neon installation that quotes a stanza by the Russian poet Anna Akhmatova in an effort to find the words to describe the experience of the Great Purge under the Stalinist regime, "So much to do today / kill memory / kill pain / turn heart into a stone / and yet / prepare to live again." Connecting a massive murder in the 1930s Soviet Union to the multiple genocides of the present, that is, thinking and creating through an aesthetic of transnational solidarities across time and sites, the line "and yet," which is also the title of the work, is rendered by Jaar in red, different from all the other lines in the poem, which are rendered in black and illuminated from behind. "And yet," therefore, means continuity, existence, living *adentro pero en contra*. It means decolonial time and an aesthetics of the unfinished.

REPRESENTATION AND LIABILITY

To name names and therefore to denounce perpetrators and those complicit with fascist regimes globally is undoubtedly a daunting task. In modernity, censorship has prevailed, and speaking out has often meant punishment from the ruling class not only in strictly political and activist but also in editorial, academic, and cultural circles. This is not so different in the Chilean case, where

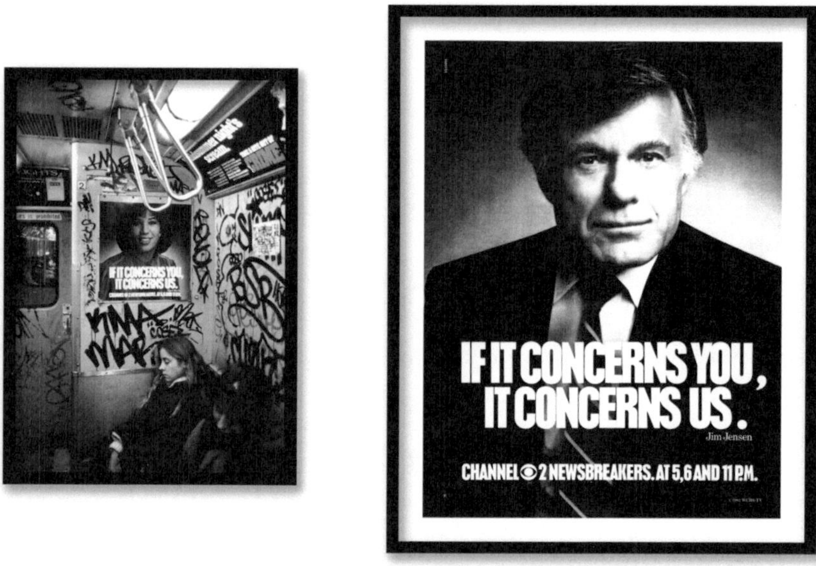

2.11 Alfredo Jaar, *You and Us*, 1984. Courtesy of Alfredo Jaar.

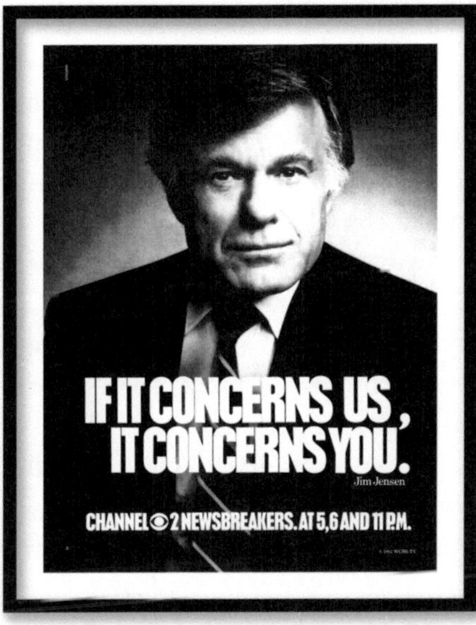
IF IT CONCERNS US,
IT CONCERNS YOU.
Jim Jensen
CHANNEL 2 NEWSBREAKERS. AT 5,6 AND 11 P.M.

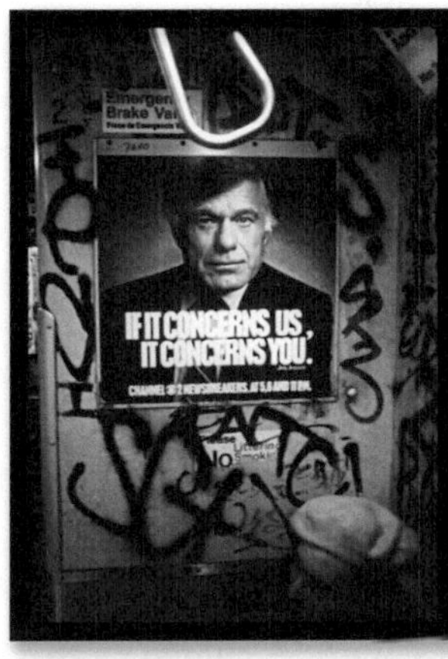
IF IT CONCERNS US,
IT CONCERNS YOU.

those who benefited from the coup have, in most cases, evaded accountability. Alongside the return of democracy in 1990, truth commissions such as the National Commission for Truth and Reconciliation Report (Rettig Report, 1991) and the National Commission on Political Imprisonment and Torture Report (Valech Report, 2004) did not include the names of perpetrators in an effort to bring them to trial, either domestically or by universal jurisdiction. Protecting those who have profited from the regime, these reports have problematically advanced toward the neoliberal progressive paradigm aiming to close the book on the dictatorship, celebrating ideas of pardon and reconciliation and therefore embracing oblivion. Equally problematic has been the misuse in Chile of Primo Levi's concept of the "gray zone," which describes the psychological processes that underlay the living conditions endured in the Nazi Lager, where a group of deportees, the *Sonderkommandos*, would become complicit in their own destruction.[82] This is a well-known concept in testimonial literature and cultural criticism assimilated in Chile as a neoliberal tool to pardon those who collaborated with the regime and who are today repentant. Said opportunistic appropriation not only shows the problems of understanding experiences of atrocity as universal, with a universality that "naturally" begins in the Holocaust as the primary source of human suffering. It also blends and undoes the clear distinction between victim and victimizer in Chile, itself different than other Cold War Latin American conflicts with clear guerrilla uprisings, such as the Sandinistas in Nicaragua or the Shining Path in Peru.

Famous is the case of Marcia Merino, a former militant of the Movimiento de Izquierda Revolucionaria (MIR; Revolutionary Left Movement of Chile) who, after being tortured by DINA, began collaborating with the dictatorship, torturing her former comrades. "I was too weak to endure torture," she apologized.[83] Writing about art, literature, and politics, writer Diamela Eltit identifies in Merino a "chameleon-like" persona that attaches itself to places of power: first to the revolutionary left and then to DINA/CNI (Central Nacional de Informaciones), culminating in the "reconciliatory" pardon given by the neoliberal transition. "Within certain political entities there is a tendency, due to weakness or a desire for belonging and status, to shift in the direction of the more dominant ideological winds," explains Eltit.[84] Considering that this "chameleon-like" tendency is typically experienced by members of the lower, the middle, and the military classes, for the "small privileged group that benefited from Economic Freedom," as Letelier put it, these desires are absent from their agenda.[85] For instance, Edwards, *El Mercurio*'s tycoon, died in 2017 wealthy and unreprimanded, and the elite who continue profiting from the coup have been appointed to top political positions and mourned with honors. The commemorative events around the 2024 drastic death of former President Sebastián Piñera, the billionaire "democratic hero" who drowned after the helicopter he was piloting crashed into a lake in southern Chile, are not an exception. Indeed, this internal policy of repentance, shame, and seeking forgiveness is controlled by the privileged, such as the late Edwards, in a twisted ethical strategy that aims to give the people and human rights organizations the *idea* of justice. But again and again, the people know. And because they know, they recognize that since the Chilean dictatorship developed in the context of Operation Condor, this complex neoliberal policy also involves Kissinger.

Memory studies scholar Michael Lazzara has stated that the key role of the privileged civilian in Chile's Machiavellian architecture and its connection to global power and complicity *are still* to be developed in Chile's law, public policy, studies on memory and history, and cultural practices alike.[86] Since the early 1980s, however, Jaar's art surrounding Henry Kissinger has been doing just that, embracing a memory politics that calls for the continuing search for those responsible for the crimes. This is why Jaar's project shows the victimizer not as a "victim of [their] circumstances" but as a "wanted" criminal. In doing so, he activates in the viewer a transnational consciousness of the coloniality between US and Latin American relations, and the elite and its others.[87] While this conceptual strategy is directly shown in *Searching for K* through red circles around Kissinger's head, it is also present in later works such as *Manhattan's Milosevic* (2001) (figure 2.12). For this occasion, Jaar appropriates the August 21, 2001, cover from the *Village Voice* featuring Kissinger wearing a suit and his black-frame glasses. In this portrait, in which Kissinger is directly illuminated by a frontal, overhead flash and thus reminding us of Schoeller's portraiture (figure 2.1), the harsh light creates shadows over the lower half of Kissinger's face, providing not only an image of personal devastation but also the depiction of a wanted criminal. The main text, rendered below Kissinger's chin and adopted by Jaar for the title of the work, reads "Manhattan's Milosevic," and a second, smaller text placed at the center left reinforces the criminal meaning of the image by quoting a provocative statement by Christopher Hitchens that reads: "How You Can Arrest Henry Kissinger for War Crimes."[88]

Instead of exposing and critiquing the fascist agenda in the mainstream media, as he did with *Time* magazine in *Untitled (Handshake)* (plate 13), here Jaar celebrates a newspaper cover that is critical of Kissinger's Realpolitik, showing the complexity of his approach to media. "I am a frustrated journalist," he often explains, and it is precisely in that complex relationship with information where an important aspect of his art expands, which he calls

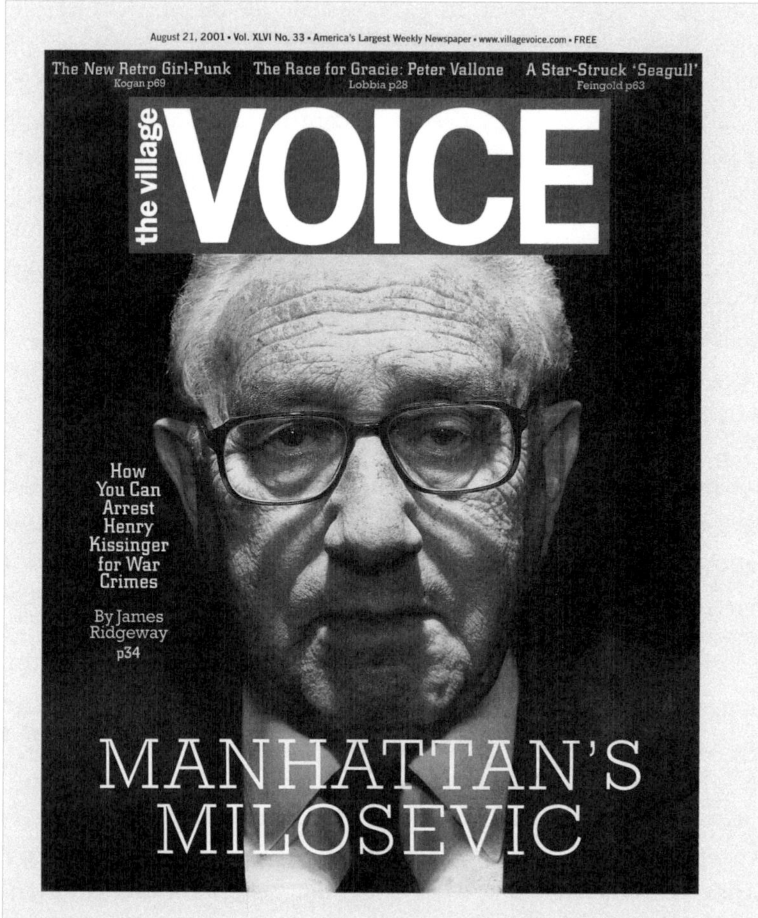

2.12 Alfredo Jaar, *Manhattan's Milosevic*, 2001, from the series *The Kissinger Project* (ongoing from 1983). Courtesy of Alfredo Jaar.

the "politics of image." In this sense, if the artist "will not act before understanding [because] context is everything," as he also often maintains, that context is how visual and textual journalism represents, transforms, or simply ignores the world's events.[89] In the case of *Manhattan's Milosevic,* for instance, Jaar underlines and applauds the journalist's and editor's decision to associate Kissinger with Slobodan Milošević, a comparison that, taking into account that the International Court was at that moment trailing the former Yugoslav president at The Hague, was unequivocal in its condemnation.

Also in 2002, when the image was published in the *Village Voice* and appropriated by Jaar, Corbis, the image agency owned by Bill Gates, moved its Bettmann Archive to "an old limestone mine . . . in western Pennsylvania [and] bur[ied it] 220 feet below the surface in a subzero, low-humidity storage vault," as Jaar himself writes in his famous installation *Lament of the Images* (plate 16). Ironically, among those millions of photographs was the famous image of Kissinger shaking hands with Pinochet.[90] This "coincidence" means that while the photograph of Kissinger as *Manhattan's Milosevic* shows Kissinger's other side, his coloniality—at least in the reproducibility of its iconic image for the Chilean case—remains hidden from view, way below the ground. As art critic Dore Ashton, a longtime friend of Jaar, told the artist in a short film he made about her in 2015, "What happened you know . . . horrible story . . . and definitely Kissinger is the villain, in my opinion . . . but people still don't say that, do they?"[91]

In 1988, because of pressure and assistance from the United States, which by that time had broken ties to the dictatorship as a result of Letelier's assassination in Washington, DC, Pinochet lost the presidential referendum, in which Chileans voted on whether he would remain president for eight more years. Unsatisfied with the results, he sought to enact a second coup, which did not come to fruition as he did not have the support of other generals.[92] No, the popularized idea of the transition as a democratic and constitutional process is *not* accurate; it is merely a facade, an image of democracy fabricated only after the failure of yet another coup. Put differently, the iconic photograph in which president-elect and Christian Democrat party cofounder Patricio Aylwin shakes hands with Pinochet, who smiles as a sign of support, is, after all, an image. And images, as Jaar tells us, whether manipulated before or after the shot, that is, before or after the event, have much more to do with the idea of truth than with mimesis or reproduction. Understanding the transition as an image thus allows us to realize that Pinochet not only did not accept his defeat; he also did not accept his accountability in a future trial. Underscoring a temporal linearity that would keep him free from charges, that is, a philosophy that equals the traumatic past with oblivion, Pinochet, through a constitution that still rules in Chile, protected himself with an amnesty law ensuring lifetime immunity.

A decade after the referendum, in 1998, Pinochet was arrested in London for crimes against humanity. A milestone event within international law, Pinochet's detention left no one indifferent, from the mainstream and independent media to human rights activists and critical journalists such as Christopher Hitchens, and from victims of the dictatorship to academics, politicians, and public figures such as former UK Prime Minister Margaret Thatcher. Thatcher, for instance, denounced Baltasar Garzón, the Spanish judge who ordered the arrest, by expressing her "outrage at the callous and unjust treatment of Senator Pinochet."[93] Recalling Kissinger's own secret 1976 declarations to Pinochet, the title of her speech was clear and simple: "Pinochet was this country's staunch, true friend."[94]

Despite Pinochet ending up returning to Chile, where he was received as a hero and died unpunished, his detention in London, in the words of Peter Kornbluh, "empowered the concept of universal jurisdiction, the ability of any state to hold gross violators accountable to international codes of justice."[95] In this new judicial context, Kissinger feared he could be the next held accountable, so he wrote and published his third and last memoir in quite a *timely* manner. Similar was the no less calculated reaction of the Bill Clinton administration, which following Pinochet's arrest released more than twenty-four thousand secret documents from the CIA, the White House, and the NSC, among them the 1976 Kissinger/Pinochet conversation. Accordingly, Kissinger, in his self-defense-like memoir, put particular emphasis on his relationship to the dictator. Addressing the now-public content of their 1976 meeting, which Kissinger described as "aloof, courteous, and to the point," he deliberately tried to contrast the information declassified, writing, "A considerable amount of time in my dialogue with Pinochet was devoted to human rights, which were, in fact, the principal obstacle to close United States relations with Chile. I outlined the main points in my speech to the OAS which I would deliver the next day. Pinochet made no comment."[96] Kissinger's narration of the meeting in his third volume is the opposite of the candid, sympathetic, and friendly account revealed in declassified archives, and these mechanisms of distortion are exactly what Jaar's *The Kissinger Project* in particular and his exercises of memory overall aim to underscore in an effort to unveil truth, that is, truth as these declassified documents expound.

The *Village Voice* cover and its appropriation by Jaar in *Manhattan's Milosevic* responded to a threefold historical moment in 1988: Pinochet's detention in

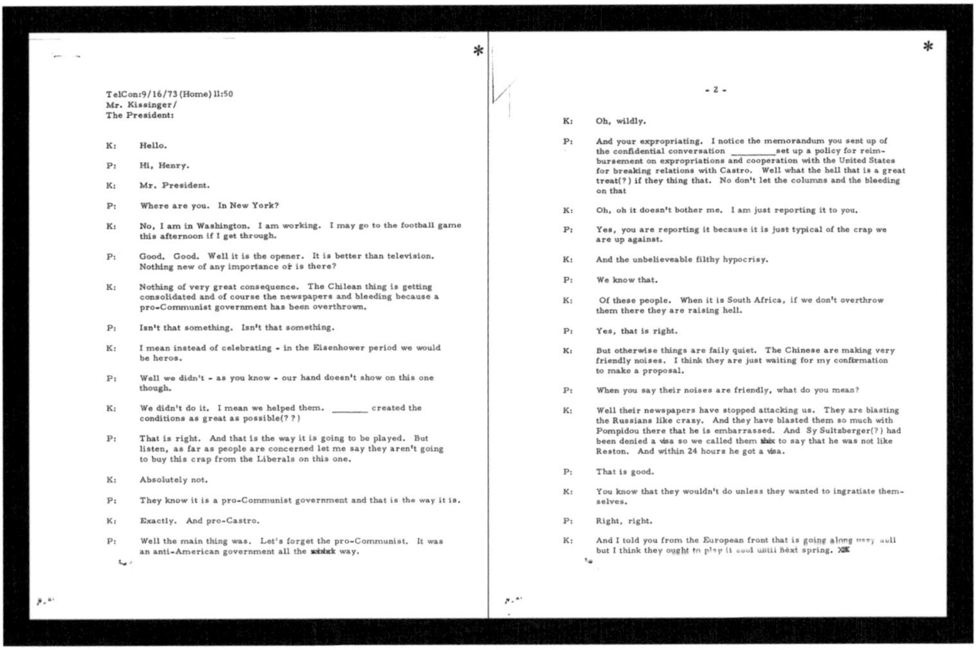

TelCon:9/16/73 (Home) 11:50
Mr. Kissinger/
The President:

K: Hello.

P: Hi, Henry.

K: Mr. President.

P: Where are you. In New York?

K: No, I am in Washington. I am working. I may go to the football game this afternoon if I get through.

P: Good. Good. Well it is the opener. It is better than television. Nothing new of any importance or is there?

K: Nothing of very great consequence. The Chilean thing is getting consolidated and of course the newspapers and bleeding because a pro-Communist government has been overthrown.

P: Isn't that something. Isn't that something.

K: I mean instead of celebrating - in the Eisenhower period we would be heros.

P: Well we didn't - as you know - our hand doesn't show on this one though.

K: We didn't do it. I mean we helped them. _______ created the conditions as great as possible(? ?)

P: That is right. And that is the way it is going to be played. But listen, as far as people are concerned let me say they aren't going to buy this crap from the Liberals on this one.

K: Absolutely not.

P: They know it is a pro-Communist government and that is the way it is.

K: Exactly. And pro-Castro.

P: Well the main thing was. Let's forget the pro-Communist. It was an anti-American government all the way.

- 2 -

K: Oh, wildly.

P: And your expropriating. I notice the memorandum you sent up of the confidential conversation _________ set up a policy for reimbursement on expropriations and cooperation with the United States for breaking relations with Castro. Well what the hell that is a great treat(?) if they thing that. No don't let the columns and the bleeding on that

K: Oh, oh it doesn't bother me. I am just reporting it to you.

P: Yes, you are reporting it because it is just typical of the crap we are up against.

K: And the unbelieveable filthy hypocrisy.

P: We know that.

K: Of these people. When it is South Africa, if we don't overthrow them there they are raising hell.

P: Yes, that is right.

K: But otherwise things are faily quiet. The Chinese are making very friendly noises. I think they are just waiting for my confirmation to make a proposal.

P: When you say their noises are friendly, what do you mean?

K: Well their newspapers have stopped attacking us. They are blasting the Russians like crazy. And they have blasted them so much with Pompidou there that he is embarrassed. And Sy Sultzberger(?) had been denied a visa so we called them to say that he was not like Reston. And within 24 hours he got a visa.

P: That is good.

K: You know that they wouldn't do unless they wanted to ingratiate themselves.

P: Right, right.

K: And I told you from the European front that is going along very well but I think they ought to play it cool until next spring.

2.13 Alfredo Jaar, *Nothing of Very Great Consequence*, 2008, from the series *The Kissinger Project* (ongoing from 1983). Courtesy of Alfredo Jaar.

London, Kissinger's publication of his last memoir, and the massive declassification of secret documents regarding US Chile affairs. In 2008, further elaborating on this threefold historical moment, Jaar created a work based on one of those telephone conversations (TELCONS) between Kissinger and Nixon from September 16, 1973 (figure 2.13). The artist divides this document's reproduction in half and places the parts in two light boxes measuring 30.5 × 45.7 cm, recalling the size of A3 paper. The only intervention is the support: two light boxes that do nothing but emit an intense cold light. A strategy adopted in Jaar's more famous, theater-like, large-scale installations, notably in *Lament of the Images* (plate 16) and *Shadows* (figure I.12), light and lighting have been used by the artist since the mid-1980s to address the ambivalence between what is visible and what is not. Considering the association of images of extreme human suffering with spectacle aesthetics, when these images resist spectacle, they are often ignored by Western media. In this case, the artist underscores how those words, especially Kissinger's evaluation of the coup as "nothing of very great consequence," were so easily spoken and so long censored, appearing by means of light and in the aftermath of the dictatorship as simultaneously enormous and banal.

Transcribing that entire TELCON in two light boxes, Jaar emphasizes how Kissinger disparaged the human and intellectual genocide that followed the coup. After telling Nixon that what happened in Chile was "nothing of very great consequence," a statement Jaar adopted as the title of the work, Kissinger continued: "I mean instead of celebrating—in the Eisenhower period we would be heros [sic]," complaining about the fact that many international reports had immediately blamed the United States for backing the coup. "We didn't—as you know—our hand doesn't show on this one," Nixon replied. "We didn't do it," Kissinger agreed. "I mean, we helped them," he concluded.[97]

Kissinger's condescending words toward Chile led literary critic Adriana Valdés to observe that Jaar's works on Kissinger recall what Hannah Arendt coined as the "banality of evil."[98] "What was a national tragedy is dismissed with no other thought than that of ranting at the liberal media in the U.S., demonstrating a mediocrity that is unable to recognize or gauge the effects of its own actions," writes Valdés.[99] Yet Kissinger's words—which expose his philosophy about the coloniality of time—are far from transparent; they don't really mean how they sound. Following his ideology of power, Kissinger, and by extension Nixon, knew they had to be linguistically strategic even in secret conversations, as they knew they were being recorded and their words would eventually be declassified.[100] "We didn't do it," they said, for which they meant: "We didn't plan the coup and have no blood on our hands. The September 16, 1973, TELCON is there to prove it." Not quite. In transforming that declassified document into art through the simple yet charged gesture of transcribing, enlarging, and illuminating, Jaar's *Nothing of Very Great Consequence* shows that words, just as images, can also shape the events and the way we remember them.

Considering that this chapter and the series it examines rely so centrally on declassified documents and critical journalistic records, that is, evidence, we can also add that Jaar's series expands and problematizes the neutrality of archives as definitive forms of truth. We can even say that their declassification, despite their immense impact on the search for justice, has not been enough. Human rights activists know. The people know. Kissinger knew. Otherwise, Kissinger wouldn't have published his last memoir to avoid culpability by affirming that heroes such as him, the "Super Secretary," never do wrong. He would have died in prison. But the story of coloniality, being the story of the world as it is, is quite different: on November 30, 2023, Kissinger died in his home in Connecticut in glory and peace, and he did so after proving that as a centenarian he was still highly influential in global affairs. In the summer of

2023, for instance, he went on a trip to China to meet with Chinese President Xi Jinping in the context of the Joe Biden administration. We can therefore also say that Jaar's series on Kissinger shows that while archives have been declassified, a more significant cultural acceptance of the truth has yet to come. The role of art in this sense is its potential to offer creative and moving avenues from which to critically reflect on ways to represent truth, testimony, and searching for accountability in the pursuit of justice from the realm of culture.

In *Nothing of Very Great Consequence*, Jaar reproduces the document exactly as it is, that is, as a TELCON, creating a silent space in which outrage might appear. Jaar does, however, intervene in the materiality of the archive by replacing paper with light, addressing the presence of complex political agendas informing what is visible and what is not, or what is shown and what is censored. In lighting up Kissinger's transcribed evaluation of the military coup as "nothing of very great consequence," Jaar demonstrates that words, even when displayed, also hide the aims of coloniality.[101] The phrase "Nothing of very great consequence," therefore, means not so much the simultaneously enormous and banal results left by the coup. It means the huge costs in the life and dignity of millions and the role of the United States in shaping the event, which Kissinger disguised as irrelevant, even in secret conversations. Moreover, the TELCON's iconography of two redacted words shows that the consequences are ongoing, which is precisely why those words are still kept secret. This unveils the incomplete state of the declassification project regarding US-Chile Cold War relations. As of today, many documents are still classified, and Kissinger's papers, which are archived by Yale University, may only be accessed by a representative he has designated until five years after his death, that is, in 2028. And then, even after being declassified, language will continue to hide, burning the memory of the victims in the ashes of linear time. And thus we wonder: Who has the right to write history and its "consequences," and how is a deferred memory administered by specific groups, both aiming to show or conceal truth? Using light, *Nothing of Very Great Consequence* exposes and dazzles the gaze, and in so doing it shows how a politics of visualization and occultation organize history, memory, and representation in the fabrication and perception of knowledge.

In the 1980s, with the emergence of the field of memory studies, cultural practices and research in the humanities and the social sciences centered primarily on testimonies of trauma and the experience of mourning.[102] In the 1990s and 2000s, during Latin America's postconflict period, the field focused on collective memories and new topics, including archives, memorials, and memory sites. And later, with the next wave of research, it has concentrated on the repercussions of regimes on subsequent generations.[103] Together, as Michael Lazzara states, the field has maintained that "to remember past violence has meant, above all, to reflect on the victims."[104] At the same time, the institutionalization of memory studies in academia in the 2000s triggered a crisis in both Latin America and the world, leading memory scholar Andreas Huyssen to argue that the field is in need of renewal.[105] Responding to this need, Lazzara offered a list of "themes and methods that might provide a refreshing turn for the future of the field within the Americas," including "thinking about dictatorships and civil conflicts in relation to broader histories of colonialism."[106] Jaar's series on Kissinger has been doing just that since its inception in the early 1980s—from the perspective of decolonial time, it has countered the violence of modernity's progress and oblivion by focusing on a victimizer and coloniality from a transdisciplinary and transnational approach. As such, Jaar's series proposes refreshing themes, methods, and forms to the field of memory studies in the hemisphere and the world while depicting a clear victimizer: Henry Kissinger (and by extension Nixon and Edwards) not as an "indirect" architect of the Chilean civic-military regime but as a complicit perpetrator.

Yet Jaar's message can be, and indeed has been, seriously misread, even in art discourses and the art museum. Such was the case of the 2018 exhibition *Everything Is Connected: Art and Conspiracy*, organized by Doug Eklund and Ian Alteveer at the now-closed Met Breuer in New York. At this exhibition, the only time in which Jaar's *Searching for K* has been exhibited in the United States, the label accompanying the work reads, "Kissinger himself *indirectly* helped install a brutally violent coup in 1973" (emphasis added), with the photograph of Pinochet shaking hands with Kissinger described as "an image that neither author nor publisher would presumably ever allow in print."[107] Considering that museums are extensions of the colonial world, it is difficult not to relate the word *indirectly* chosen by the curators to the fact that, at the time, Kissinger himself was listed as a trustee emeritus of the Met's board, turning the very theme and title of the exhibition into a mirror of itself. Regarding meaning, on the other hand, the exhibition includes no reference to critical journalism informing Jaar's project, ignoring the historical and cultural component of the central photograph in *Searching for K* and *Untitled (Handshake)*, and confusing how Jaar addresses the role of the mainstream media in the Cold War context. As the description of *Untitled (Handshake)* reads in the show's exhibition catalog: "The work concludes . . . showing a street poster of Allende splattered with red paint, recasting him as a foe of his people rather than its sacrificial lamb."[108] Not only is the "conclusive" image of the work the photograph of Kissinger shaking hands with Pinochet, but also the image of Allende described in the catalog shows a purported villain *after* being defeated by a hero and his "anti-communist" Cold War agenda, revealing the complex strategies of visual propaganda used by the mainstream media and its narrative of modernity's victory. Furthermore, to identify Allende as a "sacrificial lamb" is at odds with Allende's and Popular Unity's secular non-imperialistic ideals and instead lends support to the Catholic neoliberal "pardon" of the (lower-, middle-, and military-class) victimizers and the country's "civilized" reconciliation in postdictatorship life.

Equally problematic is the curators' affirmation that *Dear Mr. Jaar, 1976* (1984) was the first work of the series made by Jaar, "in 1976 [while] living under the dictatorship," and that had the artist made *Searching for K* in Chile, it "would have resulted in [his] imprisonment or death."[109] This twofold affirmation is wrong in strict historical terms. First, *Dear Mr. Jaar, 1976* was made in 1984 in New York and the inclusion of 1976 in the title signals a specific moment in Kissinger/Pinochet relations, when Kissinger visited Chile to give the green light to the dictatorship's past, present, and future. In this sense, Jaar's complex meditation on decolonial and colonial temporalities goes entirely unnoticed. And second, we can go even further and question the sensationalist tone of the statement about Jaar's risking "imprisonment or death" had he made the series in Chile. For one, it reveals a lack of engagement with critical Latin American art history, as it fails to acknowledge a well-known strategy used by artists under dictatorships to create political meaning and avoid censorship by means of conceptualism. "No," we hear over and over through the different echoes of imperialism in the temple of colonialism that is the museum: "nothing important can come from the South."[110] Furthermore, had Jaar shown *Searching for K* in Chile during the Pinochet years, it would likely have been celebrated by the Junta and its supporters, as the moment represented in its central image—Kissinger shaking hands with Pinochet—circulated widely in Chilean media, as an image that applauded Kissinger as an "extraordinary chancellor of the world." In other words, the work could have been interpreted as being wholly aligned with the dictatorship. Therein lies its relevance as an unfinished aesthetic project that obstructs the strict look of political binaries as effective and not just quick forms of persuasion.

Considering the role of museums in identifying, selecting, and disseminating meaning, it is clear that the institution has a long road toward decolonization, as its policies of diversity, inclusion, and anti-imperialism are, as Eve Tuck and K. Wayne Yang state, a "metaphor," a term they relate to trivial and superficial strategies of incorporation and care.[111] Specifically in the case of the Met, itself compromised by its long-standing relationship with Kissinger, Jaar's project was exhibited only to undermine its message as a shallow "metaphor," proving the validity of Kissinger's influence not only in international politics but also in the arts. Indeed, Kissinger's interest in the arts did not come late in his life. In 1978, that is, two years after his meeting with Pinochet and five years after the Chilean coup, Kissinger was appointed to the Met's Board of Trustees. As the press release (figure 2.14) of this event reads, "At a time when cultural exchanges among nations are increasing, a man of Dr. Kissinger's stature and wide range of interests will be of invaluable assistance to the Museum. His familiarity with world leaders and his known commitment to the value of cultural exchange in advancing understanding among nations will stand us in good stead as we plan future international exhibitions."[112] This statement, together with the ways Jaar's project was presented and described at the Met in 2018, ended up celebrating the role of Kissinger as a savior not only of transnational relations but also of the global arts.

TIME AND CRIME

On April 10, 2022, the *New York Times* published an opinion column titled "How Do We Deal with a Superpower Led by a War Criminal?" Its author, Thomas Friedman, maintains that solidity and affluence in post–Cold War life has been threatened by Russian President Vladimir Putin's 2022 invasion of Ukraine, inaugurating a "new" shift in global relations that is breaking the world's stability. As Friedman's opening paragraph reads: "It is hard to believe, but now impossible to deny, that the broad framework that kept much of the world stable and prospering since the end of the Cold War has been seriously fractured by Vladimir Putin's invasion of Ukraine." With Putin going "from 'bad boy' to 'war criminal' [and thus] testing the limits of the world order," Friedman argues, "the world as we've known it is profoundly changed. Nothing can work the same."[113]

"Is it?" Jaar may have asked himself, appropriating the photograph accompanying Friedman's article (figure 2.15). Shot from below, the photograph in the print shows Putin at the military parade in St. Petersburg on July 25, 2021. In the foreground, filling the left half of the frame, is a navy sailor wearing a surgical face mask, as by the time of the parade, Russia's COVID-19 death toll was hitting its record high since the beginning of the pandemic. Using a large aperture, which results in a shallow depth of field, the image of the sailor is blurred, contrasting with the figure of Putin, depicted in crisp detail in the right half of the frame. Unmasked and in complete focus, Putin wears a black suit, white shirt,

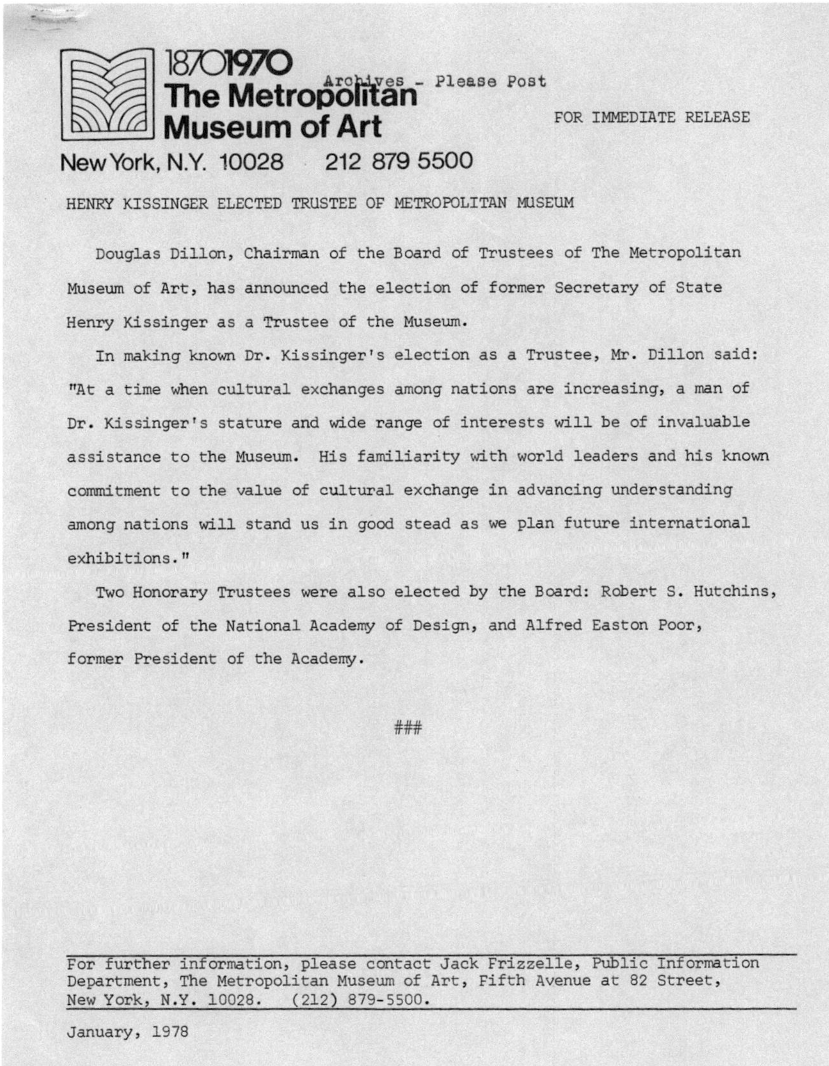

1870 1970
The Metropolitan
Museum of Art
New York, N.Y. 10028 212 879 5500

Archives - Please Post

FOR IMMEDIATE RELEASE

HENRY KISSINGER ELECTED TRUSTEE OF METROPOLITAN MUSEUM

Douglas Dillon, Chairman of the Board of Trustees of The Metropolitan Museum of Art, has announced the election of former Secretary of State Henry Kissinger as a Trustee of the Museum.

In making known Dr. Kissinger's election as a Trustee, Mr. Dillon said: "At a time when cultural exchanges among nations are increasing, a man of Dr. Kissinger's stature and wide range of interests will be of invaluable assistance to the Museum. His familiarity with world leaders and his known commitment to the value of cultural exchange in advancing understanding among nations will stand us in good stead as we plan future international exhibitions."

Two Honorary Trustees were also elected by the Board: Robert S. Hutchins, President of the National Academy of Design, and Alfred Easton Poor, former President of the Academy.

###

For further information, please contact Jack Frizzelle, Public Information Department, The Metropolitan Museum of Art, Fifth Avenue at 82 Street, New York, N.Y. 10028. (212) 879-5500.

January, 1978

2.14 Press release issued by the Metropolitan Museum of Art upon selecting Kissinger as a trustee, 1978.

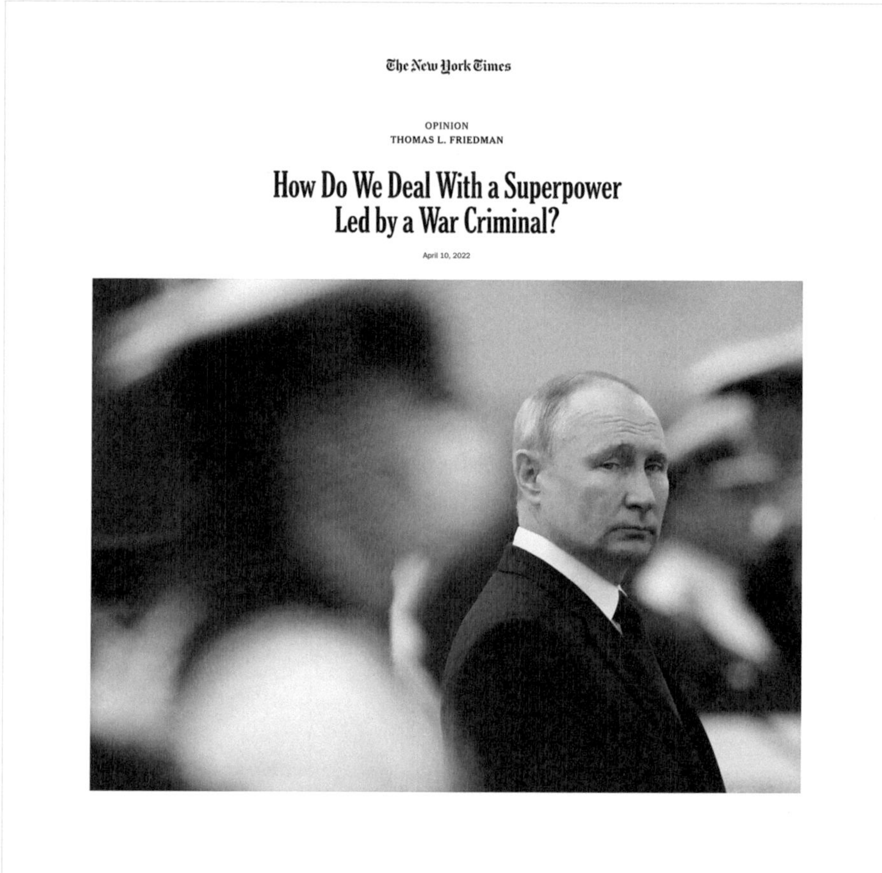

The New York Times

OPINION
THOMAS L. FRIEDMAN

How Do We Deal With a Superpower Led by a War Criminal?

April 10, 2022

2.15 Alfredo Jaar, *War Criminal* (detail), 2022. Courtesy of Alfredo Jaar.

and vermilion tie. Behind him are more sailors in uniforms, wearing face masks and similarly blurred. Technically and symbolically distinguished as a privileged civilian with a single identity and "clarity," Putin directs his gaze toward the lens, the viewer, the world. He looks defiant, serious, embracing power and conviction. At the same time, his drooping eyelids and frown isolate him within the image, as if the camera had found what it was searching for: a war criminal.

This is why this photograph, also owned by Getty Images, has been recurrently used by media outlets condemning Putin for war crimes. Such was the case of the *New York Times*, where the image accompanies Friedman's column as its "anchorage" of meaning.[114] This is also why Jaar uses it through the conceptualist practice of appropriation that adds yet another layer: the fact that, in his column, Friedman not only ignores the neoliberal legacies of the Cold War but even celebrates the "evenness" and "success" of this model in the post-Soviet world. Universalizing war into one single and *more important* conflict between two imperial nations, Friedman denies the suffering of others battling and resisting in other wars. He also negates their existence, ignoring the ongoing pain and mourning of, for instance, those affected by Kissinger's Cold War crimes in Chile, Argentina, Brazil, Vietnam, Laos, and Cambodia. Yet, as we learn over and over from critical memory studies: pain, trauma, and loss cannot be measured.

Jaar places this photograph at the beginning of a series composed of seven prints and titled *War Criminal*. Replicating its text and graphic design, Jaar changes the photograph's iconography—or Putin's portrait—for that of other war criminals (plate 17). From left to right, next to Putin are the following US statesmen: George W. Bush, Dick Cheney, Donald Rumsfeld, Richard Nixon, and Henry Kissinger, depicted through Martin Schoeller's photograph showing a deplored villain (figure 2.1). At the end of the series is Robert McNamara, secretary of defense under John F. Kennedy and Lyndon B. Johnson and a key promoter of US crimes in the Vietnam War, just as was Kissinger. Seen left to right, Jaar's temporal progression recedes in clock time, looking at the past to connect the present to crimes from early in the Cold War. Indeed, the present is denoted on each print separately, keeping Friedman's headline as-is. In so doing, Jaar groups these world criminals from the perspective of decolonial time, showing the political and historical bias of the media as well as their agency in rendering truth.

No wonder that Friedman, whose coverage of the "war on terror" and defensive reporting on the Israeli airstrikes in Lebanon granted him three Pulitzer Prizes, has also faced criticism from scholars who are critical of linear time. "The hypocrisy is, again, routine," writes Chomsky about a 2006 column by Friedman on Israel and the Middle East. "While instructing us on how the lesser breeds are to be 'educated' by terrorist violence, [he] writes that Israel's invasion of Lebanon in 2006, once again destroying much of southern Lebanon and Beirut while killing another 1000 civilians, was a just act of self-defense."[115] In 2024, in the wake of global student-organized manifestations asking campus administrators for divestment and pleading for a ceasefire in Gaza, the meaning of Friedman's May 8, 2024, weekly column at the *New York Times*, titled "Why the Campus Protests Are So Troubling," is, as Chomsky and Jaar would say, part of the same routine.[116]

In another work from 2022, *Mea Culpa*, Jaar adopts a similar conceptual strategy by appropriating a cover, replicating its textual graphic design, and changing its iconography (plate 18). The cover in this case was published by *The Economist* for its March 5, 2022, edition and portrays the blue and yellow colors of the Ukrainian flag with blood emerging from it. Next, also from left to right, Jaar adds eight more prints of flags and blood emerging from other national emblems, such as that of Palestine, which he places at the end of his narrative. As an artist who responds to context, in 2022 Jaar was affected by images of war in Ukraine in the media landscape. "But the fixation in Ukraine has erased many tragedies," Jaar has said. "Ukraine is using more shells—more guns, tanks, missiles—per month than the United States [can] produce in one year, [benefiting] business for these companies."[117] Jaar's words remind us of Letelier's 1976 article for *The Nation*, in which he stated that repression and economic freedom were constitutive to each other.[118] And in that relation, as Jaar's art reveals, the media plays a central role.[119] By adding flags of Ukraine, Yemen, Afghanistan, Ethiopia, Iraq, Myanmar, South Sudan, Syria, and Palestine, Jaar demonstrates that crimes in these places are not being exposed by the mainstream media, demanding visibility and acknowledgment even after the death of perpetrators such as Kissinger.

There is much work to do with the reframing of history and legal actions *through* representation, as culture has proven to be a key component in the fight for justice. In turn, since the museum can also operate as a site of imperial power, the public space as a site of production of meaning may also prove fruitful for the understanding of time through the aesthetics of the unfinished. This is shown in *The Kissinger Project (Berlin)*, a 2012 collaboration between Jaar and the European Center for Constitutional and Human Rights (ECCHR) (figure 2.16). A media intervention in which three major Berlin newspapers published the phrase "Arrest Kissinger!" along with German and English transcriptions, the ads also appeared in Spanish, Vietnamese, Khmer, Portuguese, and Timorese dialects, the languages of the people living in countries affected by Kissinger's Realpolitik. "And for these policies [Kissinger] is still lauded by many today," stated ECCHR founder and General Secretary Wolfgang Kaleck.[120] In modernity's racial and capitalist hypocrisy, only some are sentenced, as in, let us say, those responsible for 9/11. In this case, as cultural studies scholar Marita Sturken writes, this happens "within the myth of American exceptionalism, [where] terrorism has been narrated as something that comes from elsewhere [and] attack[s the] 'freedom' [of] an undeserving, innocent nation."[121] And that myth, as modernity has made clear, is built upon the violence of progressive time, with a market-oriented semantics that seeks to eliminate the past to avoid perpetrators' accountability. In the words of Greg Grandin, "Those support[ing] the 'war on terror' in the name of progressive values, while admitting the base motives and baleful legacy of the United States in the region, argue that the past does not necessarily have to determine the future."[122] In turn, considering modernity's understanding of (clock) time and its universal role in History (with a capital *H*), 9/11 became the most symbolic date of devastation after World War II, and, as such, it turned Chile's coup into "the Other 9/11."[123] In othering, diminishing, and considering less relevant the crimes against humanity committed outside the Northern–Western axis, this expression proves the role of language in affirming the Gregorian calendar as the hegemonic time of world history. It also shows that under modernity, human lives—and deaths—can be classified, with some considered more relevant than others that can even be made to disappear. In this design of life and time, the media plays a central role, calling 9/11, for instance, the *most* atrocious crime of the twenty-first century and its perpetrators the criminals of the world. This is why "al-Jazeera TV was condemned for showing shots of the results of US bombing in Fallujah," writes Slavoj Žižek. "Why should Kissinger, when he ordered the carpet bombing of Cambodia that led to the deaths of tens of thousands, be less of a criminal than those responsible for the Twin Towers collapse?"[124] The answer, once again, is modernity's linear time.

Importantly, by representing multiple languages, Jaar's *The Kissinger Project (Berlin)* not only denounces coloniality by signaling the sites of crimes committed by Kissinger. It simultaneously shows a decolonial solidarity that critiques monolingual understanding in our "chaos-world," as Édouard Glissant would say.[125] The artist, lawyer, and human rights institutions all connect shared histories of civic repression and human rights violations perpetrated by the United States globally, recalling works such as *Manhattan's Milosevic* or *Buscando a Kissinger* by activating the relationship between memory acts and the field of transitional justice studies by calling for liability to Kissinger using language. Significantly regarding language, time, and a transnational approach to memory, *The Kissinger Project (Berlin)* action took place on September 11, 2012, for the thirty-ninth anniversary of the Chilean coup. Regarding the date of mourning not only for Chileans within and beyond the nation but also for anti-imperialist minds and hearts, Kaleck describes the action: "September 11 . . . carries a terrible significance for Chile, for Latin America as a whole and for the Left movement everywhere."[126]

Jaar's works on victimizers aim at the same goal as every image depicting victims of global neoliberalization: they demand "*juicio y castigo*" from perpetrators within a system that has not been able to bring forth justice.

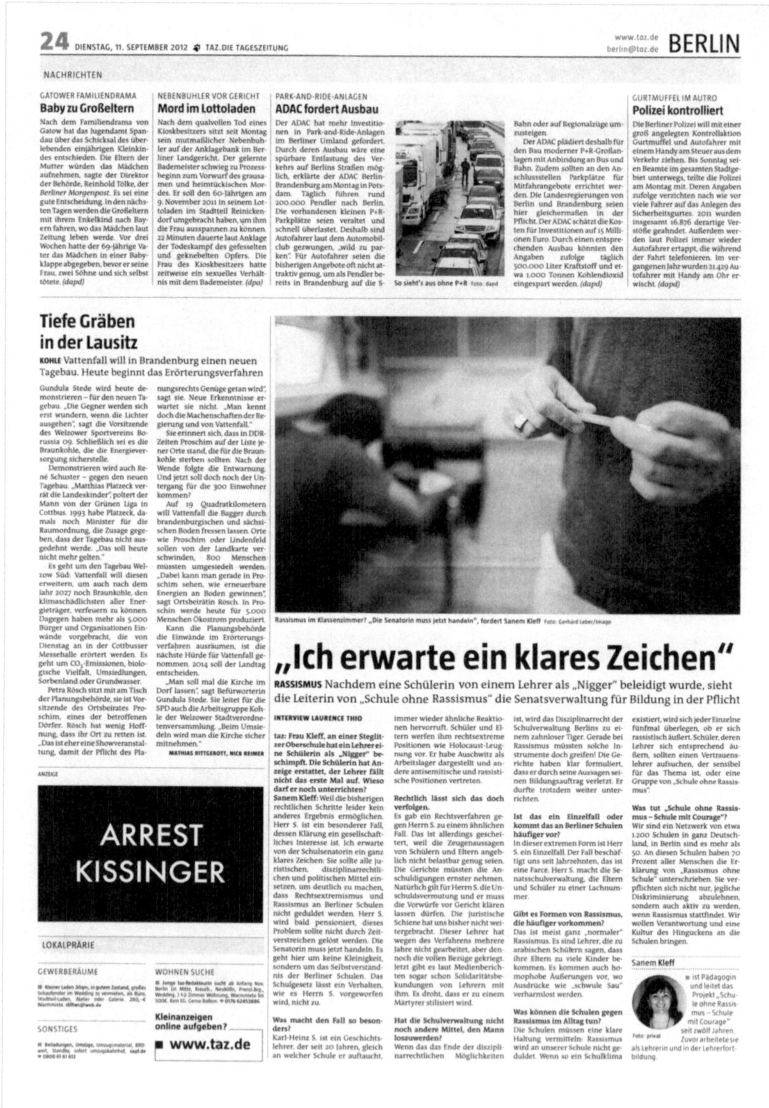

24 DIENSTAG, 11. SEPTEMBER 2012 TAZ.DIE TAGESZEITUNG

www.taz.de berlin@taz.de **BERLIN**

NACHRICHTEN

GATOWER FAMILIENDRAMA

Baby zu Großeltern

Nach dem Familiendrama von Gatow hat das Jugendamt Spandau über das Schicksal des überlebenden einjährigen Kleinkindes entschieden. Die Eltern der Mutter würden das Mädchen aufnehmen, sagte der Direktor der Behörde, Reinhold Tölke, der *Berliner Morgenpost*. Es sei eine gute Entscheidung. In den nächsten Tagen werden die Großeltern mit ihrem Enkelkind nach Bayern fahren, wo das Mädchen laut Zeitung leben werde. Vor drei Wochen hatte der 69-jährige Vater das Mädchen in einer Babyklappe abgegeben, bevor er seine Frau, zwei Söhne und sich selbst tötete. *(dapd)*

NEBENBUHLER VOR GERICHT

Mord im Lottoladen

Nach dem qualvollen Tod eines Kioskbesitzers sitzt seit Montag sein mutmaßlicher Nebenbuhler auf der Anklagebank im Berliner Landgericht. Der gelernte Bademeister schwieg zu Prozessbeginn zum Vorwurf des grausamen und heimtückischen Mordes. Er soll den 60-Jährigen am 9. November 2011 in seinem Lottoladen im Stadtteil Reinickendorf umgebracht haben, um ihm die Frau ausspannen zu können. 22 Minuten dauerte laut Anklage der Todeskampf des gefesselten und geknebelten Opfers. Die Frau des Kioskbesitzers hatte zeitweise ein sexuelles Verhältnis mit dem Bademeister. *(dpa)*

PARK-AND-RIDE-ANLAGEN

ADAC fordert Ausbau

Der ADAC hat mehr Investitionen in Park-and-Ride-Anlagen im Berliner Umland gefordert. Durch deren Ausbau wäre eine spürbare Entlastung des Verkehrs auf Berlins Straßen möglich, erklärte der ADAC Berlin-Brandenburg am Montag in Potsdam. Täglich führen rund 200.000 Pendler nach Berlin. Die vorhandenen kleinen P+R-Parkplätze seien veraltet und schnell überlastet. Deshalb sind Autofahrer laut dem Automobilclub gezwungen, „wild zu parken". Für Autofahrer seien die bisherigen Angebote oft nicht attraktiv genug, um als Pendler bereits in Brandenburg auf die S-Bahn oder auf Regionalzüge umzusteigen.

Der ADAC plädiert deshalb für den Bau moderner P+R-Großanlagen mit Anbindung an Bus und Bahn. Zudem sollten an den Anschlussstellen Parkplätze für Mitfahrangebote errichtet werden. Die Landesregierungen von Berlin und Brandenburg seien hier gleichermaßen in der Pflicht. Der ADAC schätzt die Kosten für Investitionen auf 15 Millionen Euro. Durch einen entsprechenden Ausbau könnten den Angaben zufolge täglich 500.000 Liter Kraftstoff und etwa 1.000 Tonnen Kohlendioxid eingespart werden. *(dapd)*

So sieht's aus ohne P+R Foto: dapd

GURTMUFFEL IM AUTRO

Polizei kontrolliert

Die Berliner Polizei will mit einer groß angelegten Kontrollaktion Gurtmuffel und Autofahrer mit einem Handy am Steuer aus dem Verkehr ziehen. Bis Sonntag seien Beamte im gesamten Stadtgebiet unterwegs, teilte die Polizei am Montag mit. Deren Angaben zufolge verzichten nach wie vor viele Fahrer auf das Anlegen des Sicherheitsgurtes. 2011 wurden insgesamt 16.876 derartige Verstöße geahndet. Außerdem werden laut Polizei immer wieder Autofahrer ertappt, die während der Fahrt telefonieren. Im vergangenen Jahr wurden 21.429 Autofahrer mit Handy am Ohr erwischt. *(dapd)*

Tiefe Gräben in der Lausitz

KOHLE Vattenfall will in Brandenburg einen neuen Tagebau. Heute beginnt das Erörterungsverfahren

Gundula Stede wird heute demonstrieren – für den neuen Tagebau. „Die Gegner werden sich erst wundern, wenn die Lichter ausgehen", sagt die Vorsitzende des Welzower Sportvereins Borussia 09. Schließlich sei es die Braunkohle, die die Energieversorgung sicherstelle.

Demonstrieren wird auch René Schuster – gegen den neuen Tagebau. „Matthias Platzeck verrät die Landeskinder", poltert der Mann von der Grünen Liga in Cottbus. 1993 habe Platzeck, damals noch Minister für die Raumordnung, die Zusage gegeben, dass der Tagebau nicht ausgedehnt werde. „Das soll heute nicht mehr gelten."

Es geht um den Tagebau Welzow Süd: Vattenfall will diesen erweitern, um auch nach dem Jahr 2027 noch Braunkohle, den klimaschädlichsten aller Energieträger, verfeuern zu können. Dagegen haben mehr als 5.000 Bürger und Organisationen Einwände vorgebracht, die von Dienstag an in der Cottbusser Messehalle erörtert werden. Es geht um CO_2-Emissionen, biologische Vielfalt, Umsiedlungen, Sorbenland oder Grundwasser.

Petra Rösch sitzt mit am Tisch der Planungsbehörde, sie ist Vorsitzende des Ortsbeirates Proschim, eines der betroffenen Dörfer. Rösch hat wenig Hoffnung, dass ihr Ort zu retten ist. „Das ist eher eine Showveranstaltung, damit der Pflicht des Planungsrechts Genüge getan wird", sagt sie. Neue Erkenntnisse erwartet sie nicht. „Man kennt doch die Machenschaften der Regierung und von Vattenfall."

Sie erinnert sich, dass in DDR-Zeiten Proschim auf der Liste jener Orte stand, die für die Braunkohle sterben sollten. Nach der Wende folgte die Entwarnung. Und jetzt soll doch noch der Untergang für die 300 Einwohner kommen?

Auf 19 Quadratkilometern will Vattenfall die Bagger durch brandenburgischen und sächsischen Boden fressen lassen. Orte wie Proschim oder Lindenfeld sollen von der Landkarte verschwinden, 800 Menschen müssten umgesiedelt werden. „Dabei kann man gerade in Proschim sehen, wie erneuerbare Energien an Boden gewinnen", sagt Ortsbeirätin Rösch. In Proschin werde heute für 5.000 Menschen Ökostrom produziert.

Kann die Planungsbehörde die Einwände im Erörterungsverfahren ausräumen, ist die nächste Hürde für Vattenfall genommen. 2014 soll der Landtag entscheiden.

„Man soll mal die Kirche im Dorf lassen", sagt Befürworterin Gundula Stede. Sie leitet für die SPD auch die Arbeitsgruppe Kohle der Welzower Stadtverordnetenversammlung. „Beim Umsiedeln wird man die Kirche sicher mitnehmen."

MATHIAS RITTGEROTT, NICK REIMER

ANZEIGE

ARREST KISSINGER

LOKALPRÄRIE

GEWERBERÄUME

Kleiner Laden 30qm, in gutem Zustand, großes Schaufenster im Wedding zu vermieten, als Büro, Stadtteil-Laden, Atelier oder Galerie. 280,-€ Warmmiete.

SONSTIGES

Beiladungen, Umzüge, Umzugsmaterial, BRD-weit, Standby, sofort umzugsbahnhof, sapf.de

WOHNEN SUCHE

Junge taz-Redakteurin sucht ab Anfang Nov. Berlin (in Mitte, Kreuzb., Neukölln, Prenzl.Brg., Wedding...) 1-2 Zimmer Wohnung, Warmmiete bis 500€. Kein EG. Gerne Balkon. ☎ 0176 62453886

Kleinanzeigen online aufgeben?

www.taz.de

Rassismus im Klassenzimmer? „Die Senatorin muss jetzt handeln", fordert Sanem Kleff Foto: Gerhard Leber/image

„Ich erwarte ein klares Zeichen"

RASSISMUS Nachdem eine Schülerin von einem Lehrer als „Nigger" beleidigt wurde, sieht die Leiterin von „Schule ohne Rassismus" die Senatsverwaltung für Bildung in der Pflicht

INTERVIEW LAURENCE THIO

taz: Frau Kleff, an einer Steglitzer Oberschule hat ein Lehrer eine Schülerin als „Nigger" beschimpft. Die Schülerin hat Anzeige erstattet, der Lehrer fällt nicht das erste Mal auf. Wieso darf er noch unterrichten?

Sanem Kleff: Weil die bisherigen rechtlichen Schritte leider kein anderes Ergebnis ermöglichen. Herr S. ist ein besonderer Fall, dessen Klärung ein gesellschaftliches Interesse ist. Ich erwarte von der Schulsenatorin ein ganz klares Zeichen: Sie sollte alle juristischen, disziplinarrechtlichen und politischen Mittel einsetzen, um deutlich zu machen, dass Rechtsextremismus und Rassismus an Berliner Schulen nicht geduldet werden. Herr S. wird bald pensioniert, dieses Problem sollte nicht durch Zeitverstreichen gelöst werden. Die Senatorin muss jetzt handeln. Es geht hier um keine Kleinigkeit, sondern um das Selbstverständnis der Berliner Schulen. Das Schulgesetz lässt ein Verhalten, wie es Herrn S. vorgeworfen wird, nicht zu.

Was macht den Fall so besonders?

Karl-Heinz S. ist ein Geschichtslehrer, der seit 20 Jahren, gleich an welcher Schule er auftaucht, immer wieder ähnliche Reaktionen hervorruft. Schüler und Eltern werfen ihm rechtsextreme Positionen wie Holocaust-Leugnung vor. Er habe Auschwitz als Arbeitslager dargestellt und andere antisemitische und rassistische Positionen vertreten.

Rechtlich lässt sich das doch verfolgen.

Es gab ein Rechtsverfahren gegen Herrn S. zu einem ähnlichen Fall. Das ist allerdings gescheitert, weil die Zeugenaussagen von Schülern und Eltern angeblich nicht belastbar genug seien. Die Gerichte müssten die Anschuldigungen ernster nehmen. Natürlich gilt für Herrn S. die Unschuldsvermutung und er muss die Vorwürfe vor Gericht klären lassen dürfen. Die juristische Schiene hat uns bisher nicht weitergebracht. Dieser Lehrer hat wegen des Verfahrens mehrere Jahre nicht gearbeitet, aber dennoch die vollen Bezüge gekriegt. Jetzt gibt es laut Medienberichten sogar schon Solidaritätsbekundungen von Lehrern mit ihm. Es droht, dass er zu einem Märtyrer stilisiert wird.

Hat die Schulverwaltung nicht noch andere Mittel, den Mann loszuwerden?

Wenn das das Ende der disziplinarrechtlichen Möglichkeiten ist, wird das Disziplinarrecht der Schulverwaltung Berlins zu einem zahnloser Tiger. Gerade bei Rassismus müssten solche Instrumente doch greifen! Die Gerichte haben klar formuliert, dass er durch seine Aussagen seinen Bildungsauftrag verletzt. Er durfte trotzdem weiter unterrichten.

Ist das ein Einzelfall oder kommt das an Berliner Schulen häufiger vor?

In dieser extremen Form ist Herr S. ein Einzelfall. Der Fall beschäftigt uns seit Jahrzehnten, das ist eine Farce. Herr S. macht die Senatsschulverwaltung, die Eltern und Schüler zu einer Lachnummer.

Gibt es Formen von Rassismus, die häufiger vorkommen?

Das ist meist ganz „normaler" Rassismus. Es sind Lehrer, die zu arabischen Schülern sagen, dass ihre Eltern zu viele Kinder bekommen. Es kommen auch homophobe Äußerungen vor, wo Ausdrücke wie „schwule Sau" verharmlost werden.

Was können die Schulen gegen Rassismus im Alltag tun?

Die Schulen müssen eine klare Haltung vermitteln: Rassismus wird an unserer Schule nicht geduldet. Wenn so ein Schulklima existiert, wird sich jeder Einzelne fünfmal überlegen, ob er sich rassistisch äußert. Schüler, deren Lehrer sich entsprechend äußern, sollten einen Vertrauenslehrer aufsuchen, der sensibel für das Thema ist, oder eine Gruppe von „Schule ohne Rassismus".

Was tut „Schule ohne Rassismus – Schule mit Courage"?

Wir sind ein Netzwerk von etwa 1.200 Schulen in ganz Deutschland, in Berlin sind es mehr als 50. An diesen Schulen haben 70 Prozent aller Menschen die Erklärung von „Rassismus ohne Schule" unterschrieben. Sie verpflichten sich nicht nur, jegliche Diskriminierung abzulehnen, sondern auch aktiv zu werden, wenn Rassismus stattfindet. Wir wollen Verantwortung und eine Kultur des Hinguckens an die Schulen bringen.

Sanem Kleff

Foto: privat

■ ist Pädagogin und leitet das Projekt „Schule ohne Rassismus – Schule mit Courage" seit zwölf Jahren. Zuvor arbeitete sie als Lehrerin und in der Lehrerfortbildung.

2.16 Alfredo Jaar, *The Kissinger Project (Berlin)*, 2012, from the series *The Kissinger Project* (ongoing from 1983). Courtesy of Alfredo Jaar.

Unearthing the decolonizing potential of images and words to deconstruct existing power structures by means of representation, Jaar's works on accountability embrace a task that is not yet resolved. In so doing, they bring to the realm of art political slogans such as "*No a la impunidad. Ni perdón ni olvido*" (No to impunity. Neither forget nor forgive), further revealing in turn the hidden meanings of neoliberal mottos such as "*Empezar de cero*" (Start from scratch). They reveal the logic of modernity's colonial time. By representing accountability through the conceptual metaphor of incompleteness, Jaar's project on Kissinger and his works on other world criminals invite us to imagine that things could be otherwise, participating in the linguistic decolonial idea that "*La lucha continua*" (The struggle continues).

3

FAILURE

For representation to convey the human, then, representation must not only fail, but must *show* its failure.
—Judith Butler

In 1987, Alfredo Jaar projected his animation *A Logo for America* in Times Square, New York City (plate 19). Part of the "Messages to the Public" program—a series of computer-generated artworks with social and political content broadcast from a twenty-by-forty-foot Spectacolor lightboard from 1982 to 1990—Jaar's thirty-five-second animation was shown every six minutes from April 19 to May 2 on the lightbulb screen. The work opens with an outline of the contiguous US territory and continues with a statement written across the map that reads: "This Is Not America." The font is then pixelated while the map turns into the US flag with a second negation that reads: "This Is Not America's Flag." The word *America* then blinks on the screen and transforms into the continental landmass of the Western Hemisphere, which is then duplicated as the word *America* disappears. The animation concludes with the Americas rendered in a single graphic at the center of the screen, while the word *America* multiplies on both sides. Through a conceptual strategy that overlaps images and text regarding the nomenclature *America* as both a noun and an adjective, Jaar's work challenges the term's appropriation in the United States, creating a linguistic tension as a metaphor for US colonial designs in Latin America.

A signature work in Jaar's and Latin American art, *A Logo for America* has been a recurrent and even iconic example used by critics, art historians, and curators since the early 1990s, all aiming to designate what, where, and how is "Latin American" and, more recently, (US) "American art." It has also been reenacted in multiple cities worldwide, with the vast literature around the work typically praising the animation for its success. In the summer of 2016, for instance, when shown at London's Piccadilly Circus, a critic noted that the animation "resembles a pair of eyeglasses, as if to confirm that a misunderstanding is being couched and clarified."[1] After all, in life under modernity, so the story goes, history—and for that matter, art history—is written mainly by the victors.[2] Yet, Jaar has described his animation in quite different terms: "The work was a reaction to the fact that the word America has been misused by the U.S. and that we (Latin Americans) are erased from the map. It was a subversive gesture, but of course, it did not work at all."[3] Indeed, Jaar's entire body of work regarding the idea of America is about representing such a failure, reminding us that, although initially developed as colonial linguistic constructs, the terms *America* and *Latin America*, to paraphrase historian Miguel Rojas Mix, have one hundred names.[4]

This chapter is about failure, or about the ways in which Jaar's art on the idea of America not only fails but also aims at representing such failure.[5] In this sense, the works discussed here express that failure is what keeps cultures of resistance alive, fighting collectively in an *in-process* project as a vehicle to understand the past, represent the present, and transform the future. More specifically, the chapter elaborates on how, why, and under what circumstances Jaar has been representing failure by resisting the coloniality of language, time, and art together. By providing an alternative analysis of Jaar's art in relation to the question of *America* through the notions of reenactment, combat, liberation, and revolution, this chapter not only challenges linear (art) history and critiques the nation-state as a site of modernity's oppression. It further elaborates on two central theoretical debates in decolonial theory as formulated from the Americas: the ongoing wounds of coloniality and the way these are expressed through the coloniality of language; and a hemispheric genealogy of utopia and liberation with which Jaar's works are inscribed, one that offers historical and theoretical counternarratives regarding the terms *America* and *Latin America* as anti-imperialist constructs.

REENACTMENTS

Since its first reenactment in Times Square in 2014, *A Logo for America* has been projected in multiple cities around the world, from New York to Los Angeles, Miami, Des Moines, Bentonville, Vancouver, and London, and from Buenos Aires to Bogotá, Porto Alegre, Mexico City, and beyond. In all cases, the analysis of the work as a successful public intervention and the understanding of the term *America* as a single nation-state have coexisted, albeit paradoxically. Examples abound. "The phrase 'This is not America' was sometimes taken as an indictment of the seediness of Times Square," wrote for instance an art critic when the animation was first reenacted.[6] In this case, the linguistic and thus cultural negation created by Jaar is read, first, through an affirmation: "America *is* the US." And second, through a negation that rejects places such as Times Square from the colonial affirmation of the United States *as* America. In 2018, when installed on a boat in the sea near Miami, the curator went even further by implying that "America" is both universal and transcendental: "[Jaar's work] explore[s] America as bigger than the waters and borders that frame it."[7] Or, more recently, as an influential United States–based curator of Latin American art maintained, "Fortunately, artists like Alfredo Jaar and his 1987 work *A Logo for America* . . . continue to teach 'Americans' (those born in the United States) that the 'American territory'—even if its name dives into European colonialism—lies beyond the borders of their country."[8] Turning the discourse of coloniality upside down instead of challenging it, this statement refers to Jaar as an artist who *successfully* educates the ignorant US empire in the progressive era of modernity. Statements like this further assume that First Nations and Black people, who are also "born in the United States," likewise appropriate the land "beyond the borders of their country." Or, inversely, they overlook these communities as if their members were born elsewhere, erasing them again. As Eddie Chambers maintains in an essay about art history in the age of Black Lives Matter, "We need to put academic pressure on the noun and adjective 'American.' Dictionary definitions might have it as 'relating to or characteristic of the United States or its inhabitants,' but we know that within art history departments, more often than not, 'American' pretty much means 'white American,' and it pretty much is never presumed to mean 'Black American,' 'Latin American,' 'Latinx American,' and so on."[9]

Jaar's work has also been read in relation to its mobility of meaning, considering its sites and dates of display throughout the years, all the while keeping the contradictory twofold paradigm of triumph and the nation-state. Katerina Stathopoulou—curator at the Public Art Fund in New York, the institution responsible alongside the Guggenheim Museum for the work's first reenactment in 2014—states that in 2014 "Latin American immigration was central to the conversation, as the Obama Administration was felt by many to be disappointing on the issue." She goes on to explain that "in Mexico City in 2016, the work took on additional meaning, as a result of Trump's xenophobic rhetoric and initiative to build a border wall to keep migrants out.

For those who disagree with Trump's policies, the work can be interpreted as signifying, 'This is not the America that represents them.'"[10] "I completely lost control over [the work]," Jaar said in 2014, responding to his animation's reenactment in Times Square and the responses it generated (plate 20).[11]

In this sense, one might reflect on the slogan "Make America Great Again" (MAGA), created during Donald Trump's successful 2016 presidential campaign and rapidly transformed into a popular cultural phenomenon that continues growing today. "No president in the history of the Republic has used the word 'America' as effectively as Donald Trump," stated historian Greg Grandin in 2025 at the beginning of Trump's second term in office. '"America," as Grandin continues by quoting Trump's deputy chief of staff Stephen Miller, "is for Americans and Americans only."[12] And thus, we wonder: How would Jaar's work be perceived by those opposing "Trump's xenophobic rhetoric" in the aftermath of the January 6, 2021, right-wing insurrection, in which thousands of rioters from the MAGA universe attacked the US Capitol wearing the signature red MAGA cap? How would it be perceived in the performativity of language as a wearable commodity? Or, inversely: How would titles such as the 2024 book *Filibustered! How to Fix the Broken Senate and Save America*, by democratic Senator Jeff Merkley and his chief of staff, Mike Zamore, be seen by those opposing US interventionism?[13] And, more recently, one might also reflect on how both sides of the political establishment would see Jaar's work if one considers, for example, the renaming of the Gulf of Mexico as the Gulf of America. The list is long, showing that the semiotics that relates language to meaning through imperialist convention mirrors the violence of history and therefore of war. Whether addressing the administrations of Trump, Joe Biden, Barack Obama, George W. Bush, Bill Clinton, or a long train of presidents that we can trace back to the nineteenth century, Jaar's message is directed away from the hemispheric and toward the nation-state. Put differently, the artist's series of linguistic negations—"This is not America," "This is not America's flag"—become affirmations of American exceptionalism. And, in the context of neoliberalism that drives this study, what is ignored, as Esther Gabara argues, is Jaar's "negation of the U.S.'s hegemonic Americanity—from its early 'laboratory' in Chile to its homeland in Times Square."[14]

Indeed, precisely because the equation between the nomenclature *America* and a single nation-state in both politics and the arts has not only continued but expanded, Jaar, in response, has reenacted his animation time and time again. Central to this aesthetics of reenactment is the issue of form, which fluctuates in the animation only to return to the same meaning. Form and content in this sense are not opposed methods, agencies, or heuristics in Jaar's art. Nor is art from life, or form from time. In 2014, for instance, for its first reenactment in Times Square, *A Logo for America* was shown through a remastered version of high-definition LED technology on fifteen signs and forty-five screens, all of different sizes (plate 20). This remastered version was used again in 2015 at the Museo Jumex in Mexico City, and then again in 2016 at the South London Gallery in London. While in Mexico City, the work was broadcast from one screen at the top of a vertical concrete structure located in a parking lot adjacent to the National Auditorium on the avenue Paseo de la Reforma. And, in London, it was projected simultaneously as three adjacent videos, at the bottom left of the large Piccadilly Lights screen in the heart of the West End. These projections differ from one another and from the work's inaugural reenactment in terms of repetition, singularity, multiplicity, size, and relation to iconic touristic sites. It is also significant that since 2014, the work has not always used its high-definition LED technology. In 2018, for instance, it was shown from a highway billboard in Iowa's capital, Des Moines, through its original 1987 technology of lightbulbs. This technology was used again in 2019, when the animation was broadcast from a single screen at the Plaza de la República in Buenos Aires in Argentina, facing the city's iconic obelisk at the Plaza de la República.

Considering the work's variations in regard to technology, form, and relation to site, one may wonder if there is a pattern designed by the artist to match, for instance, the remastered high-definition version with iconic sites surrounded by LED and neon billboards illuminating massive gatherings and the circulation of traffic, humans, and promotional consumerism in major cities, as in the case of Times Square. Yet this is not the case: A parking lot in Mexico City is not exactly an iconic site, and in Buenos Aires' iconic Plaza de la República, currently known for its LED and neon technology, the animation was shown using the lightbulb version, that is, a technology from the past. Within these variations, the artist is not only contextualizing the work in the present through current technology but also insisting on the importance of presenting it as a work from the past whose pulsating meaning continues inhabiting the ongoing present. In this sense, the strategy (or pattern) is to repeat *and* vary, that is, to insist *and* differ, in order to present the work's reenactment as it expands and formally (not conceptually) changes. The work's meaning, past and present, is to make visible from the realm of language and the political and ethical tactic of conceptualism as developed from Cold War Latin America that decolonial struggle against human degradation and thus of ethical reparation is essentially incomplete, unresolved.[15]

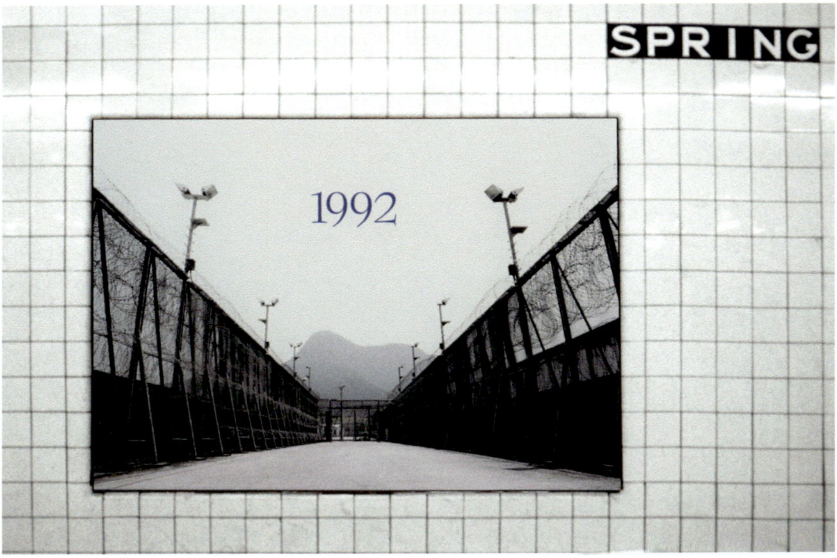

P1 Alfredo Jaar, *1992*, 1992. Courtesy of Alfredo Jaar.

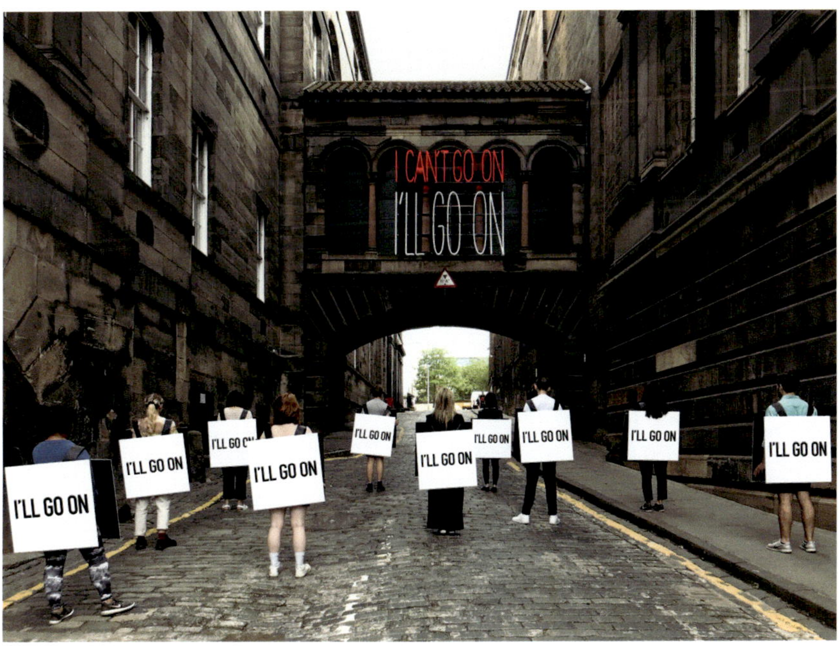

P2 Alfredo Jaar, *I Can't Go On, I'll Go On*, 2019. Courtesy of Alfredo Jaar.

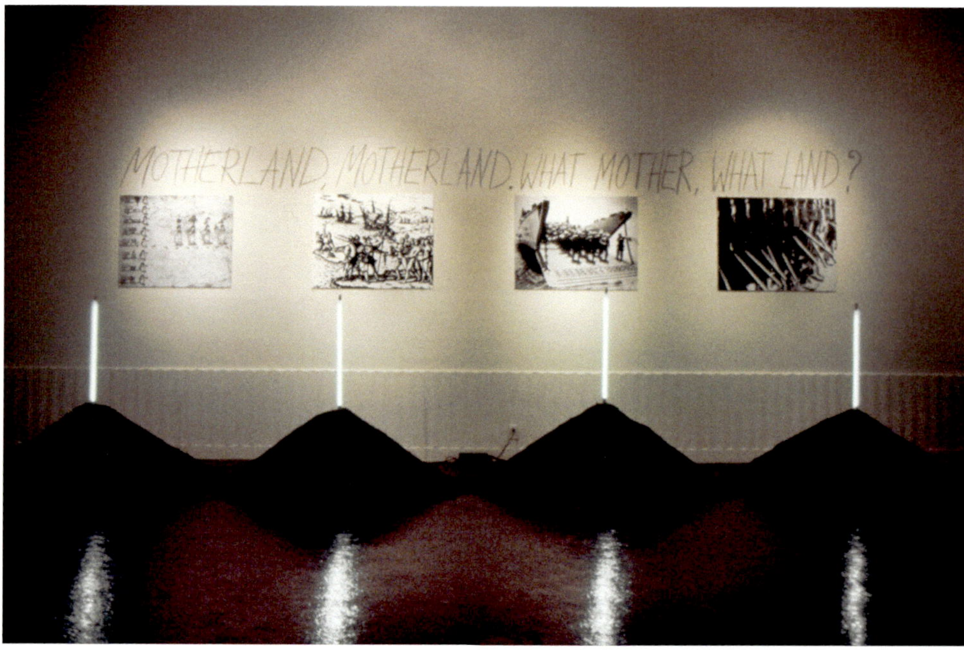

P3 Alfredo Jaar, *Motherland, Motherland. What Mother, What Land?*, 1984. Courtesy of Alfredo Jaar.

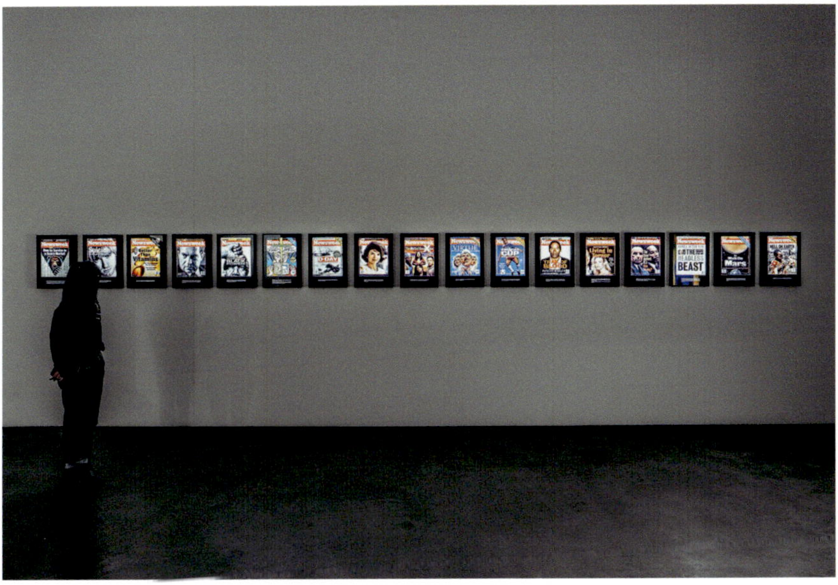

P4 Alfredo Jaar, *Untitled (Newsweek)*, 1994, from the series *The Rwanda Project* (1994–2000). Courtesy of Alfredo Jaar.

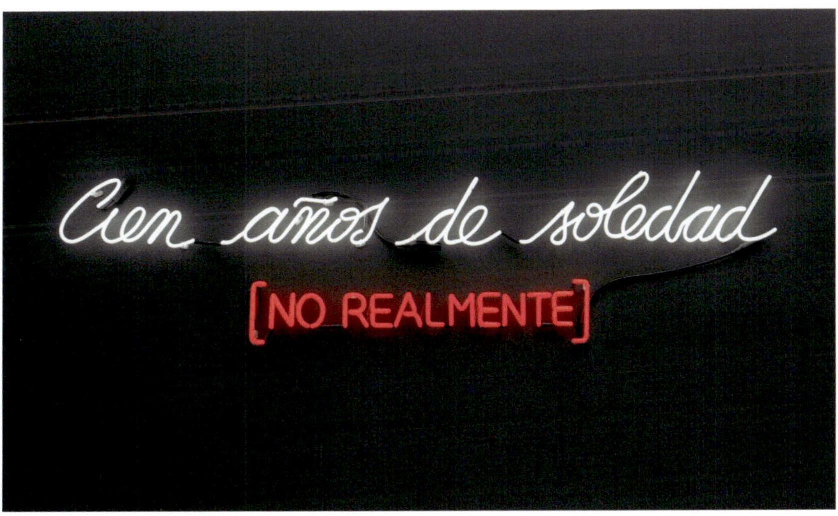

P5 Alfredo Jaar, *Cien años de soledad (no realmente)*, 1985. Courtesy of Alfredo Jaar.

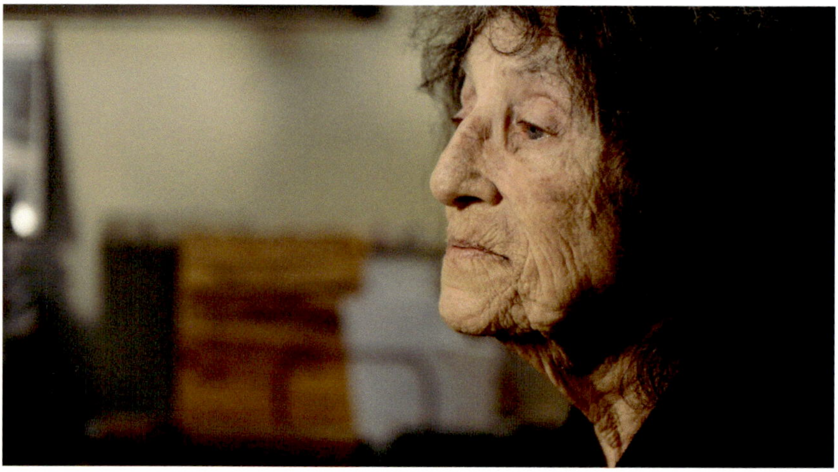

P6 Alfredo Jaar, *Dore Ashton, You Know*, 2015. Courtesy of Alfredo Jaar.

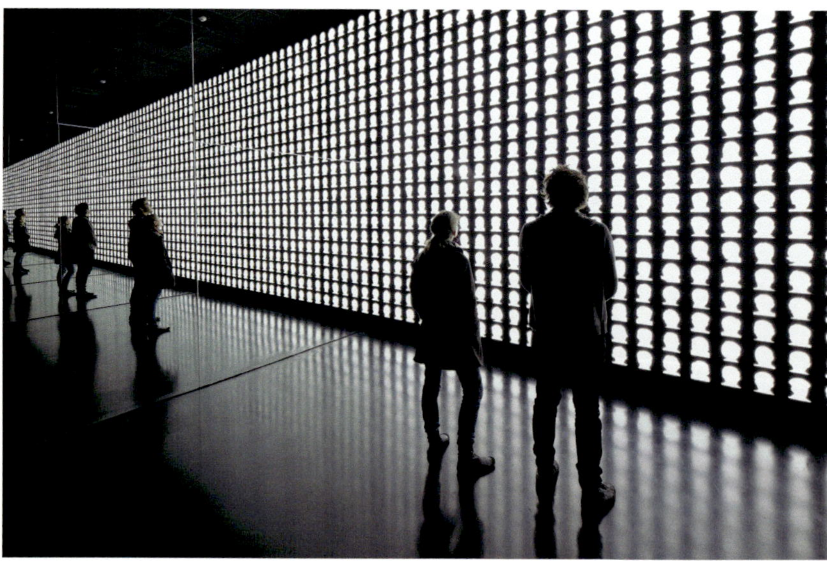

P7 Alfredo Jaar, *The Geometry of Conscience*, 2010. Courtesy of Alfredo Jaar.

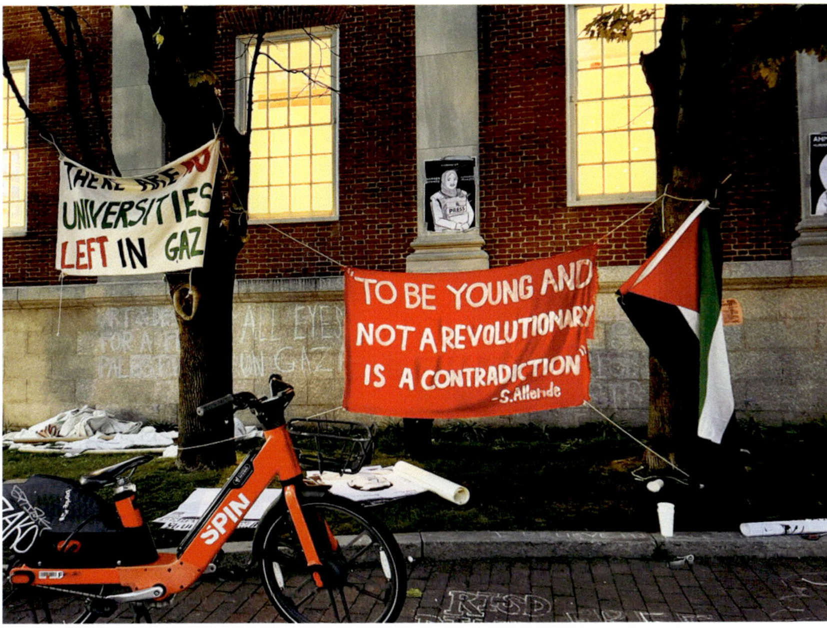

P8 Daniel Enrique Torres Marrero, Gaza Solidarity Encampment at Rhode Island School of Design (RISD), May 2024. Courtesy of Daniel Enrique Torres Marrero.

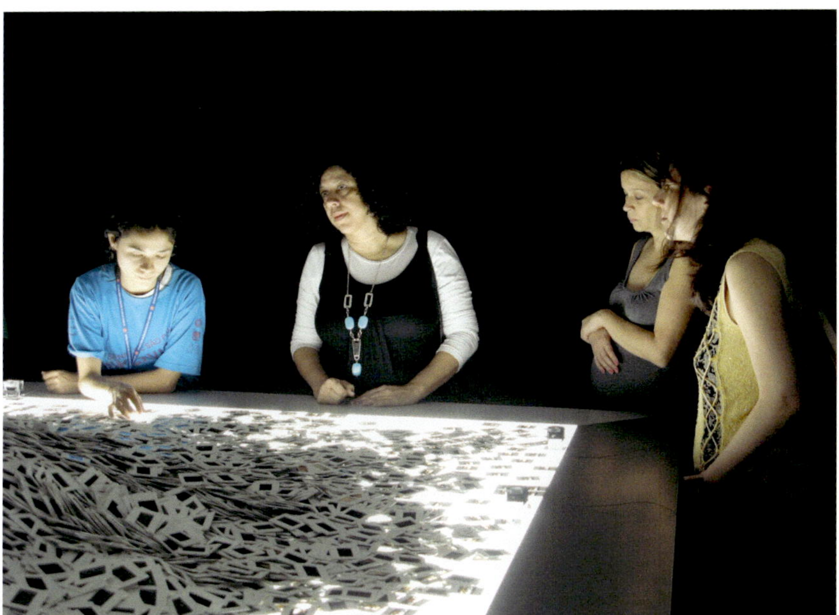

P9 Alfredo Jaar, *The Eyes of Gutete Emerita* (exhibition view), 1996, from the series *The Rwanda Project* (1994–2000). Courtesy of Alfredo Jaar.

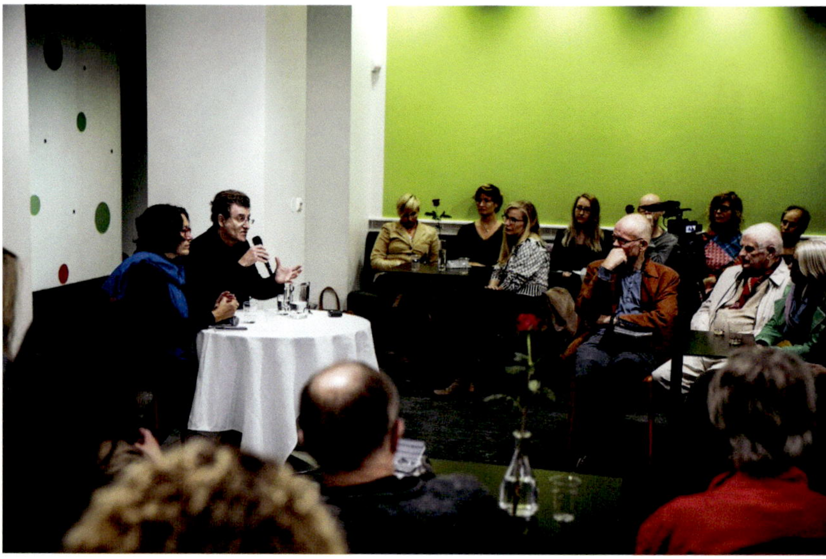

P10 Amira Hass and Alfredo Jaar in conversation in October 2014 at the Sørlandets Kunstmuseum in Norway.

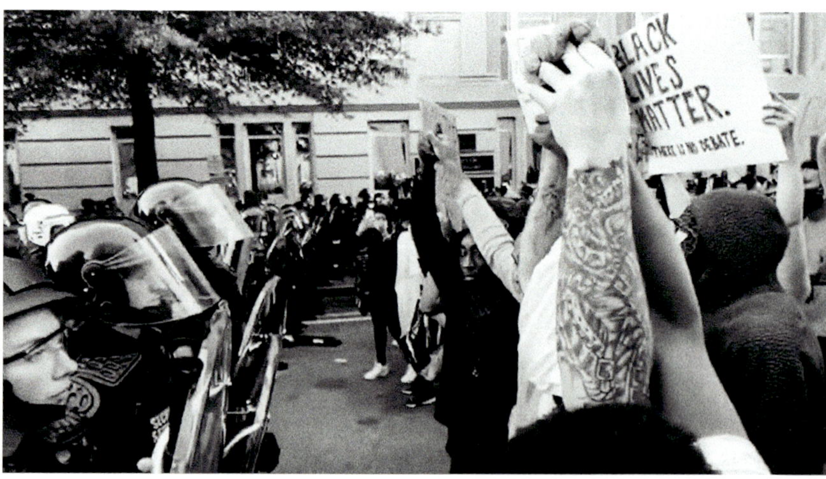

P11 Alfredo Jaar, *06.01.2020 18.39*, 2022. Courtesy of Alfredo Jaar.

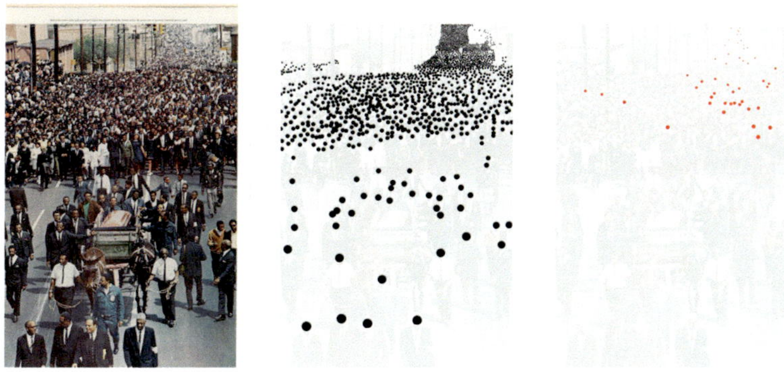

P12 Alfredo Jaar, *Life Magazine, April 19, 1968*, 1995. Courtesy of Alfredo Jaar.

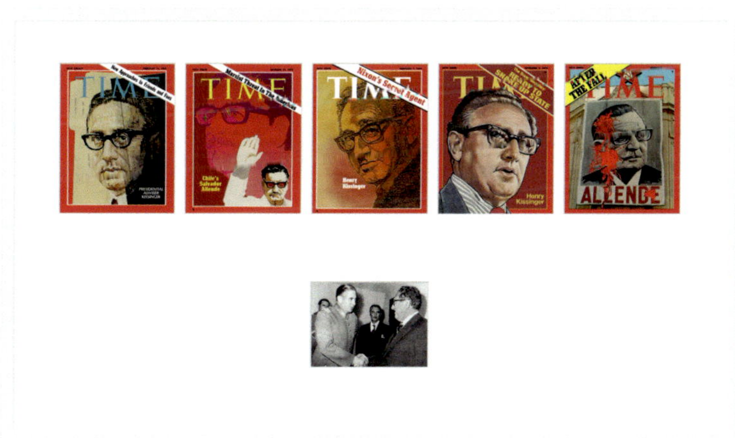

P13 Alfredo Jaar, *Untitled (Handshake)*, 1985, from the series *The Kissinger Project* (ongoing from 1983). Courtesy of Alfredo Jaar.

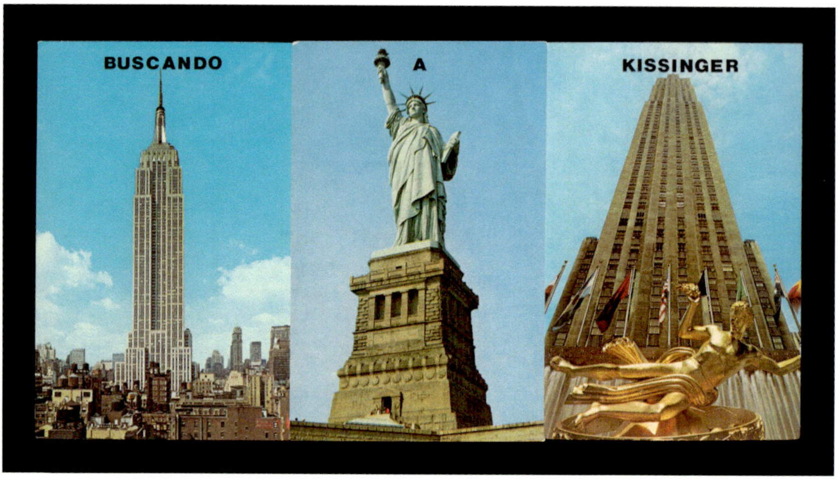

P14 Alfredo Jaar, *Buscando a Kissinger*, 1983, from the series *The Kissinger Project* (ongoing from 1983). Courtesy of Alfredo Jaar.

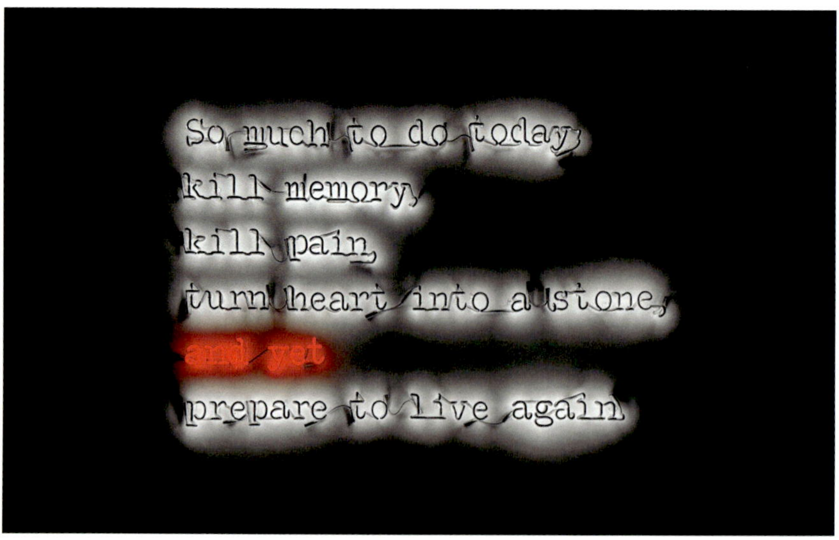

P15 Alfredo Jaar, *And Yet*, 2019. Courtesy of Alfredo Jaar.

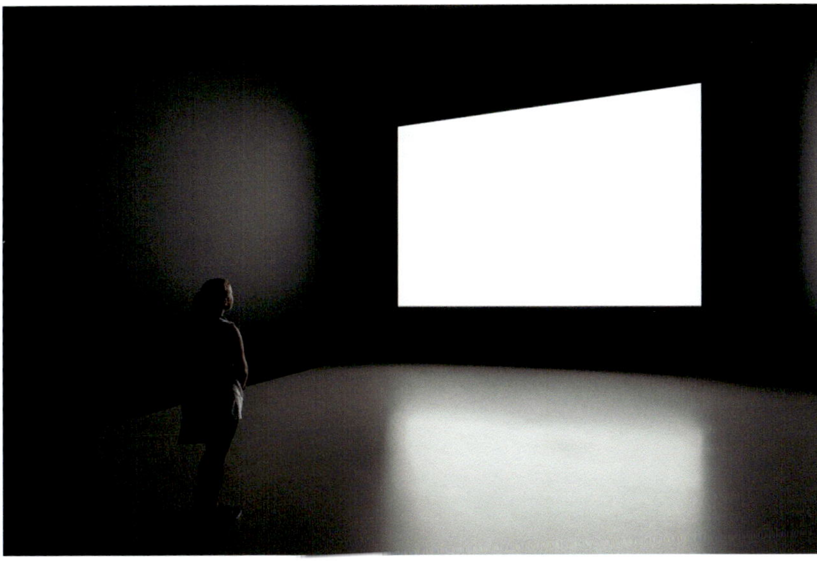

P16 Alfredo Jaar, *Lament of the Images*, 2002. Courtesy of Alfredo Jaar.

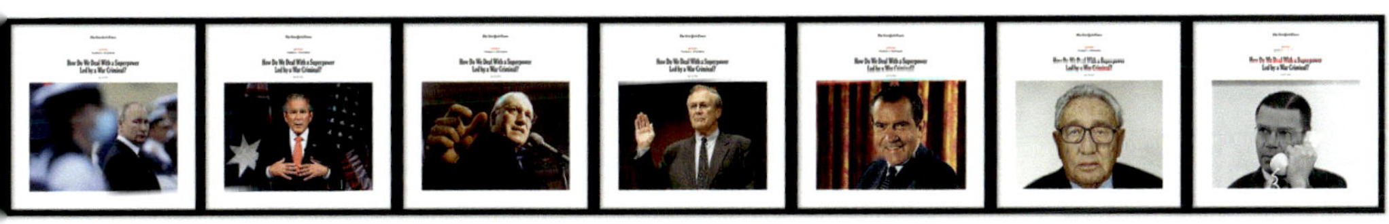

P17 Alfredo Jaar, *War Criminal*, 2022. Courtesy of Alfredo Jaar.

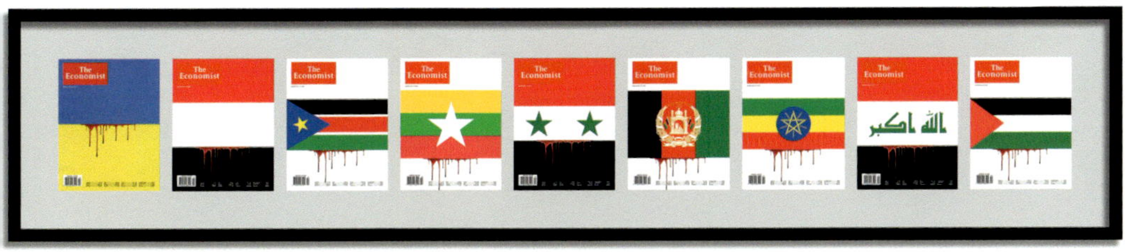

P18 Alfredo Jaar, *Mea Culpa*, 2022. Courtesy of Alfredo Jaar.

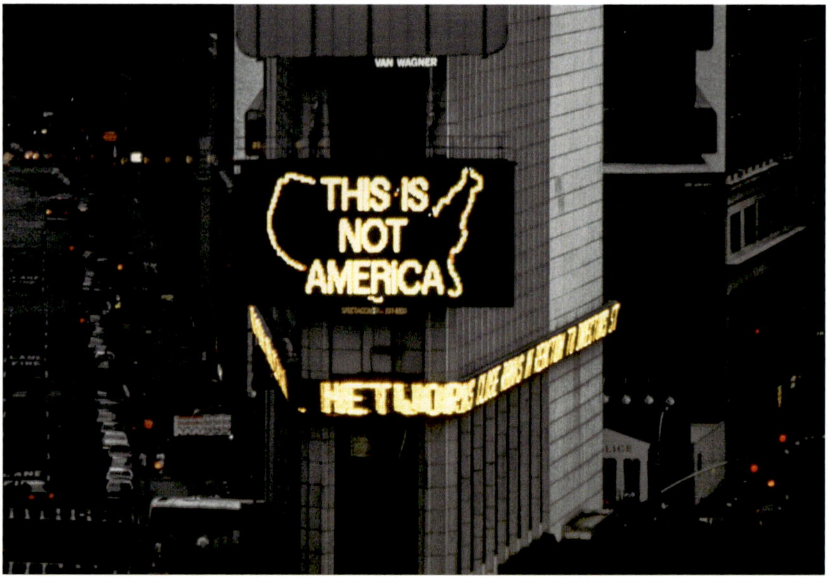

P19 Alfredo Jaar, *A Logo for America*, 1987. Courtesy of Alfredo Jaar.

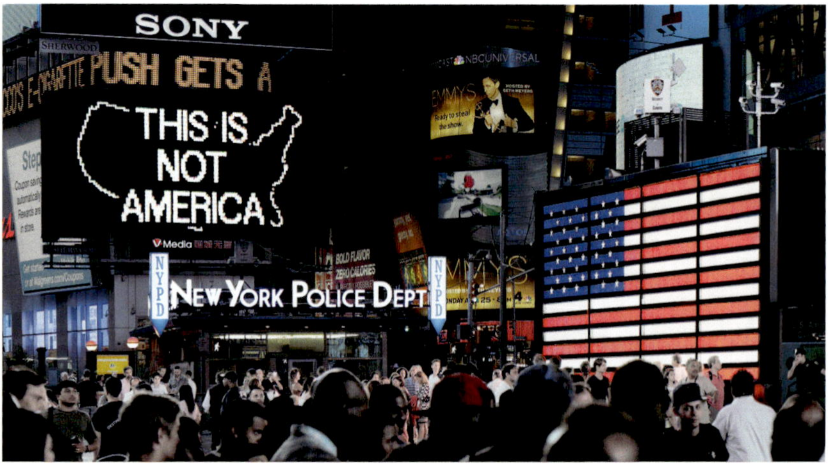

P20 Alfredo Jaar, *A Logo for America*, 1987/2014. Courtesy of Alfredo Jaar.

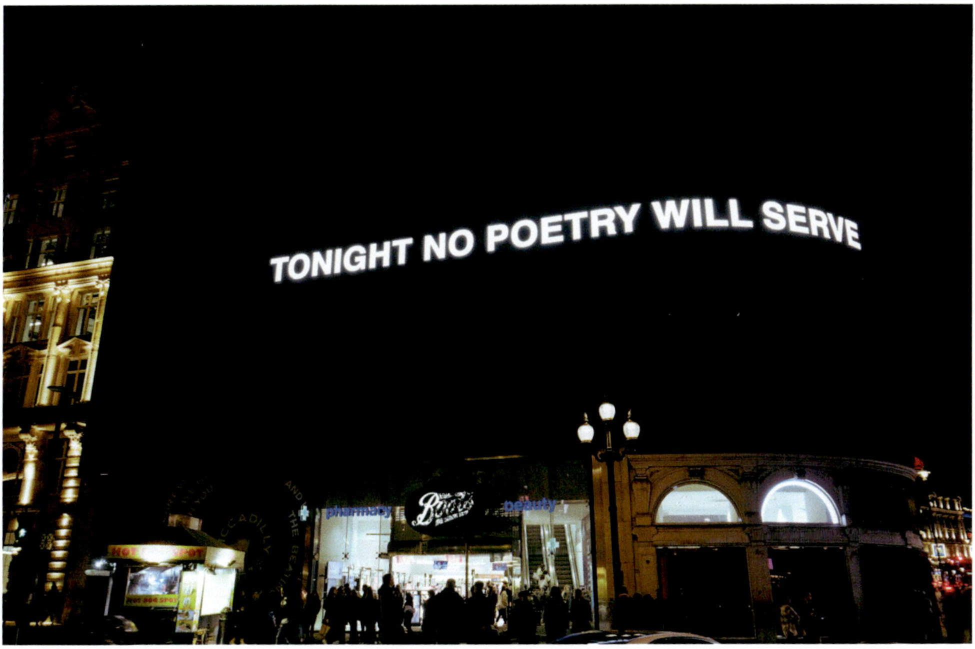

P21 Alfredo Jaar, *Tonight No Poetry Will Serve*, 2023. Courtesy of Alfredo Jaar.

P22 Gracia Barrios, *América, no invoco tu nombre en vano,* 1970. Courtesy of Museo de Arte Contemporáneo de Chile (MAC).

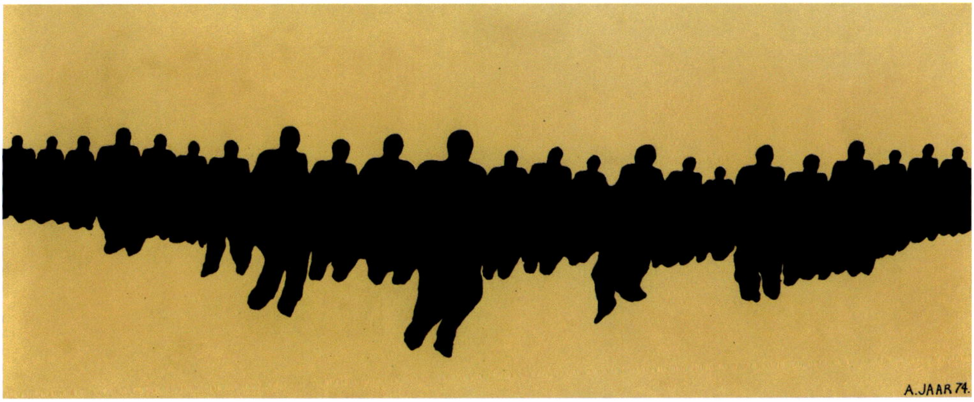

P23 Alfredo Jaar, *Exclamación, pánico y muerte,* 1974. Courtesy of Alfredo Jaar.

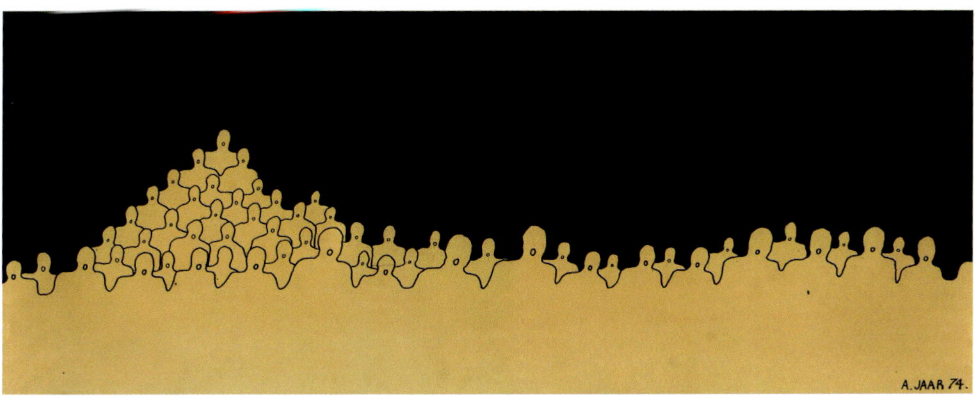

P24 Alfredo Jaar, *Exclamación, pánico y muerte,* 1974. Courtesy of Alfredo Jaar.

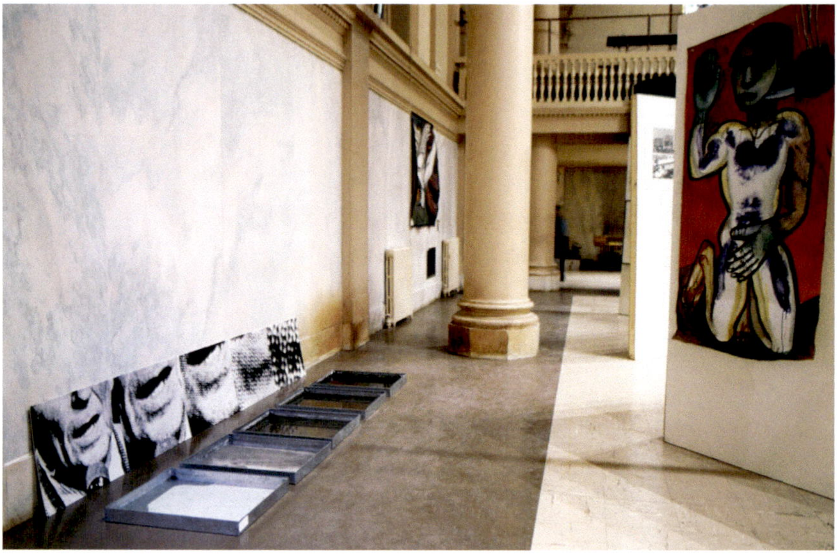

P25 Alfredo Jaar, *Strawberries*, 1983. Courtesy of Lucy Lippard.

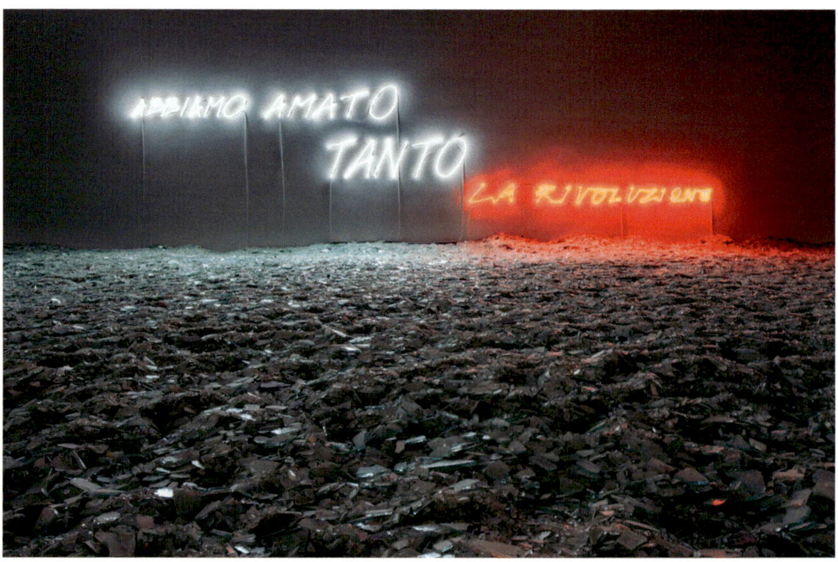

P26 Alfredo Jaar, *Abbiamo amato tanto la rivoluzione*, 2013. Courtesy of Alfredo Jaar.

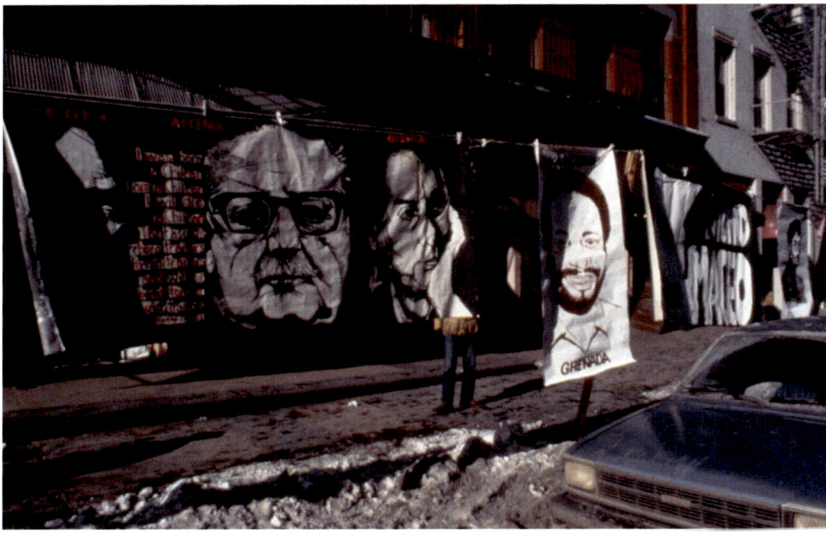

P27 Exhibition *La Verdadera Avenida de las Américas*, 1984. Courtesy of Lucy Lippard.

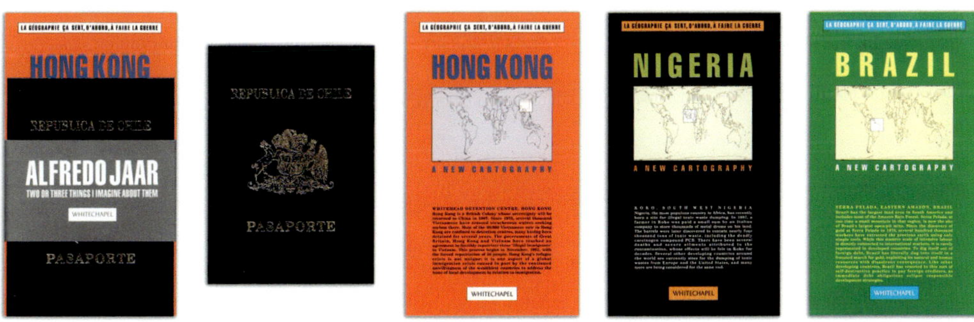

P28 Alfredo Jaar, *Two or Three Things I Imagine About Them*, 1992. Courtesy of Alfredo Jaar.

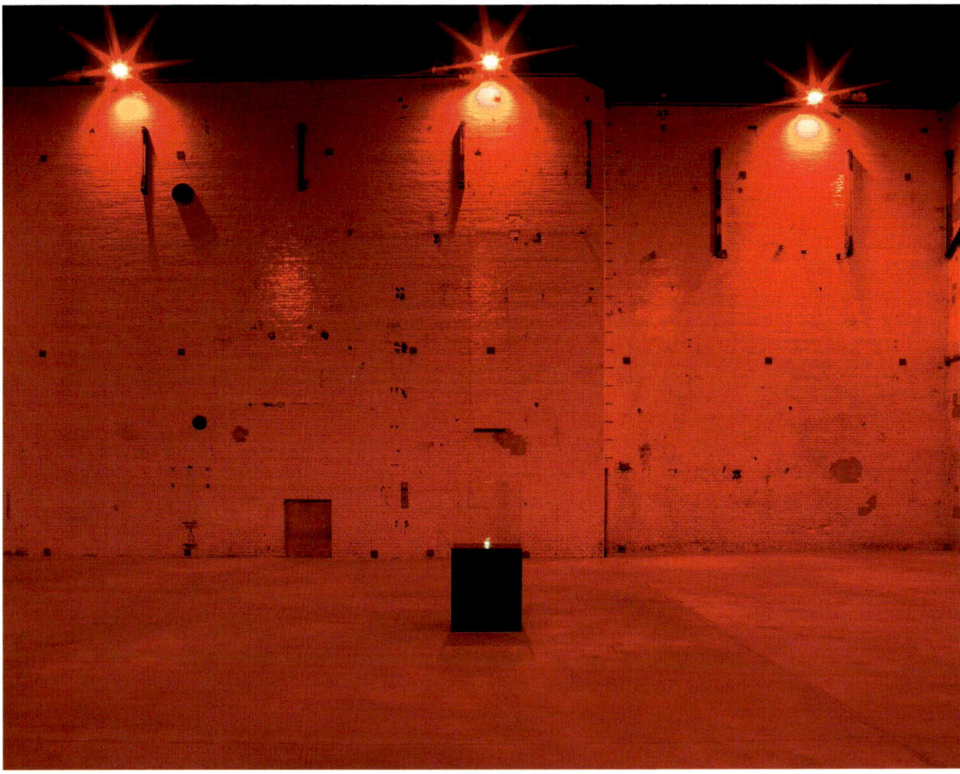

P29 Alfredo Jaar, *The End of the World*, 2024. Courtesy of Alfredo Jaar.

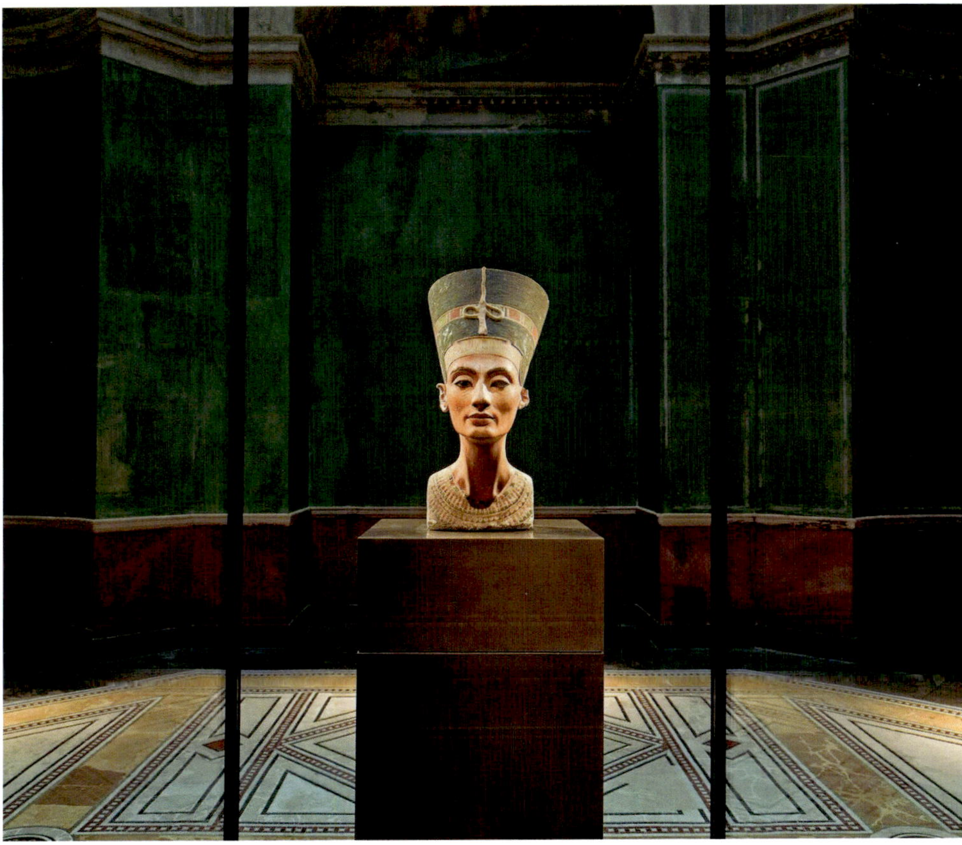

P30 Nefertiti bust, New Kingdom, Eighteenth Dynasty, Tell el-Amarna, Egypt, ca. 1340 BC. Neues Museum, Berlin.

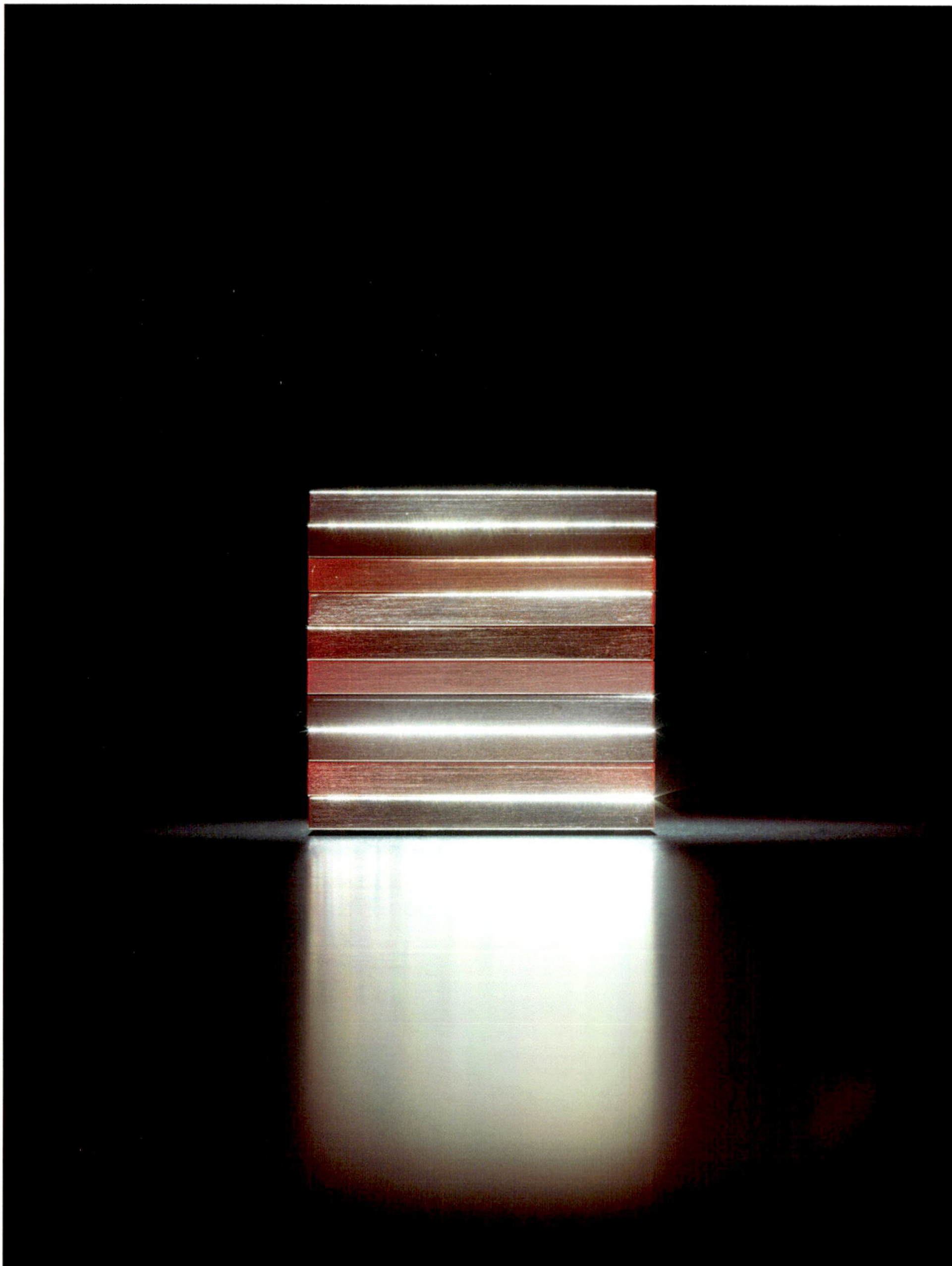

P31 Alfredo Jaar, *The End of the World* (detail), 2024. Courtesy of Alfredo Jaar.

So is the aesthetics of the unfinished within the heuristic of decolonial time. Accordingly, the work is a failed project that, as such, exposes the continuity of colonial rule in every aspect of human relations, including language, but also the hopes of a world that is yet to come.

In this sense, Jaar's animation and the words he uses to describe it remind us, as Judith Butler writes, that "for representation to convey the human, then representation must not only fail, but must *show* its failure."[16] With this in mind, one may deduce that if there is one equation that is not conflicted in Jaar's animation it is that semantics cannot be extricated from coloniality, or the conceptual continuity of a colonial world in our present modernity. Language is represented by Jaar as an extension of, in his words, "that reality that is out there."[17] And "that reality that is out there" is neither erased nor resolved. It is also not inverted in the binary model of modernity through a cartographic correction, as is the case with a genealogy of Latin American art commenced with Joaquín Torres García's famous 1943 drawing, *Inverted Map of South America*. In contrast, Jaar's work represents "that reality that is out there" as such, approaching it by outlining the appropriation of the word *America* by the United States to refer exclusively to itself as, in the words of literary and cultural critic Sacvan Bercovitch, an "over-arching synthesis, *e pluribus unum*."[18] As Jaar told a National Public Radio reporter in 1987 in the midst of the Times Square crowds while *A Logo for America* was being broadcast: "[the work] just reflects a certain reality that is out there, so when that reality changes, maybe language is going to change."[19]

Jaar's aim in *A Logo for America* is both to note that reality and *hopefully* to change it, fostering in the viewer the decolonial idea that things could be otherwise and that liberation is yet to come. Until the United States stops projecting itself as the single "America," representation of this problem *must* continue, just as decolonial struggles for liberation must endure. Furthermore, in continuing, representation *as* and *of* failure works as a decolonial project that contests the linear temporality of modernity and as such recalls that the reality shown by Jaar did not change in 2014, when the work was reenacted in a neoliberal Times Square and *formally* camouflaged with dozens of corporate signs including the word *America*. Neither was it begun in 1987, when he first created the work, but in the nineteenth century, with US imperialist expansionism and its relation to a more extensive history of coloniality, commencing with the conquest. It began with Americanity. As Jaar wrote in 1986 for his proposal for the work, "1492 is the year in which the conquest and colonization of the Americas began and the moment to which we can trace the emergence of a firm imperial Europe conceiving itself as the center of the whole world and the telos of civilization."[20] Acknowledging the coexistence of colonialism, its legacies, and linguistic imperialism, Jaar's aesthetics reenact failure as that which activates awareness of coloniality and a decolonial hope for change, reminding us that representation will not stop since decolonial hope will not stop. Thus the animation's loop is continuous, rendering an absence of a conclusive, final statement. Because it fails, it repeats; because it fails, it insists; because it fails, it resists, again and again.

Writing in the wake of decolonization struggles in Africa, Asia, and the Caribbean in the mid-twentieth century, Jean-Paul Sartre, who would soon after write the preface of Frantz Fanon's *The Wretched of the Earth* (1961), maintained: "[The poet] is certain of the total defeat of the human enterprise and arranges to fail in [their] own life in order to bear witness, by [their] individual defeat, to human defeat in general."[21] Advocating for the transformative potential of literature in our perception of the world, for Sartre the role of the poet and of poetry is to represent failure, repeatedly. Jaar, whose work is often informed by radical poetry, represents such entanglement in *Tonight No Poetry Will Serve* (plate 21). A three-minute film broadcast in November 2023 simultaneously from London's oval-like screen of Piccadilly Lights and public screens in Berlin, Milan, Seoul, and Tokyo, the work commences with the name of the artist rendered with bold black lettering over a white background.[22] After a few seconds, the screen turns to total darkness, until a sentence in bold white lettering appears slowly and subtly. Inverting light and dark as an allegory of photographic reproduction, a tactic often used by Jaar to insist on the decolonial joints between representation and failure, the sentence reads: "Tonight no poetry will serve."

"Tonight no poetry will serve" is the title of a poem written by the late Jewish poet and essayist Adrienne Rich. Published in 2011 in an eponymous book, the poem was a response by Rich to the declassification of US officials' atrocities committed in Guantánamo Bay against "presumed terrorists" during the George W. Bush administration.[23] "'Tonight I think no poetry will serve' thus suggests that no poetry can serve to mitigate such acts, they nullify language itself," Rich contended.[24] As such, the stanza recalls the limits of words in the face of human atrocities as well as how said atrocities are rendered through language describing personal experiences as an extension of the political. "One begins to write of the sensual body, but other bodies 'elsewhere' are terribly present," Rich said.[25] In light of that presence, which regards the world as war, Rich describes war as the following: "a texture of possession and deprivation, economic and religious dogmas, racism, colonialist exploitation, nationalism [and] unequal power."[26] War is everywhere. It has been naturalized under modernity. And as such, as Nelson Maldonado-Torres argues, war is increasing "the radical suspension or displacement of ethical and political relationships in favor of the propagation of a particular death ethic that renders massacre and different forms of genocide as natural."[27]

Rich's statement about poetry therefore is not about the inadequacy of this genre after war, as there is not an after to be found in modernity's continuum. It is not about reproducing Theodor Adorno's popularized statement that "to write poetry after Auschwitz is barbaric."[28] It is instead about the complexities of representation, or about representation after all. Viewed in this way, Rich's statement recalls René Magritte's 1929 negation of a pipe through its iconic and verbal renderings, or the fact that representation is never its reference or the thing it copies. It recalls that while images, and for that matter aesthetics, represent paradigms that cannot "serve" the criminalized and dehumanized under modernity, disobedient cultures are still there, here, designating instead of concealing, showing instead of hiding.[29] And, in the context of neoliberalism, they are here embracing, representing, and performing an aesthetic that radically negates hegemony's logic of production and creativity.[30] Similarly, in *A Logo for America*, Jaar's negation operates by denying a map and flag as "natural" and "universal" representations of "America," showing a linguistic problem that is yet not resolved. What has not been resolved is the ongoing presence of war and its effects on the oppressed, considering that war, as naturalized by modernity, prominently benefits the surplus aspirations of capitalism and the imperial nation-state.

In 2014, nine years before his work at Piccadilly Lights, Jaar used Rich's phrase to title his retrospective at the Museum of Contemporary Art Kiasma in Finland. The show included a little-known work created by Jaar in 2013 that was also titled *Tonight No Poetry Will Serve* (figure 3.1). Recalling the artist's 1974 series made in Chile, where he addressed the temporal massacre that resulted from the coup using a series of calendars, in this 2013 work, seven square prints are arranged in three rows. At the top of each print, Jaar adds the day of the week with red lettering over a black background. At the bottom, he adds the phrase "Tonight no poetry will serve." As the week passes, this phrase gradually appears to the viewer's eye, turning from its rendering with dark gray into a stark white. With the dark gray camouflaging itself with the black background on Monday and the stark white clearly distinguishing itself from the same background on Sunday, Jaar would use this temporal dimension of the text's visibility again nine years later in his film at Piccadilly Lights. And

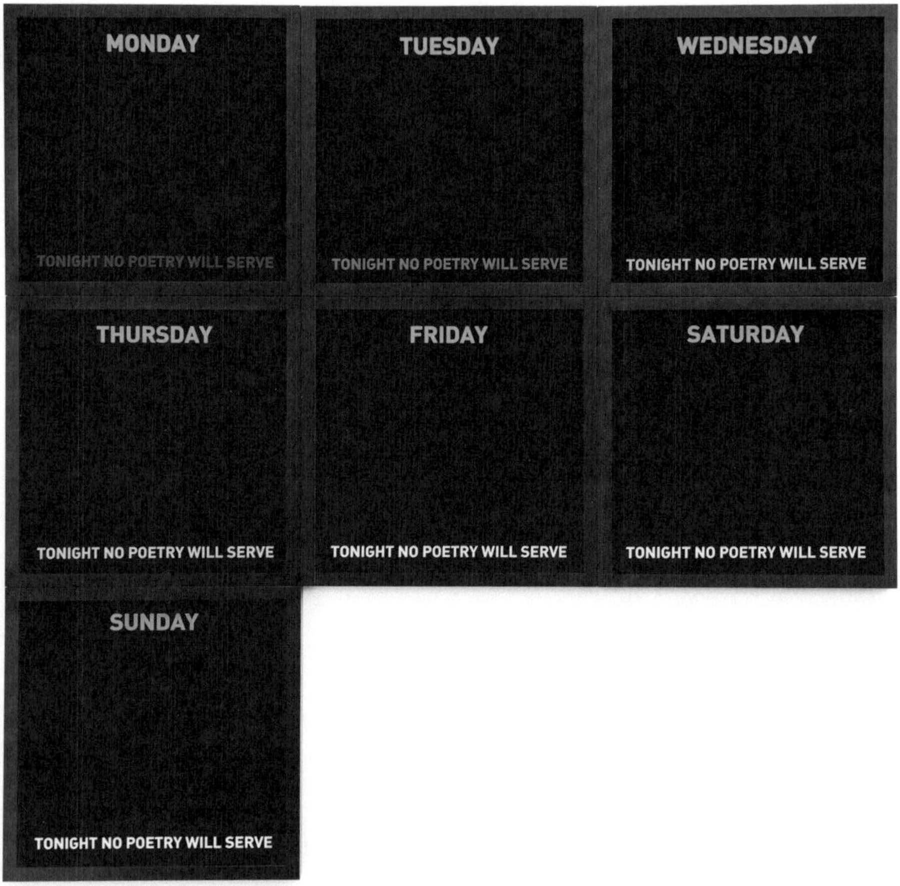

3.1 Alfredo Jaar, *Tonight No Poetry Will Serve*, 2013. Courtesy of Alfredo Jaar.

yet, regardless of its visibility, the phrase is still there, in print, just as coloniality's aggression is always there, undetachable from our "cruel modernity," as literary critic Jean Franco would say.[31] "The mentality and practice of conquest [have] extended well into [the] present," Franco remarks.[32]

Announcing Jaar's 2023 film at Piccadilly Lights, the press release declares: "The singular statement is the result of Jaar's ambition to strip language to stark essentials, which has already produced his landmark *A Logo for America*."[33] But this ambition, of course, is not free of danger. After all, thinking clearly about colonialism means thinking dangerously, as Césaire famously argued.[34] This means that under modernity, those participating in counter-representational acts such as anti-imperialist protests and radical poetry risk their life. "Our demands for ceasefire . . . have resulted in speakers facing reprimand or censorship, rather than determined actions being taken to make peace," said Jaar when referring to his 2023 film, which was made in response to the genocide in Gaza.[35] He explains:

> We are going through a very repressive moment when nuance is lost and free speech is threatened. . . . In this environment, I have turned to the words of anti-war campaigner and poet Adrienne Rich to reflect both the limits of language and the frustration felt by many that voices for peace and justice cannot sound out as clearly as we wish. . . . I am turning to today's poets, writers, and artists to support a forum for creative expression where the clear-sighted demands of humanity and empathy can be heard. In these times when politics have failed us miserably, art and culture are our only hope. Art is like the air we breathe, [as it] creates spaces of resistance, spaces of hope.[36]

In embracing hope, a noun that regards a feeling of expectation for something different to occur that has not yet happened, that is, that has so far failed, these spaces denoted by Jaar show that, in Maldonado-Torres's words, "projects of decolonization and liberation [are also projects] of happiness and hope, [and as such they] refer to forms of resistance and transformation that seek to undo dehumanizing practices and the suffering that ensues from them."[37] In this sense, in *A Logo for America*, Jaar demonstrates that the question of "America" as signifier and signified, or as term and meaning, is neither just one, nor can it easily be resolved, nor does it aim at being resolved at all. However, it can still be addressed critically from multiple scopes embracing hope and thus temporal relationalities through the reenactment of ongoing failure.

"Working with failures (cognitive and political) with their sensitive information is part of the process of reshaping thought, again and again, into a state of rebellion," writes sociologist Verónica Gago.[38] Failure thus propels resistance, and resistance to hegemony (of language, semantics, cartography, etc.) is enunciated from below. Joining a genealogy of subaltern modes and discourses in which political dissent and decolonial hope together are articulated from beneath, Jaar's works on failure, or his art on decolonial time at large, inhabit the same place of ruins, covered by modernity's buildings, and of wounds, covered by scars.[39] Ruins and wounds are not visible in modernity's public policies; they are not visible in modernity's cities, plazas, urban design, and iconic monuments and signs. But they still exist from below, in the time of behind, battling from multiple fronts, one of them being the coloniality of language embedded in the word *America*. In turn, failure from this perspective reminds us that memory matters, and thus that time is not linear. It reminds us that pasts and futures are contained in the presents, in the "open veins" of decolonial thinking, as Eduardo Galeano would say.[40] In effect, Jaar's works on failure reveal the coloniality that has caused such wounds to remain unhealed. Or, better said, they show that the ignored wounds of the before are still used in our neoliberal world to design the now, instead of the *nows*. That is why, in light of a dominant singular world in which time advances to progress and erase, the nomenclature *America* is still being used as the linguistic designation of the United States as an imperial nation-state.

COMBAT ZONES

In his 1999 book *Times Square Red, Times Square Blue*, Black queer science fiction writer Samuel R. Delany describes Times Square before its gentrification in the early 1990s as a "zone of contact" in which encounters between peoples beyond their class, sexuality, and race took place, creating circumstances that allowed new modes of solidarity.[41] "The population was incredibly heterogeneous—white, black, Hispanic, Asian, Indian, Native American, and a variety of Pacific Islanders. In the Forty-second Street area's sex theaters . . . I've met playwrights, carpenters, opera singers . . . guys with trust funds, guys on crutches, [and] guys who washed windows on the Empire State Building," writes Delany.[42] As he continues describing the type of encounters in Times Square that detached from traditional linguistic relations and personal interest: "Many encounters were wordless. Now and again, though, one would blossom into a conversation lasting hours, especially with those men less well-off, the out-of-work, or the homeless with nowhere else to go."[43] Resisting capitalism and opposing "networking," which Delany describes as encounters seeking profitable benefits, in Delany's thought the "zone of contact" signals spaces of communal belonging that are historically situated and deprived of surplus value, as with Times Square before its gentrification.[44] In the 1990s, however, these forms of interaction were drastically dismantled with the "cleaning," "zero tolerance," and "security" policies designed by then-Mayor of New York City Rudolph Giuliani, himself a lawyer, who, three decades later, would be a member of Donald Trump's legal team that sought to overturn the 2020 presidential election results.[45] Aiming to attract massive tourism and consumption in the age of neoliberal global expansionism by preventing tourists' fear of "zones of contact," Times Square was redesigned through a radical urban development plan, which has been maintained by policing and surveillance. "Toward the Eighth Avenue end, sandwiched between the subway arcade and the Georgia Chicken Kitchen, a mini grocery sold sodas and beer at only a dime per can more than you'd pay around the corner. Today they're gone," Delany laments.[46] Replacing small red sites such as pornographic theaters, stores, and kiosks with postmodern skyscrapers and chains of restaurants and stores, this design also increased the number of corporate billboards and signs, all advertising neoliberal consumption. It was in this "clean" or "contactless" plaza, as Delany would put it, that Jaar reenacted *A Logo for America* for the first time in 2014, twenty-seven years after its original projection (plate 20).

This was also the first time I saw an exhibition by Jaar in the United States. I remember that moment well. It was a humid night by the end of the summer, and I walked from my fifth-floor walkup apartment on Twenty-Ninth Street and Tenth Avenue to Forty-Second Street and the junction of Broadway and Seventh Avenue, arriving at Times Square a few minutes before midnight. At 11:57 p.m., the work started its reenactment. Mirroring Times Square's neoliberal advertising spectacle and consumerist abundance, the animation was broadcast on sixty different screens, camouflaging itself with dozens of signs and billboards from corporations including the word *America*, such as Bank of America, American Apparel, American Eagle, and the ABC morning news program *Good Morning America*. In this context, as one critic noted, the work showed "how easily and casually [the problem formulated by Jaar] has come to pass."[47]

Meanwhile, dozens of popular characters from Disney, *Sesame Street*, and Marvel wandered the streets in Times Square, interacting with tourists, commuters, and the art audience of Jaar's piece through capitalist techniques of profitable "networking," in Delany's terms. Also present at the plaza were characters from popular culture, such as Elvis, Marilyn Monroe, and Naked Cowboy, the latter a well-known character in New York City who, in short, represents himself. I remember him holding an acoustic guitar and wearing only a pair of boots, a Western hat, and underwear—all items showing his name and that of Trump rendered with the colors of the "American" flag. Indeed, it is worth mentioning that in 2009, representing his desire to lead New York City, Naked Cowboy campaigned to run for mayor, denoting the fine line between humans and advertising and, for that matter, companies. After all, as the US Supreme Court ruled in 2014, corporations are people in the eyes of the law.[48]

From the paradigm of modernity, Delany's "zone of contact" has vanished in the past, buried in oblivion under the ground of Times Square *as* an amusement park. This is what Jean Baudrillard meant in his critique of the hyperreal: "Disneyland [is] presented as imaginary in order to make us believe that the rest is real, whereas all of Los Angeles and the America that surrounds it are no longer real, but belong to the hyperreal order and the order of simulation."[49] It should be pointed out, however, that Baudrillard (not to mention translations of his work) still uses "*l'Amérique*" to refer to the United States, "naturalizing" the imperial relation between signified and signifier in the French language. As Jaar himself notes, "[The misuse of the word *America*] has become a global problem. [In France, they] talk about America, or *l'Amérique*, to refer only to the U.S."[50] In assuming such form of identification, Baudrillard equates the "real" with "liberal America," ignoring other forms of inhabiting through decolonial practices of relating in a memory politics that resists assimilation. As the Chilean-born, New York–based Two-Spirit writer, performer, and sex worker Iván Monalisa Ojeda writes in *Las Biuty Queens* (2021): "We're nocturnal butterflies at the end of the twentieth century, and in the heart of Times Square, no less."[51] Jaar's *A Logo for America* likewise acknowledges the continuity of these relational modes of existing and caring, embracing hope through the work's reenactments. Context in this sense means not only corporate "America" but the presence of radical practices that, although made invisible or criminalized by (white) "America," still gravitate on the earth from the perspective of decolonial time. Put differently, Delany's "zones of contact" are still there, where ruins dwell in the form of wounds, and, as such, they exist in what cultural theorist Mary Louise Pratt calls the "contact zones."[52]

According to Pratt, who introduced this concept in 1990, contact zones are "social spaces where cultures meet, clash, and grapple with each other, often in contexts of highly asymmetrical relations of power, such as colonialism, slavery, or their aftermaths as they are lived out in many parts of the world today."[53] From the perspective of the Americas, these spaces have existed since the conquest, as shown in Inka intellectual Felipe Guamán Poma de Ayala's artist's book–like chronicle *El primer nueva corónica y buen gobierno*.[54] Finished around 1615 and composed of 1,200 pages that include images and text, in the chronicle, which he sent to King Philip III of Spain, Guamán Poma argues that a peaceful instead of asymmetrical encounter would benefit both cultures, with the term *encounter* here meaning just that: a proposal for a reciprocal future.[55] Mixing Quechua and ungrammatical Spanish to revisit the conquest's account, "Guamán Poma mirrors back to the Spanish (in their language, which is alien to him) an image of themselves that they often suppress and will therefore surely recognize," as Pratt explains. "Such are the dynamics of language, writing, and representation in contact zones."[56] Defying annihilation and thus assimilation by using the colonizer's representational epistemologies, albeit altered through intentional grammatical mistakes, Guamán Poma's text demonstrates that the colonized knew their message could be understood by the monolingual and monocultural oppressor, even if only in terms of form. They knew, we could add, that for the colonizer to "find in colonized peoples the ability to express complex cosmological, social, scientific, erotic, economic meaning is at odds with their reduction to inferior, animal-like beings," as philosopher Gabriela A. Veronelli argues, drawing from Quijano's concept of coloniality of power.[57] Put another way, they knew that "if the idea of race constructs the perception of the colonizers, then the colonized must have been for them less than human beings, and thus without any complex form of communication, that is without language."[58] And, while there is no record that this work ever reached the king—this document so famous today was "discovered" only in the early twentieth century in the Danish Royal Archive—its performativity at the outset of coloniality shows the long-standing existence of the complexities of decolonial struggles, including that of language, within the contact zone, as well as the power of language as a form of representation that can simultaneously resist coloniality.

In *A Logo for America*, Jaar uses the language of advertising, just as did Guamán Poma de Ayala with Spanish, not to assimilate power but to enter into the conversation with neoliberal totality. Put differently, he uses the market's representational patterns so that the work can be at least formally understood as the first step for an encounter *as* a "contact zone." The message, however, from the perspective of the art world, ended up placing Jaar's animation at the very throne of Latin American art's emergence into the global market. Curator Mari Carmen Ramirez explains: "Jaar's animation worked because it was direct and used the language of advertising. In the late 1980s and early 1990s, auction houses such as Sotheby's and Christie's started collecting Latin American art artists such as Alfredo Jaar, Doris Salcedo and Guillermo Kuitca, all who entered the market with their most advertising works. Alfredo represents that."[59]

Revealing the colonial nature of art history, criticism, and certainly the art world, success has paradoxically placed Jaar's work as a victorious example of anti-imperialism within a discipline that has so prominently relied on progressive time. But since success erases the "contact zone" and thus the representation of decolonial time, success is precisely what Jaar's work rebuts. And so the artist fails, yet again. His message has been heard, yes, but within the paradigm of the neoliberal encounter. In allowing the subaltern to speak, the binominal time of modernity remains intact, inverting the colonial idea of the North with that of the South. As we have learned from literary theorist Gayatri Spivak, if the subaltern speaks, then resistance is over.[60] Or, as we observe in mainstream curatorial practices celebrating the paradigm of the encounter in art fairs, museums, biennials, and so on, art discourses, just as language is an extension of the world, are not yet decolonized. As such, the practice of representing failure must continue. Speaking *within* the conditions of modernity means silence. Speaking *adentro y en contra* those conditions means decolonial resistance within the "contact zones," yes, but from a position of combat that Maldonado-Torres calls "combat zones."[61]

Drawing from Fanon's *The Wretched of the Earth*, Maldonado-Torres argues that, for the Martinican-born psychiatrist, writer, and activist, "the goal or telos of global modern/colonial catastrophe is the complete eradication or domestication of the ideas, symbols, practices, and institutions that are fundamentally different from or that challenge the idea of modern Western civilization."[62] Highlighting the unfinished state of both coloniality and the decolonial, Maldonado-Torres further states that since "the catastrophe is still in the making . . . , it continues to generate, not so much *contact zones* between the colonizer and the colonized, but combat zones where coloniality is not only resisted but also countered and defied."[63] From this perspective, resistance differs from combat, with the former embracing a position of negation toward modernity and the latter a position of fight. Put differently, the former embraces the acknowledgment of coloniality, and the latter a radical mode of being, thinking, and praxis together against coloniality. Identifying this difference after Fanon's three stages experienced by intellectuals working in colonial contexts, Maldonado-Torres maintains that, for Fanon, the first stage regards epistemological assimilation; the second, a "precombat stage," where the intellectual notices the colonial difference or the zones of contact; and the third, in Maldonado-Torres's words, regards the "combat stage, that comes into being when the intellectual is part of the struggle and when writing is no longer the unique domain of the intellectual, both because intellectuals do not only contribute to the combat by writing and because many other writers emerge."[64]

Jaar's art represents that third stage, writing ongoing relationalities through representational forms that display agency in those depicted by the decolonial tropes of mourning, accountability, and failure. This is shown, for instance, in works by Jaar honoring women writers and activists such as Dore Ashton, Amira Hass, and Adrienne Rich, as well as in works regarding the collectivity of cultures of resistance that mourn, as I show in chapter 1. This is also shown in artworks denouncing modernity's perpetrators, such as Kissinger, which the artist has elaborated through collaborations with human rights organizations and lawyers working from the realm of international jurisdiction, such as Wolfgang Kaleck, as I show in chapter 2 (figure 2.16). And, as discussed in this chapter and across this book, the third stage is also visible in Jaar's art critique of Americanity, which he offers not only from the museum but also in the public space as a site of combat. This is the case for *A Logo for America* and *Tonight No Poetry Will Serve*. Commenting on the latter, Jaar said:

> When they invited me to create a work at Piccadilly Lights that responded to what was happening in Gaza, I wanted to write something like: "Ceasefire Now" or "Stop the Genocide." They didn't allow me, so I almost withdrew and then said to myself: Alfredo, you live within the system and have handled censorship before in Chile. If I said no, that three-minute advertising space was going to be used by another advertiser selling potato chips during November 2023, so I used it and projected the phrase from Rich: "Tonight No Poetry Will Serve." In saying "tonight," Rich suggests that it could work tomorrow. While declaring herself helpless, she also declares the usefulness of poetry and art.[65]

Jaar's words reveal the combative zone of decolonial discourse and praxis, one that is aware of its incompleteness and the role of culture in such a struggle. They also reveal that Jaar is aware of living within modernity—"within the system," he says—and that it is from this awareness that he can act and fight back, acknowledging the failure of the present and the possibility of liberation in the future. From a zone of combat, Jaar's art is about representing hope. And, of course, he is not alone. As British writer Annie Rockson maintains in her poem accompanying Jaar's intervention: "I hope you can wait for the future you so long to see."[66] Broadcast from CIRCA's website alongside other poems addressing Rich's verse in relation to Jaar's film, Rockson's words advocate for decolonial time and thus critical hope. The same can be said about Ghanaian artist Joseph Awuah-Darko, whose poem is broadcast from the same platform. Elaborating on the potential of decolonial language to defeat genocide, Awuah-Darko says: "Let our words serve as architects / constructing bridges of empathy, / let us shine a light in the shadows, / allowing truth to permeate. / Let us draw a line on the dead counted. / Cease. / Cease. / Cease."[67]

"When I moved to New York in 1982, I realized that Latin America didn't exist there. It was then that the program I gave to myself began."[68] This program Jaar mentions refers to works on the question of America he started developing well before he projected his famous animation in Times Square in 1987. *America, America* is one example (figure 3.2). In a series of five black-and-white Photostats made in 1982, on each of the five units, overlapped with an image of the White House facade shown at the center and slightly angled to the right, Jaar writes different sentences with the following words: *America, north, south, us, our, their, them, plus, minus, and equals.* Creating linguistic equations such as "South America (us), plus North America (them), equals America (our)," and "America (our) minus America (their) equals South America (us)," Jaar concludes his series with the phrase "Our America Is Our America" (figure 3.3). In concluding the work with this phrase, Jaar evokes Cuban revolutionary and writer José Martí's (1853–95) 1891 manifesto, "Nuestra América" (Our America).

Written in the years leading up to the Spanish-US War of 1898, Martí's "Nuestra América" denounces the emergence of the United States as a new hemispheric power. After all, the United States had appropriated almost half of Mexico in 1848, becoming, in the words of Miguel Rojas Mix, "a continent that goes from the Atlantic to the Pacific."[69] "What is 'Ours'?" Martí asks, responding to that question in the very title of the essay: "America." And that America, Martí continues, resists not only the tiger's (an allegorical figure of the United States) "violence . . . inherited from four centuries" and a "Greece which is not ours" but also "nineteen centuries of monarchy in France."[70] This latter is significant, as in the decades prior to Martí writing "Nuestra América," French intellectuals and Francophile Latin American elites began to use the nomenclature *Latin America* to define the republics newly independent from the Portuguese and Spanish crowns.

This idea of "Latin America" comes from another idea: "Latinidad" (Latinity), which served to differentiate "Latin" countries from the Teutonic north, represented at that time by Germany, England, and the United States.[71] With the entire world as European, as French statesman Michel Chevalier stated in his 1836 *Lettres sur l'Amérique du Nord*, the Anglo-Saxon and Protestant North belonged to England, and the Latin, Catholic South to France. By

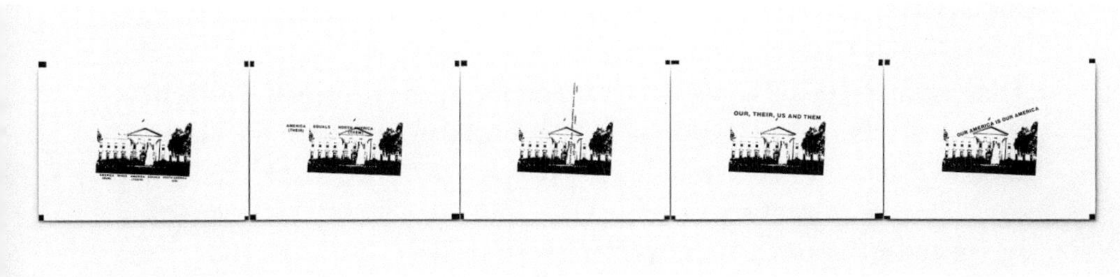

3.2 Alfredo Jaar, *America, America*, 1982. Courtesy of Alfredo Jaar.

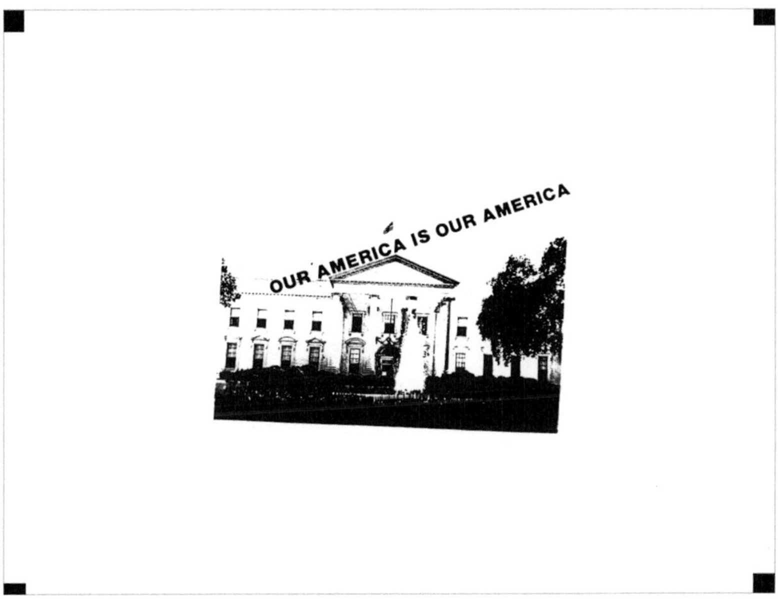

3.3 Alfredo Jaar, *America, America* (detail), 1982. Courtesy of Alfredo Jaar.

turning its face to France and its back to Spain and Portugal, Colombian José María Torres Caicedo wrote, "[if] there is Anglo-Saxon America . . . what other scientific name applies but Latin to the Spanish, French, Portuguese America?"[72] Providing French and Latin American elites with the linguistic tools to depict the region as its own "prey," as the United States was rapidly expanding its control across the region, this new idea of "Latin America" meant and continues to mean a colonial enterprise.

This is why Martí deliberately uses the word *America* without the qualifier "Latin."[73] He writes: "The history of America, of the Incas"; "[the America of] the black man [who] sings at night the music in his heart"; and "our mestizo America," including in his idea of "mestizo" Indigenous and Black peoples.[74] In this sense, Martí's Latin America as Ours is a call for hemispheric hope and resistance against capitalist and imperialist powers, as well as a critique of Latinidad as a colonial construct that reproduces not only Indigenous but also Black erasure.[75] In the US nation-state context, these erasures were noted by Sylvia Wynter: "The exclusion of the Black and the Red . . . was correlated with a school curriculum whose system of knowledge represented the nation as being bonded by the shared biogenetic characteristic of 'Whiteness.'"[76] From this perspective, America as discovered and appropriated by the United States means whiteness, and to exist as the guard of capitalism and vice versa, it entails the empirical invisibility of racial minorities living in the United States as well as low-income peoples and the unhoused. However, it does so paradoxically by the very appropriation of Indigenous land as private property and the development of various forms of labor.

These two ideas of America—the utopian, unified, and liberated Our America imagined by Martí, on the one hand, and the United States as a nation-state that excludes racial, ethnic, and economic minorities while aiming at regional control through neoliberal expansionism, on the other hand—are represented by Jaar in his *America, America*. This can be explained both historically and conceptually. Regarding the former, Jaar created the work in a historical moment in which Martí's manifesto had just become known in US intellectual circles through the work of the Cuban poet and intellectual Roberto Fernández Retamar.[77] It was also the moment in which Jaar had just self-exiled from the dictatorship in Chile. Upon his arrival in New York, he realized, through a linguistic designation that "shocked" him, about the relation between America and whiteness as described by Wynter.[78] On the other hand, regarding the conceptual presence of these ideas in Jaar's *America, America*, it is essential to note that while Martí's "Our América" is literally quoted in Jaar's work—he writes "Our America is our America" in capital letters (figure 3.3)—the artist reframes Martí's discourse. While in Martí's manifesto, "Nuestra América" triumphs, in Jaar's *America, America,* it fails, again and again, showing over time the continuity of such failure by insisting on the presence of an imperial nation-state built upon settler colonialism and racial erasure. In the last Photostat, the artist keeps the image of the White House in the background, formulating an equation in which text and image correspond. In so doing, Jaar evokes Martí's call for hemispheric liberation while also acknowledging that said call has not yet been resolved. In other words, the artist expands Martí's manifesto by highlighting the continuity of a decolonial project that is still unfolding, adding to Martí's strategies for resisting imperialism in the very notion of decolonial failure in and beyond the nation-state, and in and beyond the contact zones.

In the mid-nineteenth century, observing the US appropriation of a major territory of Mexico in the Mexican-American War (1846–48) and its intervention in Nicaragua in 1856, Chilean writer Francisco Bilbao (1823–65) began using the term *Latin America* as a concept of liberation, social inclusion, racial belonging, and certainly decolonial hope.[79] Freely interchanging the term with the nomenclature *America,* in his famous 1856 speech "Iniciativa de la América," Bilbao called upon the "Latin American world" to collectively resist "Yankee consumerism," stating: "America [is] in danger. Whoever does not see it should renounce to the future."[80] The "earl[iest] promoter of the idea of Latin America as a democratic, all-inclusive polity," Bilbao would later influence Martí's thinking on the question of America.[81] "The scorn of our formidable neighbor who does not know us is our America's greatest danger," wrote Martí.[82]

This genealogy of danger expanded further into the mid-twentieth century, when Césaire called for a critical and thus dangerous subjectivity, insisting on the "essential" question of colonization and its corollary institution: the market.[83] More recently, for the Zapatistas in Chiapas, Mexico, "it's all about the question [of] how to live in a dangerous world defined by lack of equality, respect, and care."[84] Responding and reacting to the dangers of coloniality, the Zapatistas disobey sequential time, living in an alternative world in which "many worlds are possible" and thus multiple temporalities. So did Martí in the late nineteenth century: from the front of a united "Our America," he battled the same danger through the allegory of the tiger, wherein he defeated it. That Martí defeated the tiger *only* in literature—he died in 1895 in Cuba during a military action while fighting against Spanish troops—is no less real than how the Zapatistas live in Chiapas. The locus of knowledge in decolonial action and thinking exceeds mono-temporal subjects in mono-spatial life.

Put differently, the power of imagination to fight coloniality can also generate possibilities of existence and thus realities despite, or precisely because of, the dismissal of a decolonial imagination by Western reason.

In the case of Bilbao, however, danger is not defeated. This is also not the case of Jaar and many others in cultures of resistance, or at least not yet. Still, in the battle against danger, acknowledgment of war and ongoing hope coexist. In this sense, Bilbao's thought remembers the letter Gramsci sent from prison to his brother Carlo: "My mind is pessimistic, but my will is optimistic."[85] It remembers the philosophical impulse that motivates Jaar to create his art, relocating its origins before and beyond Gramsci, in the invention of the Americas in the sixteenth century, or in the origins of both the contact and the combat zones.

LIBERATION

In her groundbreaking text, *Ch'ixinakax Utxiwa: On Decolonising Practices and Discourses*, Bolivian theorist Silvia Rivera Cusicanqui states that under the logic of modernity, a coloniality of language is "particularly evident in the republican phase, during which the state adopted egalitarian ideologies while at the same time erasing the citizenship rights of the majority of the population."[86] This also holds true for the term *Latin America*. In the mid-nineteenth century, Bilbao, upon learning about the imperialist meaning of the term bestowed on it by French and Latin American elites while Napoleon III was invading Mexico, stopped using the term, publishing his signature book on hemispheric unity against imperialism as *La América en peligro* (America in danger, 1862).[87] This means that Bilbao's use of the term *Latin America* was not just a "sporadic" and "occasional" concept, as has been argued.[88] Instead, this discontinuity responded to the power of language in the era of "egalitarian" struggles, that is, in the epoch of the nation-state.

A century passed, and in the late 1960s and early 1970s, Bilbao's idea of Latin America as decolonial liberation was resumed, and quite widely. This linguistic turn emerged simultaneously to a distinct philosophy in Latin America, the philosophy of liberation, which merges theory and praxis, or aesthetics and politics.[89] Formulated from ethical and situated experiences and epistemologies, the philosophy of liberation was informed by political uprisings against fascism in the region and Martinican writer Frantz Fanon's critique of "the colonial experience in its racial dimension [through] the trauma of the encounter with the imperial and racist Other."[90] Liberation, therefore, means not to emancipate within a given reality or *within* modernity. It means to transform that reality from epistemic and aesthetic paradigms that, to start, acknowledge the hopes of the past. It means the decolonial: "The notion of decolonization, as opposed to the concepts of independence or emancipation, contains less of a sense that it can be granted by another. Decolonization implies action on the part of the colonized. For this reason, the concept is more directly linked to the notion of Liberation than to the other terms," writes Maldonado Torres.[91]

In Chile, this idea of Latin America as a regional project against imperialism was promoted by Salvador Allende.[92] Interweaving culture and politics as an aesthetic juncture from where to enact the anti-imperialist fight, in his Popular Unity program Allende notes: "The social process that emerges from the triumph of the people will develop a new culture with a critical position about our reality, Latin America. . . . The deep transformations to come need a pueblo that is socially conscious and solidary; one that struggles against capitalism, individualism, and cultural colonization, making art closer to the masses and vice versa."[93]

Within this context, the 1969 exhibition *América, no invoco tu nombre en vano* (*America, I Do Not Invoke Your Name in Vain*) developed. Supported by Allende and installed in front of the Museum of Contemporary Art in Santiago in a circus-like tent as a symbol of a transitional instead of a permanent time, the show featured artworks in traditional and experimental media and literary readings. Curated by Miguel Rojas Mix, founder of the Instituto de Arte y Cultura Latinoamericano at the Universidad de Chile, the exhibition was titled after a poem by Pablo Neruda that Rojas Mix described as a declaration of "love" and "hope" toward "Nuestra América" and thus a memorial to Jose Martí.[94] As Neruda wrote elsewhere: "But Martí with hope and gunfire / awakened the daydreamer and the peasant / building with blood and thought / the architecture of the new light."[95] Celebrated by the local media, the show represented, according to one critic, "our dangerous reality" through "art that engaged with life."[96] Likewise acknowledging the show's relation to Allende's program and Bilbao's *La América en peligro*, another critic put it this way: "Addressing social, racial, political, economic and cultural issues—including the Indigenous, black, and European tradition in Latin America—the show represents our [Latin American] reality through artistic expressions."[97]

One of the works in the show was Gracia Barrios's *América, no invoco tu nombre en vano* (*America, I Do Not Invoke Your Name in Vain*) (plate 22). Titled like the poem and exhibition, the work is a large horizontal painting made with loose brushstrokes and a minimal pallet of black, white, and earth hues. In it, women and men walk together, a conglomeration in the streets, filling the canvas completely from left to right and top to bottom. Protesting in collectivity for the transformation of society and the dismantling of conventions, this critique is formulated by Barrios in both content and form, challenging the binominal logic of modernity and modern art by blurring the limits between foreground and background, figuration and abstraction, and positive and negative.[98] Representing the masses as a testimony of "Nuestra América Latina," the pueblo in Barrios's painting is an allegory of a "Latin" America as "Ours."[99] It is an allegory of liberation.

In 1974, Alfredo Jaar created a diptych composed of two horizontal drawings. The drawing on the top showcases black silhouettes against the light, creating a collective body of liberation that evokes Barrios's painting in both content and form (plate 23). The drawing on the bottom showcases light silhouettes against the dark, with every figure in the image having a rounded, open mouth (plates 24). The figures in this component of Jaar's diptych, created a year after the overthrow of Allende and the Popular Unity, are making exclamations, panicking about the risk of being imprisoned, tortured, killed, or made to disappear. And thus the work's title is *Exclamación, pánico y muerte* (*Exclamation, panic and death*). Together, both drawings recall the twofold aspects of life under modernity: colonial danger and liberatory revolution. They recall the statement so often used by Jaar—inspired by the life and literature of Samuel Beckett and Antonio Gramsci—which interlaces war and hope: "I can't go on, I'll go on." And more specifically in this case, they recall the US-backed Chilean troops advancing violently and dangerously to attack La Moneda on the day of the coup while also honoring Barrios's painting depicting a Pueblo Americano that resists the world's atrocities through hope. They recall, in short, the analytic of failure that motivates Jaar and many others in cultures of resistance to continue creating, searching for a paradigm shift that embraces a decolonial liberation that is yet to come. As Diné artist Demian DinéYazhi' writes with red neon light in an installation for the Whitney Biennial in New York City in 2024: "We must stop imagining destruction + extraction + deforestation + cages + torture + displacement + surveillance + genocide! we must stop predicting apocalypses + fascist governments + capitalist hierarchies! we must pursue + predict + imagine routes toward liberation!"[100]

In the ruins of the Cold War, the idea of Latin America as Ours, despite the advent of fascist regimes and the failure of utopia, has remained, or "at least ideally."[101] As Jaar himself told an interviewer in 1984 when asked about whether or not he missed Chile: "What I miss is Latin America, that Latin America that could be." "Has it ever existed?" the interviewer continued.

"No," Jaar responded, "never. But I am working on that. Well, that is probably what my work is all about!"[102] Or, as poet Raúl Zurita tells Jaar in the video-recorded interviews of his *Studies on Happiness* (1979–81): "Then, crushing my burned cheek / Against the rough grit of this rocky soil / —like a good South American— / for a minute more I'll raise my face toward heaven / because I who believed in happiness / shall have seen once more the radiant stars."[103] The idea of Latin America is embedded in Zurita's body, in his face touching the stony road and rising to see the stars. Latin America is therefore represented in a twofold metaphor that announces and denounces, embracing both pain and hope, history and memory, and dictatorship and resistance. And poetry is there to prove it.

In 1981, Alfredo Jaar made a video performance inspired by a 1979 photograph by Susan Meiselas, which she had taken in Matagalpa in the last days of the Sandinista uprising against the Anastasio Somoza dictatorship of Nicaragua (figure 3.4).[104] In Meiselas's image, three young members of the Frente Sandinista de Liberación Nacional (FSLN, Sandinista National Liberation Front) stand in the foreground. At the center right, two of them take cover behind sandbags. They hold M16 rifles, likely obtained from Cubans who, in turn, likely obtained them from the United States, which had confiscated the weapons in Vietnam.[105] They are ready to attack, to defend, to fight. On the left, a third Sandinista stands with what seems to be a bolt-action rifle on his back. He looks forward, his gaze detached from the action, while playing a clarinet. From a decolonial approach, this last unexpected scene in the barricade represents hope and liberation from the US-sponsored regime of Somoza. More broadly, it represents a longer struggle against the Somoza dynasty, which seized power in 1936 after the assassination of Augusto César Sandino, the anti-imperialist leader who had revived Martí's project of "Our America" in Nicaragua in the second quarter of the twentieth century.

Jaar, as he recalls, was "deeply touched" by this "fragment," by this "detail" in Meiselas's photograph.[106] Evoking Roland Barthes's *punctum* as that element that "rises from the scene [and] shoots out of it like an arrow," in his video performance titled *OPUS 1981/Andante Desesperato*, Jaar reenacts the *punctum* through sonic repetition, blowing a clarinet as hard as he can until utter exhaustion.[107] He blows for seven minutes and fifteen seconds, until he fails to continue, yet not without trying to do so. Created at the outset of the Reagan-sponsored Contra war in Nicaragua, Jaar's work speaks to a regional sense of hope, liberation, and solidarity, while also denoting the constraints in dictatorship Chile, where he created the work in total isolation to avoid censorship and

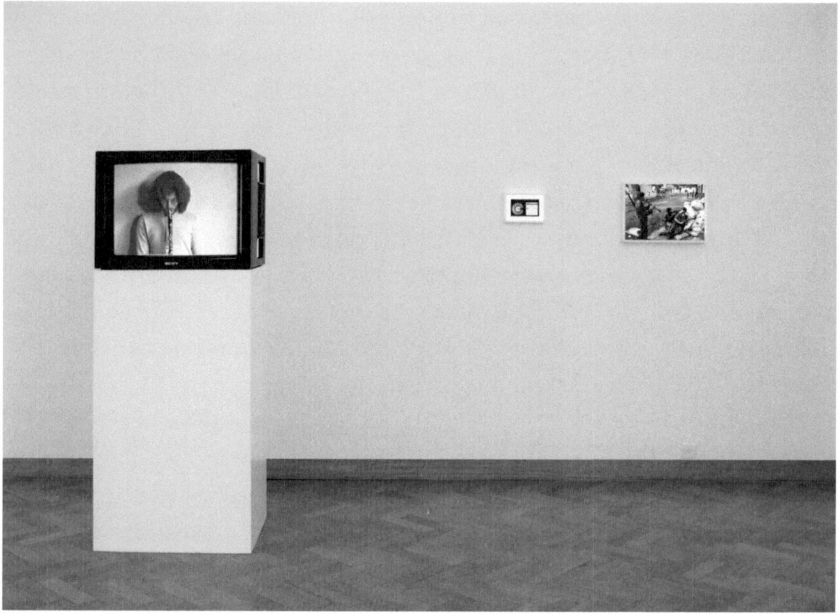

3.4 Alfredo Jaar, *OPUS 1981/Andante Desesperato*, 1981. Courtesy of Alfredo Jaar.

thus punishment. It is about "a voice that cannot form words but can only emit strident sounds in order to let its owner's agony be heard," one critic wrote.[108] Celebrating Meiselas's solidarity with "Our America" by appropriating one of her most famous photographs of the Nicaraguan Revolution, Jaar, as Peruvian liberatory theologian Gustavo Gutiérrez Merino would say, signals "what is not yet but will be."[109] It signals a project of liberation that is in progress; an aesthetics of the unfinished within a world of decolonial time.

In 1983, when Jaar's *America, America* (figures 3.2 and 3.3) was on view at the Washington Project for the Arts (WPA), a community-driven venue that promoted contemporary experimental art half a mile from the White House, President Ronald Reagan delivered his famous speech on US intervention in Central America.[110] Addressing the "American people" from the US Capitol, Reagan asked for "a greater commitment" to what he would later call "freedom fighters," the Contra guerrillas in Central America trained with CIA-produced manuals on torture under the School of the Americas, a US Army academy at the Panama Canal. In doing so, Reagan offered a clear geographic and linguistic idea of the United States *as* "America"—that is, a country that can intervene in

Latin American democracies and cultures as it wills, watching over the "safety," "freedom," and "democratic values" of the "American" people.[111]

But freedom *as* liberty is not the same as liberation. With its etymological origins in Libertas, the Roman goddess representing "universal" freedom, *liberty*, as Enrique Dussel maintains, carries "the same connotations of epistemological violence that we find on a larger scale, in modern rationality."[112] This is why Reagan's co-option of the term *freedom fighters* to refer to US-backed Contra guerrillas resonated significantly with Jaar. In his 1983 mixed-media installation *Strawberries* (plate 25), Jaar represents Reagan's action of speaking that day at the Capitol by blowing up a photograph of his mouth and reproducing it five times.[113] The photographs are lined up horizontally along the wall; located below each photograph is a tray filled with water, recalling the actions of development and reproduction that take place in the darkroom.[114] Paradoxically, however, the more he insisted on turning the latent image into a permanent reproduction, the more he failed, repeating said failure in the trays. Put differently, the more the series "advances," the more detailed the fragment of the image becomes, transforming it into total abstraction by the last reproduction. By literalizing and physicalizing the photographic process of enlargement—in which images are blown up to reveal aspects of their subjects that elude the naked eye—and by turning the last image into an abstraction, Jaar creates a metaphor of photography's subjective relation to truth.[115] He doubts, questions, and reframes, connecting cultural associations between photography and veracity and between words and meanings.

"For those who stubbornly seek freedom, there can be no more urgent task than to come to understand the mechanisms and practices of indoctrination in societies in the system of brainwashing under freedom," writes linguist Noam Chomsky in the exhibition catalog for *Disinformation: The Manufacture of Consent*.[116] A group exhibition organized in 1985 by Geno Rodríguez at the Alternative Museum in New York, the show, which was drawn from Chomsky and his collaborator Edward S. Herman's critique of the media's intervention in "truth," included a work by Jaar.[117] Made in 1984 and titled *The Power of Words*, the work is an installation composed of a typewriter and sixteen color slides (figure 3.5). Projected one by one above the typewriter, images here are appropriated and rephotographed by Jaar from photojournalistic records. Some of them show humans in sorrow: They show victims of modernity. Others depict scenes involving the US military, including an official funeral for fallen soldiers, gathered around the US flag and the Contras, including Honduran counterforces staging a mock landing against Sandinista Nicaraguans, whom Reagan called "freedom fighters."[118]

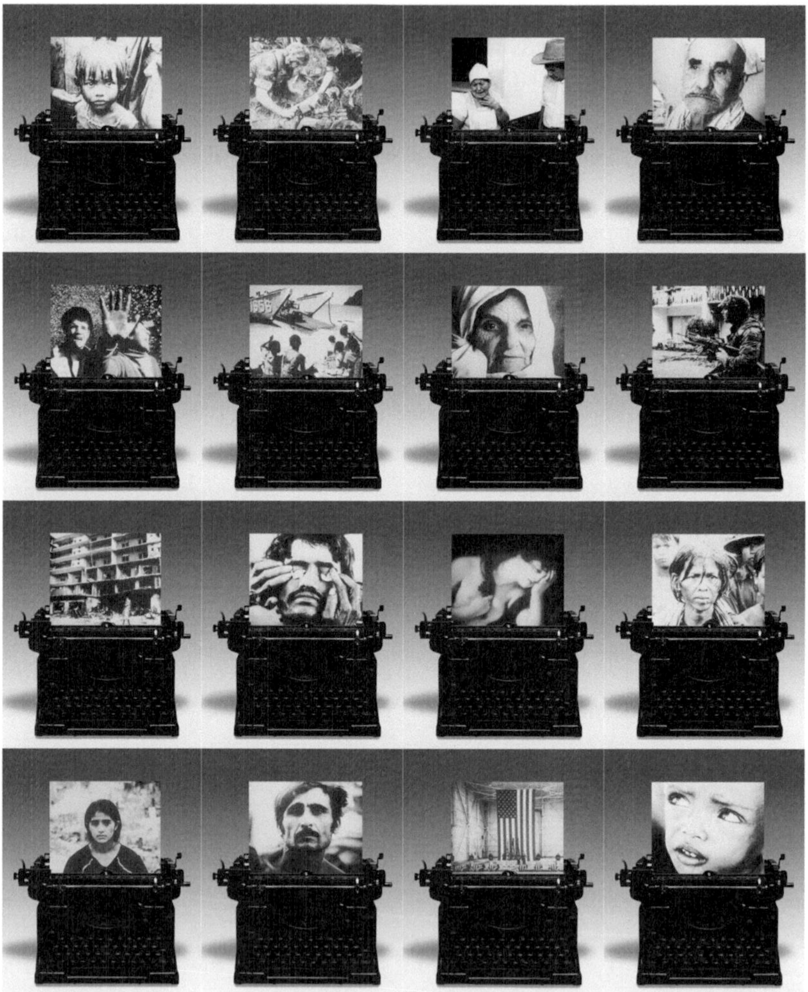

3.5 Alfredo Jaar, *The Power of Words*, 1984. Courtesy of Alfredo Jaar.

Jaar's installation raises the following questions: What is the power of language in the fabrication of truth, and how do these truths vary from media to media and from institution to institution? "Most of the terms of political discourse have double meanings—their literal meaning and the meaning assigned for political warfare," Chomsky states.[119] In effect, as scholars of liberation have argued, unveiling the imperial undercurrents of linguistic paradigms within media outlets that supposedly disseminate information is a key task of the hemispheric project of liberation and its desire to effect tangible political and social change.[120]

REVOLUTION

In a 2013 neon installation by Jaar at the Fondazione Merz in Turin, the artist writes: "We Loved It So Much, the Revolution" (plate 26). Transcribed in the language spoken in Turin and rendered with red and white neon light, the text is taken by Jaar from the title of a book by Daniel Cohn-Bendit, a former leader of the May 1968 student uprising in Paris.[121] Across the way, as shown in this installation shot, is Jaar's *OPUS 1981/Andante Desesperato* (figure 3.6). Providing a grating sonic background to a phrase denoting revolt and love, here dictatorship Chile, solidarity with the Sandinistas, and a student upheaval in 1968 Europe all intersect. Seen in retrospect, they also fail: the dictatorship's neoliberal ghost still defines life in Chile, and fascism has upsurged in Nicaragua, France, and most of the Western world.

Theorists of revolution, however, as Tatiana Flores argues, have read these events in terms of success.[122] Such is the case of Hannah Arendt, who, in her 1963 book, *On Revolution,* contends: "Only when this pathos of novelty is present and where novelty is connected with the idea of freedom are we entitled to speak of revolution."[123] Likewise connecting progress and the political, Stefan Jonsson, in a volume on art and upheaval, introduces a work by Jaar by asserting: "Strictly speaking . . . there are no unsuccessful revolutions."[124] From the lens of the decolonial, on the other hand, revolutions do not happen within history's developmentalist narratives of victory. Instead, they happen within a relational memory politics that interlaces love and time, embracing a radical utopia that announces what is yet to come.

The revolution for what is yet to come has also exposed the coloniality of words, as in the term *America.* In early 1980s New York, where Jaar commenced the program of work that this chapter is about, the question of "America" was a central theme of *Artists Call: Against U.S. Intervention in Central America,* a 1984 nationwide political and artistic endeavor organized

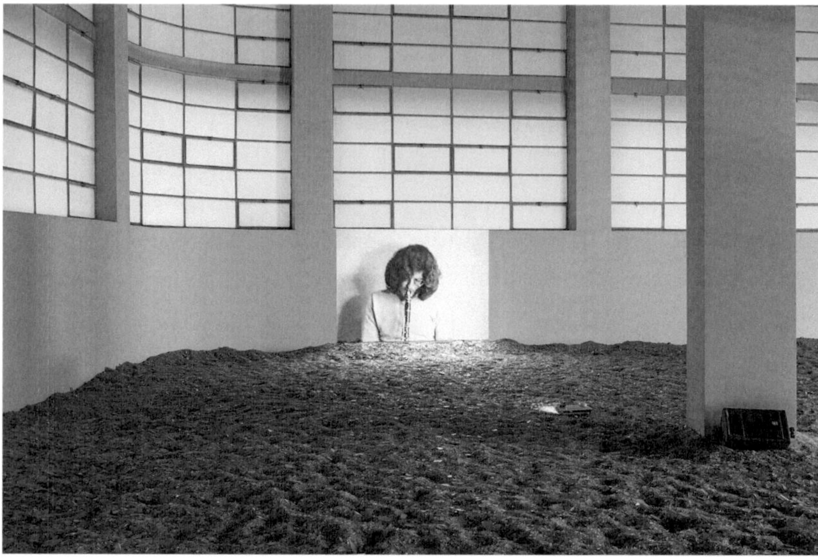

3.6 Alfredo Jaar, *Abbiamo amato tanto la rivoluzione*, 2013. Courtesy of Alfredo Jaar.

from New York by Lucy Lippard, Dore Ashton, and Salvadoran art worker Daniel Flores Ascensio.[125] This endeavor comprised more than three hundred events, including art exhibitions, poetry readings, film screenings, and performance, music, and dance festivals that were held in a variety of venues, from public space and media outlets to museums, galleries, cultural centers, schools, theaters, churches, and more. *Artists Call*, as Chilean-born New York–based artist Cecilia Vicuña recalls, "was an exciting moment of mobilization! After that, I do not remember another similar mobilization of artists here in New York."[126]

Regarding the term *America* more specifically, as part of the *Artists Call* programming, Ariel Dorfman, playwriter and cultural adviser under Allende, organized *Todas las Américas, All the Americas*, an evening of poetry, theater, music, and dance that took place at PS41, a public elementary school in Greenwich Village. Likewise invoking the Americas in plural, Flores Ascencio read the text "Ambos mundos; sangre unánime" (Both worlds; unanimous blood") at Kenkeleba Gallery in New York, where Jaar's *Strawberries* was on view (plate 25).[127] Exposing solidarity and belonging through the pronouns "Todas" (All) and "Ambas" (Both), these events also challenged previous cultural productions made from New York by Latin American intellectuals with similar linguistic designations, as famously shown in the magazine *Ambas Américas*. Launched by Argentinian writer and statesman Domingo Faustino Sarmiento in 1867, the magazine promoted Latinidad, commemorating the United States as "the educational, industrial, and agricultural model to [be] follow[ed by] the rest of the continent" and calling for "the US intelligentsia to recognize the intelligence of the other America."[128] This considered, Dorfman's *Todas las Américas,* Flores Ascencio's "Ambos mundos," and certainly Jaar's *America, America* are not only projects of a failed revolution in the hemisphere's open veins; they also act as ironic subversions of linguistic coloniality within the intellectual history of Latin America.

A central event in *Artists Call* was the exhibition *La Verdadera Avenida de las Américas* (*The True Avenue of the Americas*). Organized by Ashton, Lippard, and Eva Cockcroft, along with artists Rudolf Baranik, Catalina Parra, May Stevens, and Cecilia Vicuña, among others, the show took place on January 21, 1984, at the intersection of West Broadway and Sixth Avenue, also known as the Avenue of the Americas. Among the works exhibited were dozens of banners and murals as well as street signs and posters plastered in the streets honoring those who were "fighting and dying for the right to live, to work, to make art and to stroll down their own streets in their own towns," as the promotional flyer for the event reads.[129] Embracing a sense of hemispheric belonging and collective revolution in the aesthetic fight for life and in the representation of mourning, the flyer continues: "We want to remember our own struggle for liberation and those that are going on right now in countries that are our neighbors—neighbors with whom we share a respect for culture."[130]

In a silk-screened poster advertising the action, the event's title is written in Spanish with white lettering over a black background, and includes its English translation and information about the art action in small print below the image (figure 3.7). In the image, women and men raise their voices and stretch their arms out in the streets, forming a mass as a means of revolution that recalls Barrios's *América, no invoco tu nombre en vano* and thus Jaar's *Exclamación, pánico y muerte*. Another flyer promoting the event shows a list of thirty revolutionaries whose portraits and iconic phrases were rendered by participants on the banners.[131] First on the list is José Martí, joined by Salvadorian theologian of liberation and human rights defender Óscar Romero, who was assassinated by the Contras in 1980 while celebrating Mass in a small chapel in a hospital for the terminally ill. Additional revolutionaries in the list include the early twentieth-century activists Augusto César Sandino and Jamaican Marcus Garvey, nineteenth-century abolitionists such

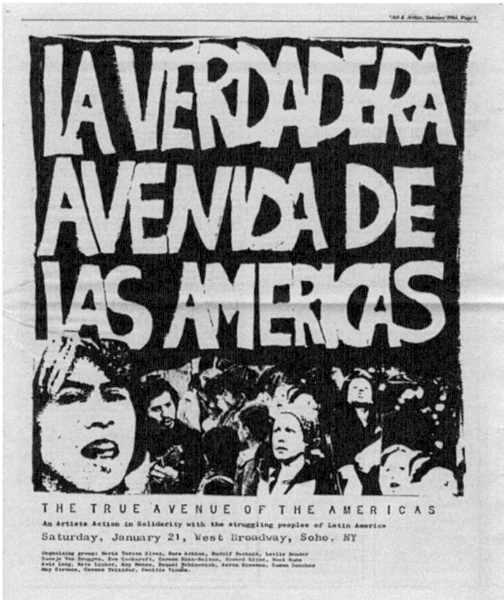

3.7 Promotional flyer for the *Artists Call* exhibition *La Verdadera Avenida de las Americas*, 1984.

as Puerto Rican Ramón Emeterio Betances, and eighteenth-century revolutionaries such as Túpac Amaru II and the Peruvian Indigenous and mestizo rebels who led the revolt against the Spanish viceroyalty of Peru.[132] Built upon the recognition of the liberatory work of ethnic and gender minorities, all often omitted from nationalistic and triumphant discourses, the list further unwraps the role of the masses—the collective—in the revolution toward reparation. This is shown in the inclusion of the Madres de la Plaza de Mayo in Argentina, the regional collective No más lágrimas, Campesinos, and the four US nuns who were raped and murdered in 1980 by US-sponsored death squads in El Salvador. Turning their names and faces into moving and lived memorials, participants of *La Verdadera Avenida de las Américas* were clearly thinking about "Our America" as a hemispheric project of liberation and revolution, one in which politics, poetry, art, and solidarity all intersect. This is also why the list included Salvador Allende, Pablo Neruda, and Orlando Letelier. Hence one of the banners at the exhibition, a painting made by May Stevens and Rudolf Baranik, displayed a portrait of the three, taken together (plate 27).[133]

Indeed, as explained in chapter 1, Allende's, Neruda's, and Letelier's revolutionary struggles and subsequent deaths inspired many of the events of the New York solidarity movement with Chile in the 1970s. And this movement, specifically its aesthetic denoting contingency, disobedience, and agitation, served as a reference for *Artists Call* a decade later.[134] In turn, it is central to note that while the main focus of *Artists Call* was "to raise consciousness" and "affect public opinion" regarding Reagan's "disastrous" international policies in Central America, its temporal and spatial scope was much broader, as it honored the fight against neoliberalism and oppression not only in 1970s Chile but also against capitalism and coloniality across the hemisphere since the very origins of modernity in 1492.[135] This is apparent in several *Artists Call* events. One is the exhibition *Reconstruction Project*. Organized at Artists Space, one of the first independent art venues in Lower Manhattan, the show consisted of the reconstruction of two pages of the Dresden Codex—one of the few Mayan codices to survive the Spanish invasion—and linked that invasion to the current US intervention in Guatemala.[136] Another instance is a reading by artist Jimmie Durham at Kenkeleba Gallery accompanying the exhibition that included Jaar's *Strawberries*. Using the figure of Columbus to expose modernity's wounds by allegorically turning the proper name of Columbus into the concept of coloniality, the text was titled "Columbus Day." "Columbus [is] gone but not forgotten," writes Black feminist scholar and activist bell hooks.[137]

The genealogy this chapter unearths shows that in the Cold War and its ruins, artists and intellectuals in cultures of resistance have denounced Americanity to reframe critical discourses about art *as* politics, or about decolonial time. As the decolonial is ongoing, in this genealogy, art, as shown through the study of Jaar's practice, means mourning, accountability, and failure. It means the insistence of representing the life and memory of the victims of modernity so that we do not forget them twice, in the progressive time of history and art. And thus, we ask once again: Can *America* mean anything more than a pathological construct of a given superiority that justifies interventionism in the name of a civilizing mission?[138] Can it mean a revolutionary project that, despite failing again and again, can still exist and resist even if only in the form of words, images, ideas, and utopias? The answer is yes, it can. As Gabriel Boric said in his last addresses as President of Chile at the United Nations Assembly on September 23, 2025, "What is history if not a permanent utopian journey?"[139] And while it is true that language, including terms such as *utopia*, is not only a "cultural" phenomenon but also the location where knowledge is inscribed, its dynamic and fluid potential can indeed embrace a cultural and epistemological liberation in becoming, within an aesthetics of decolonial time.[140]

This is what Jaar does in *A Logo for America* (plate 19). Using the Mercator projection to bring attention to those who continue associating the same image with the same imperial meanings and terms, Jaar's animation provides a critical aesthetic dialogue from the location of the contact zone, enacting a combat zone from the realm of representation.[141] In doing so, he interferes in those images and terms by noting that the meaning of words is not unique, fixed, and thus not universal or modern, as in the case of freedom, revolution, America, or *libertad*. He intervenes in the coloniality of language by insisting on the failure of the decolonial project and thus on the urgency of its continuity, acknowledging the link between empire and nation-state. In this sense, we can further contend that the second negation in the animation, in which the US map and flag are overlapped, is rather impossible, since the empire, despite its nationalistic and enraged construction of militarized walls, actually erases borders for its neoliberal domination across the region. In so doing, it denies Latin America's autonomy by imposing the neoliberal logic of freedom as a rhetoric of "salvation" for its hemispheric "backyard." "Latin America as the United States' 'backyard' is a ruling assumption of official ideology and political practice," writes Fernando Coronil, "as when President Clinton, in describing U.S. vital interests in Haiti, stated, 'First of all, it's in our backyard.'"[142] Likewise, in 2019, national security advisor John Bolton told a reporter after Trump's recognition of former opposition leader Juan Guaidó as Venezuela's legitimate ruler, "The Monroe Doctrine is alive and well. It's our hemisphere."[143] An indicator that the idea of hemispheric control has not changed at all is that on January 5, 2026, during Trump's second term in office, the State Department posted on X: "This is OUR Hemisphere." On this basis, the argument revolves not so much around the fact that the United States calls itself America but in the fact that America—from that perspective—takes on another connotation that is essential to acknowledge. Jaar's animation does so by *not* presenting a counternarrative—that is, a counter or corrected flag and map—but the decolonial idea that America was "invented" instead of "discovered" has multiple meanings. It has meant and will continue to mean liberation, Our America, revolution, hope, and utopia but also imperialism, whiteness, exclusion, Americanity, and so on.

In fact, while it is true that "words have a peculiar function in colonialism: they conceal rather than designate," as Rivera Cusicanqui argues, it is also true that acknowledging the complexities of language has the potential of advancing the decolonial project of liberation.[144] Writing about the struggles of the Algerian people, Fanon put it this way: "Expressing oneself in French, understanding French, was no longer tantamount to treason or to an impoverishing identification with the occupier. Used by the Voice of the Combatants, conveying in a positive way the message of the Revolution, the French language also becomes an instrument of liberation."[145] Thus exists the use of Spanish in Guamán Poma de Ayala's chronicle and the recurrent invocation of the terms *America* and *Latin America* in Jaar's art. And then we wonder, again: What, why, and how is America? In strict historical ways, the name honors the sixteenth-century Italian navigator Amerigo Vespucci, who while looking at the stars from the coast of Brazil "discovered" he was in the "New World" and not in Asia. In this context, the origins of "America" as "new" come to justify the erasure of all Indigenous lands, meanings, and languages.[146] Under the name "America," therefore, the "civilized" began their colonial practice of wiping out everything they "encountered," from complex architectural cities and forms of social organization to peoples, knowledges, and certainly words. Metaphorically speaking, since the "discovery," the conqueror, the missionary, the developer, the extractivist have all been burying the "primitive" and "non-rational" past, in singular. No, from the paradigm of the discovery, the past of the other has no name and thus no grave, and as a time without history, it should not be remembered. Yet, as I have shown in this chapter and in this book, since modernity's very onset with the conquest, cultures of resistance have fought back, enacting the multidimensional project of decolonial time. Using language as one of its tools to contest the world as it is, they have often reframed and reimagined the very words that so exemplary "conceal," such as *America, Latin America, history, research, freedom, maps,* and even *revolution*. Challenging the rules of semiotics, in which a word regards its meaning through cultural convention, a main question in this chapter comes to mind again: What is covered under a name, a noun, or a verb? The quick answer is coloniality. The longer one is the decolonial potential of language to contest its coloniality.

Alfredo Jaar's works discussed in this chapter invite us to remember that the colonial logic inaugurated in 1492 continues to resonate clearly and loudly. It resonates in the arts, in political discourses, and most certainly in words. It also resonates in images and maps in the Americas and the world. "To fight, then, against domination [is] to transform lack of power into potency . . . through acts, gestures, words, writings, images," writes Georges Didi-Huberman.[147] This is all shown, again, in *Two or Three Things I Imagine About Them* (plate 28), an artist's book created by Jaar not coincidentally in the year 1992. Four parts are held together with a paper band. The first contains a passport from Chile, the artist's country of birth and the place in which neoliberalism first developed, informing Jaar's art ever since. The next three parts show full-page color reproductions of maps, which are folded and placed behind the Chilean passport. Rendered with the Peters instead of the Mercator projection to contest the Western locus of orientation and thus of imperial power, the maps represent Nigeria, Hong Kong, and Brazil. As they fold out, each map reveals a large photograph. The map of Nigeria shows children among a toxic waste site. The map of Hong Kong displays thousands of Vietnamese migrants at the infamous Whitehead detention center, with a second photograph on the back displaying the center's entrance rendered in blue and earthy tones, which Jaar also uses in his *1992* to critique the linguistic paradigm of the encounter between two worlds (plate 1). Finally, the map of Brazil shows miners in Serra Pelada, Brazil's open-pit gold mine at the south of the mouth of the Amazon rainforest. As Dore Ashton wrote for the exhibition catalog for Jaar's *Gold in the Morning* series exhibited a year prior at the Venice Biennial: "Gold, after all, started all the trouble in Latin America."[148] Furthermore, Ashton's reading is reinforced by Jaar a year later through the design he made for the exhibition catalog for his participation at *documenta*. Reproducing on a translucent page a circular design by Amerigo Vespucci on the following page, Jaar reproduces a text by the explorer originally published in his 1505 "Mundus Novus." Vespucci writes: "Thus comes about that we are on an upright line, but they on a line down sidewise. A kind of orthogonal triangle is thus formed, the position of whose upright line we occupy, but they the base; and the hypotenuse is drawn from our zenith to theirs, as is seen in the diagram."[149] As Vespucci's words show, not only race and capitalism but also a specific spatial orientation were injected with the invention of America, whose name honors those coordinates and cultural meanings of north, south, east, and west.

Looking at this artist's book in relation to Jaar's exercises of memory overall, we can add that the result of such trouble is the dumping of European toxic waste in Africa, the refugee crisis in Hong Kong, or, in total, the racial capitalism that defines life under modernity's current neoliberal phase. Furthermore, we can also say that in our colonial society, not all citizens, despite sharing the same passport, share the same rights: waste is systematically being dumped in low-income communities in West Virginia and southern Ohio, and in Chile, a country described in 2019 by Piñera as "Latin America's oasis," 1 percent of the population controls almost half of the total wealth. In our world without borders, so the narrative of globalization says, opportunities, connections, or "networks," in Delany's terms, abound. And yet the reality for the majority is quite different. Passports represent less a symbol of circulation and access and more a document of restraint. And maps, instead of touristic brochures, symbolize the world as it is: an image built upon a binominal system that began with the Americas' invention in 1492. Looked at from a decolonial approach, they show, as Eduardo Galeano argues, that Europe's extension to the Americas was not a "descubrimiento but an encubrimiento" (not a discovery but a cover-up).[150] They also show that diagrams—icons—can be challenged as forms of communication's coloniality from an ongoing revolution, recalling, as Argentinian historian Adolfo Gilly states in the introduction of Fanon's *Dying Colonialism*, that "revolution is [human]kind's way of life."[151] This is why the masses, as Gilly continues, "never ceased to resist, to fight as well as they could, to live in combat. The combatant dignity of humanity was maintained in an unbreakable though not always visible line, in the depths of the life of the masses and in the uninterrupted fight."[152] And in such a fight, where the conceptual tactic of reenactment, a positionality of combat, a search for liberation, and a practice of revolution overlap, at stake is the dismantling of the coloniality of language and the acknowledging of failing, again and again.

All in all, Jaar's works in this chapter show that terms such as *America* and *Latin America* are intrinsically linked to coloniality and imperialism, as their locus of enunciation is formulated from the perspective of the modern savior and the paradigms of discovery, civilization, reason, and universality. They simultaneously show that these exact terms can display their decolonial difference through their very presence as words, mobilizing meaning and propelling hope as forms of utopian actions that call for reciprocity, solidarities, linguistic reparation, kinship, and togetherness. "Together we are America," wrote the Puerto Rican rapper and singer Benito Antonio Martínez Ocasio, known professionally as Bad Bunny, on a football while performing at the 2026 Super Bowl halftime show. Together, both forms of linguistic meaning insist that "America" and "Latin America" have not been invoked in vain, critiquing the nation-state's authority through an aesthetics that shows decolonial failure and thus its radical hope. As Gabriela Mistral wrote in her 1922 collection of poems, *Recados para América*: "America, America! All for her / because from her will come misfortune or good!"[153]

CONCLUSION

The End of the World

What can I do?
One must begin somewhere.
Begin what?
The only thing in the world worth beginning:
The End of the world of course
—Aimé Césaire

In the fall of 2024, while working on revisions for this book, I met with German human rights attorney Wolfgang Kaleck at a small café in Berlin. Best known for representing former National Security Agency (NSA) intelligence contractor and whistleblower Edward Snowden, Kaleck has been prosecuting war criminals through universal jurisdiction for more than thirty years. Among other cases, he has filed proceedings against former members of the US government such as George W. Bush's Secretary of Defense Donald Rumsfeld and defended the mothers of the disappeared in Argentina's Dirty War. My interest in interviewing Kaleck, apart from a general curiosity about the hopes and limitations of universal jurisdiction, was twofold. Considering his collaboration with Alfredo Jaar in 2012, when they printed the phrase "Arrest Kissinger!" (figure 2.16) in three major Berlin newspapers, I wished to learn more about the intersections of culture and justice from the perspective of the law, and about Chile's historical and symbolic role in this context. "There is a before and an after with respect to Pinochet's arrest in London in 1998," he told me at the beginning of our meeting. "That marked an important precedent for what many human rights lawyers are doing today."[1]

This precedent meant hope, I thought—hope, for instance, for the detention of Israeli Prime Minister Benjamin Netanyahu under the arrest warrant issued by the International Criminal Court (ICC) on November 21, 2024. "[If he travels] abroad, as Augusto Pinochet did in 1998 [and] enters the territory of any of the 124 parties to the ICC statute, . . . that country would be obligated to arrest and transfer him to the court," said legal scholar Michael Byers.[2] Still, in Jaar's words, "he is still traveling around the world because countries don't have the courage to arrest him when they should by law."[3] In the history of modernity, such a case—as with any similar case—is never so simple; it is never completed. Pinochet, for instance, the infamous fascist general who led Chile's dictatorship from 1973 to 1990, managed to avoid a trial in Europe and died in Santiago in 2006 without being condemned. He was ninety-two years old, and while the government denied him a state funeral, he was still mourned with the symbolic honors of an army general by nearly sixty thousand tearful Chileans. Meanwhile, at Pinochet's wake the day prior, Cardinal Archbishop of Santiago Francisco Javier Errázuriz stated: "We thank God for all the qualities he gave him and all the good he did for our country."[4] In the unchanged narrative of modernity, so the story goes, only those Frantz Fanon called "the wretched of the earth" are subject to the punishments of the law. Adding the moral ideal of Christianity into the equation, Fernando J. Rosenberg contends: "[In] the incommensurability of justice at the foundation of biblical and modern Western thought . . . the attempt to identify state law with justice would appear to be transparently misguided."[5] And, in Latin America specifically, as Rosenberg further maintains, recalling the words of Argentinian writer Jorge Luis Borges, "aphorisms such as Hegel's 'The state is the reality of the moral ideal' strike [us] as sinister jokes."[6]

Centering our conversation on such irony, cynicism, contradiction, and double standard—in short, on the darker side of modernity when it comes to the law—Kaleck, who is also the founder and general secretary of the European Center for Constitutional and Human Rights (ECCHR), continues: "This is why we call the work that we do at ECCHR as 'interventions.' We know we are not achieving victory, but we also know that small achievements such as Pinochet's arrest in London can do much to inform our work as lawyers and keep up society's hopes for accountability."[7] Accountability, in the minds and hearts of anti-imperialist lawyers, politicians, and resistance fighters, extends beyond the court and into the public space, where performativity and artistic interventions can also criminalize perpetrators in society. This is what Jaar aimed for in his newspaper intervention calling for the arrest of Henry Kissinger, and this is why, as Kaleck also mentioned in our meeting, "I am interested in collaborating with artists like Alfredo."[8]

In this book, I have argued that while justice is bound to fail, failure does not mean giving up but continuing the struggle for accountability through interventions shaped by collective efforts and sustained by hope. I have also argued that such efforts and hope arise from those who mourn in emancipatory temporalities and those who stand in solidarity with them as well as from those with shared histories of liberation. As Syrian-born author Shifa Saltagi Safadi stated when accepting the 2024 US National Book Award for Young People's Literature: "All of our liberations are tied together."[9] Or, as she states elsewhere about the fall of the Assad regime in December of that year: "Syrians [in] the country and in the diaspora . . . are filled with hope."[10] Likewise, referring to the case of Chile from the realm of the law, Kaleck states elsewhere that with Pinochet's arrest, "criminal proceedings emerged from exiled Argentine and Chilean communities in Spain and human rights networks around the world," adding that "only through the spirit of global solidarity can the fight for human rights generate the possibility of their enforcement."[11]

This conceptualization of the relationship between human rights, transnational solidarities, and transdisciplinarity recalls the three main concepts of this book: mourning, or the enacting of decolonial memory within decolonial pasts; accountability, or the search for horizontal and reciprocal enforcement; and failure, or what the ECCHR calls interventions (plural). They all overlap. It also recalls the work of so many poets, artists, intellectuals, activists, and scholars whose theories have accompanied me in the writing of this book: It recalls, for instance, Glissant's "relational poetics" and Mistral's "Anniversary," the latter a poem that dismantles the clock time of the Gregorian calendar—or the time of Chronos in Greek mythology and thus the foundation of "universal" history—with the verse "And we go on and on."[12] And, of course, it recalls the work of Alfredo Jaar, which I have conceptualized here through his aesthetics of the unfinished. Yet, in light of Jaar's *The End of the World* (2024) (plate 29), a recent exhibition at KINDL, a center of contemporary art in Berlin and the reason I traveled to Germany that fall, a central issue about all of this comes to the fore. Considering the linguistic in the present that drives this volume's temporal and conceptual flows, or what Humberto Maturana calls *lenguajear* (languaging), this issue originates with this exhibition's very title; even the phrase "The End of the World," although linguistically structured in the present tense, still avows its very collapse.[13]

Let me explain. "The End of the World" does not mean "The World Has Ended," as if Jaar were portraying a postapocalyptic moment that humans have already witnessed. Nor does it mean "After the End of the World," as if he were inhabiting the liberal future of the postmodernist plurality articulated in 1976 by the art critic Arthur Danto in *After the End of Art*. In turn, "The End of the World" neither reflects or affirms what Francis Fukuyama coined “the end of history” in a book published in 1992. No, Jaar’s art tells us, over and over, if 1992 means anything it is not the celebration of the universalization of Western liberal democracy but a historical turn in decolonial genealogy where critique of modernity’s origins with the conquest and its continuity in the ongoing present became more massive. Still, the title of Jaar’s work, despite being grammatically suggestive of the present tense, invokes a moment in the now that *affirms* a total fall, its end, as if hope had given up and the time of liberation were sealed, closed off. With this affirmation offering no room for decolonial inquiry and praxis—or optimism, in Gramsci’s terms—this title (and the work, which I describe in this chapter), as provocative as it can be, still leads to several questions. Have Jaar’s aesthetics of the unfinished ended with the end of this book? And, if so, what arises when the world ends? What hopes, challenges, relationalities, and disarray emerge? Or, perhaps, they have always been there, gravitating in the seas and earths, in speech, joy, and in a poetics of decolonial time?

This conclusion is about the latter, or about the presence of the three main concepts of this book in Jaar’s lesser-known line of work, wherein the effects of capitalism’s inexorable pursuit of profit in our environmental and humanitarian crises are at stake. At stake, in other words, is the Capitalocene: how Jaar’s art has responded to the interconnectedness of power, class, race, and the environment, under the conditions of global neoliberal rule.[14] In turn, from the starting point of Jaar’s *The End of the World*, at stake is the acknowledgment of the museum as a colonial institution built under the imperial paradigms of appropriation, extractivism, and aesthetic universalization. Offering some final remarks about how Jaar, a living artist, reflects and expands on current critical debates, including the coloniality of international law, this conclusion ultimately highlights a central aspect in this study: that the ongoing collective struggle for justice and human rights and the practice of art made through care and hope are constitutive to one another, and that, as such, in Jaar’s words, “a life without art would be unlivable. Art is life.”[15]

At the center of the Kesselhaus, KINDL’s main space, is a small cube (plate 29). Made by Jaar in 2024 and under the same name as the exhibition—*The End of the World*—the cube is only four centimeters in each direction, contrasting with the Kesselhaus’s colossal dimensions of twenty square meters. Importantly, as in any installation by Jaar, a spatial design has been built to contextualize the object and its surroundings, the world. In this case, the design is quite simple, encompassing only a narrow, dark hallway that leads the viewer into the main space. It also includes light, which the viewer encounters by the end of the hallway, where a door at the right leads to the main space or, let us say, the larger cube. Evenly illuminated by multiple red bulbs lined up along the ceiling, the diffuse lighting of this space contrasts with the single direct, hard, and bright source illuminating the small cube from above. Through a centripetal force of bodily motion created by Jaar through formal decisions regarding light, space, and scale, which he formulates through a series of opposites—soft and hard, color and value, and minuscule and colossal—the viewer is drawn toward the center. There, the small cube brightly stands out in the vastness of the red space. In the center, more visual information is provided: more colors, shapes, and lights. All of them are rendered in the form of a diminutive cube made of ten thin slices of metal. These elements include cobalt, coltan, copper, germanium, lithium, manganese, nickel, platinum, rare earths, and tin. Organized by Jaar in a formal pattern such that no one metal matches the color and tone of the one next to it, these metals are essential to the manufacturing and maintenance of our digital life (the production of computer chips, cables, screens, and so forth) and of renewable technologies (solar panels and electric vehicles, for instance, which are all connected to computers). Writing for the exhibition catalog of *The End of the World,* political geologist Adam Bobbette states, "The drive to extract precious minerals is contributing to displacement and murder. Mining companies are profiting from ecological destruction and the devastation of Black, Brown, and Indigenous communities. The energy transition is a contemporary form of colonialism."[16] With the cube of ten critical minerals in Jaar's work standing in for the planet and the vast emptiness of the red space emphasizing the seriousness of its collapse, Bobbette further contends, "The extraction of each is the end of the world."[17]

Considering that such extractivism or "end," in Bobbette's words, has been ongoing in what environmental studies scholar Rob Nixon defines as the "slow violence" of the Capitalocene, *The End of the World,* as formulated here, reminds us of Aníbal Quijano's statement about coloniality and decolonial resistance quoted in the introduction of this book: "Vivimos adentro, pero en contra" (We live inside and against), he said, acknowledging the ongoing catastrophe that is the world and the task of challenging this by different means, as Jaar does in his project on decolonial time.[18] From this perspective, *The End of the World*—the exhibition, the object, the title, the language—affirms not so much the end of the planet and thus the end of resistance but a denunciation of our present global crisis, namely, the current place of metals and critical minerals as our most profitable source of genocide, ecocide, and epistemicide. It also acknowledges that, at this rate, the world will indeed end and that the universe—or modernity—will eventually fall.

And while this is frightening, it is nothing new for "the wretched of the earth." It is frightening for those of us writing from privileged academic positions, benefiting from digital technologies such as cell phones and computers, and traveling using airplane fuel for research purposes instead of crossing borders for survival. It is frightening for those of us who have not faced forced migration from militarized Indigenous land, who do not live in villages where the water is ever more contaminated and the rivers, plants, trees, birds, and seeds ever more extinct. It is frightening for those of us who are not battling lung cancer from the toxic and poisoned air we breathe from the informal mining settlements in our towns, and for those of us whose parents and grandparents and their parents did not die of that, either. As investigative journalist Tom Burgis writes in the epilogue of his book *The Looting Machine*, which he titles "Complicity": "We all enjoy the profits of the giant corporations of oil and mining industries."[19]

Importantly, the acknowledgment of such complicity—instead of its absence or self-censorship in the name of some idealized moral equivalency—is present in Jaar's exhibition by different means, including the artist's reflections about his work. "[The] little cube stands for the planet itself. It's so minuscule, and then you realize how in danger we are because of our irresponsibility and our criminality," he says.[20] In turn, various publications on the themes of the exhibition are available for visitors in the small library at KINDL's café. This includes, among others, Burgis's *The Looting Machine*. It also includes Anna Lowenhaupt Tsing's *The Mushroom at the End of the World*, a study on the relations between collaborative survival within multispecies landscapes amid capitalist destruction. There is "possibility of life in capitalist ruins," reads this book's subtitle, which is to say: The world has not yet ended, resistance is still possible, and this is why those who mourn will not stop mourning, fighting for accountability, and failing, time and time again. From this perspective, *The End of the World*—the work, the artist's reflections, and the library—not only affirms the ongoing present and presence of liberation struggles. It also engages with an aesthetics of humility, solidarity, care, and cooperation that takes a distance from the rapid artistic responses to political, cultural, and environmental agitations so recurrent in our neoliberal art world. It further complicates and extends the colonial binarism of victim and victimizer into other forms and knots of positionalities, where "epistemic and cultural humility invite us to listen, learn, grow, and change," as applied ethics scholar Cornelius Ewuoso argues: "Epistemic and cultural humility may help prevent decolonization projects that unintentionally reinforce what they seek to dismantle."[21] All this considered, we can thus say that Jaar's *The End of the World* does not dismantle the world by locating critical discourse as the last recourse for ethical salvation. Instead, he shows the world just as it is, in the present tense, acknowledging complicity while creating forms to resist the ongoing war in which we live: one that, as Jaar's art also demonstrates, exists in the museum as an extension of the world.

Standing on a black rectangular pedestal and theatrically illuminated from above, Jaar's small cube is protected by glass, guarding the cube, the artwork, and the world. As such, it echoes traditional modes of exhibition in the museum, an institution created at the height of imperialism following the Enlightenment doctrine of universal reason. This echoes, more specifically, the bust of Nefertiti (plate 30), the "main attraction" at the Egyptian museum on Berlin's Museum Island, located in the district of Neukölln, only a few miles away from the KINDL. A painted limestone featuring the Egyptian queen, with her long neck, arched brows, high cheekbones, slim nose, graceful and well-proportioned smile, red lips, and inlaid right eye, Nefertiti's bust, just like Jaar's cube, is not only solemnly protected by a cubic glass. It is also the single object displayed at the center of a large room; when seen from a decolonial approach, it further represents, like Jaar's *The End of the World*, a stolen "jewel" appropriated by colonial extractivism.[22]

Nefertiti's bust was found by the German archaeologist Ludwig Borchardt during an excavation in Tell el-Amarna in 1912, when Egypt was still under British control and archaeologists from England, France, and Germany were digging up the land in search of treasures for their "encyclopedic" museums. It soon became an icon of Egyptian antiquity, a symbol of universal and timeless beauty, and a major tourist attraction in Germany's Neues Museum. It also became a prominent symbol of colonialism, with Egypt demanding its repatriation since its first public display in 1924. "The government, the people of Egypt, and worldwide citizens are eager for [the bust] to be returned," reads a petition from 2022.[23] Importantly, from a feminist perspective in Egypt, such "eager" regards not simply the relocation of an object whose name literally means "the beautiful one has come forth." It regards the struggles of the present *in* relation to those of the past. Herself a co-pharaoh frequently depicted as a resilient leader with fertility strength, Nefertiti means an emblem for contemporary Egyptian "women [who] in the process of fighting for [equality] look up to women in history," as archaeologist Monica Hanna maintains.[24] Repatriation thus means the right to care for and preserve one's heritage at home and also the experience of a situated presence that emancipates gender struggle *through* time, before and after Dynastic Egypt and before and after the Ottoman Empire and British colonial rule. And, if by the time of Borchardt's excavation, "the law [was to follow] the conditions of empire," meaning that in repatriation discourse, "the laws themselves and their legitimacy need to be questioned," as historian Sebastian Conrad argues, the museum's jewels and their glassed-in display are exemplars of the darker side of modernity: coloniality. From this perspective, Jaar's *The End of the World* is not so much about a "space of contrasts and discrepancies" between, for instance, "the cube's refined display . . . evoking the aesthetics of a jewelry showcase [versus] the 'dirty business' of its extraction," as curator Kathrin Becker writes in the exhibition's catalog.[25] It is more about how one mirrors the other or about the museum as a mirror of the world, where a jewel equals coloniality and extractivism and where art equals life.

Importantly, Jaar's understanding of the museum as a site of coloniality is nothing new. In 1992, for instance, when he created *1992* (plate 1) to show the global reach of the conquest through the case of Vietnamese refugees in Hong Kong in the context of the Quincentenary, he also made *The Aesthetics of Resistance* (figure C.1). A site-specific installation he began developing in 1991 as a Deutscher Akademischer Austauschdienst (DAAD) fellow at the Artist in Berlin Program, this work consists of fifteen words in neon installed on the grand staircase of the Pergamon Altar at the eponymous museum in Berlin. With the neon's cold, white, and fluorescent light contrasting with the Altar's gray-veined marble, these words represent the names of fifteen cities in Germany where attacks against immigrants' and asylum seekers' homes were conducted by neo-Nazis and right-wing extremists in 1992. Indeed, while in the year 1992 massive critiques of coloniality came to symbolize a third turn in decolonial genealogy as seen from the Americas, in Germany, the early decade also saw the rise of an openly neo-Nazi new right.[26] In the post–Cold War epoch, this migration crisis—the biggest xenophobic crime in Germany since World War II—is signaled in Jaar's installation using more than light and site; he also designed a booklet listing more than thirty acts of violence against migrants and refugees. As we learn from the booklet, one of these acts occurred on August 22, 1992, in the northeast city of Rostock. That day, early in the evening, a far-right mob gathered at the front of the Sunflower Tower, an eleven-story shelter for asylum seekers and immigrants from Vietnamese and Roma communities. Chanting xenophobic slogans, the rioters threw stones, bottles, fireworks, and Molotov cocktails at

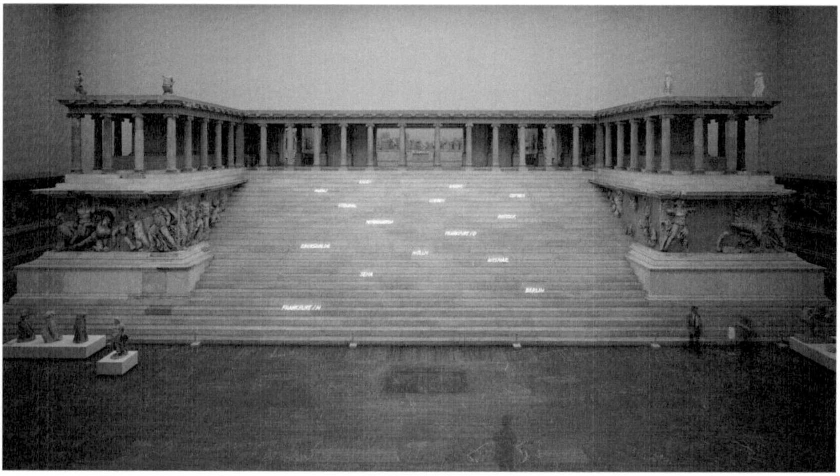

C.1 Alfredo Jaar, *The Aesthetics of Resistance*, 1992. Courtesy of Alfredo Jaar.

the building. The attack continued and grew over the following days, with rioters setting a fire on the ground floor.[27] "Even after 30 years, there are no real political consequences, no real judicial consequences [for perpetrators]," said Vietnamese German theater director Dan Thy Nguyen in 2022, on the occasion of the thirtieth anniversary of the massacre, collectively embracing the decolonial concepts of mourning, accountability, and failure.[28] Further, as historian Gudrun Heinrich contends, if 1992 meant anything in German politics, it is a "victim-perpetrator reversal" that narrowed asylum laws, just as Jaar shows in the twofold context of international law and neoliberal globalization with *1992* (plate 1).[29] After all, as legal scholar Noura Erakat states, "the first seeds of international law were . . . planted during a violent conquest to afford that conquest a veneer of objective legality."[30]

Significantly, Jaar's *The Aesthetics of Resistance* is titled after Peter Weiss's three-volume novel about antifascist resistance, which commences with the narrator and two dissident characters visiting the Pergamon Altar to contemplate the friezes.[31] Depicting the mythological overthrow of the Giants by the Olympian gods Athena and Zeus, in the novel, these battles represent the failed struggle against fascism in a period spanning from the late 1930s to World War II, with the defeated symbolizing the risks entailed when resisting injustice. However, injustice has been the norm since the outset of the Western history of antiquity. As Rosenberg contends, "*Oresteia*'s highest tribunal of law embodying justice for the whole community is already partial, as

Athena's ideal of civil order responds to a logocentric masculine injunction coming right out of Zeus's head."[32] In the Pergamon's friezes, Athena and Zeus are depicted as being in total control, with the former battling a giant while being crowned by Nike, the winged goddess of victory, and the latter, while rushing forward, still securing success. They know they will win, just as in the history of modernity, the battles of the present mean the fates of the future. Put differently: Modernity is well aware of its triumph in a linear progression, represented here in both the arts and the law. In *The Aesthetics of Resistance,* Jaar confronts this heuristic with the Pergamon Altar as a backdrop to critique the current crises of immigrants and asylum seekers. Past and present, the museum and the public space, and aesthetics and politics all overlap.

Such conjuncture, however, went unnoticed by most visitors to Jaar's installation. As one art critic noted, "most [were] upset that classical art, which is supposed to simply please the eye, [was] being 'misused' for political manifestation [with] some even feeling the installation to be the 'desecration of the sacred altar.'"[33] From the perspective of those who believe in hallowed universal beauty, modernity's past cannot be contested. Nor can its present, as famously demonstrated in the multifaceted duet performance *The Year of The White Bear* by Cuban American artist Coco Fusco and Chicano artist Guillermo Gómez-Peña. Shown first at the University of California at Irvine in 1992 and later in multiple art institutions—from Madrid, London, Minneapolis, and Washington, DC, to Sydney, Chicago, and New York—in this performance Fusco and Gómez-Peña locked themselves in a cage and presented themselves as aboriginal inhabitants of an island off the Gulf of Mexico that was somehow overlooked by Columbus. Ironically addressing the Quincentenary's rhetoric of multicultural encounter, the artists engaged in various "ritual" activities, including watching TV, sewing voodoo dolls, drinking Coca-Cola, and lifting weights. Following their colonial desires, some audiences assumed that Indigenous people could be confined in a cage, while others "demanded more 'authenticity,' noting that the performers were not 'dark enough' to be 'undiscovered Amerindians.'"[34] However people understood the work—as an anthropological finding or as a contemporary performance—they accepted that humans could be exhibited as curiosities, just as works of "universal beauty" discovered by colonial excavations, such as Nefertiti's bust, could be shipped to cities like Berlin and displayed in their museums as symbols of their art, their nation, and their desires for a linear past, present, and future.

Indeed, as with Nefertiti's bust, the relief panels of the Pergamon Altar were brought to Berlin during the German Empire. Furthermore, their return has also been demanded, in this case to present-day Turkey, where they were built in the first half of the second century BC in Hellenistic Greece. However, there are "no plans to return Berlin's star museum attractions Nefertiti and Pergamon Altar," as the *Art Newspaper* reported on January 20, 2023.[35] Indeed, as Nelson Maldonado-Torres writes, "Since war is anchored in the catastrophic order of things and is perpetual, neither land, resources, or any sense of dignity are meant to be given back."[36] This means that, in the late nineteenth and early twentieth centuries, modernity's "looting machine" created the conditions for the Pergamon Altar and the bust of Nefertiti to be stolen, just as today it ensures the colonial paradigm that allows them to *remain* stolen, exhibited at the museum as a gem of universal, atemporal, and transcendental beauty. As such, modernity affirms the art history canon as we know it; after locating its Western origins in ancient Egypt, paradoxically a country in Africa, art history did not look "back" in time until the turn of the 1980s and 1990s, when the so-called rest of the world (Africa, Asia, the Americas, Oceania) became legitimated as sources of aesthetic discourse as a product of neoliberal globalization.[37] Within this linear succession we can find, for instance, the bust of Nefertiti, Leonardo's *Mona Lisa,* and, let's say, Andy Warhol's *Double Liz Cleopatra.* "Our *Mona Lisa* must stay in Berlin," claimed an art critic in response to demands for the repatriation of Nefertiti.[38] And Warhol's silkscreen, while critiquing US society's consumerism in the postwar period, also shows that Egypt was "recovered" by Western contemporary art, film, and popular culture only to prove its continued fascination with orientalism.[39] Also included in this art history are archaeological discoveries informed by modernity's paradigms of salvation and conservation of universal treasures. This is what the director of the Neues Museum in Berlin, Friederike Seyfried, meant when she was asked why Germany hasn't returned Nefertiti's bust to Egypt. "The theory that the object was smeared [when discovered], I don't think anyone would ever have done that," she said, implying that modernity will continue to protect, preserve, and display itself with the solemnity it deserves.[40] In this sense, petitions for repatriation mirror the world itself, where, as Noura Erakat states with regard to the question of Palestine, "justice [applies only] for some."[41] Or, as Palestinian-descendant organizer of the student solidarity movement Mahmoud Khalil wrote in March 2025 while he was detained in an Immigration and Customs Enforcement (ICE) detention center in Louisiana: "Rights are granted to those who align with power."[42]

As a reproduction of itself, or as a "document of civilization which is [at the same time] a document of barbarism," as Walter Benjamin would say, the museum is complicit with the world as we know it, just as cultures of resistance will continue fighting for repatriation even when failing under the law.[43] The museum is also complicit with the end of the world, that is, with those benefiting from war, genocide, and death in the context of neoliberal extractivism. As I noted in chapter 2, Kissinger, who for more than four decades, until his death in 2023, served as trustee emeritus of the Metropolitan Museum of Art, did not orchestrate the military coup in Chile for an ideological purpose only. He did not—nor did the US establishment—design this event in fear of another left-wing regime in Latin America after the Cuban Revolution, even when a harsh critique of communism was the leading impulse of US Cold War propaganda. For Kissinger and the US economic class, as I have maintained throughout this book, the coup meant a green light to put in place an advanced model of capitalism in a country that Milton Friedman called a "miracle."[44] It also meant that if such a model succeeded, it could be implemented globally so that the private sector could eventually control a multinational economic and cultural order. And it worked so efficaciously that for those benefiting from neoliberalism it became a "miracle," one that offered conditions—a fascist dictatorship led by Pinochet—under which "developed" nations (or nations with imperialist desires) could magnify their interests by extracting and acquiring multiple resources, including copper and lithium, two of the metals present in Jaar's *The End of the World* (see plate 31).

In effect, it was during the dictatorship that the United States regained control of the world's largest open-pit copper mine in Chuquicamata, northern Chile, which was previously expropriated by Salvador Allende's socialist policies from the Rockefeller family and the US company Kennecott Copper. Such a history of multinational control has been demonstrated by Jaar for decades, as evident in his 1983 conceptual postcards, through which he advertises the search for Kissinger with the Rockefeller building in New York in the background (plate 14), as analyzed in chapter 2. In doing so, Jaar's work also acknowledges the complicity of the museum and its patrons (the Rockefeller family, for instance, has maintained a deep connection to the Museum of Modern Art in New York since its founding in 1929) with colonial extractivism and denigration of *some* lives, past and present. The same can be said about Kennecott Copper, a company that in the early twentieth century began digging for nitrates in the Chilean desert with financing from the Guggenheim family, which, in turn, made its fortune from the mining industry and became art philanthropists.[45] Using a "tele-production" system to manage the Chilean mines from New York so that the company could ensure its political and legal immunity from Chilean authorities, under the Guggenheims' control, as one reporter wrote for Chile's *La Nación*, the desert was "a lonely place, lacking essential comforts, where the laborers work incessantly [to satisfy the] extraction of the wealth."[46] And, since coloniality is not only external but also internal, it is no wonder that during the dictatorship, when the world's largest lithium reserves in the Chilean desert were privatized, Pinochet handed over the state lithium company, known as Sociedad Química y Minera de Chile (SQM), to his own son-in-law, Julio Ponce Lerou, who, in turn, has been "internationalizing" this metal through global acquisitions and multinational alliances. "Board members have links to oligarchs," writes Bobbette in the exhibition catalog for *The End of the World*. "It is no surprise that global mining conglomerates direct the extractive practice of sovereign states or that states use extractive capitalism as one of their central tools of wealth accumulation."[47] Indeed, it is no surprise either that, as international human rights lawyer and scholar Philippe Sands notes, "Pinochet opened numerous bank accounts in the United States under various names, into which moneys were deposited, in amounts that could not have come from his modest presidential salary."[48]

"Beben litio, comen cobre" (They drink lithium, they eat copper), reads a silkscreen by the Atacama-based graphic arts collective Laboratorio de Artes Gráficas del Desierto de Atacama (LAGDA) (figure C.2).[49] In this image, which adopts Guamán Poma de Ayala's signature graphics, a European settler kneels in profile, offering a dish of typical Chilean empanadas to two human cadavers. Behind him, at the edge of the frame, a hand holding a mining tube drops liquid into a jar with the inscription "SQM." With the European settler representing his "barbaric reproduction" in the embodiment of a CEO who wears a suit, a tie, and a mining helmet, the inscription of SQM on the jar and on the cadavers of miners and Indigenous peoples living in proximity to Chuquicamata speaks to the catastrophic consequences of neoliberal extractivism. And thus the earth burns, the rivers run dry, and the waters grow tainted. "[Since] copper mines consume a lot of water, most rivers have dried up except the Loa" says Sergio Chamorro, an environmental lawyer who represents many Indigenous peoples in the area. Addressing the genocide and ecocide provoked in the Chilean desert by Aurubis, one of the world's largest copper recyclers with its headquarters in Hamburg, Germany, Chamorro adds: "The most important source of life in the Atacama Desert, [the Loa] could be the most toxic river in Chile."[50]

LAGDA's silkscreen—made in 2021 in the context of Chile's *estallido social*—critiques how multinational mining companies, including those

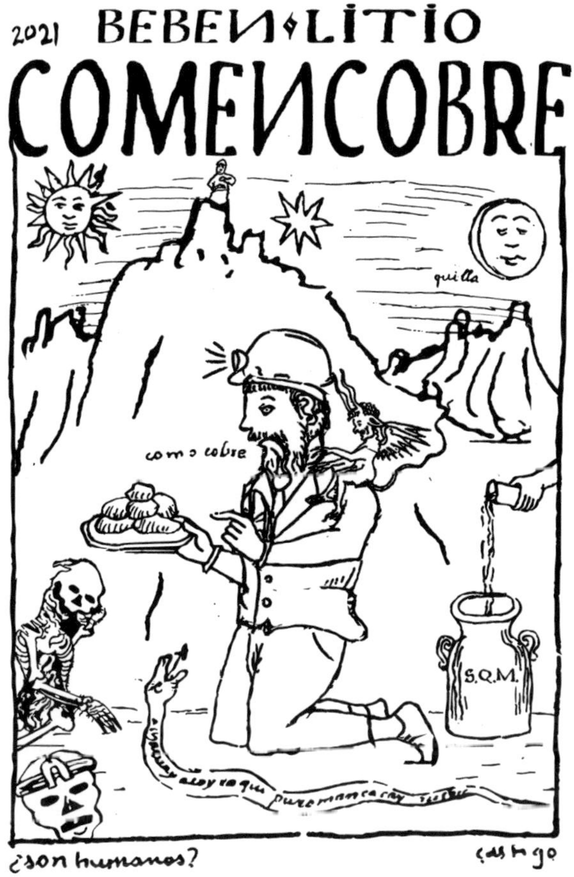

C.2 LAGDA collective in collaboration with Fundación Desierto de Atacama, Colectivo Pésimo Servicio, Ángela Ormeño, Javier Díaz, Valentina Pallacán, Francisco Bahamondes, Antonieta Clunes, Valeria Valenzuela, Gonzalo Bravo, René Reyes, Carmen Aramayo, Kristell Heine, and Alejandro Herrera, *Beben litio, comen cobre,* 2021. Courtesy of LAGDA.

controlled by Pinochet's descendants, have profoundly damaged human life and the environment in the vast Chilean desert. By adopting and adapting Guamán Poma de Ayala's iconography, the work also shows that extractivism and its critiques emerged immediately after the conquest in the sixteenth century and have continued into the present, following an aesthetics of decolonial time. And, if we read the work in connection to Jaar's *The End of the World*, it further demonstrates that the accumulation of capital and our desires within digital and "green" life are only possible through the devastation of human beings and the ecosystem in the colonial time of modernity. Indeed, just as the world's largest radio telescope and ground-based observatory looking only *up* to the sky in the Chilean desert can be figured as a spatial metaphor for neoliberal forgetting of the bodies that the military buried *under* the earth, as I explained in chapter 1, mining excavators in Chuquicamata and the desert's salt flat dig deep into the soil in search of cooper, lithium, metals: profit. In both cases, the technologies of the present look to the future, all the while ignoring that the traces of the past continue to inform relational lives and hopes from the perspective of decolonial time.

Importantly, Jaar's interest in exposing and denouncing our planetary crises and human degradation did not begin in 2024, when he made *The End of the World*. It started as early as 1984, when a plant from the US chemical company Union Carbide leaked tons of toxic gas in Bhopal, India, killing roughly 22,000 and injuring more than 100,000 people who are still fighting for their lives.[51] Two weeks after the tragedy, on December 24, 1984, *Business-Week Magazine* mourned not the victims in Bhopal but the challenges Union Carbide faced, publishing a portrait of the company's CEO on its cover with the headline "Union Carbide Fights for Its Life." As I explained in chapter 2, Jaar appropriates this cover (figure 2.7) and offers it as a document of modernity's barbarism, exposing the crimes of a multinational chemical business and the media's complicity with those crimes. In doing so, he also shows that under neoliberalism, the lives of human beings and companies are indeed different, with the latter mattering more, far more.

Indeed, this colonial paradigm has paralleled Jaar's career: In 1985, ironically supported by a Guggenheim Fellowship, the artist traveled to Serra Pelada, the largest open-pit gold mine in Brazil, to denounce the effects of modernity on the lives of miners who searched for gold debris using only handheld tools. The result was his well-known series *Gold in the Morning* (discussed in chapter 3), which includes the installation *1+1+1* (figure C.3). Exhibited in 1987 at *documenta 8* in Kassel, Germany, the work comprises three square light boxes,

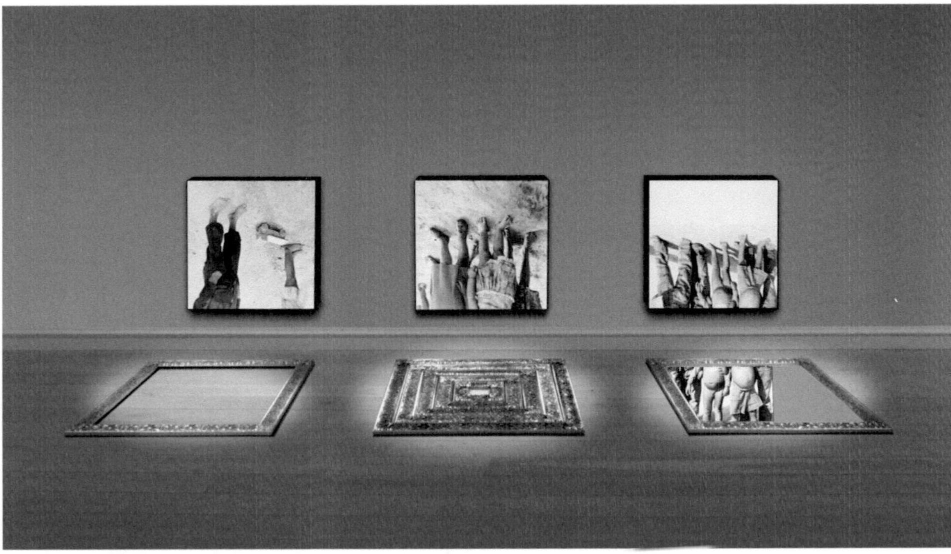

C.3 Alfredo Jaar, *1 + 1 + 1*, 1987. Courtesy of Alfredo Jaar.

placed on a wall. Each light box contains one sepia-toned photograph placed upside-down and depicting children. In turn, three gold frames of the same size are placed on the floor beneath each image. The frame on the left is empty. The one at the center repeats its shape through gradually smaller frames positioned within. Lastly, the frame on the right contains a large mirror, where the image from the third light box is projected upright. Jaar's work exposes the denigration of Black and Indigenous children searching for gold, a means through which early capitalism, with its exploitation of labor and extractivism, first came into play with the "discovery" of the Americas. Columbus's searching for the island of "endless gold" or Cipangu (Japan)—which he had learned about from Marco Polo's thirteenth-century *Travels* but never reached due to a miscalculation of the circumference of the globe—was not in vain.

Thus, the endless colonial desire for gold soon became the project of modernity itself, and its historical shifts and turns left the linear paradigm of discovery unchanged, as Edmundo O'Gorman would say.[52] Today, this boundless desire for precious metals means a global war among multinational corporations and imperial nation-states for critical minerals. It means the tyrannic and insatiable project of imperial nation-states for economic supremacy and the naturalization of war. "Ukraine controls eighty percent of lithium in Europe. . . . This is well-known in the scientific press but not in political discussions about the 2022 Russian invasion of Ukraine," said Jaar.[53] Acknowledging this relation, an article the artist used for his research for *The End of the World* states: "Ukraine was poised to become an important rare earth exporter. Then came the invasion."[54] Recognizing such relationships between power, expansionism, war, and metals, a month after assuming his second term in office, Donald Trump said: "I want them to give us something for all the money we put up [so] we're asking for rare earth."[55] Proudly using the linguistic rhetoric of technological "innovation," "intelligence," "efficiency," and "connectivity," modernity is currently performed in a deep scenario of neoliberal extractivism that allows outspoken violations of human rights and the law, whether at *Oresteia*'s tribunal of justice or at juridical interventions advocating for human and nonhuman dignity.

Considering that the time of coloniality is a linear progression that links the singular past, present, and global future, Jaar, referring in 2024 to the role of rare earths in the war *yet to come* between the United States and China over Taiwan, maintained: "This *next* war is not about democracy or land but about rare earth. Taiwan controls 80 percent of the world's production of microchips, with rare earth playing a crucial role in this manufacturing process."[56] In satisfying the user's experience, that is, humans' interaction with digital devices, the war on metals has even further widened the gap between rich and poor, between "smart" technologies and critical thinking, and between human and nonhuman beings, with everything that this entails. "We are living through another industrial revolution, a traumatic re-enactment of the past where geopolitical plate tectonics are shifting and we are on the precipice of a new, terrifying world," writes Bobbette for Jaar's *The End of the World*.[57] Gold, copper, lithium, rare earth: metals. Extractivist desires have long provided the means of war. And, in our epoch of total digitization, this has also facilitated cyber-arms companies' production of spyware used by these nations not only to fight "terrorism" but also to surveil cultures of resistance. "Things are going to get worse before they get better," says political scientist Ronald Deibert.[58] Indeed, this is why "there will be more urgent need for the work of activists and researchers bringing this out of the shadows," adds investigative journalist Ronan Farrow in the documentary *Surveilled*, clearly embracing an aesthetics of radical hope.

As I have elaborated in this book, Jaar has been embracing such aesthetics throughout his career by different means and in different eras. Significantly, when transatlantic elites were celebrating the Quincentenary in 1992, Jaar created *The Conference* (figure C.4), a work demanding Indigenous rights and critiquing the role of imperial nation-states in our planetary crisis. The occasion was an invitation from the Museum of Modern Art of Rio de Janeiro

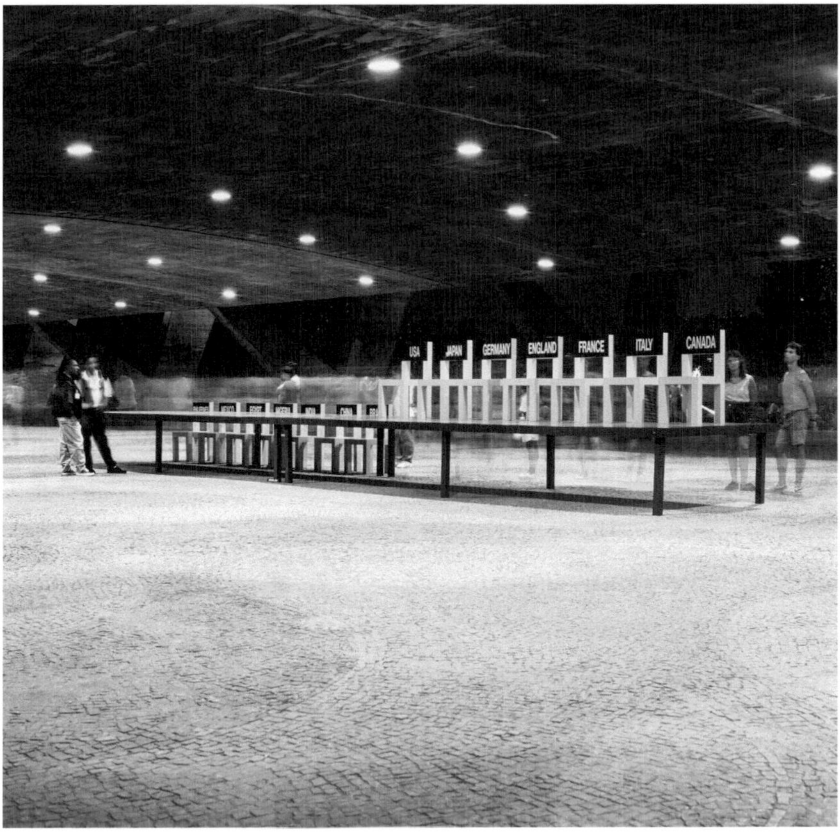

C.4 Alfredo Jaar, *The Conference*, 1992. Courtesy of Alfredo Jaar.

(MAM) to create a work in the context of the Earth Summit of Rio '92.[59] Installed on MAM's ground floor, where a series of *pilotis* lifting the building allow a utopian architecture of communality, the work consists of a very long table with fourteen chairs, all lined up along one side of the table. Divided into two groups, on the left are seven chairs placed on the ground. On the right, the remaining seven chairs are placed on the table. In turn, the names of some of the countries attending the Summit are inscribed on the front of the backrest of each chair. The chairs on the ground read: "Philippines," "Mexico," "Egypt," "Nigeria," "India," "China" and "Brazil," all countries that, at the time, in Jaar's words, were "emerging" from their so-called underdevelopment. The chairs on the table, on the other hand, read: "USA," "Japan," "Germany," "England," "France," "Italy," and "Canada." "This is the work's *punctum*," Jaar said. "Instead of sitting at the table, these countries are sitting on the table, showing the world's imbalance [in which] the supposedly developed countries . . . are also the ones that have created the maximum pollution on the planet."[60] The *punctum* here, as I discussed in chapter 1, is collective, involving a shared critique by those in cultures of resistance against our ecological and humanitarian crises.

Importantly, in *The Conference*, such criticism is not only rendered formally through the spatial hierarchy at the table as a metaphor for unequal power in global decision-making. It also takes the form of a series of manifesto-like statements created by Jaar that, in turn, are reproduced on the back of the chairs' backrests. Rendered in yellow capital letters over a blue background—all colors that, along with the green of the table, represent the Brazilian flag—one reads: "End all nuclear weapon testing, which is a crime against the environment and a waste of resources." Another states: "Stop protecting the interests of transnational corporations who are responsible for many of the world's worst environmental problems." A third, directly addressing the fight for Indigenous rights in the context of the Capitalocene, reads: "Support land and cultural rights of Indigenous peoples. Save the few remaining natural forests and cultures that live in them" (figure C.5). Structured in the present tense, Jaar's statements recall the multiple signs used today in public-space protests demanding environmental reciprocity and Indigenous sovereignty, calling for modernity to stop the ongoing genocide, ecocide, and epistemicide of those it considers part of the remote past of nonhistory. They recall, in other words, that land and profit are not always the same, certainly not for those combating modernity.

For the Mapuche, for instance, the largest Indigenous group in modern-day Chile, the systematic loss of ancestral land justified by Chilean law means not an economic but an ontological issue. It signals the loss of sacred sites, where the living and the dead, as well as the past, present, and future, all coexist, as anthropologist Ana Mariella Bacigalupo maintains.[61] It further entails the rejection of the Mapuche as a people for whom land and language converge: "The dream of the land / screams / in my heart," writes the Mapuche poet Leonel Lienlaf in Mapudungun, connecting territory and sound.[62] The sonic experience of inhabiting, poetry in this sense, as Mapuche scholar Luis E. Cárcamo-Huechante states, resists "acoustic colonialism imposed by the dominant state, corporate, and media actors in neoliberal, contemporary Chile."[63] Poetry sounds. Put differently, just as poetry is not only representation or words, neoliberalism is not merely an epoch in progressive time but a paradigm within modernity. As such, it hurts, and quite deeply, the lands, waters, languages, relationalities, lives, and poems, all of which fight back,

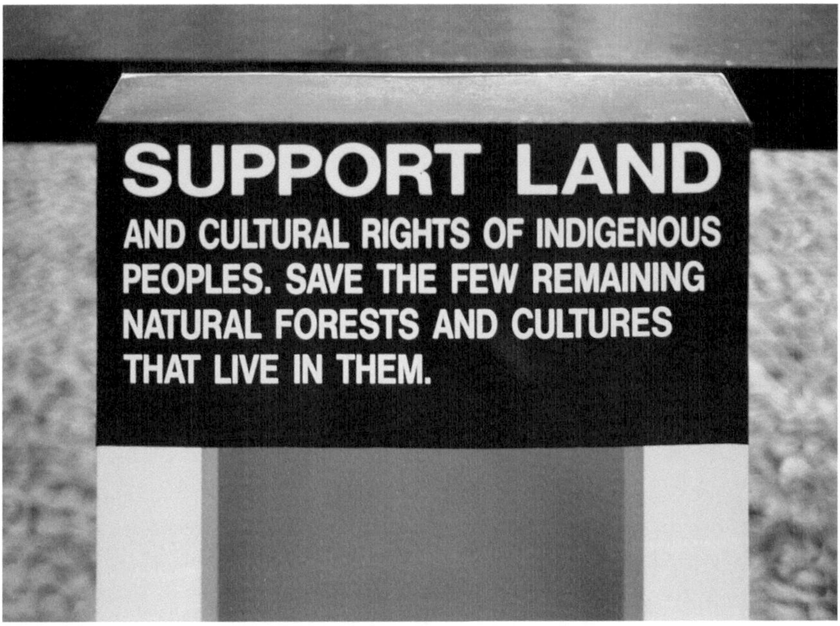

C.5 Alfredo Jaar, *The Conference* (detail), 1992. Courtesy of Alfredo Jaar.

again and again. They fight and mourn, fight and fail, but continue fighting nonetheless for justice and accountability across the world and nations such as Chile, where the legacies of the dictatorship's extractivist constitution still define life and thus death. And, importantly, they all fight in the present tense. "La Tierra no se vende" (Land is not for sale), reads the title of a song by the Mapuche band Wechekeche Ñi Trawün, meaning "young people together" in Mapudungun.[64] Recalling a linguistic in the present—or Maturana's concept of *lenguajear*—and Allende's famous words about the central role revolutionary youth played in the collective project of liberation and radical hope, these cultural practices offer spaces outside the traditional poetry book, the Aristotelian theater, and for that matter the Western and westernized museum, to create forms and experiences with and about decolonial time. Such is the case with *The End*, a series of documentary photographs of the Great Salt Lake in Utah created by Jaar in 2025. A central ecosystem in the Western Hemisphere that is currently drying up, Jaar's photographs, in his words, expose the "tragic fate of the lake and simultaneously reveal its extraordinary beauty and potential" as sources of hope.[65] In doing so they insist—as does Jaar's body of work—that "vivimos adentro, pero en contra," where another world is in becoming, and that this is why we keep going, despite failing, in our pursuit of justice and accountability through ongoing mourning, reciprocity, and decolonial hope.

Alfredo Jaar's exercises of memory invite us to think, look, listen, learn, and unlearn from multiple and often divergent perspectives at once, acknowledging the complexities of coloniality and the many forms and fronts of resistance that decolonial praxis and intellectual inquiry entail. As such, Jaar's exercises of memory concern not only the Americas but the world. This is what Jaar's art is about, as shown in *1992* (plate 1), the work that opens this volume, or *The End of the World* (plates 29 and 31), the work that closes the conceptual framework of this book, only to open it yet again. And then we wonder, insatiably and insistently, as Diana Taylor queries in the introduction of this book: "What can we do when apparently nothing can be done, and doing nothing is not an option?"[66] Jaar's answer is *art*: art as a form of representation that acknowledges the relationship between world and war and contests it, time and time again.

This is what Jaar means when explaining one of his references for *The End of the World*: Piero Manzoni's 1961 *Socle du Monde* (Base of the world) (figure C.6).[67] Describing this iron sculpture in a park in the Danish town of Herning that bears the inscription "Socle du monde" turned upside-down, Jaar said: "You have to turn around to read it, and then you realize that Manzoni was suggesting that the world is resting on this little piece . . . transforming the entire world into a work of art."[68] From the perspective of the decolonial analysis of Jaar's art that this book enacts, Manzoni's upside-down world shows modernity (the world) and its darker side (being reversed) together, locating this twofold reality as the metaphor of the artwork supported by the pedestal. In this sense, the sculpture—or Manzoni's cube—becomes an ongoing inquiry instead of a finished answer that might take the form of an isolated object *about* the world. And, considering the eruption of global neoliberalism in post-1990s history, we can further say that while in Manzoni's work the world is spatially and allegorically *below* the ground, in Jaar's it is *on view* and over the pedestal, just as in *The Conference* the seven chairs representing the role of "developed" countries in global environmental policies are *on top of* the table.[69] In *The End of the World*, this is all rendered in the form of a small cube (the object) and a large cube (the museum), showing that in our present, where digitalization has become the norm, the slow violence of the Capitalocene has drastically accelerated.

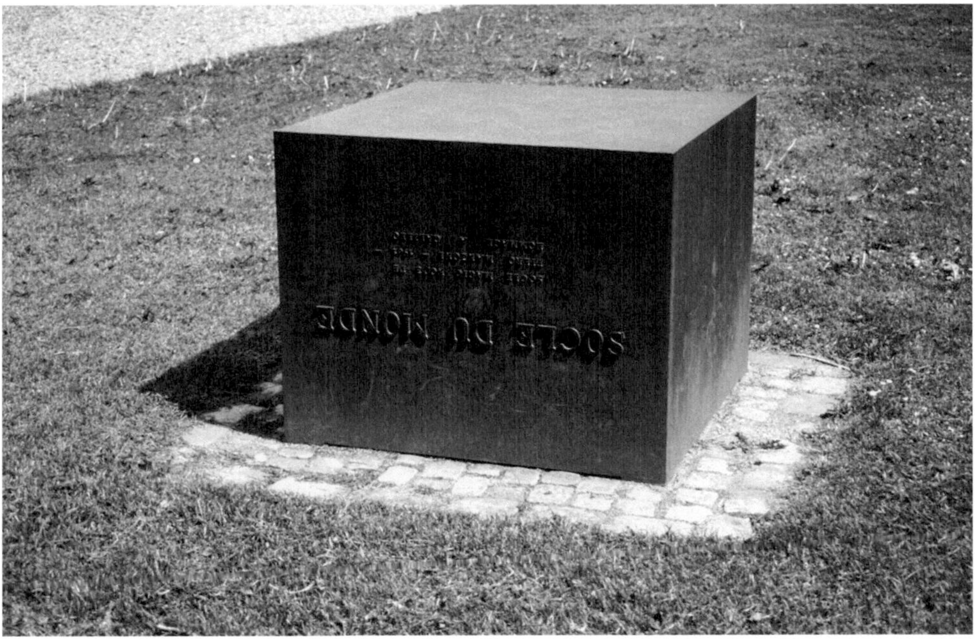

C.6 Piero Manzoni, *Socle du Monde*, 1961.

"Metals for Progress," reads the slogan of Aurubis, the German metal company with operations in Chile I referred to previously. "Being smart and connected doesn't work without metals. Whether renewable energies, electric vehicles, digitalization, or urbanization, the demand for metals will continue to rise," the company's website maintains, clearly embracing the efficiency and brutality of coloniality's ongoing rhetoric of progressive time.[70] Hence, it should come as no surprise that for the 2024 presidential election in the United States, technology titan and the world's wealthiest person, Elon Musk, supported Donald Trump's campaign with no less than a quarter of a billion dollars, even though Trump's "dream is . . . to allow the market to function freely at its most destructive, from brutal profiteering to dismissing all ethical limitations."[71] And these limitations, of course, are not detached from the law. "He who saves his Country does not violate any Law," wrote Trump in February 2025 on the Musk-owned social media platform X, by which he meant that as president, he is above the law.[72] Pinochet similarly "felt himself to be above the law, and [therefore] had no regrets about his actions."[73] Recalling the Chilean regime, where the general "appointed judges that would look after him and lawyers that would protect him," in the current dictatorial context in the United States, Trump, through executive orders, has aimed to dismantle all forms of non-supremacist and non-imperialist programs, identities, actions, behaviors, words, and institutions, including the university as a site of critical thinking and scientific inquiry.[74] "Universities are under attack," said Jaar. And yet, "students continue to speak out."[75]

In the collapse of politics and society, where plate tectonics and technologies are shifting *within* the paradigm of modernity, at stake is a radical fight for justice that acknowledges the likelihood of its own failure, as Jaar does in his project on decolonial time. Both *The End of the World* and Jaar's art practice overall are about that fight and its continuity—even though, or perhaps precisely because, they present themselves to us as the end of the world. They are also rendered in the present tense to show that the world *is* ending, linguistically and allegorically. "And yet," as Jaar writes in an installation from 2019 (plate 15), we must "prepare to live again," that is, to continue mourning, failing, and creating in the search for accountability, inhabiting the ongoing practice of hope that drives collective efforts for liberation.

In this sense, Jaar's *The End of the World* is a decolonial response to the colonial temporality celebrated in Fukuyama's and modernity's "end of history," reminding us about the unfinished nature of the decolonial as a result of liberation's ongoing failures. This is what Frantz Fanon meant in *Black Skin, White Masks* when he argued that a truly universal world history is only possible with the "end of the world" as we know it.[76] And thus we wonder if such an end may propel the emergence of something else, or, as noted earlier, if that something has always been there, here, gravitating in the seas, earths, sounds, languages, memories, and forms—if it has always been there, here, in the poetics of decolonial time. As Césaire writes in *Notebook of a Return to the Native Land*: "What can I do? / One must begin somewhere. / Begin what? / The only thing in the world worth beginning: / The End of the world of course."[77] Beginning, from this perspective, is always tied to hope, just as hope is tied to mourning *as* reparation, accountability *as* resistance, and repetition *as* failure. Hope, in other words, is always tied to live, exist, resist, and remember, again and again. In this sense, Jaar's art—*The End of the World* as well as his entire oeuvre on modernity or the world—refuses to forget the decolonial combats of the pulsating pasts, creating dynamic temporalities that are essentially transdisciplinary, in solidarity, and ongoing.

This is what Kaleck meant at the end of our meeting in that small café in Berlin when he told me about the concept of "concrete utopia," which he developed in his 2024 book of the same name.[78] Advocating for the potential of human rights to intervene in our current global crises if they are reinvented through reexamination of their utopian roots through feminist, decolonial, and ecocritical interventions, Kaleck said: "Utopia is the right to hope."[79] Utopia from this perspective means a way of thinking, being, and relating that acknowledges the relationalities between pasts, presents, and futures, harking back to Jaar's exercises of memory and the work of so many artists, writers, poets, scholars, architects, activists, students, and lawyers. It recalls and honors all of those in cultures of resistance that create, remember, and imagine a world in becoming, or a world in decolonial time.

ACKNOWLEDGMENTS

This book would not have been possible without the support of multiple individuals and institutions across the years. First, I offer my most profound gratitude to Alfredo Jaar, who believed in this project from the start in 2014 when I visited his studio on Twenty-Sixth Street and Tenth Avenue in New York and told him I wanted to write about his work. He listened carefully, smiled, and agreed to collaborate. For the next ten years, he shared his archives and memories with me, inspiring every aspect of this book. I extend my deepest admiration to an artist and intellectual who has not stopped fighting for a more just world from the realm of aesthetics and a positionality of care, courage, and radical hope.

This book would also not have been possible without the multiple scholars, poets, journalists, artists, and thinkers who accompanied me throughout this process. Their names, narratives, and critical imaginaries are acknowledged across this volume, showing the collectivity that drives scholarly work even when "produced" in the "solitary" space of single-authored research. Writing alone does not really mean *being* alone. It means a relational, dialogic mode of ongoing inquiry that spans different disciplines, places, periods, and languages. In this book, such a dialogue involved multiple and diverse phases of learning and unlearning, reading, writing, rewriting, and multiple revision processes. It also had numerous forms of sharing, including presentations at conferences and talks, fellowship applications, informal conversations, and more. Tatiana Flores, my former advisor at Rutgers and now a great colleague and dear friend, was present at all these phases, and her brilliant intellectual insights are imprinted throughout this book. She advised me with the wisest scholarly sources, supported and encouraged my transdisciplinary and cultural bilingualism, provided me with the best tools to navigate the complexities of academia, and made herself available to chat over the phone whenever I needed. I am grateful for the opportunity to have had Tatiana as my mentor. In turn, I will be forever grateful to human rights lawyer Wolfgang Kaleck for writing the foreword to this book and for his tireless work in promoting human rights and international jurisdiction. Having his words included in this book means the world.

In 2022, after coediting two academic volumes—one on decolonial art history and the other on Chilean contemporary art—and relocating twice, from New York to Los Angeles and from Los Angeles to Montgomery County in Pennsylvania, I found myself ready to turn to completing this book. This was, of course, a challenging task but also one full of intellectual growth, inquiry, and radical joy. I am grateful to Ken Wissoker, senior executive editor at Duke University Press, for believing in this project from the start, when I emailed him in February 2024 and later met at the College Art Association (CAA) Annual Conference in Chicago. Ken's support, guidance, and enthusiasm about this project gave me the energy and trust I needed for this book's final stages. I am also grateful to project editor Lisa Lawley, assistant editors Alejandra Mejía and Ryan Kendall, and all the staff at Duke University Press. I always considered Duke the ideal place to publish this book, and I am forever grateful that this study has found its home.

Financial support received over the years was key for researching, writing, and publishing this book. This includes a Millard Meiss Publication Fund from the CAA; a Tyson Scholar Fellowship at Crystal Bridges Museum of American Art; a Patricia and Phillip Frost Fellowship at the Smithsonian American Art Museum (SAAM); a University and Louis Bevier Dissertation Completion Fellowship from the School of Graduate Studies at Rutgers University; and a predoctoral fellowship from the Center for Cultural Analysis (CCA) at Rutgers. It also includes research and travel grants from the College of Arts and Sciences at Lehigh University; the College of Arts and Letters at California State University, San Bernardino; the Center for Latin American Studies at Rutgers; the Latin American Studies Association (LASA); the Association of Historians of American Art (AHAA); and SECAC (formerly the Southeastern College Art Conference).

As with any first academic monograph researched in multiple phases and sites, many colleagues and friends provided feedback throughout the years. First, my deep gratitude to the two anonymous reviewers for their dedicated analysis of this study's theoretical debates, their bibliographic recommendations, and their intellectual kindness. Their feedback and encouragement were central to this volume's current shape. I am likewise grateful to Carl Fischer, who made me think further about the connections between extractivism, culture, and transnational wealth in Chile before and after the dictatorship, all while providing incredibly valuable editorial suggestions. Hannah

Shaw shared with me her insights on photography, representation, and repetition; Sophie Halart helped me think further about the relations between the museum, commodification, and failure; and Abbe Schriber caused me to expand more on the poetic aspect of this book. Jennifer Sichel offered critical advice at different stages of this book, and I will never forget our reading workshop at her home in Louisville, Kentucky, in the summer of 2024, when we would read our manuscripts aloud for hours and then go for walks, only to come back and read again. It was fun. I am also grateful to Matías Celedón, Paula Recart, María Gracia San Martín, and Alina Tenser for reading versions of the conclusion and providing profound critical feedback from their perspectives as fiction writers, cultural organizers, architects, and artists. Finally, I am deeply thankful to my Lehigh students Emma Wright, Jackson Darling, and Mira Principe, whose brilliant young minds helped me identify parts of this volume that needed more work from their perspectives as undergraduates in the arts and humanities. In times of obscene marketable individualism, frenetic digital excess, and euphoric celebration of ignorance, arrogance, and repression—that is, in times of profound neoliberal totality, where the market is literally governing from the state—this book is dedicated to all the students who find in the university a space for learning, unlearning, relating, and belonging through emancipatory thinking and critical practices.

In its initial phase, this study benefited from the feedback and support of E. Carmen Ramos, who encouraged me to continue thinking about the question of America within hemispheric and global art histories, Andrés Mario Zervigón, who made me think deeper about photojournalism's ethical tensions in relation to truth and doubt, and Jane Sharp, who pushed me to engage further with conceptual global debates on exhibition making and curating in relation to Jaar's art. In these early years, feedback from my peers was also central, and I am particularly grateful to Hannah Shaw and Jeff Fraiman. Living in New York at the time, we all commuted multiple times from Penn Station to New Brunswick, New Jersey, and back and studied for our orals at NYU's Bobst Library, visiting museums and exhibitions in the city, and sharing memorable dinners, ideas, and laughs—many laughs. The challenges of living abroad and studying in English as a second language, all while facing the limitations of an F1 international student visa and a narrow understanding of the complexities of US academia, were certainly not easy, and many times those years were met with frustration. Yet these friends' enthusiasm, encouragement, patience, and guidance were always there. Reciprocal friendship in academia is a powerful resource for critical thinking, confidence, and emancipatory writings.

Across the years, versions of portions of this book were presented at different symposiums, conferences, and talks, and I am grateful to their organizers for inviting me to participate in such exchange of ideas. While word-length limitations make it impossible to name them all, some of these events include a Terra Foundation conference organized by Martin Lüthe at the Freie University in Berlin in 2025; a lecture at Paloma Checa-Gismero's class on Latin American art at Swarthmore, also in 2025; a keynote talk organized by the Facultad de Artes at Universidad Católica in Temuco, Chile, in 2023; a writing workshop organized by the California Modern and Contemporary Latin American and Latino/a/x AH Network and hosted by Rosalia Romero at Pomona College in 2022; a lecture at the Rhode Island School of Design organized by Angela Dufresne in 2021; and a conversation with Jaar organized by ARTBO, Feria Internacional de Arte de Bogotá, in 2020. In turn, support from colleagues from the two institutions where I have worked was key. At Lehigh University, where I currently serve as an assistant professor of art history, I am grateful to Nicholas Sawicki and Matthew Bush, who have been incredible mentors in the process of navigating first monograph publishing. I am also deeply thankful to Jane Chin Davidson for her brilliant and invaluable mentorship from 2020 to 2022, when I served as assistant professor of art history and global cultures at California State University, San Bernardino.

In turn, I offer my gratitude for editorial feedback and support in versions of this book published previously as an essay and book chapter. An early version of debates in chapter 2 was published as "Decolonial Temporality in Alfredo Jaar's *The Kissinger Project*" in *ASAP/Journal* in spring 2019. A Portuguese translation of this article was published as "Temporalidade Decolonial no *The Kissinger Project* de Alfredo Jaar" in *Revista Poiésis* from the Universidade Federal Fluminense in 2020. Furthermore, an early version of debates in chapter 3 was published as "On Failure and the Nation State: A Decolonial Reading of Alfredo Jaar's *A Logo for America*," in *The Routledge Companion to Decolonizing Art History*, edited by Tatiana Flores, Charlene Villaseñor Black, and myself in 2023.

This book was heavily researched at archival centers and libraries in multiple cities, from New York, Houston, Chicago, New Haven, Storrs, Waterville, and Washington, DC, to Santiago, Madrid, and Berlin. I am particularly grateful to Elizabeth Botten from the Archives of American Art at the Smithsonian Institution for her dedicated and generous assistance over the years. I am also thankful to Bill Casari from the Hostos Community College Archive; Elizabeth Finch from the Colby College Museum of Art archive; Kelly R. Haydon and John M. Zarrillo from Fales and Tamiment archives at

New York University's Elmer Holmes Bobst Library; Nora Heymann from the International Center for the Art of the Americas; Martin Maischberger and Beate Ebelt-Borchert from the Central Archive of the Berlin State Museums; Jenny Tobias from the Museum of Modern Art; Jonathan Trinque from the Archives and Special Collections at the University of Connecticut Library; Jordan Wright from the Hanna Holborn Gray Special Collections Research Center at the University of Chicago; and staff from Yale University Library, the Library and Documentation Centre at Museo Reina Sofía, and the Ibero-American Institute in Berlin; and from Chile's Centro de Documentación de Artes Visuales, Biblioteca Nacional, and Museo de la Memoria y los Derechos Humanos. In turn, this book would have not been possible without the support of studio assistants, museum professionals, and fellowship coordinators. At Jaar's studio, I offer my deep gratitude to Daniel Felix, Capucine Gros, Pablo Montealegre, and John Rohrer. I am also grateful to Carola Chacón and Pamela Navarro Carreno from Chile's Museo de Arte Contemporáneo; Denhart V. Harling from KINDL in Berlin; Amelia Goerlitz and Stacy Weiland from the Smithsonian American Art Museum; Mindy N. Besaw and Taylor Pecktal from Crystal Bridges Museum of American Art; and Pam Mongi from the Department of Art, Architecture and Design at Lehigh University. Furthermore, I would like to thank Sheila McMahon for copyediting and Andrew Ascherl for preparing the index..

For a book on a living artist and contingent critical debates, conversations with people across disciplines was essential, and I am thankful for all those individuals who shared with me their memories, knowledge, and perceptions about art, culture, politics, and history through interviews, email correspondence, telephone conversations, and more. I am particularly grateful to art critic Lucy Lippard, whose writings, email correspondence, and archives significantly helped shape this research. I am also thankful to art historians David Kunzle and Emma Oslé; curators and art professionals Taína Caragol, Julia P. Herzberg, Nilda Peraza, and Mari Carmen Ramírez; journalists John Dinges and Peter Kornbluh; artists Papo Colo, Rafael Máximo Colón, Mario Fonseca, Jerry Kearns, Nicolás Manning, Susan Meiselas, Freddy Rodríguez, Juan Sanchez, Jake Scharbach, Jorge Tacla, Cecilia Vicuña, Manuela Viera Gallo, and Marshall Weber; architects Jorge Dalmazzo, Isabel Devés, Humberto Eliash, Jorge Iglesis, Miguel Lawner, Pedro Murtinho, and Bernardo Urquieta; writers Mark Eisner, Alejandro Moreno, and Ivan Monalisa Ojeda; and poets Carmen Berenger and Raúl Zurita. I also extend my deepest gratitude to design and architecture historian Evelyn Maynard (Jaar's wife), and to family and friends who offered hospitality and care when I conducted research in various cities, from Santiago to the Atacama Desert and from Berlin to Paris, and Madrid. You all make me feel at home. To Carmen, Pedro, Gabriela, Maggie, Beatriz, Arturito, Josefina, Danielita, Cristóbal, María Paz, Felipe, Alejandro, Yael, Jesús, and Emmanuel: *Gracias*.

Lastly, my profound gratitude to my parents, Eduardo and Verónica, for their unconditional support. *Por escucharme hablar de mi investigación tantas veces y por tantos años, por existir y por hacerme existir. Gracias por ser personas tan compresivas, tan generosas, por entender tanto. Este libro y todo lo que hago es por y gracias a ustedes.* My gratitude also goes to my sisters, best friends, and admired artists and architects, María Verónica and María Gracia, as well as to my thirteen-year-old nephew, Salvi. Finally, I extend my deepest gratitude to my husband, Josh, whom I met in a Scottish pub in Brooklyn in the summer of 2012, and who has accompanied me ever since, walking this journey alongside me with immense support, patience, criticality, humor, care, and love.

NOTES

FOREWORD. VIVIMOS ADENTRO, PERO EN CONTRA

1. Telephone conversation (hereafter TELCON) between Nixon and Kissinger, 11:50 a.m., September 16, 1973, Freedom of Information Act (hereafter FOIA) website, https://www.foia.gov/.

2. Jaar, *Eine Ästhetik des Widerstands*, 174.

3. Donoso, "Obra de Alfredo Jaar," 26.

INTRODUCTION. DECOLONIAL TIME AND THE AESTHETICS OF THE UNFINISHED

1. "New York Columbus Day 1992 October 12th," Helga Vintage, May 9, 2020, https://www.youtube.com/watch?v=hVYacklSYbE.

2. The work was commissioned by the Public Art Fund, an organization that supports the development and exhibition of contemporary art in public spaces, in collaboration with the Whitney Museum of American Art and the American Center in Paris. It was also part of the multimedia exhibition *Trans-Voices*, in which fifty artists intervened with social and political content in publicity announcements in New York's Spring Station and subways in Paris.

3. Typescript of exhibition *Trans-Voices*, 1992, Series VI, Subseries A, Box 44, Folder 17, Public Art Fund Archive, Fales Library and Special Collections, Elmer Holmes Bobst Library, New York University (NYU) (hereafter Public Art Fund Archive).

4. Sachs, "Introduction," 457.

5. Jaar, "Questionnaire."

6. "Deep Dive: Alfredo Jaar," interview with Gary Carrion-Murayari, New Museum, November 8, 2022, https://www.youtube.com/watch?v=NAbA7CTiMWA.

7. For more on modernity/coloniality, see, among others, Dussel, "Eurocentrism and Modernity"; Lugones, "Heterosexualism"; Maldonado-Torres, "Thinking Through the Decolonial Turn"; Mignolo, *Darker Side of Western Modernity*; Mignolo, "Geopolitics of Knowledge"; Moraña et al., *Coloniality at Large*; Quijano, "Coloniality and Modernity/Rationality"; and R. Vázquez, "Translation as Erasure."

8. Mignolo, *Darker Side of Western Modernity*, 217.

9. Quijano and Wallerstein, "Americanity as a Concept," 549.

10. Quijano and Wallerstein, "Americanity as a Concept," 549.

11. Quijano and Wallerstein, "Americanity as a Concept," 549.

12. Quijano and Wallerstein, "Americanity as a Concept," 551.

13. Quijano, *Vivir adentro y en contra*, 54.

14. For more on coloniality of power, see Quijano, "Coloniality of Power, Eurocentrism, and Latin America."

15. Donoso, "Obra de Alfredo Jaar," 26. Unless otherwise indicated, all translations are mine.

16. Beckett, *Unnamable.*

17. Gramsci, *Letters from Prison*, 159.

18. Quijano, *Vivir adentro y en contra*, 54.

19. Dominic Rushe, "Art Provocateur Alfredo Jaar: 'I Want to Change the World. I Fail All the Time,'" *Guardian*, August 1, 2019.

20. Taylor, *¡Presente!*, 2.

21. Jaar and Levi Strauss, "Temptation to Exist."

22. Jaar and Levi Strauss, "Temptation to Exist."

23. Batchen, *Negative/Positive*, xxi.

24. Pelaez Lopez, "Alán Pelaez Lopez—Art of the Matter."

25. R. Vázquez, "Modernity Coloniality and Visibility," 112.

26. Maldonado-Torres, "Thinking Through the Decolonial Turn," 1–2.

27. Williams, "Structures of Feeling," 128. I want to thank Matthew Bush for sharing this reference with me.

28. Du Bois, "Comet."

29. R. Vázquez, "Modernity Coloniality and Visibility," 113.

30. R. Vázquez, "Museum, Decoloniality and the End of the Contemporary," 182.

31. For more on this, see Hutton, "Overcoming Art History's Meta-Narrative."

32. For more on this, see San Martín, "Time, Love and the Museum."

33. Ellis, "Being an Indigenous Art Historian," 64.

34. Beckett, *Worstward Ho*, 39.

35. O'Gorman, *Invention of America*, 10.

36. Mignolo, *Idea of Latin America*, 13.

37. Césaire, *Discourse on Colonialism*, 32–33.

38. See Quijano Valencia, "Reseña," 255–62.

39. Titled *Aquí: 27 Latin American Artists Living and Working in the United States*, this exhibition included the work of Latin American and Latinx artists living in the United States, including, among others, Cuban American Ana Mendieta, Uruguayan Luis Camnitzer, Puerto Rico–born Papo Colo, and Argentines Liliana Porter and Leandro Katz. See Lugo-Saavedra and Spray, *Aquí.*

40. Castañeda de la Paz, "Tira de la peregrinación," 183–84.

41. Taylor, *¡Presente!*, 43–44.

42. Taylor, *¡Presente!*, 43–44.

43. Ingold, *Lines*, 2.

44. For more on this sense of superiority, see Rivera Cusicanqui, "Ch'ixinakax utxiwa."

45. See de Las Casas, *In Defense of the Indians*. Significantly, according to Maldonado-Torres, this debate represents "a staging of some of the most fundamental questions and terms about the meaning of the human in the context of Western modernity." Maldonado-Torres, "Liberation Philosophy," 17.

46. Cabral, "National Liberation and Culture," 14.

47. Rivera Cusicanqui, "Ch'ixinakax utxiwa," 99.

48. Rivera Cusicanqui, "Ch'ixinakax utxiwa," 99.

49. Cabral, "National Liberation and Culture," 15.

50. Mignolo, "Crossing Gazes," 183.

51. Mignolo, *Idea of Latin America*, 76.

52. Mignolo, *Idea of Latin America*, 77.

53. For more on the concept of coevalness, see Fabian, *Time and the Other*.

54. Rosenberg, *After Human Rights*, 5.

55. Friedman, "Free Markets and the Generals," 59.

56. Friedman, "Free Markets and the Generals," 59 (author's emphasis).

57. Grandin, *Empire's Workshop*, 165. For critical approaches to Friedman's miracle, see Klein, *Shock Doctrine*; Richards, *Race and the Chilean Miracle*; Winn, *Victims of the Chilean Miracle*.

58. Kornbluh, *Pinochet File*, 591.

59. Avelar, "Dictatorship and Immanence," 75–76.

60. Orlando Letelier, "The 'Chicago Boys' in Chile," *Nation*, August 28, 1976.

61. Memorandum of Conversation (hereafter MEMCON), "U.S.-Chilean Relations" (Kissinger—Pinochet), June 8, 1976, FOIA website.

62. For more on Guzmán and the political ideology of *gremialismo*, see Castro, "Jaime Guzmán."

63. See Kornbluh and Schlotterbeck, "Reagan y Pinochet."

64. Gómez-Barris, *Where Memory Dwells*, 3.

65. Bachelet's father, Alberto Bachelet, was brigadier general of the Chilean Air Forces under Allende. He died in 1974 after being tortured by the military for opposing the coup, and his family was detained, tortured, and forced into exile. For more on critical accounts on the end of the transition, see Barton and Murray, "The End of Transition?," 329–38.

66. Trump White House Archives, "Remarks by President Trump and President Piñera of Chile Before Bilateral Meeting," September 28, 2018, https://trumpwhitehouse.archives.gov/briefings-statements/remarks-president-trump-president-pinera-chile-bilateral-meeting.

67. "La inusual sorpresa que mostró el Presidente Piñera en reunión con Trump," Meganoticias, September 28, 2018, https://www.youtube.com/watch?v=3H1-Lon-kE4&APS/APS.

68. Mignolo, *Idea of Latin America*, 57–58.

69. Grandin, *Empire's Workshop*, 15.

70. Grandin, *Empire's Workshop*, 15.

71. Main, "Is Latin America Still?"

72. "Secretary of State Marco Rubio and Mexican Foreign Secretary Juan Ramón de la Fuente at a Joint Press Availability," U.S. Department of State, September 3, 2025, https://www.state.gov/releases/office-of-the-spokesperson/2025/09/secretary-of-state-marco-rubio-and-mexican-foreign-secretary-juan-ramon-de-la-fuente-at-a-joint-press-availability.

73. For more on the social outbreak in relation to the arts, see San Martín et al., *Dismantling the Nation*; and Gordon-Zolov and Zolov, *Walls of Santiago*. For more on the transnational scope of the social outbreak, see, for instance, Draper et al., "Feminist Performance."

74. "'We Are at War': Chile's Pinera Extends State of Emergency," *Al Jazeera*, October 21, 2019.

75. "Chile Launches Fresh Talks to Calm Deadly Unrest," *Straits Times*, November 1, 2019.

76. Jaar, "Es difícil" (2021).

77. Jaar, "I Can't Go On, I'll Go On."

78. Hernandez, "Why Trump Is Talking."

79. Smith, *Decolonizing Methodologies*, 20.

80. Chomsky and Pappé, *On Palestine*, xiii.

81. Santayana, *Life of Reason*, 284.

82. Yamashita and Ly, "Going Backward to Move Forward."

83. Yamashita and Ly, "Going Backward to Move Forward."

84. Jaar, "Message from the Artist," 15.

85. Maldonado-Torres, "Thinking Through the Decolonial Turn," 2.

86. See Jaar and Siitari, "I Need to Understand the World," 69.

87. Pérez-Oramas, *Power of an Idea*, 29.

88. Cohen-Aponte, "Pathways to Art History," 208; Love, *We Want to Do More Than Survive*, 100–101.

89. Love, *We Want to Do More Than Survive*, 100–101.

90. Donna Ristorucci, "Angela Davis Case Stirs World Peace Council Assembly," *Daily World*, June 17, 1971, 6.

91. "Angela Davis Leads Allende Rally Here," *New York Times*, September 12, 1973, 18.

92. Lawner, "Solidaridad internacional," 58.

93. Alfredo Jaar, interview with the author, New York City, March 10, 2017.

94. Jorge Dalmazzo, Skype interview with the author, October 17, 2017.

95. Dalmazzo, interview.

96. Isabel Devés, Skype interview with the author, September 24, 2017.

97. Bernardo Urquieta, Skype interview with the author, September 26, 2017.

98. Jorge Iglesis, Skype interview with the author, September 24, 2017.

99. Frank, *Manifestos and Polemics*, 215–16.

100. Chambers, "Writing About Art History," 49.

101. Ricoeur, *Time and Narrative*, 258.

102. Ferraz, *Lina Bo Bardi*, 327.

103. Coronil, "Beyond Occidentalism," 61.

104. Grandin, *America, América,* 448. For more on the relations between the dictatorship and education in Chile, see Errázuriz, "Dictadura militar en Chile"; and C. Ruiz, *De la república al mercado.*

105. For a comprehensive historical study on this project, see Vazquez, *Alfredo Jaar*; and Valdés, *Alfredo Jaar.*

106. Segal, *Radical Happiness,* 5.

107. Muriel Alarcón, "El mundo del arte en Chile no me entendió, no me daban pelota," *El Mercurio* (Santiago, Chile), November 7, 2017.

108. Foxley, "Felicidad en la mira," 41.

109. Lispector, *The Hour of the Star,* 11. I thank Paula Recart for sharing this reference with me.

110. Alfredo Jaar, interview with the author, New York City, October 8, 2017.

111. Césaire, *Discourse on Colonialism*; B. Benjamin, *Invested Interests,* 114.

112. Carmen Castillo, "Mi felicidad es la lucha," *Jacobin,* October 5, 2024, https://jacobinlat.com/2024/10/mi-felicidad-es-la-lucha2/.

113. Castillo, "Mi felicidad es la lucha."

114. Works of nonfiction, novels, documentary films, and essays by and about former victims of the regime who collaborated with the military abound. See, for instance, Luz Arce, *Inferno: A Story of Terror and Survival in Chile,* trans. Stacey Alba Skar (Madison: University of Wisconsin Press, 2004); Diamela Eltit, "Cuerpos Nómadas," *Debate Feminista* 14 (1996): 101–17; Arturo Fontaine, *La vida doble* (Barcelona: Tusquets Editores, 2010); and Michael J. Lazzara, ed., *Luz Arce and Pinochet's Chile: Testimony in the Aftermath of State Violence* (Palgrave Macmillan, 2011).

115. Gabara, *Non-Literary Fiction,* 13.

116. Gabara, *Non-Literary Fiction,* 19.

117. Gabara, *Non-Literary Fiction,* 19; Valdés, *Alfredo Jaar.*

118. Valdés, *Alfredo Jaar.* The original quote from Achebe reads: "Actually, art is man's constant effort to create for himself a different order of reality from that which is given to him; an aspiration to provide himself with a second handle on existence through his imagination." Achebe, "Truth of Fiction," 139.

119. Jaar "Peripatetic Artist," 131.

120. Jaar, "Peripatetic Artist," 131.

121. W. Benjamin, "Work of Art," 41.

122. Jaar, "Peripatetic Artist," 131.

123. Lowenhaupt Tsing, *Friction,* 11–12.

124. Pollock, "Not Forgetting Africa," 117.

125. Jaar and Siitari, "I Need to Understand the World," 69.

126. Sky O'Brien, "Person-to-Person with Alfredo Jaar," *Dispatches Magazine* (July 26, 2023): 28–33.

127. Ikenberry, "Why the Liberal World Order Will Survive," 18.

128. Typescript of exhibition *Trans-Voices,* 1992, Series VI, Subseries A, Box 44, Folder 17, Public Art Fund Archive.

129. Shah, "Trump Invokes the Alien Enemies Act."

130. "J.D. Vance | The Universities Are the Enemy | National Conservatism Conference II," National Conservatism, November 10, 2021, https://www.youtube.com/watch?v=oFR65Cifnhw.

131. Jaar, "End of the World."

132. Alfredo Jaar, Zoom interview with the author, October 10, 2024.

133. Jaar, "Understanding the World Before Acting in It."

134. Jaar, "End of the World."

135. Jaar, "End of the World."

136. Jaar, "Alfredo Jaar Accepts."

137. Alfredo Jaar, review, author not identified, 1985, Box 1:6, Folder 11, Alfredo Jaar, Installation Projects, 1980–1985, Grey Art Gallery and Study Center Archive 1975–1997, Fales Library and Special Collections, New York University.

138. Bush, *Other Americans*, 23.

139. See, for instance, Ramírez, "Beyond 'The Fantastic'"; Goldman, "Booming Spirit of Latin America"; and Caragol, "Boom and Dust."

140. Barriendos Rodríguez, "La idea del arte latinoamericano," 47–51.

141. Baddeley and Fraser, *Drawing the Line*, 4.

142. Franco, *Decline and Fall of the Lettered City*, 125.

143. Benitez-Rojo, *Repeating Island*, 186–87.

144. Jaar, "Photography and Politics."

145. Avelar, *Alegorías de la derrota*, 10.

146. Franco, "Memoria, narración y repetición," 116.

147. Avelar, *Untimely Present*, 33.

148. Gerald M. Boyd, "Reagan Terms Nicaraguan Rebels' Moral Equal of Founding Fathers," *New York Times*, March 2, 1985.

149. Quijano and Wallerstein, "Americanity as a Concept," 550.

150. Jaar, "Understanding the World Before Acting in It."

151. Shah Stamets, "Were His Priorities Out of Focus?"

152. Sontag, *Regarding the Pain of Others*, 117.

153. Sontag, *Regarding the Pain of Others*, 117.

154. "Video interview with Koen Wessing," in *Alfredo Jaar: Shadows*, Galerie Lelong. New York, 2014.

155. Such was the case of photojournalist Rodrigo Rojas de Negri, who was burned alive during a street demonstration against the dictatorship in 1986.

156. Roberta Smith, "One Image of Agony Resonates in Two Lives," *New York Times*, April 14, 2009.

157. R. Smith, "One Image of Agony."

158. Rancière, "Theater of Images," 76.

159. Azoulay, *Civil Imagination*, 59.

160. Azoulay, *Civil Imagination*, 59.

161. Linfield, *Cruel Radiance*.

162. For more on this aspect of photography, see Linfield, *Cruel Radiance*.

163. Giunta, "Politics of Representation," n.p.

164. Avelar, *Untimely Present*, 21.

165. W. Benjamin, *Illuminations*, 256.

166. W. Benjamin, *Illuminations*, 256.

167. Alfredo Jaar, Zoom interview with the author, October 11, 2024.

168. Glissant, *Poetics of Relation*, 32.

169. Glissant, *Poetics of Relation*, 32.

170. Glissant, *Poetics of Relation*, xii.

171. Glissant, "Robben's Rocks," n.p.

172. For more on Glissant's idea of *tout-monde*, see Glissant, *Philosophie de la Relation*. For more on archipelagic thinking in relation to the visual arts, see Flores and Stephens, *Relational Undercurrents*.

173. Glissant, *Poetics of Relation*, 26; Jaar, interview, October 11, 2024.

174. For more on clock time, see Barad, "Troubling Time/s."

175. Césaire, *Notebook of a Return*, 27.

176. Ly, "Of Performance," 109. See also Williams, "Structures of Feeling," 128.

177. Maturana, "What Is It to See?"; see also Veronelli, "La colonialidad del lenguaje," 152.

CHAPTER ONE. MOURNING

1. Jaar and Siitari, "I Need to Understand the World," 67.

2. Estimates place the number of tortured individuals at around 40,000; and as many as 3,200 were killed or disappeared during the dictatorship.

3. In this regard, Idelber Avelar argues: "Allegorically speaking, it could be argued that [with] the bombing of Allende's presidential palace [and] the Chilean Popular Unity's demise [in September 1973], all modernization in the Southern Cone came to spell integration into the global capitalist market. . . . This was, let us make no mistake, the central role of the military regimes: to purge the social body of all elements that could offer some resistance to a generalized opening to multinational capital." Avelar, *Untimely Present*, 35–36.

4. Lazzara and Unruh, *Telling Ruins in Latin America*, 4.

5. Hartman, "Time of Slavery," 769.

6. For a critical approach to these protests, see Kaplan, *Taking Back the Streets*.

7. Kaplan, *Taking Back the Streets*, 66–67.

8. Paul Rosenstein-Rodan, "Allende's Big Failing: Incompetence," *New York Times*, June 16, 1974.

9. Nathan Thornburgh, "Chile's 9/11: President Piñera Speaks with TIME on 40th Anniversary of the Coup," *Time* magazine, September 11, 2013.

10. "José Antonio Kast: 'La primera dictadura en Chile fue la Salvador Allende,'" esRadio, October 12, 2022, https://www.youtube.com/watch?v=cHtXidBEylA.

11. Jack Anderson, "Memos Bare ITT Try for Chile Coup," *Washington Post*, March 21, 1972.

12. Secretaría General de Gobierno, *Documentos secretos de la ITT*, 79.

13. Kornbluh, *Pinochet File*; Qureshi, *Nixon, Kissinger, and Allende*.

14. "Jack Anderson Interview with Chilean Television," FOIA, March 27, 1972, https://www.cia.gov/readingroom/docs/CIA-RDP74B00415R000300020011-1.pdf. The interviewer, José Miguel Varas, was a Chilean journalist who in 2006 was awarded the National Prize for Literature. A member of the Communist Party, Varas exiled after the coup in the Soviet Union, where he hosted "Escucha Chile" in Radio Moscú, a key event in the transnational solidarity movement. See Lawner, "Solidaridad internacional."

15. Secretaría General de Gobierno, *Documentos secretos de la ITT*, 5.

16. Pratt, *Planetary Longings*, 15.

17. Neruda, "Victory," poem VIII in *Call for the Destruction of Nixon*, n.p. The English translation of Neruda's last collection of poems was published as a bilingual edition in 1980 by West End Press, a US publishing house founded in New York City in 1975 that specializes in politically progressive literature.

18. Notes on Meeting with the President on Chile, September 15, 1970, National Security Archive, https://nsarchive.gwu.edu/document/23592-cia-notes-meeting-president-chile-15-25-sept-15-70-september-15-1970.

19. Allende, "Speech to the United Nations."

20. Greg Grandin, "The TPP Will Finish What Chile's Dictatorship Started," *The Nation*, September 11, 2015.

21. Robert Aldendec, "Mr. Allende Follows Outline of Speech," *New York Times*, December 5, 1972.

22. Aldendec, "Mr. Allende Follows Outline of Speech."

23. Máximo Rafael Colón, interview with the author, New York City, June 15, 2018.

24. Máximo Rafael Colón, interview.

25. Colón, interview.

26. For more on this museum and collection, see Zaldívar, *40 años Museo de la Solidaridad*.

27. Allende Gossens, "A los artistas del mundo," 170.

28. Dore Ashton, transcript of an oral history conducted 2010–11, Dore Ashton papers, 1849, ca. 1928–2014, Archives of American Art (hereafter AAA), Smithsonian Institution, Washington, DC.

29. Dore Ashton, "Critical Exercise of Freedom," in Zaldívar, *40 años Museo de la Solidaridad*, 311.

30. Call for Participation, El Museo de la Solidaridad, Chile, Dore Ashton papers, 1849, circa 1928–2014, AAA.

31. Orlando Letelier, thank-you letter, Dore Ashton papers, 1849, circa 1928–2014, AAA.

32. For more on artistic practices engaged with the solidarity movement with Vietnam, see Bryan-Wilson, *Art Workers*. See also Ho, *Artists Respond*.

33. Call for Participation, El Museo de la Solidaridad, Chile.

34. Dinges, "Expats After the Coup."

35. Alfredo Jaar, Zoom interview with the author, March 10, 2022.

36. For more on the burning of books, see Collyer, "De las hogueras a la imprenta."

37. Lopez Lloreda, "Pablo Neruda Was Poisoned to Death, a New Forensic Report Suggests," *Sifter*, February 15, 2023. See also Pascale Bonnefoy, "Cancer Didn't Kill Pablo Neruda, Panel Finds. Was It Murder?," *New York Times*, October 21, 2017.

38. Graciela Mochkofsky, "The Second Death of Pablo Neruda," *New Yorker*, February 6, 2024.

39. Nicolás Valencia, "¿Es usted feliz?," *ArchDaily*, October 27, 2017.

40. Neruda, "A Brief Explanation," in *Call for the Destruction of Nixon*, n.p.

41. Neruda, "I Begin by Invoking Walt Whitman," poem I in *Call for the Destruction of Nixon*, n.p.

42. Qureshi, *Nixon, Kissinger, and Allende*, 60–69.

43. Neruda, "My General, Good-Bye," poem XXIX in *Call for the Destruction of Nixon*, n.p.

44. Carmen Castillo, interview with the author, Santiago, Chile, November 8, 2023.

45. Conger, *Nilton da Silva Rosa*, 23.

46. "Chilean Jailing Prompts Inquiry," newspaper clipping, Chicago Committee to Save Lives in Chile Records, 1973–2009, Hanna Holborn Gray Special Collections Research Center (SCRC), University of Chicago Library.

47. Castillo, interview.

48. North American Congress on Latin America (NACLA) Archive of Latin Americana, Archives and Special Collections, Thomas J. Dodd Research Center, University of Connecticut Libraries, Storrs, CT.

49. Etcheverry Arcaya, "Da Silva Nilton."

50. S. Ruiz, *Left Turns in Brown Study*, 6.

51. Patricio Guzmán, dir., *Nostalgia for the Light* (Brooklyn, NY: Icarus Films, 2016), DVD.

52. Patricio Guzmán, dir., *Chile, Obstinate Memory* (New York: First Run / Icarus Films, 1997), DVD.

53. Richard, "La escena de avanzada," 260.

54. See Silvio Caiozzi, dir., *Fernando ha vuelto* (Santiago: Andrea Films, 2006), DVD.

55. Label for section "Politics" in exhibition *En el aire conmovido . . .* (*In the Troubled Air . . .*), curated by Georges Didi-Huberman at the Museo Reina Sofía, viewed on January 15, 2025.

56. Mistral, "Aniversario," 90–91.

57. Valencia, "¿Es usted feliz?"

58. Alfredo Jaar, Zoom interview with the author, March 10, 2018.

59. Millán, "Poem 48 from The City," 115.

60. Millán, "Poem 48 from The City," 115.

61. Demonstration at Columbia University, US Committee for Justice to Latin American Political Prisoners (hereafter USLA), Lucy R. Lippard papers, 1930s–2010, bulk 1960–1990, AAA.

62. Colón, interview.

63. USLA, newsletter, 1973, Lucy R. Lippard papers, 1930s–2010, bulk 1960–1990, AAA.

64. USLA, Lucy R. Lippard papers, 1930s–2010, bulk 1960–1990, AAA.

65. Carla Machiavello, "Entrevista a Dore Ashton," in Zaldívar, *40 años Museo de la Solidaridad*, 61.

66. I have written in depth about this elsewhere. See, for instance, San Martín, "Aesthetics of Disobedience"; San Martín, "Politics of Collectivity"; and San Martín, *Todavía somos el tiempo*.

67. An Evening of Solidarity with the Victims of Repression in Chile, 1973, Lucy R. Lippard papers, 1930s–2010, bulk 1960–1990, AAA.

68. Lucy Lippard, email to author, February 22, 2018.

69. Chile Emergency Exhibition, Lucy R. Lippard papers, 1930s–2010, bulk 1960–1990, AAA.

70. Poster for *Chile Emergency Exhibition*, Ivan Karp's Gallery, 1974, Dore Ashton papers, 1849, circa 1928–2014 (oversize), AAA.

71. Documents for *Chile Emergency Exhibition*, Dore Ashton papers, 1849, circa 1928–2014, Box 27, AAA.

72. Documents for *Chile Emergency Exhibition*, Dore Ashton papers, 1849, circa 1928–2014, Box 27, AAA.

73. Documents for *Chile Emergency Exhibition*, Dore Ashton papers, 1849, circa 1928–2014, Box 27, AAA.

74. Documents for *Chile Emergency Exhibition*, Dore Ashton papers, 1849, circa 1928–2014, Box 27, AAA.

75. Ximena Rojas, letter to Dore Ashton, November 20, 1973, Dore Ashton papers, 1849, circa 1928–2014, AAA.

76. Notes on the Solidarity Movement with Chile, 1973, Lucy R. Lippard papers, 1930s–2010, bulk 1960–1990, AAA.

77. Transcript of Orlando Letelier's Speech at the Felt Forum, Madison Square Garden, September 10, 1976, Transnational Institute, https://www.tni.org/en/article/transcript-of-orlando-leteliers-speech-at-the-felt-forum.

78. Letelier, "'Chicago Boys' in Chile." For more on Letelier's assassination, see Dinges, *Condor Years*.

79. Brochure for the Memorial Exhibition for Letelier organized by Dore Ashton at Cayman Gallery, Political Art Documentation/Distribution (hereafter PAD/D) Archive, Museum of Modern Art (MoMA), New York. For more information on Cayman/MoCHA, see Caragol, "Boom and Dust."

80. Call for Participation, October Solidarity with Chilean Democracy: A Memorial to Orlando Letelier, PAD/D Archive, Museum of Modern Art (MoMA), New York. Among other organizers of the event were Chilean-born, New York–based artist Juan Manuel Gomez-Quiroz and US artists Rudolf Baranik, Irving Petlin, and Carl Andre.

81. Call for Participation, October Solidarity with Chilean Democracy: A Memorial to Orlando Letelier.

82. Brochure for the memorial exhibition for Letelier organized by Dore Ashton at Cayman Gallery, New York, PAD/D Archive, pamphlet file: miscellaneous uncatalogued material.

83. Brochure for the memorial exhibition for Letelier organized by Dore Ashton at Cayman Gallery, New York.

84. Alfredo Jaar, *Dore Ashton, You Know*, 2015, video, 9 min., 25 sec., https://www.youtube.com/watch?v=sDPcYsT8Y6I.

85. Jaar and Ashton were introduced by Juan Downey, a Chilean-born artist who, like Jaar, was a trained architect.

86. Jaar, "Art in Conversation."

87. Walsh, "Open Letter to the Military Junta."

88. March 24, the date of Walsh's letter, is celebrated as Argentina's Day of Remembrance for Truth and Justice.

89. Walsh, "Open Letter to the Military Junta."

90. Jaar, "It Is Difficult" (2015).

91. Jaar, "It Is Difficult" (2015).

92. Jaar, "It Is Difficult" (2015).

93. Giunta, "Politics of Representation."

94. Giunta, "Politics of Representation."

95. Richard, *Políticas y estéticas de la memoria*, 11–12.

96. Jaar, "It Is Difficult" (2015).

97. Jaar, "It Is Difficult" (2015).

98. Jaar, "It Is Difficult" (2015).

99. Jaar, "It Is Difficult" (2015).

100. For more on the term *anchoring*, see Barthes, "Rhetoric of the Image," in *Image, Music, Text*.

101. Jaar, "It Is Difficult" (2015).

102. Rosler, "In, Around and Afterthoughts," 315.

103. Nathan Thornburgh, "40 years After Pinochet's Bloody Coup, War Photographer David Burnett Travels Back to Chile in Search of His Most Famous Subject," *Roads and Kingdoms*, September 12, 2013.

104. In 1996, for instance, Jaar created *Camera Lucida*, an "homage" project to Barthes on photography, social engagement, criminalization, and the need for a decolonial museum in the city of Catia in Venezuela. For more on this project, see Julia Bryan-Wilson, "Alfredo Jaar: Catia," in *Collaboration: A Potential History of Photography* (New York: Thames and Hudson, 2024), 150–51.

105. Barthes, *Camera Lucida*, 27.

106. Barthes, *Camera Lucida*, 26–27.

107. Barthes, *Camera Lucida*, 51.

108. See Batchen, "Palinode: An Introduction to *Photography Degree Zero*."

109. Barthes, *Camera Lucida*, 73.

110. Richard, "Sitios de la memoria."

111. Sekula, "Dismantling Modernism," 860, 859.

112. For more on circulation of photographs in the context of regimes in Latin America, see Giunta, "Politics of Representation."

113. Feinstein, *Pablo Neruda*, 395.

114. "Funeral de Pablo Neruda 1973," Manuel Ubalde, December 10, 2011, https://www.youtube.com/watch?v=xF7s8CM-dTY.

115. Millán, "Poem 48 from The City," 115.

116. Millán, "Poem 48 from The City," 115.

117. Taylor, *¡Presente!*, 10.

118. Juan Williams, "Thousands March in Memorial Exhibition to Letelier," *Washington Post*, September 27, 1976, copy in Orlando Letelier Folder, Tamiment Library Archives, Fales Library and Special Collections, Elmer Holmes Bobst Library, New York University.

119. Williams, "Thousands March in Memorial Exhibition to Letelier."

120. Wolfgang Kaleck, "Edward Snowden's Lawyer Wolfgang Kaleck on the Global Fight for Human Rights," *Democracy Now!*, January 25, 2019, https://www.youtube.com/watch?v=oFQUG-MQCOw.

121. For more on the Chilean student movement, see Espinoza et al., "Student Movement in Chile."

122. See Salvador Allende, "Discurso del presidente salvador allende en el auditorio central del instituto de ciencias sociales y humanidades de la universidad de Guadalajara," Fundación Salvador Allende, December 2, 1972, https://fundacionsalvadorallende.cl/discurso-del-presidente-salvador-allende-en-el-auditorio-central-del-instituto-de-ciencias-sociales-y-humanidades-de-la-universidad-de-guadalajara/. For more on Allende's idea of youth and revolution, see Moraga Valle, "'Ser jóven y no ser revolucionario.'"

123. Moraga Valle, "'Ser jóven y no ser revolucionario,'" 370.

124. Mas Vall, "Per què la Guerra?"

125. Importantly, this same banner was used in previous demonstrations by Brown University students on campus, including marches in solidarity with the Federación Universitaria Pro Independencia (FUPI, Pro-Independence University Federation of Puerto Rico) and labor strikes by facilities staff. Daniel Enrique Torres Marrero, email to author, May 13, 2024.

126. Butler, *Precarious Life*, 19.

127. Freud, "Mourning and Melancholia."

128. Freud, "Mourning and Melancholia."

129. Butler, *Precarious Life*, 21.

130. Jaar, "Photography and Politics."

131. Butler, *Precarious Life*, 32.

132. Hartman, "Time of Slavery," 769.

133. Amira Hass, "Israeli Journalist Amira Hass, Daughter of Holocaust Survivors, Calls for Gaza Ceasefire Now," *Democracy Now!*, October 20, 2023.

134. Marcelo Garzo Montalvo, presentation at Florencia San Martín's Latin American Art class, Lehigh University, April 11, 2024.

135. Garzo Montalvo, presentation, April 11, 2024.

136. "FUNA a Alejandro Saez Mardones, Caso Degollados," Señal 3 La Victoria, April 3, 2016, https://www.youtube.com/watch?v=Rs1vmR7jY6g.

137. Gómez-Barris, *Where Memory Dwells*, 5–6.

138. For more on this case, see "Guerrero Ceballos Manuel Leonidas," Memoria Viva, accessed January 15, 2025, https://memoriaviva.com/nuevaweb/ejecutados

-politicos/ejecutados-politicos-g/guerrero-ceballos-manuel-leonidas/; "Santiago Nattino Allende (1921–1985)," Memoria Chilena, accessed January 15, 2025, https://www.memoriachilena.gob.cl/602/w3-article-93231.html; and "José Manuel Parada," Memoria Chilena, accessed January 15, 2025, https://www.memoriachilena.gob.cl/602/w3-article-98137.html.

139. Butler, *Precarious Life*, 32.

140. Eva Cockcroft, "Chile Murals, After 1973 September 11," ca. October 1973, p. 1, Lucy R. Lippard papers, 1930s–2010, bulk 1960s–1990, AAA.

141. Nora, *Realms of Memory*.

142. Patricio Guzmán, dir., *Allende* (New York: First Run/Icarus Films, 2004), DVD.

143. Pratt, *Planetary Longings*, 145.

144. Pratt, *Planetary Longings*, 145.

145. Sarah Cascone, "'This Work Is About the Abuse of Power': Alfredo Jaar on His Immersive Black Lives Matter Protest Piece at the Whitney Biennial," *ArtNews*, April 13, 2022, https://news.artnet.com/art-world-archives/alfredo-jaar-whitney-biennial-2022-2093016.

146. Raiford, *Imprisoned in a Luminous Glare*, 7.

147. Martin Luther King Jr., "Draft of Chapter X, 'Shattered Dreams,'" The Martin Luther King, Jr. Research and Education Institute, Stanford University, July 1, 1962–March 31, https://kinginstitute.stanford.edu/king-papers/documents/draft-chapter-x-shattered-dreams#ftnref1.

148. Correa Morandé, *La guerra de las mujeres*; Bernd Debusmann Jr., Madeline Halpert, and Mike Wendling, "'It's Simple, Really'—Why Latinos Flocked to Trump's Working-Class Coalition," BBC News, November 8, 2024, https://www.bbc.com/news/articles/cze3yr77j9wo.

149. Žižek, "After Trump's Victory."

150. Christian Leal, "Manifestantes expulsan a Checho Hirane de marcha pro Palestina," Biobio Chile, March 17, 2024, https://www.biobiochile.cl/noticias/nacional/region-metropolitana/2024/03/17/manifestantes-expulsan-a-checho-hirane-de-marcha-pro-palestina-no-te-queremos-aca.shtml.

151. Judith Butler, "Judith Butler: Jewish Prof. Among 160 Named in UC Berkeley 'Antisemitism' Files Handed to Trump Admin," *Democracy Now!*, September 15, 2025, https://www.democracynow.org/2025/9/15/judith_butler.

152. For more on the historic Palestinian migration in Chile and its relation to the elite, see Baeza, "Palestinians in Latin America." For more on the Palestinian diaspora in Chile and their different experiences regarding decolonial time and solidarities, see Winn, *Weavers of Revolution*; and Meruane, *Palestina en pedazos*.

153. Cristian Aravena, "Memoriales sónicos" (paper presented at the Symposium "Todavía somos el tiempo: Arte y resistencia a 50 años del golpe," CNAC, Santiago, Chile, November 9, 2023).

154. Segal, *Radical Happiness*, 157.

155. Chomsky and Pappé, *On Palestine*, xiii.

CHAPTER TWO. ACCOUNTABILITY

An early version of debates covered in this chapter was published as "Decolonial Temporality in Alfredo Jaar's *The Kissinger Project*," ASAP/*Journal* 4, no. 2 (May 2019): 345–76. A Portuguese translation of this article was published as "Temporalidade Decolonial no *The Kissinger Project* de Alfredo Jaar," translated by Rafael Melo, Caroline Alciones de Oliveira Leite, and Luiz Sérgio de Oliveira, in "O que pode uma curadoria descolonial?," special issue, in *Revista Poiésis* 21, no. 35 (2020):193–234, https://periodicos.uff.br/poiesis/article/view/40436.

1. Jaar, "It Is Difficult" (2015).

2. Jaar, "It Is Difficult" (2015).

3. Sebenius et al., *Kissinger the Negotiator*, ixi.

4. Sebenius et al., *Kissinger the Negotiator*, xxxii.

5. Kissinger, *White House Years*; Kissinger, *Years of Upheaval.*

6. See captions in Kissinger, *White House Years*; and Kissinger, *Years of Upheaval.*

7. This is shown, for instance, on the cover of the Spanish translation of Peter Kornbluh's groundbreaking *The Pinochet File: A Declassified Dossier on Atrocity and Accountability* (2003), published in Spanish in 2023 for the fiftieth anniversary of the coup as *Pinochet desclasificado: Los archivos secretos de Estados Unidos sobre Chile* (Santiago, Chile: Catalonia).

8. For more on the international dimension of crimes committed during the Latin American dictatorships, see Dinges, *Condor Years.*

9. John Dinges, "A Harsh Warning on Human Rights," *Time* magazine, June 21, 1976, 31.

10. Dinges, "Harsh Warning on Human Rights," 31.

11. MEMCON between Henry Kissinger and Augusto Pinochet, June 8, 1976, FOIA website, https://www.foia.gov/.

12. Dinges, "Harsh Warning on Human Rights," 31; MEMCON between Kissinger and Pinochet, June 8, 1976.

13. MEMCON between Kissinger and Pinochet, June 8, 1976.

14. Kissinger, *Years of Renewal*, 749, emphasis added.

15. "Con promesa de amor de nos va Kissinger," *La Tercera de la Hora* (Santiago, Chile), June 10, 1976; "Augusto Pinochet y Henry Kissinger se reunieron ayer en una cordial reunion en el Edificio Diego Portales," *El Mercurio* (Santiago, Chile), June 9, 1976, archive, Archivo de Fondos y Colecciones, Museo de la Memoria y los Derechos Humanos (hereafter MMDH), Santiago, Chile.

16. Dinges, "Harsh Warning on Human Rights," 31; MEMCON between Henry Kissinger and Augusto Pinochet, June 8, 1976.

17. "Visita de Henry Kissinger a Chile—Parte 1—1976 | Buenos días a todos," TVN (Televisión Nacional de Chile), November 12, 2015, https://www.youtube.com/watch?v=2bHSTUsHPHQ.

18. "Visita de Henry Kissinger a Chile—Parte 1—1976 | Buenos días a todos."

19. Avelar, *Untimely Present*, 37–38.

20. Memorandum of Record, "U.S.-Chilean Relations" (Richard Helms—Donald Kendall—Agustin Edwards), September 14, 1970, Department of State, FOIA website.

21. Memorandum of Record, "U.S.-Chilean Relations" (Richard Helms—Donald Kendall—Agustin Edwards).

22. Peter Kornbluh, "Nuevo informe de cita de Agustín Edwards con el jefe de la CIA devela su rol clave en el Golpe," CIPER, May 27, 2014, https://ciperchile.cl/2014/05/27/nuevo-informe-de-cita-de-agustin-edwards-con-el-jefe-de-la-cia-devela-su-rol-clave-en-el-golpe/.

23. Kornbluh, "Nuevo informe de cita de Agustín Edwards."

24. MEMCON between Viron Vaky and Henry Kissinger, September 14, 1970, FOIA website.

25. Notes on Meeting with the President on Chile, September 15, 1970, FOIA website. In a series of notes handwritten by Helms recording the Nixon/Kissinger conversation declassified as early as 1975 by the Church Committee, a special Senate investigation on US intelligence involvement in Chile, the entire archive reads: "1 in 10 chance perhaps, but save Chile! worth spending; not concerned; no involvement of embassy; $10,000,00 available, more if necessary; full-time job—best men we have; game plan; make the economy scream; 48 hours for plan of action."

26. For more information on the first coup plan, see Kornbluh, *Pinochet File*; and Dinges, *Condor Years*.

27. Avelar, "Dictatorship and Immanence," 75–76.

28. Alfredo Jaar, interview with the author, New York, August 15, 2016; Didi-Huberman, "Emotion Does Not Say 'I,'" 61.

29. Carlos Naudon, "La OEA: ¿De la coalición a la collision?," *Mensaje* (Santiago, Chile), June 1976, 204, MMDH archive.

30. Cristián Pretch Bañados, "Carta del vicario de la Solidaridad a El Mercurio," *Revista Solidaridad*, July 1976, MMDH archive.

31. "Sistema interamericano y sistema mundial," *Mensaje*, no. 250 (July 1976), MMDH archive.

32. Iñigo Herrera, "Los derechos humanos: Reflexión en tres niveles," *Mensaje*, no. 249 (June 1976), MMDH archive.

33. Jaar, interview, August 15, 2016.

34. O'Brien, "Person-to-Person with Alfredo Jaar."

35. Hersh, *Price of Power*, 263.

36. Barthes, *Camera Lucida*, 96.

37. For more on the relationship between photography and truth, see Kriebel and Zervigón, *Photography and Doubt*.

38. See illustrations in Kissinger, *White House Years*; and Kissinger, *Years of Upheaval*.

39. Kissinger, *Years of Upheaval*, 374–76.

40. Dinges, "Harsh Warning on Human Rights," 31.

41. Dinges, "Harsh Warning on Human Rights," 31.

42. Jaar and Siitari, "I Need to Understand the World," 69.

43. Lübecker, "Politics of Images," 392.

44. Lübecker, "Politics of Images," 392.

45. Malhotra, "Ray of Hope."

46. Chemam, "Alfredo Jaar."

47. Pratt, *Planetary Longings*, 5.

48. Maturana and Verden-Zöller, *Origin of Humanness*, 223.

49. "Amnesty International: Dow's Failure to Offer Remedy for Bhopal Disaster Has Created a 'Sacrifice Zone,'" *Envirotec Magazine*, April 2024, https://envirotecmagazine.com/2024/04/08/amnesty-international-dows-failure-to-offer-remedy-for-bhopal-disaster-has-created-a-sacrifice-zone/.

50. Hitchens, *Trial of Henry Kissinger*, 71.

51. John Dinges, interview with the author, Washington, DC, April 14, 2016.

52. MEMCON between Kissinger and Pinochet, June 8, 1976.

53. MEMCON between Vaky and Kissinger, September 14, 1970. For more on the meaning of anchoring an image with a text, see Barthes, *Image, Music, Text*, 39–41.

54. Peter Kornbluh, "The Pinochet File" (presentation, Politics and Prose Bookstore, Washington, DC, September 16, 2003), https://www.c-span.org/program/public-affairs-event/the-pinochet-file/197520.

55. Peter Kornbluh, interview with the author, Washington, DC, December 15, 2023.

56. Chomsky and Herman, *Manufacturing Consent*, 306.

57. "Diplomacy, Eccentrics: The Pursuit of Peace and Power," *Time* magazine, February 7, 1972.

58. Describing Kissinger's celebrity-like persona, Grandin wrote that Kissinger is remembered by many for his "wry sense of humor and fondness for intrigue, good food, and high-cheeked women. [He] dated Jill St. John and Marlo Thomas, was friends with Shirley MacLaine, and was affectionately known as Super K, Henry of Arabia, and the Playboy of the West Wing." Grandin, *Kissinger's Shadow*, 6.

59. Suri, *Henry Kissinger and the American Century*, 241.

60. Lübecker, "Politics of Images," 392.

61. Suri, *Henry Kissinger and the American Century*, 241.

62. Grandin, "Sucking Up to P," 12.

63. Niall Ferguson, "The Jewish Key to Henry Kissinger," *UK Times Literary Supplement*, May 28, 2008.

64. Niall Ferguson and Mary Sarotte, "Niall Ferguson on Kissinger," Institute of Politics, Harvard Kennedy School, November 6, 2015, https://www.youtube.com/watch?v=tx-E6AxTwYc.

65. Greg Grandin, "The Kissinger Effect," *The Nation*, September 10, 2015.

66. Ikenberry, "Why the Liberal World Order Will Survive," 18.

67. Tedde, "Trump the Neoliberal President.".

68. Tedde, "Trump the Neoliberal President."

69. Orlando Letelier, "The 'Chicago Boys' in Chile," *The Nation*, August 28, 1976. See also Mignolo, *Darker Side of Western Modernity*, 42.

70. Letelier, "'Chicago Boys' in Chile." See also Mignolo, *Darker Side of Western Modernity*, 42.

71. Naomi Klein, "40 Years Ago, This Chilean Exile Warned Us About the Shock Doctrine. Then He Was Assassinated," *The Nation*, September 21, 2016.

72. "Decreto Supremo que priva de la nacionalidad chilena a Orlando Letelier del Solar, 15 de junio de 1976," Archivo Nacional de la Administración, Fondo Orlando Letelier, Memoria Chilena, National Library of Chile, https://www.memoriachilena.gob.cl/602/w3-article-79520.html.

73. Transcript of Orlando Letelier's Speech at the Felt Forum, Madison Square Garden, September 10, 1976, https://www.tni.org/en/article/transcript-of-orlando-leteliers-speech-at-the-felt-forum.

74. For more information on Letelier's assassination, see Dinges and Landau, *Assassination on Embassy Row*.

75. Associated Press, "Cable Ties Kissinger to Chile Scandal," *Boston Globe*, April 10, 2010.

76. For more information about copper, see chapter 1.

77. Hersh, *Price of Power*, 266.

78. David Stout, "Edward Korry, 81, Is Dead; Falsely Tied to Chile Coup," *New York Times*, January 30, 2003.

79. MEMCON between Henry Kissinger and Augusto Pinochet, June 8, 1976, FOIA.

80. Todd Haynes, dir., *Dark Waters* (New York: Focus Features, 2019).

81. "If It Concerns Us, It Concerns You: Alfredo Jaar at Goodman Gallery," Art Breath, 2023, https://artbreath.org/coffee-talk/if-it-concerns-us-it-concerns-you-alfredo-jaar-at-goodman-gallery.

82. Levi, *Drowned and the Saved*, 46.

83. Carmen Castillo and Guy Girard, dirs., *La flaca Alejandra* (Paris: Institut National de l'Audiovisuel [INA], 1994).

84. Eltit, *Emergencias*, 51.

85. Eltit, *Emergencias*, 51.

86. Lazarra, "Complicity and Responsibility," 59. See also Osorio and Cabezas, *Los hijos de Pinochet*; and Rebolledo, *La danza de los cuervos*.

87. Lazzara, "Complicity and Responsibility," 62.

88. See Hitchens, *Trial of Henry Kissinger*; and Christopher Hitchens, "The Case Against Henry Kissinger, Part One and Part Two," *Harper's Magazine*, February and March 2001.

89. Elena Shtromberg, "'I Will Not Act Before Understanding. Context Is Everything': The Work of Alfredo Jaar," *Los Angeles Book Review*, December 8, 2013.

90. Suri, *Henry Kissinger and the American Century*, 241.

91. Alfredo Jaar, *Dore Ashton, You Know*, 2015, video, 9 min., 25 sec., https://www.youtube.com/watch?v=sDPcYsT8Y6I.

92. Kornbluh, interview. See also "Operación Chile: Top Secret," Chilevisión, 2023, https://www.chilevision.cl/operacion-chile-top-secret/capitulo-completo/operacion-chile-top-secret.

93. Margaret Thatcher, "Pinochet Was This Country's Staunch, True Friend," *The Guardian*, October 6, 1999.

94. Thatcher, "Pinochet."

95. Kornbluh, *Pinochet File*, x.

96. Kissinger, *Years of Renewal*, 758.

97. TELCON between Nixon and Kissinger, 11:50 a.m., September 16, 1973, FOIA website.

98. Valdés, "Missing Chile"; and Arendt, *Eichmann in Jerusalem.*

99. Valdés, "Missing Chile," 196.

100. See TELCON between Nixon and Kissinger, 11:50 a.m., September 16, 1973. See also Qureshi, *Nixon, Kissinger, and Allende*, 132.

101. Rivera Cusicanqui, *Ch'ixinakax utxiwa*, 12.

102. Stern, *Battling for Hearts and Minds.*

103. Stern, *Battling for Hearts and Minds*, 16. See also Jelin, *State Repression and the Labors of Memory.*

104. Lazzara, "Memory Turn," 18–20.

105. Lazzara, "Memory Turn," 14; Huyssen, *Present Pasts.* See also Richard, *Crítica de la memoria.*

106. Lazzara, "Memory Turn," 26.

107. Label in exhibition *Everything Is Connected: Art and Conspiracy*, curated by Doug Eklund and Ian Alteveer at the Met Breuer, viewed September 28, 2018.

108. Eklund, "Wilderness of Mirrors," 52.

109. Eklund, "Wilderness of Mirrors," 52.

110. Hersh, *Price of Power*, 263.

111. Tuck and Yang, "Decolonization Is Not a Metaphor."

112. "Henry Kissinger Elected Trustee of Metropolitan Museum" (press release issued by the Metropolitan Museum of Art, 1978), Thomas J. Watson Library Digital Collections, the Met, New York.

113. Thomas Friedman, "How Do We Deal with a Superpower Led by a War Criminal?," *New York Times*, April 10, 2022.

114. Barthes, *Image, Music, Text*, 156.

115. Noam Chomsky, "'Exterminate All the Brutes': Gaza 2009," chomsky.info, January 19, 2009 (revised June 6, 2009), https://web.archive.org/web/20201111230440/https://chomsky.info/20090119/.

116. Thomas Friedman, "Why the Campus Protests Are So Troubling," *New York Times*, May 8, 2024.

117. O'Brien, "Person-to-Person with Alfredo Jaar."

118. Letelier, "'Chicago Boys' in Chile."

119. Tom McDonough, "Alfredo Jaar," *OSMOS Magazine*, no. 24 (July 16, 2024).

120. Kaleck, "Arrest Kissinger!"

121. Sturken, *Terrorism in America Memory*, 16.

122. Grandin, *Last Colonial Massacre*, xiv.

123. For more on the expression "the Other 9/11," see Ariel Dorfman, "50 Years After 'the Other 9/11,'" *The Nation*, September 11, 2023.

124. Žižek, *Violence*, 38.

125. Glissant, *Introduction to a Poetics of Diversity*, 76.

126. Kaleck, "Arrest Kissinger!"

An early version of debates discussed in this chapter was published as "On Failure and the Nation-State: A Decolonial Reading of Alfredo Jaar's *A Logo for America*," in *The Routledge Companion to Decolonizing Art History*, edited by Tatiana Flores, Florencia San Martín, and Charlene Villaseñor Black, 151–63. (New York: Routledge, 2023).

1. Blitzer, "Logo for America."

2. Ellis, "Being an Indigenous Art Historian," 64.

3. Jaar et al., *Jaar SCL 2006*, 71.

4. Rojas Mix, *Los cien nombres de América*. For more on the relevance of Rojas Mix's book on the origins and challenges of the term *Latin America* and a critique of the term's association with imperial and racial connotations only, see Tenorio-Trillo, *Latin America*, 19.

5. Butler, *Precarious Life*, 144.

6. Blitzer, "Logo for America."

7. Shaw, "We Are All America."

8. Fonseca, "Introduction," 12.

9. Chambers, "Writing About Art History" 55.

10. Stathopoulou, "Timeless Relevance."

11. Blitzer, "Logo for America."

12. Greg Grandin, "Trump Is Waging War on His Own Citizens." *New York Times*, July 4, 2025.

13. Stathopoulou, "Timeless Relevance."

14. Gabara, *Non-Literary Fiction*, 17.

15. For more on conceptualism, see Camnitzer, *Global Conceptualism*; and Calirman, *Brazilian Art Under Dictatorship*.

16. Butler, *Precarious Life*, 144.

17. Alfredo Jaar, interview with the author, New York, April 8, 2019.

18. Bercovitch, "America as Canon and Context," 104.

19. Alfredo Jaar folder, Messages to the Public Archive, Fales Library and Special Collections, New York University (hereafter NYU).

20. Alfredo Jaar folder, Messages to the Public Archive.

21. Sartre, *What Is Literature?*, 37.

22. This work was commissioned to Jaar by the Cultural Institute of Radical Contemporary Arts (CIRCA), an art and culture platform that broadcasts socially committed public art every evening in a network of public advertising screenings in cities in Western Europe and East Asia.

23. Waldman, "Adrienne Rich."

24. Waldman, "Adrienne Rich."

25. Waldman, "Adrienne Rich."

26. Waldman, "Adrienne Rich."

27. Maldonado-Torres, *Against War*, xi.

28. Adorno, "Cultural Criticism and Society," 34. For more about Adorno's concept of the term *barbaric*, see Rowland, "Re-Reading 'Impossibility' and 'Barbarism.'"

29. For more on the dehumanized, see Wynter, "Unsettling the Coloniality."

30. For more on an aesthetics of negation, see Gabara, *Non-Literary Fiction.*

31. Franco, *Cruel Modernity.*

32. Franco, *Cruel Modernity.* 5

33. "Press Release: Alfredo Jaar, Tonight No Poetry Will Serve," CIRCA, November 2023, https://circa.art/press/press-release-alfredo-jaar-tonight-no-poetry-will-serve/.

34. Césaire, *Discourse on Colonialism,* 32–33.

35. "Press Release: Alfredo Jaar, Tonight No Poetry Will Serve."

36. "Press Release: Alfredo Jaar, Tonight No Poetry Will Serve."

37. Maldonado-Torres, *Against War,* xiii.

38. Gago, "Introduction," xxvi.

39. For more on decolonial practices formulated from below, see Cornejo, "Writing Art Histories from Below"; and Nelson Maldonado-Torres, "Recognition from Below: The Meaning of the Cry and the Gift of the Self in the Struggle for Recognition," in Maldonado-Torres, *Against War,* 122–59.

40. Galeano, *Open Veins of Latin America.*

41. Robert F. Reid-Pharr, "Foreword," in Delany, *Times Square Red, Times Square Blue,* xii.

42. Delany, *Times Square Red, Times Square Blue,* 15.

43. Delany, *Times Square Red, Times Square Blue,* 15.

44. Delany, *Times Square Red, Times Square Blue,* 129.

45. Delany, *Times Square Red, Times Square Blue,* 96.

46. Delany, *Times Square Red, Times Square Blue,* 5.

47. Blitzer, "Logo for America."

48. Holloway, "Are Corporations People?"

49. Baudrillard, *Simulacra and Simulation,* 12.

50. Jaar et al., *Jaar SCL 2006,* 71.

51. Ojeda, *Las Biuty Queens,* 62.

52. Pratt, "Arts of the Contact Zone."

53. Pratt, "Arts of the Contact Zone," 34.

54. Guamán Poma de Ayala, *First New Chronicle.*

55. Guamán Poma de Ayala, *First New Chronicle.*

56. Pratt, "Arts of the Contact Zone," 35.

57. Veronelli, "Coloniality of Language," 113.

58. Veronelli, "Coloniality of Language," 113.

59. Mari Carmen Ramirez, interview with the author, Hudson, TX, October 2, 2018.

60. Spivak, "Can the Subaltern Speak?"

61. Maldonado-Torres, "Liberation Philosophy."

62. Maldonado-Torres, "Liberation Philosophy," 15.

63. Maldonado-Torres, "Liberation Philosophy," 15, emphasis added.

64. Maldonado-Torres, "Liberation Philosophy," 12. See also Fanon, *Wretched of the Earth,* 159.

65. Jaar, conversation, April 8, 2019.

66. Jaar, "Tonight No Poetry Will Serve."

67. Jaar, "Tonight No Poetry Will Serve."

68. Jaar et al., *Jaar SCL 2006*, 71.

69. Rojas Mix, *Los cien nombres de América*, 24–25.

70. Martí, "Our America," 209.

71. See, for instance, Michel Chevalier, "Ancient and Modern Mexico," in Ramírez et al., *Resisting Categories*, 111–17; Charles Calvo, "Latin America," in Ramírez et al., *Resisting Categories*, 107–10; and Mignolo, *Idea of Latin America*, 51–94.

72. Quoted in Ardao, *Génesis de la idea*, 19.

73. For more on this, see Ardao, *Génesis de la idea*, 19.

74. Martí, "Our America," 211.

75. For more on Latinidad and Black erasure, see Flores, "'Latinidad Is Cancelled.'"

76. Wynter, *Do Not Call Us Negroes*, 9.

77. For more on Martí's reception in US academic circles via Roberto Fernández Retamar, see Saldívar, *Dialectics of Our America*, 5; and Franco, *Introduction to Spanish-American Literature*, 118.

78. Goldman, *Dimensions of the Americas*, 377.

79. Tenorio-Trillo, *Latin America*, 6.

80. Bilbao, *Iniciativa de la América*, 365.

81. Tenorio-Trillo, *Latin America*, 6.

82. Martí, "Our America," 114.

83. Césaire, *Discourse on Colonialism*, 32–33.

84. Taylor, *¡Presente!*, 29.

85. Gramsci, *Letters from Prison*, 159.

86. Rivera Cusicanqui, *Ch'ixinakax utxiwa*, 12.

87. Bilbao, *La América en peligro*.

88. This is a main point in Ardao's *Génesis de la idea*.

89. Specifically, this philosophy emerged in the city of Córdoba in the context of a tumultuous year in the Western World: 1968. However, as one of its key promoters, Enrique Dussel, explains, differently than in Paris and Berkeley, students and workers in Córdoba shared the same struggle: to liberate themselves from General Juan Carlos Onganía's military dictatorship (1966–70). On May 29, 1969, they took the city in an event later known as El Cordovazo. A national strike followed as well as the persecution, incarceration, and expatriation of thousands, Dussel among them. Within this context, the philosophical academic discourse had become deeply politicized, propelling the creation of a philosophy whose practical aim was clear and simple: liberation. Dussel wrote the core book of this philosophy in 1976 in Mexico at the beginning of his exile. For more on the philosophy of liberation, see Dussel, *Philosophy of Liberation*; Dussel, *Ethics of Liberation*; Alcoff et al., *Thinking from the Underside of History*; Cerutti Guldberg, *Filosofía de la liberación latinoamericana*; Gutiérrez Merino, *Theology of Liberation*; and Salazar Bondy, *¿Existe una filosofía de nuestra América?*

90. Maldonado-Torres, "Enrique Dussel's Liberation Thought," 1.

91. Maldonado-Torres, "Decolonial Turn," 20.

92. Rojas Mix, *América imaginaria*, 381. See also Salvador Allende, "Discurso en La Habana" (speech, Havana, Cuba, December 13, 1972), https://www.marxists.org/espanol/allende/1972/diciembre13.htm.

93. See Unidad Popular, *Programa básico de gobierno*, 28.

94. See Neruda, *Canto General*. For more on Neruda's relation to Martí, see Rojas Mix, "'América, no invoco tu nombre en vano'"; and Serna Arnaiz, "Jose Martí." For more on Rojas Mix's development of the show vis-à-vis his early understanding of "Our America," see Pablo Espinosa, "América se pobló de monstruos mucho antes de ser explorada," interview with Miguel Rojas Mix, *Fundación La Fuente*, December 30, 2015, https://www.fundacionlafuente.cl/entrevistas/miguel-rojas-mix-america-se-poblo-de-monstruos-mucho-antes-de-ser-explorada/.

95. Neruda, "I Remember a Man," in *Song of Protest*, 15.

96. Becerra, "Comentario," n.p., MAC-Chile Archive.

97. Carlos Maldonado, "América, no invoco tu nombre en vano," *El Siglo*, May 31, 1970, ICAA/DOC Archive.

98. For more on this work, see Andrea Giunta, "People, Mass, Multitude," in González et al., *Memories of Underdevelopment*, 168.

99. Ivelic and Galaz, *Chile Arte Actual*, 70.

100. Palumbo, "Whitney Biennial Artist's Hidden Message."

101. Tenorio-Trillo, *Latin America*, 6.

102. Lugo-Saavedra and Spray, *Aquí*, 60.

103. Jaar, *Obra abierta y de registro continuo* (1981), video copy in Jaar's archive. Zurita included this poem in his 1982 book *Anteparaíso*, which, in turn, was designed by Mario Fonseca, an artist and designer who was Jaar's closest friend in Chile. See Zurita, *Anteparadise*, 203.

104. For more on Meiselas's work in Nicaragua, see Duganne, "*Nicaragua Media Project*." For more on committed photojournalism by Nicaraguan photographs on the Sandinista revolution and the Contra war, see Selejan, "Pictures in Dispute."

105. See James Lemoynenov, "Salvador Rebels. Where Do They Get the Arms?," *New York Times*, November 24, 1988.

106. Alfredo Jaar, "It Is Difficult" (2016).

107. Barthes, *Camera Lucida*, 26. Considering Jaar's fluency in French, his early interest in photojournalism, and the wide reception of Barthes among Chilean intellectuals since the late 1960s, it is likely that the artist was familiar with the original publication of this book in 1980 as *La chambre claire*. For more on the reception of Barthes's *Camera Lucida* in Chile, see "Jornadas de discusión. Roland Barthes recepción y contextos en Chile" (symposium, Universidad de Chile, July 2014), http://www.filosofia.uchile.cl/agenda/102383/jornadas-de-discusion-roland-barthes-recepcion-y-contextos.

108. Panicelli, "Alfredo Jaar Fondazione Merz."

109. Quoted in Gogol, *Utopia and the Dialectic*, 1.

110. For more on this exhibition, see IN/OUT: *Four Projects by Chilean Artists*. For more on the WPA, see the Washington Project for the Arts Statement of Purpose, February 1983, Washington Project for the Arts records, ca. 1975–1990, Archives of American Art (AAA), Smithsonian Institution, Washington, DC.

111. Ronald Reagan, "National Address on Central America," *New York Times*, April 28, 1983.

112. Dussel, "Philosophy of Liberation," 337.

113. I am thankful to artist Jerry Kearns for helping me in identifying this work, which exists only as documentation in the archive at Colby College Museum of Art, Waterville, Maine. I am also thankful to the Kenkeleba Gallery director Corine Jennings for sharing her memories about this piece in email correspondence on September 28, 2018.

114. He would later do the same in works such as his 1987 installation *1 + 1 + 1*, where he recalls the chemical and mechanical actions of development and reproduction that take place in the darkroom (see this book's conclusion). Jaar would repeat this formal engagement with photography a decade later in another famous work, *Blow-Up*, an installation created specifically for MoMA's 1993 exhibition *Latin American Artists of the Twentieth Century*.

115. For more on the relationship between photography and truth, see Kriebel and Zervigón, *Photography and Doubt*.

116. Chomsky, "Disinformation," 20.

117. Other artists in the show included Juan Downey, Leon Golub, Jerry Kearns, Antoni Muntadas, Nancy Spero, and May Stevens.

118. Gerald M. Boyd, "Reagan Terms Nicaraguan Rebels 'Moral Equal of Founding Fathers,'" *New York Times*, March 2, 1985.

119. Grandin, "Chomsky in Sandinista Nicaragua," 94.

120. Grandin, "Chomsky in Sandinista Nicaragua," 90.

121. Cohn-Bendit, *Nous l'avons tant aimée, la revolution*.

122. Flores, "Revolution," 169.

123. Arendt, *On Revolution*, 34.

124. Jonsson, *A Brief History of the Masses*, 125.

125. For more on *Artists Call*, see Artists Call Against U.S. Intervention in Central America files, Political Art Documentation/Distribution (hereafter PAD/D) Archive, Museum of Modern Art (MoMA), New York.

126. Cecilia Vicuña, email to the author, February 5, 2018. For more on *Artists Call*, see Duganne and Satinsky, *Art for the Future*.

127. Artists Call Against U.S. Intervention in Central America files, PAD/D Archive. This work by Jaar was exhibited at three *Artists Call* venues: the Judson Memorial Church and Kenkeleba Gallery, both in New York, and the Colby College Museum of Art in Waterville, Maine.

128. Tenorio-Trillo, *Latin America*, 8.

129. Flyer, *La Verdadera Avenida de las Américas, Artist Call* exhibition, Artists Call Against U.S. Intervention in Central America files, PAD/D Archive.

130. Flyer, *La Verdadera Avenida de las Américas, Artist Call* exhibition, Artists Call Against U.S. Intervention in Central America files, PAD/D Archive.

131. Posters, *La Verdadera Avenida de las Américas, Artist Call* exhibition, Artists Call Against U.S. Intervention in Central America files, PAD/D Archive.

132. For a historical discussion on the transatlantic dimension of Túpac Amaru II's rebellion in the eighteenth century, see Walker, *Tupac Amaru Rebellion*.

133. Lucy Lippard, email to the author, February 22, 2018.

134. Jerry Kearns, interview with the author, Brooklyn, NY, June 15, 2018.

135. "Artists Call General Statement, January 1984," flyer, Artists Call Against U.S. Intervention in Central America files, PAD/D Archive. In this historical context, exhibitions in New York dedicated to Chile continued. Such was the case of *Chile Chile*, a 1983 group show organized by Jaar at Cayman, a gallery on West Broadway that promoted Latin American and Latino artists underrepresented in art venues in the United States. For more on this, see *Chile Chile* exhibition, Cayman Gallery/Museum of Contemporary Hispanic Art, Hostos Library and Special Collections, Hostos Community College, CUNY.

136. This project was organized by US feminist artist Sabra Moore, and participants included, among others, Nancy Spero, Brazilian Josely Carvalho, and Catalina Parra. Writing about their intervention, they noted that by the time of the exhibition, the United States was "intervening in the same region through its military and cultural support of the government in Guatemala. The Mayan inhabitants of this region are daily facing annihilation. This same policy extends into the neighboring regions of El Salvador and Nicaragua." Reconstruction Project, *Artists Call*, Artists Call Against U.S. Intervention in Central America files, PAD/D Archive.

137. hooks, "Columbus."

138. Grosfoguel, "Decolonizing Post-Colonial Studies," 25.

139. "Presidente de la República, Gabriel Boric Font, interviene en la 80° Asamblea General de Naciones Unidas," *Prensa Presidencia*, September 23, 2025, https://prensa.presidencia.cl/comunicado.aspx?id=303969.

140. Mignolo, *Darker Side of the Renaissance*, 669.

141. The Mercator projection, as Mignolo explains, ignores the images of the world according to Indigenous people: "When Gerardus Mercator drew his world map in 1542 and represented the New World as an independent continent, he contributed to an 'American' identity that ignored and suppressed Anáhuac, Tawantisuyu, and Abya-Yala. This kind of suppression would become conceptualized as 'modernity,' as if modernity was a necessary historical force with the right to negate and suppress everything that did not fit a model of world history that is seen as 'an essential history process.'" Mignolo, *Idea of Latin America*, 26.

142. Coronil, "Beyond Occidentalism," 67–68.

143. Saldívar, *Dialectics of Our America*, 3.

144. Rivera Cusicanqui, *Ch'ixinakax utxiwa*, 12.

145. Fanon, *Dying Colonialism*, 90.

146. Quijano and Wallerstein, "Americanity as a Concept," 549–50.

147. Label for section "Politics" in exhibition *En el aire conmovido . . .* (*In the Troubled Air . . .*), curated by Georges Didi-Huberman at the Museo Reina Sofía, visited on January 15, 2025.

148. Ashton, "Alfredo Jaar: Gold in the Morning," 7.

149. *Alfredo Jaar: 1 + 1 + 1: Documenta 8*, exhibition catalog (New York: privately printed, 1987), frontispiece.

150. Galeano, *El descubrimiento de América*, 5.

151. Fanon, *Dying Colonialism*, 1.

152. Fanon, *Dying Colonialism*, 1.

153. Mistral, "El Grito," 11–12.

CONCLUSION. THE END OF THE WORLD

1. Wolfgang Kaleck, interview with the author, November 1, 2024.

2. Michael Byers, "The ICC Arrest Warrant Will Hang over Netanyahu for the Rest of His Life," *Globe and Mail*, November 21, 2024, https://www.theglobeandmail.com/opinion/article-the-icc-arrest-warrant-will-hang-over-netanyahu-for-the-rest-of-his/.

3. Alfredo Jaar, "The End of The World" (keynote talk at KINDL, Berlin, Germany, April 4, 2025).

4. "Cardenal Errázuriz: Llamado a la serenidad," Iglesia.cl, December 11, 2006, https://www.iglesia.cl/3965-cardenal-errazuriz-llamado-a-la-serenidad.html.

5. Rosenberg, *After Human Rights*, 13.

6. Borges, "Our Poor Individualism," 309. See also Rosenberg, *After Human Rights*, 13.

7. Kaleck, interview.

8. Kaleck, interview.

9. Maan Jalal, "National Book Award winner calls for end of 'US-funded Gaza genocide,'" *The National*, November 22, 2024, https://www.thenationalnews.com/arts-culture/books/2024/11/22/national-book-award-palestine-gaza/.

10. "I know many of my IG friends and followers might be confused about Syria right now, and I get it! And I am here to explain what I know." Saltagi Safadi (@muslimmommyblog), Instagram, December 7, 2024, https://www.instagram.com/p/DDSyLk-xsS2/?hl=en&img_index=1.

11. Kaleck, *Concrete Utopia*, xvi.

12. Mistral, "Aniversario," 91.

13. Maturana, *Emociones y lenguaje*, 13; Maturana, "What Is It to See?"

14. For more on the Capitalocene, see Moore, *Anthropocene or Capitalocene?*

15. Jaar, "Questionnaire."

16. Bobbette, "Political Geology," 29

17. Bobbette, "Political Geology," 37.

18. Nixon, *Slow Violence*; Quijano, *Vivir adentro y en contra*, 154.

19. Burgis, *Looting Machine*, 245.

20. Duncan Ballantyne-Way, "Alfredo Jaar: 'I Don't Think Things Have Ever Been Darker in the World Than They Are Right Now,'" *Berliner*, November 21, 2024, https://www.the-berliner.com/art/berlin-alfredo-jaar-the-end-of-the-world-kindl-gallery-installation/.

21. Ewuoso, "Decolonization Projects."

22. This is not a rare case in the history of Egyptologists, who have relied on colonial paradigms of racial superiority and universal aesthetics to present some artifacts as different from others in Africa and Egypt itself. For more on this, see, for instance, Sedra, "Imagining an Imperial Race."

23. Dr. Zahi Hawass, "Repatriation," accessed January 15, 2025, https://www.hawasszahi.com/repatriation.

24. "Why Germany Hasn't Returned Nefertiti," DW History and Culture, June 9, 2024, https://www.youtube.com/watch?v=-TA5esJJLgc.

25. Becker, "Introduction," 17.

26. For more on the decolonial turn in 1992, see Maldonado-Torres, "Decolonial Turn."

27. Artist's collection, SMB-ZA, V/ Slg. Künstler, Alfredo Jaar, Zentralarchiv (Central Archive), Staatliche Museen zu Berlin.

28. Knight, "Germany Remembers 1992."

29. Knight, "Germany Remembers 1992."

30. Erakat, *Justice for Some*, 7.

31. Weiss, *Die Ästhetik des Widerstands*.

32. Rosenberg, *After Human Rights*, 4.

33. Antikensammlung newspaper clippings, SMB-ZA, V/Slg. SMB, II.4.2, Antikensammlung, Zentralarchiv (Central Archive), Staatliche Museen zu Berlin.

34. Robles-Moreno, "'Please, Don't Discover Me!'"

35. James Jackson, "No Plans to Return Berlin's Star Museum Attractions Nefertiti and Pergamon Altar, German Official Says," *Art Newspaper*, January 20, 2023, https://www.theartnewspaper.com/2023/01/20/no-plans-to-return-berlins-star-museum-attractions-nefertiti-and-pergamon-altar-german-official-says.

36. Maldonado-Torres, "Outline of Ten Theses," 15.

37. Famously, the 1989 exhibition *Magiciens de la terre* at the Centre Georges Pompidou and the Grande halle de la Villette in Paris symbolizes the outset of such globalization. For more on this, see Barriendos Rodríguez, "La idea del arte latinoamericano."

38. DW History and Culture, "Why Germany Hasn't Returned Nefertiti."

39. For more on orientalism, see Said, *Orientalism*.

40. DW History and Culture, "Why Germany Hasn't Returned Nefertiti."

41. Erakat, *Justice for Some*.

42. Conley, "Democracy for Some."

43. W. Benjamin, *Illuminations*, 256.

44. Friedman, "Free Markets and the Generals," 59. For more on this, see Friedman, "The Fragility of Freedom."

45. I am grateful to Carl Fischer for reminding me about the Guggenheim family's interest in Chile when reading a draft of this conclusion.

46. Galaz-Mandakovic and Rivera, "Revolution and Resistance in the Desert," 605.

47. Bobbette, "Political Geology," 89.

48. Sands, *38 Londres Street*, 12.

49. This work, *Beben litio, comen cobre* (2021), was made by LAGDA in collaboration with Fundación Desierto de Atacama, Colectivo Pésimo Servicio, Ángela Ormeño, Javier Díaz, Valentina Pallacán, Francisco Bahamondes, Antonieta Clunes, Valeria Valenzuela, Gonzalo Bravo, René Reyes, Carmen Aramayo, Kristell Heine, and Alejandro Herrera.

50. "El cobre y el lado oscuro de la transición energética," DW Documental, March 10, 2023, https://www.youtube.com/watch?v=nVERa8sSML4.

51. Malhotra, "Ray of Hope."

52. O'Gorman, *Invention of America*, 10.

53. Alfredo Jaar, interview with the author, October 9, 2024.

54. Coakley, "Ukraine Was Poised."

55. Zeke Miller, "Trump Says He Wants Ukraine's Rare Earth Elements as a Condition of Further Support.," AP, February 23, 2025, https://apnews.com/article/trump-ukraine-europe-rare-earth-russia-war-9af06a9f17dbaa49a05dcba3a3363977.

56. Jaar, interview, October 9, 2024, emphasis added.

57. Bobbette, "Political Geology," 29.

58. See Matthew O'Neill and Perri Peltz, dirs., *Surveilled* (New York: HBO Documentary Films, 2024).

59. This was where the United Nations Framework Convention on Climate Change (UNFCCC) was established, with parties that would later meet annually at the Conference of the Parties (COP).

60. Jaar, interview, October 9, 2024.

61. Bacigalupo, "El tiempo del trueno guerrero mapuche," 15.

62. Lienlaf, *Se ha despertado el ave de mi corazón*, 29, translation in Cárcamo-Huechante, "No + Wingka Word," 105.

63. Cárcamo-Huechante, "No + Wingka Word," 103.

64. Blystra, "Roots in Rhythm."

65. Prix Pictet, "Alfredo Jaar Wins Eleventh Prix Pictet," September 26, 2025, https://prix.pictet.com/news/alfredo-jaar-wins-eleventh-prix-pictet.

66. Taylor, *¡Presente!*, 2.

67. Another central reference used by Jaar to create this work is Brazilian artist Cildo Meireles's 1969 *Cruzeiro do Sul* (Southern Cross), 1960–70. For more about this, see San Martín, "Alfredo Jaar: *The End of the World*."

68. Ballantyne-Way, "Alfredo Jaar."

69. I am grateful to María Gracia San Martín for noting the analogy between the pedestal and the chairs' arrangement in Jaar's *The Conference*.

70. Aurubis Metals for Progress, "About Us," accessed January 15, 2025, https://www.aurubis.com/en/about-us/group/group-profile.

71. Žižek, "After Trump's Victory."

72. Donald Trump (@realDonaldTrump), "He who saves his Country does not violate any Law," X, February 15, 2025, 1:32 p.m., https://x.com/realDonaldTrump/status/1890831570535055759.

73. Sands, *38 Londres Street*, 3.

74. Sands, *38 Londres Street*, 8.

75. Jaar, "Alfredo Jaar Accepts."

76. Fanon, *Black Skin, White Masks*, 76.

77. Césaire, *Notebook of a Return to the Native Land*, 27.

78. Kaleck, *Concrete Utopia*.

79. Kaleck, interview.

BIBLIOGRAPHY

PRIMARY SOURCES

Archivo de Fondos y Colecciones. Museo de la Memoria y los Derechos Humanos (MMDH), Santiago, Chile.

Archivo Museo de Arte Contemporáneo de Chile (MAC), Santiago, Chile.

Call and Response exhibition (March 7–April 1, 1984), exhibition folder, Colby College Museum of Art archive. Colby College, Waterville, Maine.

Chicago Committee to Save Lives in Chile Records, 1973–2009. Hanna Holborn Gray Special Collections Research Center (SCRC). University of Chicago Library.

Documents of Latin American and Latino Art (CAA/DOC), Museum of Fine Arts, Houston.

Dore Ashton papers, 1849, circa 1928–2014. Archives of American Art (AAA). Smithsonian Institution, Washington, DC.

Freedom of Information Act (FOIA) website. https://www.foia.gov/.

Grey Art Gallery and Study Center Archive 1975–1997. Fales Library and Special Collections. Elmer Holmes Bobst Library, New York University (NYU).

Lucy R. Lippard papers, 1930s–2010, bulk 1960–1990. Archives of American Art (AAA). Smithsonian Institution, Washington, DC.

Museum of Contemporary Hispanic Art (MoCHA). Hostos Archives. Hostos Community College, New York.

North American Congress on Latin America (NACLA) Archive of Latin Americana. Archives and Special Collections. Thomas J. Dodd Research Center. University of Connecticut Libraries, Storrs, CT.

Political Art Documentation/Distribution (PAD/D) Archive. Museum of Modern Art (MoMA), New York.

Public Art Fund Archive. Fales Library and Special Collections. Elmer Holmes Bobst Library. New York University (NYU).

Washington Project for the Arts records, ca. 1975–1990. Archives of American Art (AAA). Smithsonian Institution, Washington, DC.

Zentralarchiv (Central Archive). Staatliche Museen zu Berlin.

SECONDARY SOURCES

Achebe, Chinua. "The Truth of Fiction." In *Hopes and Impediments: Selected Essays*, 138–53. New York: Doubleday, 1989.

Adorno, Theodor. "Cultural Criticism and Society." In *Prisms*. London: Neville Spearman, 1967.

Alcoff, Linda, et al., eds. *Thinking from the Underside of History: Enrique Dussel's Philosophy of Liberation*. Lanham, MD: Rowman and Littlefield, 2000.

Allende, Salvador. "Speech to the United Nations." United Nations, New York, December 4, 1972. YouTube video. https://www.youtube.com/watch?v=r493eEOFXuE.

Allende Gossens, Salvador. "A los artistas del mundo." Inaugural speech for the Museo de la Solidaridad, Santiago, Chile, June 17, 1972. https://icaa.mfah.org/s/en/item/765609#?c=&m=&s=&cv=&xywh=-2001%2C-140%2C6551%2C3666.

Ardao, Arturo. *Génesis de la idea y el nombre de América Latina*. Caracas: Centro de Estudios Latinoamericanos Romulo Fallegos, 1993.

Arendt, Hannah. *Eichmann in Jerusalem: A Report on the Banality of Evil*. New York: Penguin Books, 1964.

Arendt, Hannah. *On Revolution*. New York: Penguin Books. 1990.

Ashton, Dore. "Alfredo Jaar: Gold in the Morning." In Alfredo Jaar, *Gold in the Morning*, 6–7. New York: John Simon Guggenheim Memorial Foundation, 1986. Exhibition catalog for the XVII Venice Biennale International Exhibition.

Avelar, Idelber. *Alegorías de la derrota: La ficción postdictatorial y el trabajo del duelo*. Santiago: Editorial Cuarto Propio, 2013.

Avelar, Idelber. "Dictatorship and Immanence." *Journal of Latin American Cultural Studies* 7, no. 1 (1998): 75–94.

Avelar, Idelber. *The Untimely Present: Postdictatorial Latin American Fiction and the Task of Mourning*. Durham, NC: Duke University Press, 1999.

Azoulay, Ariella Aïsha. *Civil Imagination: A Political Ontology of Photography*. Translated by Louise Bethlehem. New York: Verso, 2012.

Bacigalupo, Ana Mariella. "El tiempo del trueno guerrero mapuche: Lo silvestre, el estado chileno salvaje y las machi civilizadas." *Mitológicas* 30 (2015): 9–60.

Baddeley, Oriana, and Valerie Fraser. *Drawing the Line: Art and Cultural Identity in Contemporary Latin America*. London: Verso, 1989.

Baeza, Cecilia. "Palestinians in Latin America: Between Assimilation and Long-Distance Nationalism." *Journal of Palestine Studies* 43, no. 2 (2014): 59–72.

Barad, Karen. "Troubling Time/s and Ecologies of Nothingness: Re-turning, Re-membering, and Facing the Incalculable." *New Formations: A Journal of Culture/Theory/Politics* 92 (2018): 56–86.

Barriendos Rodríguez, Joaquín. "La idea del arte latinoamericano: Estudios globales del arte, geografías subalternas, regionalismos críticos." PhD diss., Universitat de Barcelona, 2013.

Barthes, Roland. *Camera Lucida: Reflections on Photography*. New York: Noonday Press, 1988.
Barthes, Roland. *Image, Music, Text*. London: Fontana, 1977.
Barton, Jonathan R., and Warwick E. Murray. "The End of Transition? Chile 1990–2000." *Bulletin of Latin American Research*, no. 21 (2002): 329–38.
Batchen, Geoffrey. *Negative/Positive: A History of Photography*. New York: Routledge, 2021.
Batchen, Geoffrey. "Palinode: An Introduction to *Photography Degree Zero*." In *Photography Degree Zero: Reflections on Roland Barthes's Camera Lucida*, edited by Geoffrey Batchen, 3–30. Cambridge, MA: MIT Press, 2009.
Baudrillard, Jean. *Simulacra and Simulation*. Translated by S. F. Glaser. Ann Arbor: University of Michigan Press, 1994.
Becerra, Ricardo. "Comentario." In *América, no invoco tu nombre en vano*. Santiago de Chile: MAC-Partenón/Sala Ercilla–Universidad del Norte, 1970. Exhibition catalog.
Becker, Kathrin, "Introduction." In Jaar, *The End of the World*, edited by Kathrin Becker and KINDL Centre for Contemporary Art, 7–25.
Beckett, Samuel. *The Unnamable*. New York: Grove Press, 1953.
Beckett, Samuel. *Worstward Ho*. London: John Calder, 1983.
Benitez-Rojo, Antonio. *The Repeating Island: The Caribbean and the Postmodern Perspective*. Durham, NC: Duke University Press,1996.
Benjamin, Bret. *Invested Interests: Capital, Culture, and the World Bank*. Minneapolis: University of Minnesota Press, 2007.
Benjamin, Walter. *Illuminations*. London: Fontana, 1992.
Benjamin, Walter. "The Work of Art in the Age of Its Technological Reproducibility." In *The Work of Art in the Age of its Technological Reproducibility, and Other Writings on Media*, edited by Michael W. Jennings, Brigid Doherty, and Thomas Y. Levin and translated by Edmund Jephcott, Rodney Livingstone, Howard Eiland, and others, 19–55. Cambridge, MA: Belknap Press of Harvard University Press, 2008.
Bercovitch, Sacvan. "America as Canon and Context: Literary History in a Time of Dissensus." *American Literature* 28, no. 1 (March 1986): 99–107.
Bilbao, Francisco. *Iniciativa de la América: Idea de un Congreso Federal de las Repúblicas*. Ediciones de la Facultad de Humanidades y Educación. Caracas: Universidad Central de Venezuela, 1983.
Bilbao, Francisco. *La América en peligro*. Buenos Aires: Imprenta y Litografía a vapor de Bernheim y Boneo, 1862.
Blitzer, Jonathan. "A Logo for America." *New Yorker*, August 27, 2015.
Blystra, Soffía. "Roots in Rhythm Exploring Activism in Mapuche Punk Music." *ReVista: Harvard Review of Latin America*, February 22, 2024. https://revista.drclas.harvard.edu/roots-in-rhythm-exploring-activism-in-mapuche-punk-music/.
Bobbette, Adam. "Political Geology in the Age of Critical Minerals." In Jaar, *The End of the World*, edited by Kathrin Becker and KINDL Center for the Arts, 27–259.

Borges, Jorge Luis. "Our Poor Individualism." In *Selected Non-Fictions*, edited by Eliot Weinberger and translated by Esther Allen, Suzanne Jill Levine, and Eliot Weinberger, 309–10. New York: Viking, 1999.

Bryan-Wilson, Julia. "Alfredo Jaar: Catia." In *Collaboration: A Potential History of Photography*, edited by Ariella Azoulay, Wendy Ewald, Susan Meiselas, and Leigh Raiford, and Laura Wexler, 150–51. New York: Thames and Hudson, 2024.

Bryan-Wilson, Julia. *Art Workers: Radical Practice in the Vietnam War Era*. Berkeley: University of California Press, 2010.

Burgis, Tom. *The Looting Machine: Warlords, Tycoons, Smugglers, and the Systematic Theft of Africa's Wealth*. London: William Collins, 2015.

Bush, Matthew. *Other Americans: The Art of Latin America in the US Imaginary*. Pittsburgh: University of Pittsburgh Press, 2022.

Butler, Judith. *Precarious Life: The Powers of Mourning and Violence*. New York: Verso, 2004.

Cabral, Amilcar. "National Liberation and Culture." *Transition*, no. 45 (1974): 12–17.

Calirman, Claudia. *Brazilian Art Under Dictatorship: Antonio Manuel, Artur Barrio, and Cildo Meireles*. Durham, NC: Duke University Press, 2012.

Camnitzer, Luis. *Global Conceptualism: Points of Origin, 1950s–1980s*. New York: Queens Museum of Art, 1999.

Caragol, Taína. "Boom and Dust: The Rise of Latin American and Latino Art in New York Exhibition Venues and Auction Houses, 1970s–1980s." PhD diss., City University of New York, 2013.

Cárcamo-Huechante, Luis. E. "No + Wingka Word: Sounds of Mapuche Resurgence in the Poetry of Leonel Lienlaf." *Radical History Review* 124 (2016): 102–16.

Castañeda de la Paz, María. "Tira de la peregrinación y la ascendencia chichimeca de los tenochca." *Estudios de cultura Náhuatl* 38 (December 2007): 183–212.

Castro, José Manuel. "Jaime Guzmán, Gremialismo, and the Ideological Origins of the 1980 Constitution." EIAL—*Estudios Interdisciplinarios de América Latina y el Caribe* 33, no. 2 (2022): 25–46.

Cerutti Guldberg, Horacio. *Filosofía de la liberación latinoamericana*. Mexico City: Fondo de Cultura Económica, 2006.

Césaire, Aimé. *Discourse on Colonialism*. Translated by Joan Pinkham. New York: Monthly Review Press, 1976.

Césaire, Aimé. *Notebook of a Return to the Native Land*. Edited by Clayton Eshleman. Translated by Annette Smith. Middletown, CT: Wesleyan University Press, 2001.

Chambers, Eddie. "Writing About Art History in the Age of Black Lives Matter." In Flores, San Martín, and Villaseñor Black, *The Routledge Companion to Decolonizing Art History*, 49–60.

Chemam, Melissa. "Alfredo Jaar: Poetic Visual Interventions." *Art UK*, May 2, 2023. https://artuk.org/discover/stories/alfredo-jaar-poetic-visual-interventions.

Chomsky, Noam. "Disinformation." In *Disinformation: The Manufacture of Consent*, 11–33. New York: Alternative Museum, New York, 1985. Exhibition catalog.

Chomsky, Noam, and Edward S. Herman. *Manufacturing Consent: The Political Economy of the Mass Media*. New York: Pantheon Books, 2002.

Chomsky, Noam, and Ilan Pappé. *On Palestine*. Chicago: Haymarket Books, 2015.

Coakley, Amanda. "Ukraine Was Poised to Become an Important Rare Earths Exporter. Then Came the Invasion." Coda Media, March 20, 2023. https://www.codastory.com/climate-crisis/ukraine-lithium-export/.

Cohen-Aponte, Ananda. "Pathways to Art History: Pedagogy, Research, and Praxis Through a Decolonial Lens." In Flores, San Martín, and Villaseñor Black, *The Routledge Companion to Decolonizing Art History*, 207–17.

Cohn-Bendit, Daniel. *Nous l'avons tant aimée, la revolution*. Paris: Barrault, 1986.

Collyer, Jaime. "De las hogueras a la imprenta: El arduo renacer de la narrativa chilena." *Cuadernos Hispanoamericanos* 2 (Aug.–Sept. 1990): 123–35.

Conger, Amy. *Nilton da Silva Rosa: 1973 Santiago; "We Don't Forget the Color of Blood."* Telluride, CO: Nolvido Press, 2010.

Conley, Julia. "Democracy for Some 'Is No Democracy at All,' Writes Mahmoud Khalil from ICE Detention." Common Dreams, April 18, 2025. https://www.commondreams.org/news/mahmoud-khalil-columbia-2671801014.

Cornejo, Kency. "Writing Art Histories from Below: A Decolonial Guanaca-Hood Perspective." *Latin American and Latinx Visual Culture Journal* 1, no. 3 (2019): 72–77.

Coronil, Fernando. "Beyond Occidentalism: Toward Nonimperial Geohistorical Categories." *Cultural Anthropology* 11, no. 1 (Feb. 1996):51–87.

Correa Morandé, María. *La guerra de las mujeres*. Santiago de Chile: Universidad Técnica del Estado, 1980.

Danto, Arthur. *After the End of Art: Contemporary Art and the Pale of History*. Princeton, NJ: Princeton University Press, 1997.

Davis, Angela Y. *Freedom Is a Constant Struggle: Ferguson, Palestine, and the Foundations of a Movement*. Chicago: Haymarket Books, 2016.

Delany, Samuel R. *Times Square Red, Times Square Blue*. 20th anniv. ed. New York: New York University Press, 2019.

de Las Casas, Bartolomé. *In Defense of the Indians: The Defense of the Most Reverend Lord, Don Fray Bartolomé de las Casas, of the Order of Preachers, Late Bishop of Chiapa, Against the Persecutors and Slanderers of the Peoples of the New World Discovered Across the Seas*. DeKalb: Northern Illinois University Press, 1974.

Didi-Huberman, Georges. "Emotion Does Not Say 'I': Ten Fragments on Aesthetic Freedom." In Alfredo Jaar, *La politique des images*, 57–69.

Dinges, John. *The Condor Years: How Pinochet and His Allies Brought Terrorism to Three Continents*. New York: Norton, 2004.

Dinges, John. "Expats After the Coup: A Memoir of the Road not Taken." April 4, 2017. https://thebaffler.com/latest/rebel-mother-dinges.

Dinges, John, and Saul Landau. *Assassination on Embassy Row*. New York: Pantheon Books, 1980.

Donoso, Claudia. "Obra de Alfredo Jaar: El mundo, el oro y los muros." *APSI* 15, no. 319 (Aug. 28–Sept. 3, 1989): 26–31.

Draper, Susana, Daffne Valdés Vargas, Paula Cometa Stange, Sibila Sotomayor Van Rysseghem, and Marlena Gittleman. "Feminist Performance: An Interview with Colectivo LASTESIS." *Critical Times* 7, no. 1 (April 2024): 119–27.

Du Bois, W. E. B. "The Comet." In *Darkwater: Voices from Within the Veil*, 253–75. New York: Harcourt, Brace, 1920.

Duganne, Erina. "The *Nicaragua Media Project* and the Limits of Postmodernism." *Art Bulletin* 100, no. 1 (2018): 146–68.

Duganne, Erina, and Abigail Satinsky, eds. *Art for the Future: Artists Call and Central American Solidarities*. Los Angeles, CA: Inventory Press; Boston, MA: Tufts University Art Galleries, 2022.

Dussel, Enrique. *Ethics of Liberation: In the Age of Globalization and Exclusion*. Edited by Eduardo Mendieta. Durham, NC: Duke University Press, 2013.

Dussel, Enrique. "Eurocentrism and Modernity (Introduction to the Frankfurt Lectures)." In *The Postmodernism Debate in Latin America*, edited by John Beverley, Michael Aronna, and José Oviedo, 65–76. Durham, NC: Duke University Press, 1995.

Dussel, Enrique. *Philosophy of Liberation*. Translated by Aquilina Martínez and Christine Morkovsky. New York: Orbis Books, 1985.

Dussel, Enrique. "Philosophy of Liberation, the Postmodern Debate, and Latin American Studies." Translated by Rosalia Bermúdez. In *Coloniality at Large: Latin America and the Postcolonial Debate*, edited by Mabel Moraña, Enrique Dussel, and Carlos A. Jáuregui, 335–49. Durham, NC: Duke University Press, 2008.

Eklund, Douglas. "A Wilderness of Mirrors: Conspiracy and Identity." In *Everything Is Connected: Art and Conspiracy*, edited by Ian Alteveer, Meredith A. Brown, John Miller, Kathryn Olmsted, Beth Saunders, and Jonathan Lethem, 44–75. New York: Metropolitan Museum of Art, 2018.

Ellis, Ngarino. "Being an Indigenous Art Historian in the Twenty-First Century: How Can Māori Adornment Reveal New Ways of Thinking About Art, Its Histories, and Futures." In Flores, San Martín, and Villaseñor Black, *The Routledge Companion to Decolonizing Art History*, 61–72.

Eltit, Diamela. *Emergencias: Escritos sobre literatura, arte y política*. Santiago: Planeta, 1989.

Erakat, Noura. *Justice for Some: Law and the Question of Palestine*. Stanford, CA: Stanford University Press, 2019.

Errázuriz, Luis Hernán. "Dictadura militar en Chile: Antecedentes del golpe estético-cultural." *Latin American Research Review* 44, no. 2 (2010): 136–57.

Espinoza, Oscar, Luis Eduardo González, and Noel McGinn. "The Student Movement in Chile and the Neo-Liberal Agenda in Crisis." In *Understanding Southern Social Movements*, edited by Simin Fadaee, 168–85. London: Routledge, 2016.

Etcheverry Arcaya, Jorge. "Da Silva Nilton." *Archivo Chile: Historia político social—Movimiento Popular*, June 2005. Centro de Estudios Miguel Enríquez. https://www.archivochile.com/Memorial/caidos_mir/D/da_silva_nilton.pdf.

Ewuoso, Cornelius. "Decolonization Projects: Achieving Inclusion with Cultural Sensitivity." *Voices in Bioethics* 9 (September 2023). https://doi.org/10.52214/vib.v9i.11940.

Fabian, Johannes. *Time and the Other: How Anthropology Makes Its Object*. New York: Columbia University Press, 2014.

Fanon, Frantz. *Black Skin, White Masks*. Translated by Richard Philcox. New York: Grove, 2008.

Fanon, Frantz. *Dying Colonialism*. Translated by Haakon Chevalier. New York: Grove, 1965.

Fanon, Frantz. *The Wretched of the Earth*. Translated by Richard Philcox. New York: Grove, 2004.

Feinstein, Adam. *Pablo Neruda*. New York: Bloomsbury, 2008.

Ferguson, Niall. *Kissinger*. Vol. 1, *1923–1968: The Idealist*. New York: Penguin, 2015.

Ferraz, Marcelo. *Lina Bo Bardi*. São Paulo: Instituto Lina Bo e PM Bardi e Marcelo Ferraz, 2008.

Flores, Tatiana. "'Latinidad Is Cancelled': Confronting an Anti-Black Construct." *Latin American and Latinx Visual Culture* 1, no. 3 (July 2021): 58–79.

Flores, Tatiana. "Revolution: Revolution Is a circle." In Jones and Chin Davidson, *Companion to Contemporary Art in a Global Framework*, 169–82.

Flores, Tatiana, and Michelle Ann Stephens, eds. *Relational Undercurrents: Contemporary Art of the Caribbean Archipelago*. Long Beach, CA: Museum of Latin American Art in association with Fresco Books/SF Design LLC and Duke University Press, 2017. Exhibition catalog.

Flores, Tatiana, Florencia San Martín, and Charlene Villaseñor Black, eds. *The Routledge Companion to Decolonizing Art History*. New York: Routledge, 2023.

Fonseca, Raphael. "Introduction: From Rakatá to Rakará." In *Latin American Artists: From 1785 to Now*, 11–17. Phaidon, 2023.

Foxley, Ana María. "Felicidad en la mira: Alfredo Jaar cierra un ciclo que invita a soñar, reflexionar, actuar." *Revista Hoy* 6 (Dec.–Jan. 1982): 41–42.

Franco, Jean. *Cruel Modernity*. Durham, NC: Duke University Press, 2013.

Franco, Jean. *Decline and Fall of the Lettered City: Latin America in the Cold War*. Cambridge, MA: Harvard University Press, 2009.

Franco, Jean. *An Introduction to Spanish-American Literature*. Cambridge: Cambridge University Press, 1969.

Franco, Jean. "Memoria, narración y repetición: La narrative latinoamericana en la epoca de la cultura de masas." In *Más allá del boom: Literatura y mercado*, edited by David Viñas, 111–29. Mexico City: Marcha Editores, 1981.

Frank, Patrick. *Manifestos and Polemics in Latin American Modern Art*. Albuquerque: University of New Mexico Press, 2017.

Freud, Sigmund. "Mourning and Melancholia." In *The Standard Edition of the Complete Psychological Works of Sigmund Freud*, vol. XIV, edited by James Strachey, 237–58. London: Hogarth, 1953.

Friedman, Milton. "The Fragility of Freedom." In *Milton Friedman in South Africa*, edited by Meyer Feldberg, Stephen Mulholland, and Kate Jowell, 3–10. Cape Town: University of Cape Town, Graduate School of Business, 1976.

Friedman, Milton. "Free Markets and the Generals." *Newsweek* 25 (January 1982): 59.

Fukuyama, Francis. *End of History and the Last Man*. New York: Avon, 1992.

Gabara, Esther. *Non-Literary Fiction: Art of the Americas Under Neoliberalism*. Chicago: University of Chicago Press, 2022.

Gago, Verónica. Introduction to Silvia Rivera Cusicanqui, *Ch'ixinakax utxiwa: On Practices and Discourses of Decolonization*, 6–33. Cambridge, MA: Polity, 2020.

Galaz-Mandakovic, Damir, and Francisco Rivera. "Revolution and Resistance in the Desert: The Guggenheim System's Impact on Nitrate Mining and Society in Atacama, 1926–31." *Technology and Culture* 65, no. 2 (2024): 603–22.

Galeano, Eduardo. *El descubrimiento de América que todavía no fué y nuevos ensayos*. Caracas, Venezuela: Alfadil Ediciones, 1991.

Galeano, Eduardo. *Open Veins of Latin America: Five Centuries of the Pillage of a Continent*. Translated by Cedric Belfrage. New York: Monthly Review Press, 1997.

Giunta, Andrea. "Politics of Representation: Art and Human Rights." *E-misférica* 7, no. 2 (2010). https://hemisphericinstitute.org/en/emisferica-72/7-2-essays/politics-of-representation-art-a-human-rights.html.

Glissant, Édouard. *Introduction to a Poetics of Diversity*. Translated by Celia Britton. Liverpool, UK: Liverpool University Press, 2020.

Glissant, Édouard. *Philosophie de la Relation*. Paris: Gallimard, 2009.

Glissant, Édouard. *Poetics of Relation*. Translated by Betsy Wing. Ann Arbor: University of Michigan Press, 1997.

Glissant, Édouard. "Robben's Rocks Have Confined Their Site, the Waves Released It; and Thus We Notice It." In Jaar, *The Sound of Silence*.

Gogol, Eugene Walker. *Utopia and the Dialectic in Latin American Liberation*. Boston: Brill, 2015.

Goldman, Shifra. "The Booming Spirit of Latin America." *Artweek*, July 1, 1989.

Goldman, Shifra M. *Dimensions of the Americas: Art and Social Change in Latin America and the United States*. Chicago: University of Chicago Press, 1994.

Gómez-Barris, Macarena. *Where Memory Dwells: Culture and State Violence in Chile*. Berkeley: University of California Press, 2009.

González, Julieta, Sharon Lerner, and Jacopo Crivelli Visconti, eds. *Memories of Underdevelopment: Art and the Decolonial Turn in Latin America, 1960–1985*. San Diego: Museum of Contemporary Art, 2017.

Gordon-Zolov, Terri, and Eric Zolov. *The Walls of Santiago: Social Revolution and Political Aesthetics in Contemporary Chile*. New York: Berghahn Books, 2022.

Gramsci, Antonio. *Letters from Prison*. Selected and translated by Lynn Lawner. New York: Harper and Row, 1973.

Grandin, Greg. *America, América: A New History of the New World*. New York: Penguin Random House, 2025.

Grandin, Greg. "Chomsky in Sandinista Nicaragua." NACLA *Report on the Americas* 48, no. 1 (2016): 89–97.

Grandin, Greg. *Empire's Workshop: Latin America, the United States, and the Rise of the New Imperialism*. New York: Henry Holt, 2013.

Grandin, Greg. *Kissinger's Shadow: The Long Reach of America's Most Controversial Statesman*. New York: Picador, 2016.

Grandin, Greg. *The Last Colonial Massacre: Latin America in the Cold War*. Chicago: University of Chicago Press, 2011.

Grandin, Greg. "Sucking Up to P." *London Review of Books* 29, no. 23 (November 2007): 11–13.

Grosfoguel, Ramón. "Decolonizing Post-Colonial Studies and Paradigms of Political-Economy: Transmodernity, Decolonial Thinking and Global Coloniality." *Transmodernity: Journal of Peripheral Cultural Production of the Luso-Hispanic World* 1, no. 1 (2011). https://doi.org/10.5070/T411000004.

Guamán Poma de Ayala, Felipe. *The First New Chronicle and Good Government*. Abridged. Selected, translated, and annotated by David L. Frye. Indianapolis: Hackett, 2006.

Gutiérrez Merino, Gustavo. *A Theology of Liberation: History, Politics, and Salvation*. Maryknoll, NY: Orbis Books, 1983.

Hartman, Saidiya. "The Time of Slavery." *South Atlantic Quarterly* 101, no. 4 (2002): 757–77.

Hernandez, Joe. "Why Trump Is Talking About Bringing Columbus Day 'Back from the Ashes.'" NPR, April 28, 2015. https://www.npr.org/2025/04/28/nx-s1-5380183/trump-columbus-day.

Hersh, Seymour M. *The Price of Power*. New York: Summit Books, 1983.

Hitchens, Christopher. *The Trial of Henry Kissinger*. New York: Verso, 2001.

Ho, Melissa, ed. *Artists Respond: American Art and the Vietnam War, 1965–1975*. Washington, DC: Smithsonian American Art Museum; Minneapolis: Minneapolis Institute of Art; Princeton, NJ: Princeton University Press, 2019. Exhibition catalog.

Holloway, Carson. "Are Corporations People?" *National Affairs*, no. 25 (Fall 2015). https://www.realclearpolicy.com/am_update/2015/39/.

hooks, bell. "Columbus: Gone but Not Forgotten." In *Outlaw Culture: Resisting Representations*, 231–42. New York: Routledge, 1994.

Hutton, Deborah. "Overcoming Art History's Meta-Narrative." In Flores, San Martín, and Villaseñor Black, *The Routledge Companion to Decolonizing Art History*, 196–206.

Huyssen, Andreas. *Present Pasts: Urban Palimpsests and the Politics of Memory*. Stanford, CA: Stanford University Press, 2009.

Ikenberry, G. John. "Why the Liberal World Order Will Survive." *Ethics and International Affairs* 32, no. 1 (Spring 2018): 17–29.

Ingold, Tim. *Lines: A Brief History*. New York: Routledge, 2016.

IN/OUT: Four Projects by Chilean Artists; C.A.D.A., Dittborn, Downey, Jaar. Washington, DC: Washington Project for the Arts, 1983. Exhibition catalog.

Ivelic, Milan, and Gaspar Galaz. *Chile Arte Actual*. Valparaiso: Ediciones Universitarias de la Universidad Católica de Valparaíso, 1988.

Jaar, Alfredo. "Alfredo Jaar Accepts the 65th Edward MacDowell Medal on June 29." Macdowel, June 29, 2025. https://www.macdowell.org/events/2025-medal-day.

Jaar, Alfredo. "Art in Conversation." With Phong Bui, Dore Ashton, and David Levi Strauss. *Brooklyn Rail,* April 2009. https://brooklynrail.org/2009/04/art/alfredo-jaar.

Jaar, Alfredo. *Eine Ästhetik des Widerstands. Alfredo Jaar: The Way It Is = An Aesthetics of Resistance.* Berlin: RealismusStudio; Neue Gesellschaft für Bildende Kunst, 2012.

Jaar, Alfredo. *The End of the World.* Edited by Kathrin Becker and KINDL Centre for Contemporary Art, 7–25. Berlin: Distanz, 2025. Exhibition Catalog.

Jaar, Alfredo. "The End of the World." Lecture and book launch, KINDL Centre for Contemporary Art, Berlin, Germany, April 12, 2025.

Jaar, Alfredo. "Es difícil." Keynote address, inauguration of academic year at the Faculty of Architecture, Construction, and Design, Universidad de las Américas, Santiago, Chile, April 20, 2021.

Jaar, Alfredo. "'I Can't Go On, I'll Go On.'" Public intervention commission for *Stories for an Uncertain World,* Edinburgh Art Festival. Vimeo video. Uploaded August 7, 2019. https://vimeo.com/352508393.

Jaar, Alfredo. "It Is Difficult." Presentation at Palestine at/without the Museum Conference, Museum of Contemporary Art, Barcelona, Spain, 2015. https://www.macba.cat/en/palestine-at-without-the-museum.

Jaar, Alfredo. "It Is Difficult." Keynote address at Hemispheric Institute's 10th Encuentro, "eX-céntrico: dissidence, sovereignties, performance," Santiago, Chile, July 2016.

Jaar, Alfredo. *La politique des images.* Edited by Nicole Schweizer and Lionel Bovier. Translated by Judith Hayward. Lausanne, Switzerland: Musée Cantonal des Beaux-Arts, 2007. Exhibition catalog.

Jaar, Alfredo. "Message from the Artist." In *Alfredo Jaar: The 11th Hiroshima Art Prize,* by Alfredo Jaar, Motoko Suhama, Yasufumi Nakamori, and Hiroshima-shi Gendai Bijutsukan, 15. Hiroshima: The Hiroshima City Museum of Contemporary Art, 2023.

Jaar, Alfredo. "The Peripatetic Artist: 14 Statements." Interview by Lilly Wei. *Art in America* 77, no. 7 (1989): 131.

Jaar, Alfredo. "Photography and Politics." Presentation, Frieze Masters, London, UK, October 8, 2017.

Jaar, Alfredo. "Questionnaire: Alfredo Jaar." *Frieze Magazine,* no. 143 (November 1, 2011).

Jaar, Alfredo. *The Sound of Silence.* New York: Peter Blum, 2006.

Jaar, Alfredo. "The Temptation to Exist: Alfredo Jaar." Video conversation with David Levi Strauss. *Brooklyn Rail,* June 17, 2022. https://brooklynrail.org/events/2022/06/17/the-temptation-to-exist-alfredo-jaar/.

Jaar, Alfredo. "Tonight No Poetry Will Serve." CIRCA. Accessed October 9, 2025. https://circa.art/exhibition/tonight-no-poetry-will-serve/.

Jaar, Alfredo. "Understanding the World Before Acting in It." Interview by Jalena Martinović. *Loophole*, November 15, 2024. https://loophole.art/articles/alfredo-jaar-interview.

Jaar, Alfredo, and Pirkko Siitari. "'I Need to Understand the World Before Acting in the World." In Alfredo Jaar, *Tonight No Poetry Will Serve*, 65–79 Helsinki: Museum of Contemporary Art Kiasma, 2015. Exhibition catalog.

Jaar, Alfredo, Sandra Accatino, and Adriana Valdés. *Jaar SCL 2006*. Barcelona: Actar, 2006. Exhibition Catalog.

Jelin, Elizabeth. *State Repression and the Labors of Memory*. Minneapolis: University of Minnesota Press, 2003.

Jones, Amelia, and Jane Chin Davidson, eds. *Companion to Contemporary Art in a Global Framework*. Hoboken, NJ: Wiley-Blackwell, 2024.

Jonsson, Stefan. *A Brief History of the Masses: Three Revolutions*. New York: Columbia University Press, 2008.

Kaleck, Wolfgang. "Arrest Kissinger!" European Center for Constitutional and Human Rights blog, 2014. https://www.ecchr.eu/en/publication/arrest-kissinger/.

Kaleck, Wolfgang. *Concrete Utopia: Looking Back into the Future of Human Rights*. New York: OR Books, 2024.

Kaplan, Temma. *Taking Back the Streets: Women, Youth, and Direct Democracy*. Berkeley: University of California Press, 2003.

Kissinger, Henry. *Leadership: Six Studies in World Strategy*. New York: Penguin, 2022.

Kissinger, Henry. *The White House Years*. Boston: Little, Brown, 1979.

Kissinger, Henry. *Years of Renewal*. New York: Simon and Schuster, 1999.

Kissinger, Henry. *Years of Upheaval*. Boston: Little, Brown, 1982.

Klein, Naomi. *The Shock Doctrine: The Rise of Disaster Capitalism*. New York: Picador, 2007.

Knight, Ben. "Germany Remembers 1992 Anti-Immigrant Riots in Rostock." Deutsche Welle (DW), August 22, 2022. https://www.dw.com/en/germany-remembers-the-rostock-anti-immigrant-riot-of-1992/a-62890639.

Kornbluh, Peter. *Pinochet desclasificado: Los archivos secretos de Estados Unidos sobre Chile*. Santiago: Catalonia, 2023.

Kornbluh, Peter. *The Pinochet File: A Declassified Dossier on Atrocity and Accountability*. New York: New Press, 2003.

Kornbluh, Peter, and Marian Schlotterbeck. "Reagan y Pinochet: El momento en que Estados Unidos rompió con la dictadura." Centro de Investigación Periodísta (CIPER), November 23, 2010. https://ciperchile.cl/2010/11/23/reagan-y-pinochet-el-momento-en-que-estados-unidos-rompio-con-la-dictadura/.

Kriebel, Sabine T., and Andrés Mario Zervigón, eds. *Photography and Doubt*. Florence: Taylor and Francis, 2016.

Lawner, Miguel. "Solidaridad internacional." In *Todavía somos el tiempo: Arte y resistencia a 50 años del golpe*, edited by Florencia San Martín, 55–62. Santiago: Centro Nacional de Arte Contemporáneo de Chile, 2023.

Lazzara, Michael J. "Complicity and Responsibility in the Aftermath of the Pinochet Regime: The Case of 'El Mocito.'" *Rúbrica contemporánea* 5, no. 9 (2016): 59–76.

Lazzara, Michael J. "The Memory Turn." In *New Approaches to Latin American Studies: Culture and Power*, edited by Juan Poblete, 14–31. New York: Routledge, 2018.

Lazzara, Michael J., and Vicky Unruh, eds. *Telling Ruins in Latin America*. New York: Palgrave Macmillan, 2009.

Levi, Primo. *The Drowned and the Saved*. New York: Simon and Schuster, 2017.

Lienlaf, Leonel. *Se ha despertado el ave de mi corazón*. Santiago: Editorial Universitaria, 1989.

Linfield, Susie. *The Cruel Radiance: Photography and Political Violence*. Chicago: University of Chicago Press, 2012.

Lispector, Clarice. *The Hour of the Star*. Translated by Giovanni Pontiero. New York: New Directions, 2012.

Love, Bettina L. *We Want to Do More Than Survive: Abolitionist Teaching and the Pursuit of Educational Freedom*. Boston, MA: Beacon, 2019.

Lowenhaupt Tsing, Anna. *Friction: An Ethnography of Global Connection*. Princeton, NJ: Princeton University Press, 2005.

Lowenhaupt Tsing, Anna. *The Mushroom at the End of the World: On the Possibility of Life in Capitalist Ruins*. Princeton, N J: Princeton University Press, 2015.

Lübecker, Nikolaj. "The Politics of Images." *Paragraph* 36, no. 3 (2013): 392–407.

Lugones, María. "Heterosexualism and the Colonial/Modern Gender System." *Hypatia* 22, no. 1 (Winter 2007): 186–209.

Lugo-Saavedra, Denise, and John Spray. *Aquí: 27 Latin American Artists Living and Working in the United States = 27 artistas latinoamericanos que viven y trabajan en los Estados Unidos*. Los Angeles: University of Southern California, 1984. Exhibition catalog.

Ly, Boreth. "Of Performance and the Persistent Temporality of Trauma: Memory, Art, and Visions." *East Asia Cultures Critique* 16, no. 1 (2008): 109–30.

Main, Alexander. "Is Latin America Still the US's 'Backyard'?" Center for Economic and Policy Research (CEPR), September 12, 2018. https://www.cepr.net/is-latin-america-still-the-us-s-backyard/.

Maldonado-Torres, Nelson. *Against War: Views from the Underside of Modernity*. Durham, NC: Duke University Press, 2008.

Maldonado-Torres, Nelson. "The Decolonial Turn." In *New Approaches to Latin American Studies: Culture and Power*, edited by Juan Poblete, 111–27. New York: Routledge, 2018.

Maldonado-Torres, Nelson. "Enrique Dussel's Liberation Thought in the Decolonial Turn." *TRANSMODERNITY: Journal of Peripheral Cultural Production of the Luso-Hispanic World* 1, no. 1 (2011): 1–30.

Maldonado-Torres, Nelson. "Liberation Philosophy and the Search for Combative Decoloniality: A Fanonian Approach." In *Liberation Struggles in Abya Yala*, edited by Luis Rubén Díaz Cepeda and Ernesto Rosen Velásquez, 11–28. Hoboken, NJ: Wiley-Blackwell, 2024.

Maldonado-Torres, Nelson. "Outline of Ten Theses on Coloniality and Decoloniality." Frantz Fanon Foundation, 2016. https://caribbeanstudiesassociation.org/docs/Maldonado-Torres_Outline_Ten_Theses-10.23.16.pdf.

Maldonado-Torres, Nelson. "Thinking Through the Decolonial Turn: Post-Continental Interventions in Theory, Philosophy, and Critique—An Introduction." *Transmodernity: Journal of Peripheral Cultural Production of the Luso-Hispanic World* 1, no. 2 (2011): 1–15.

Malhotra, Madhu. "Ray of Hope for Survivors of the Bhopal Disaster." Amnesty International, August 7, 2013. https://www.amnesty.org/en/latest/campaigns/2013/08/ray-of-hope-for-survivors-of-the-bhopal-disaster/.

Martí, José. "Our America." In *Resisting Categories: Latin American and/or Latino?*, edited by Mari Carmen Ramírez, Héctor Olea, and Tomás Ybarra-Frausto, 208–15. Houston: International Center for the Arts of the Americas, Museum of Fine Arts, Houston, 2012.

Mas Vall, Ariadna. "Per què la Guerra?" *El Temps de las Arts*, March 19, 2024.

Maturana, Humberto. *Emociones y lenguaje en educación y política*. Santiago: Dolmen, 2001.

Maturana, Humberto. "What Is It to See?" *Archivos de biología y medicina experimentales* 16, nos. 3–4 (1983): 255–69.

Maturana, Humberto, and Gerda Verden-Zöller. *The Origin of Humanness in the Biology of Love*. Exeter, UK: Imprint Academic, 2008.

Merkley, Jeff, and Mike Zamore. *Filibustered! How to Fix the Broken Senate and Save America*. New York: New Press, 2024.

Meruane, Lina. *Palestina en pedazos: Volverse Palestina; Volvernos otros; Rostros en mi rostro*. Santiago de Chile: Literatura Random House, 2021.

Mignolo, Walter D. "Crossing Gazes and the Silence of the 'Indians': Theodor De Bry and Guaman Poma de Ayala." *Journal of Medieval and Early Modern Studies* 41, no. 1 (2011): 173–223.

Mignolo, Walter D. *The Darker Side of the Renaissance: Literacy, Territoriality, and Colonization*. Ann Arbor: University of Michigan Press, 2007.

Mignolo, Walter D. *The Darker Side of Western Modernity: Global Futures, Decolonial Options*. Durham, NC: Duke University Press, 2011.

Mignolo, Walter D. "The Geopolitics of Knowledge and the Colonial Difference." *South Atlantic Quarterly* 101, no. 1 (2000): 57–97.

Mignolo, Walter D. *The Idea of Latin America*. Malden, MA: Blackwell, 2005.

Millán, Gonzalo. "Poem 48 from The City." In *Poets of Chile: A Bilingual Anthology, 1965–1985*, selected and translated by Steven F. White, 114–15. Greensboro, NC: Unicorn Press, 1986.

Mistral, Gabriela. "Aniversario." In *Las renegadas: Antología*, edited by Lina Meruane, 90–91. Barcelona: Lumen; Penguin Random House, 2019.

Mistral, Gabriela. "El Grito." In *Recados para América: Textos de Gabriela Mistral*, edited by Mario Céspedes, 11–12. Santiago de Chile: Revista Pluma y Pincel/Instituto de Ciencias Alejando Lipschutz, 1978. Poem first published 1922.

Moore, Jason W., ed. *Anthropocene or Capitalocene? Nature, History, and the Crisis of Capitalism*. Oakland, CA: PM Press, 2016.

Moraga Valle, Fabio. "'Ser jóven y no ser revolucionario': La juventud y el movimiento estudiantil durante la Unidad Poplar." In *Frágiles suturas: Chile a treinta años del gobierno de Salvador Allende*, edited by Francisco Zapata, 365–411. Mexico City: Colegio de México, 2006.

Moraña, Mabel, Enrique Dussel, and Carlos A. Jáuregui, eds. *Coloniality at Large: Latin America and the Postcolonial Debate*. Durham, NC: Duke University Press, 2008.

Neruda, Pablo. *A Call for the Destruction of Nixon and Praise for the Chilean Revolution = Incitación al nixonicidio y alabanza de la Revolución Chilena*. Translated by Teresa Anderson. Cambridge, MA: West End Press, 1980.

Neruda, Pablo. *Canto General: Song of the Americas*. Translated by Mariela Griffor. North Adams, MA: Tupelo Press, 2016.

Neruda, Pablo. *Song of Protest*. Translated by Miguel Algarín. New York: Morrow, 1976.

Nixon, Rob. *Slow Violence and the Environmentalism of the Poor*. Cambridge, MA: Harvard University Press, 2013.

Nora, Pierre. *Realms of Memory: The Construction of the French Past*. 3 vols. New York: Columbia University Press, 1996–98.

O'Gorman, Edmundo. *The Invention of America: An Inquiry into the Historical Nature of the New World and the Meaning of Its History*. Bloomington: Indiana University Press, 1961.

Ojeda, Iván Monalisa. *Las Biuty Queens*. New York: Random House, 2021.

Osorio, Víctor, and Iván Cabezas. *Los hijos de Pinochet*. Santiago: Planeta, 1995.

Palumbo, Jacqui. "A Whitney Biennial Artist's Hidden Message, 'Free Palestine,' Asks Viewers to Take a Long Look." CNN, March 20, 2024. https://www.cnn.com/2024/03/20/style/demian-dineyazhi-whitney-biennial-free-palestine-art/index.html.

Panicelli, Ida. "Alfredo Jaar Fondazione Merz." *Art Forum* 52, no. 9 (May 2014). https://www.artforum.com/events/alfredo-jaar-9-205184/.

Pelaez Lopez, Alán. "Alán Pelaez Lopez—Art of the Matter." Interview, Center for the Study of Race and Ethnicity in America, Brown University, August 18, 2022. https://www.youtube.com/watch?v=ot5Yf4d1OxU.

Pérez-Oramas, Luis. *Power of an Idea: A Moment in Time with Alfredo Jaar and Luis Pérez-Oramas*. Caracas: Colección Patricia Phelps de Cisneros, 2022.

Pollock, Griselda. "Not Forgetting Africa: The Dialectics of Attention/Inattention, Seeing/Denying, and Knowing/Understanding in the Positioning of the Viewer in the Work of Alfredo Jaar." In Jaar, *La politique des images*, 113–36.

Pratt, Mary Louise. "Arts of the Contact Zone." *Profession* (1991): 33–40.

Pratt, Mary Louise. *Planetary Longings*. Durham, NC: Duke University Press, 2022.

Quijano, Aníbal. "Coloniality and Modernity/Rationality." *Cultural Studies* 21, no. 2 (2007): 168–78.

Quijano, Aníbal. "Coloniality of Power, Eurocentrism, and Latin America." *Neplanta: Views form South* 1, no. 3 (2000): 533–80.

Quijano, Aníbal. *Vivir adentro y en contra: Colonialidad y descolonialidad del poder.* Lima, Perú: Universidad Ricardo Palma, Editorial Universitaria, 2022.

Quijano, Aníbal, and Immanuel Wallerstein. "Americanity as a Concept, or the Americas in the Modern World-System." *International Social Science Journal* 1, no. 134 (1992): 549–56.

Quijano Valencia, Olver B. "Reseña de 'Discurso sobre el colonialismo' Aimé Césaire." *Convergencia Revista de Ciencias Sociales* 14, no. 43 (Jan.–April 2007): 255–62.

Qureshi, Lubna Z. *Nixon, Kissinger, and Allende: U.S. Involvement in the 1973 Coup in Chile.* Lanham, MD: Lexington Books, 2009.

Raiford, Leigh. *Imprisoned in a Luminous Glare: Photography and the African American Freedom Struggle.* Chapel Hill: University of North Carolina Press, 2011.

Ramírez, Mari Carmen. "Beyond 'The Fantastic': Framing Identity in U.S. Exhibitions of Latin American Art." *Art Journal* 51, no. 4 (Winter 1992): 60–68.

Ramírez, Mari Carmen, Héctor Olea, and Tomás Ybarra-Frausto, eds. *Resisting Categories: Latin American and/or Latino?* Houston: International Center for the Arts of the Americas, Museum of Fine Arts, Houston, 2012.

Rancière, Jacques. "Theater of Images." In Jaar, *La politique des images*, 71–80.

Rebolledo, Javier. *La danza de los cuervos: El mocito y el destino final de los detenidos desaparecidos.* Santiago de Chile: Editorial Planeta, 2016.

Richard, Nelly. *Crítica de la memoria, 1990–2010.* Santiago, Chile: Ediciones Universidad Diego Portales, 2010.

Richard, Nelly. "La escena de avanzada: Photography and Writing in Postcoup Chile." Conversation with Idelber Avelar. In *Photography and Writing in Latin America: Double Exposures*, edited by Marcy E. Schwartz and Mary Beth Tierney-Tello, 259–70. Albuquerque: University of New Mexico Press, 2006.

Richard, Nelly. *Políticas y estéticas de la memoria.* Santiago de Chile: Cuarto Propio, 2000.

Richard, Nelly. "Sitios de la memoria, vaciamiento del recuerdo." *Revista de Crítica Cultural*, no. 23 (2001): 10–13.

Richards, Patricia. *Race and the Chilean Miracle: Neoliberalism, Democracy, and Indigenous Rights.* Pittsburgh: University of Pittsburgh Press, 2013.

Ricoeur, Paul. *Time and Narrative.* Vol. 2. Translated by K. McLaughlin and D. Pellauer. Chicago: University of Chicago Press, 1985.

Rivera Cusicanqui, Silvia. "Ch'ixinakax utxiwa: A Reflection on the Practices and Discourses of Decolonization." *South Atlantic Quarterly* 111, no. 1 (2012): 95–109.

Rivera Cusicanqui, Silvia. *Ch'ixinakax utxiwa: On Practices and Discourses of Decolonization.* Cambridge, MA: Polity, 2020.

Robles-Moreno, Irma Leticia. "'Please, Don't Discover Me!' On *The Year of the White Bear*." *Walker Reader*, July 19, 2018. https://walkerart.org/magazine/guillermo-gomez-pena-and-coco-fuscos-the-year-of-the-white-bear#_edn1.

Rojas Mix, Miguel. *América imaginaria.* Barcelona: Editorial Lumen, 1992.

Rojas Mix, Miguel. "'América, no invoco tu nombre en vano': De la idea de la América Latina de Neruda a la geopolítica contemporánea." *Revista de la Casa de las Américas*, no. 253 (2008): 4–19.

Rojas Mix, Miguel. *Los cien nombres de América: Eso que descubrió Colón*. Barcelona: Lumen, 1991.
Rosenberg, Fernando J. *After Human Rights: Literature, Visual Arts, and Film in Latin America, 1990–2010*. Pittsburgh: University of Pittsburgh Press, 2016.
Rosler, Martha. "In, Around and Afterthoughts (On Documentary Photography)." In *The Contest of Meaning: Critical Histories of Photography*, edited by Richard Bolton, 303–25. Cambridge, MA: MIT Press, 1992.
Rowland, Anthony. "Re-Reading 'Impossibility' and 'Barbarism': Adorno and Post-Holocaust Poetics." *Critical Survey* 9, no. 1 (1997): 57–69.
Ruiz, Carlos. *De la república al mercado: Ideas educacionales y política en Chile*. Santiago de Chile: LOM Ediciones, 2010.
Ruiz, Sandra. *Left Turns in Brown Study*. Durham, NC: Duke University Press, 2024.
Sachs, Ignacy. "Introduction: The End of the Age of Columbus? Development in Question." UNESCO, *International Social Science Journal* 44, no. 4 (1992): 457–62.
Said, Edward. *Orientalism*. New York: Vintage Books, 1979.
Salazar Bondy, Augusto. *¿Existe una filosofía de nuestra América?* Mexico City: Siglo XXI, 1968.
Saldívar, David. *The Dialectics of Our America: Genealogy, Cultural Critique, and Literary History*. Durham, NC: Duke University Press, 1991.
Sands, Philippe. *38 Londres Street: On Impunity, Pinochet in England and a Nazi in Patagonia*. London: Weidenfeld and Nicolson, 2025.
San Martín, Florencia. "Aesthetics of Disobedience." *Smithsonian Magazine*, August 23, 2018.
San Martín, Florencia. "Alfredo Jaar: *The End of the World*." *Journal of the Society of Architectural Historians* 84, no. 4 (Dec. 2025): 619–21.
San Martín, Florencia. "Decolonial Temporality in Alfredo Jaar's *The Kissinger Project*." *ASAP/Journal* 4, no. 2 (May 2019): 345–76.
San Martín, Florencia. "On Failure and the Nation-State: A Decolonial Reading of Alfredo Jaar's *A Logo for America*." In Flores, San Martín, and Villaseñor Black, *The Routledge Companion to Decolonizing Art History*, 151–63.
San Martín, Florencia. "Politics of Collectivity: Muralism and Public Space in the Practices of the Brigada Ramona Parra during the Unidad Popular." *Seismopolite Journal of Art and Politics* 10 (April 30, 2015).
San Martín, Florencia. "Time, Love and the Museum." In Jones and Chin Davidson, *Companion to Contemporary Art in a Global Framework*, 467–79.
San Martín, Florencia, ed. *Todavía somos el tiempo: Arte y resistencia a 50 años del golpe*. Santiago de Chile: Centro Nacional de Arte Contemporáneo de Chile, 2025.
San Martín, Florencia, Carla Macchiavello, and Paula Solimano, eds. *Dismantling the Nation: Contemporary Art in Chile*. Amherst, MA: Amherst College Press, 2023.
Santayana, George. *The Life of Reason*. New York: Charles Scribner's Sons, 1905.
Sartre, Jean Paul. *What Is Literature?* New York: Philosophical Library, 1949.

Sebenius, James K., R. Nicholas Burns, and Robert H. Mnookin. *Kissinger the Negotiator: Lessons from Dealmaking at the Highest Level.* New York: HarperCollins, 2018.
Secretaría General de Gobierno. *Documentos secretos de la ITT: Fotocopias de los originales en inglés y su traducción al castellano.* Santiago de Chile: Empresa Editora Nacional Quimantú, 1972.
Sedra, Paul. "Imagining an Imperial Race: Egyptology in the Service of Empire." *Comparative Studies of South Asia, Africa and the Middle East* 24, no. 1 (2004): 249–59.
Segal, Lynne. *Radical Happiness: Moments of Collective Joy.* New York: Verso, 2017.
Sekula, Allan. "Dismantling Modernism, Reinventing Documentary (Notes on the Politics of Representation)." *Massachusetts Review* 19, no. 4 (Winter 1978): 859–83.
Selejan, Ileana L. "Pictures in Dispute: Documentary Photography in Sandinista Nicaragua." *photographies* 10, no. 3 (2017): 283–302.
Serna Arnaiz, Mercedes. "Jose Martí, Pablo Neruda y la República en España." *Monteagudo Revista de literatura española, hispanoamericana y teoría de la literature* 9 (2004): 13–24.
Shah, Naureen. "Trump Invokes the Alien Enemies Act to Carry Out Mass Deportations, Explained." ACLU, March 28, 2025. https://www.aclunv.org/news/trump-invokes-alien-enemies-act-carry-out-mass-deportations-explained/.
Shah Stamets, Reena. "Were His Priorities Out of Focus?" *Tampa Bay Times,* April 14, 1994. https://www.tampabay.com/archive/1994/04/14/were-his-priorities-out-of-focus/.
Shaw, Anny. "We Are All America: First Faena Festival Aims to Unify, Not Divide." *Art Newspaper,* December 5, 2018. https://www.theartnewspaper.com/news/faena-festival-miami-beach-2018.
Smith, Linda Tuhiwai. *Decolonizing Methodologies: Research and Indigenous Peoples.* London: Zed Books, 1999.
Sontag, Susan. *Regarding the Pain of Others.* New York: Picador, 2004.
Spivak, Gayatri Chakravorty. "Can the Subaltern Speak?" In *Marxism and the Interpretation of Culture,* edited by Cary Nelson and Lawrence Grossberg, 271–313. Urbana: University of Illinois Press, 1988.
Stathopoulou, Katerina. "The Timeless Relevance of Alfredo Jaar's 'A Logo for America.'" *Art21,* April 2, 2020. https://art21.org/read/the-timeless-relevance-of-alfredo-jaars-a-logo-for-america/.
Stern, Steve J. *Battling for Hearts and Minds: Memory Struggles in Pinochet's Chile, 1973–1988.* Durham, NC: Duke University Press, 2006.
Sturken, Marita. *Terrorism in American Memory: Memorials, Museums, and Architecture in the Post-9/11 Era.* New York: New York University Press, 2022.
Suri, Jeremi. *Henry Kissinger and the American Century.* Cambridge, MA: Belknap Press of Harvard University Press, 2007.
Taylor, Diana. *¡Presente! The Politics of Presence.* Durham, NC: Duke University Press, 2020.

Tedde, Adriano. "Trump the Neoliberal President: New Language, Same Old Politics (for Now)." Australian Institute of International Affairs, March 26, 2025. https://www.internationalaffairs.org.au/australianoutlook/trump-the-neoliberal-president-new-language-same-old-politics-for-now/.

Tenorio-Trillo, Mauricio. *Latin America: The Allure and Power of an Idea*. Chicago: University of Chicago Press, 2017.

Tuck, Eve, and K. Wayne Yang. "Decolonization Is Not a Metaphor." *Decolonization: Indigeneity, Education and Society* 1, no. 1 (2012): 1–40.

Unidad Popular. *Programa básico de gobierno de la Unidad Popular*. Santiago de Chile: Horizonte, 1970.

Valdés, Adriana. *Alfredo Jaar: Studies on Happiness (1979–1981)*. Barcelona: ACTAR, 1999.

Valdés, Adriana. "Missing Chile: Far South. Far. Very Far." In *Alfredo Jaar—The Way It Is: An Aesthetics of Resistance*, edited by Frank Wagner, 180–203. Berlin: Neue Gesellschaft für Bildende Kunst, 2012.

Vazquez, Edward A. *Alfredo Jaar: Studies on Happiness*. London: Afterall Books, 2023.

Vázquez, Rolando. "Modernity Coloniality and Visibility: The Politics of Time." *Sociological Research Online* 14, no. 4 (2009): 109–15.

Vázquez, Rolando. "The Museum, Decoloniality and the End of the Contemporary." In *The Future of the New, Artistic Innovation in Times of Social Acceleration*, edited by Thijs Lijster, 181–95. Amsterdam: Valiz, 2018.

Vázquez, Rolando. "Translation as Erasure: Thoughts on Modernity's Epistemic Violence." *Journal of Historical Sociology* 24, no. 1 (2011): 27–44.

Veronelli, Gabriela A. "La colonialidad del lenguaje y el monolenguajear como práctica lingüística de racialización." *Polifonia* 26, no. 44 (2019): 146–59.

Veronelli, Gabriela A. "The Coloniality of Language: Race, Expressivity, Power, and the Darker Side of Modernity." *Wagadu: A Journal of Transnational Women's and Gender Studies* 13, no. 1 (Summer 2015): 108–34.

Waldman, Kate. "Adrienne Rich on 'Tonight No Poetry Will Serve.'" *Paris Review*, March 2, 2011.

Walker, Charles F. *The Tupac Amaru Rebellion*. Cambridge, MA: Belknap Press of Harvard University Press, 2014.

Walsh, Rodolfo. "Open Letter to the Military Junta." March 24, 1977. Argentine Commission for Human Rights Washington Information Bureau, 1977.

Weiss, Peter. *The Aesthetics of Resistance*. Translated by Joachim Neugroschel. Durham, NC: Duke University Press, 2005.

Weiss, Peter. *Die Ästhetik des Widerstands*. Frankfurt am Main: Suhrkamp, 1988.

Williams, Raymond. "Structures of Feeling." In *Marxism and Literature*, 128–35. Oxford: Oxford University Press, 1977.

Winn, Peter, ed. *Victims of the Chilean Miracle: Workers and Neoliberalism in the Pinochet Era, 1972–2002*. Durham, NC: Duke University Press, 2006.

Winn, Peter. *Weavers of Revolution: The Yarur Workers and Chile's Road to Socialism*. New York: Oxford University Press, 1986.

Wynter, Sylvia. *Do Not Call Us Negroes: How "Multicultural" Textbooks Perpetuate Racism*. San Francisco: Aspire Books, 1992.

Wynter, Sylvia. "Unsettling the Coloniality of Being/Power/Truth/Freedom: Towards the Human, After Man, Its Overrepresentation—An Argument." *CR: The New Centennial Review* 3, no. 3 (2003): 257–337.

Yamashita, Karen Tei, and Boreth Ly. "Going Backward to Move Forward: Karen Tei Yamashita in Conversation with Boreth Ly on *Traces of Trauma*." *Art Journal Open*, February 11, 2021. https://artjournal.collegeart.org/?p=15188.

Zaldívar, Claudia, ed. *40 años Museo de la Solidaridad por Chile: Fraternidad, arte y política, 1971–1973*. Santiago de Chile: Museo de la Solidaridad Salvador Allende, 2013.

Žižek, Slavoj. "After Trump's Victory: From MAGA to MEGA." *e-flux*, November 13, 2024. https://www.e-flux.com/notes/641013/after-trump-s-victory-from-maga-to-mega.

Žižek, Slavoj. *Violence: Six Sideways Reflections*. New York: Picador, 2008.

Zurita, Raúl. *Anteparadise: A Bilingual Edition*. Translated by Jack Schmitt. Berkeley: University of California Press, 1986.

INDEX

Note: page numbers followed by *f* refer to figures.